AI and Contracting

AI and Contracting

Opportunities and challenges for AI in contracting and deliberation

Georges Gielen, Maarten Herbosch and Bernard Tilleman (Eds.)

eleven

Boomjuridisch
Antwerpen

Published, sold and distributed by Eleven
P.O. Box 85576
2508 CG The Hague
The Netherlands
Tel.: +31 70 33 070 33
Fax: +31 70 33 070 30
e-mail: sales@elevenpub.nl
www.elevenpub.com

Sold and distributed in USA and Canada
Independent Publishers Group
814 N. Franklin Street
Chicago, IL 60610, USA
Order Placement: +1 800 888 4741
Fax: +1 312 337 5985
orders@ipgbook.com
www.ipgbook.com

Boom Juridisch Antwerpen
ISBN 978-94-6451-126-0
ISBN 978-94-6451-224-3 (e-book)
NUR 822
D/2024/15251/05

GPRC
Guaranteed
Peer Reviewed
Content
www.gprc.be

Eleven is an imprint of Boom uitgevers Den Haag.
ISBN 978-94-6236-814-9
ISBN 978-94-0011-456-2 (e-book)

TABLE OF CONTENTS

Introduction

A Brief Introduction to AI and Its Use in the Legal Practice

*Georges Gielen**

1 Introduction

Beyond any doubt, artificial intelligence (AI) is here to stay! It is taking our world by storm, disruptively affecting all aspects of our society. The field of law and the legal practice are no exception to this. This contribution[1] will give a brief introduction to AI and describe its huge potential and current limitations, followed by an overview of possible applications in the legal practice, such as in smart contracting, the focus of this book.

2 AI: Definition and Basic Techniques

Long before the introduction of ChatGPT, our society has been characterised by a gradual but steady process of digitisation and digitalisation (see the figure below), which is fundamentally transforming our daily way of living and working. This goes from digitally processing all data and documents (instead of using paper) over digitising all processes in companies and organisations (tax declarations, bank transactions, ordering concert or train tickets, etc.) to reshaping entire organisations.

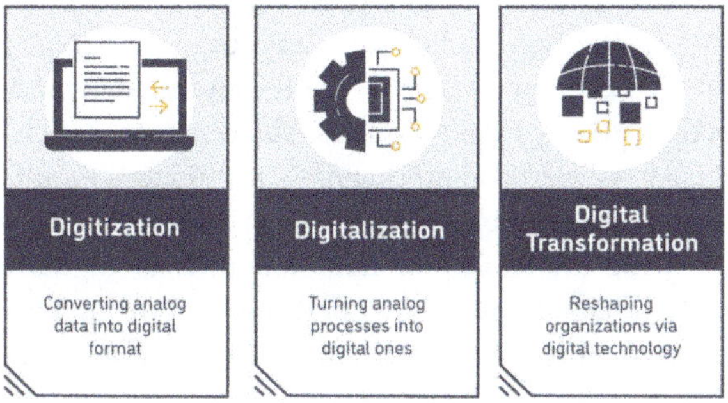

Source: www.channelinsider.com

* Prof. dr. ir. Georges Gielen. ESAT-MICAS, Department of Electrical Engineering (ESAT), KU Leuven, Belgium.

1 *This introductory text by no means pretends to be complete in any way, and – considering the fast evolutions in the field – is likely to be outdated before it is even completed.*

Apart from the socio-cultural problems that this may create (the *digital divide* between different social classes within a population or between younger and older generations or between developed and developing countries), the benefits of this digital transformation are deemed to outweigh by far its drawbacks.

Technologically, this digital transformation is, of course, enabled by the ever-continuing progress in the semiconductor technology used to fabricate electronic chips for computing. This relentless progression over many decades now, in line with the so-called 'Moore's law',[2] made it possible to continuously build ever more powerful computer chips, running ever more powerful software applications in acceptable time and/or at affordable cost.

Originally, computers were developed to compute, i.e. to perform large calculations ('number crunching'). Illustrative examples are calculating the orbit of the Apollo rockets on their journey to the moon, calculating the weather forecasts for the coming days/weeks, calculating the profit/loss account of a company, etc. Over the years, the software applications have diversified and have supported other tasks such as text processing in editors, audio filtering in hearing aids, data streaming in WiFi base stations, movie editing for social media posting, radar-based distance control in cars, to name a few. The relentless progression of hardware and software over many decades has created a wide range of products and applications we use in our daily lives today.

Although extremely powerful at computing tasks, computers, as we knew them, were not very effective at cognitive tasks, such as recognising faces on photos, creating a new poem or a new painting, summarising a discussion or debate, or understanding the nuances in a speech. Humans were believed to be superior at such cognitive tasks, and this was attributed to the way their brain functions – different from classical computers. All this has changed, however, with the recent re-emergence of techniques of AI. Originally coined in 1955 by John McCarthy, the progress in AI techniques over the years has experienced several ups and downs. Only since the mid-2010s did the right ingredients of progress in computing power, progress in artificial neural network algorithms and the growing availability of huge amounts of digital data (through digitisation, the internet, the cloud, the internet of things and the many wireless sensor networks) come together to make practical and efficient AI systems possible. The

2 Moore's law is the prediction by Gordon Moore, co-founder of Intel, in 1965 that the semiconductor technology would develop further in such a way that the number of transistors on a (computer) chip and hence its computing power would double every 1.5 years (later on modified to every 2 years). Repeating this over many decades led to an exponential increase in computing capabilities (for the same price) over time [Moore65].

capabilities seem to be limited only by the availability of proper data and the energy efficiency of the computing devices.

Roughly based on the EC JRC Flagship report on AI[3] and on the publication of Rémy Bonnaffé,[4] the following definition describes the field of AI pretty well:

> *Definition:* ***Artificial Intelligence (AI)*** is a generic term that refers to any machine or algorithm that is capable of observing its environment, learning, analysing and reasoning and, based on the knowledge and experience gained, of taking intelligent action or proposing decisions, to solve a problem at hand, comparable to human intelligence.

The AI Act of the EU[5] uses a slightly different definition:

> *Definition:* An ***AI system*** means a machine-based system designed to operate with varying levels of autonomy and that may exhibit adaptiveness after deployment and that, for explicit or implicit objectives, infers, from the input it receives, how to generate outputs, such as predictions, content, recommendations or decisions that can influence physical or virtual environments.

Essential properties of an AI system are as follows:
1. its *autonomy*: it processes the observed inputs entering the system to come to a conclusion by itself. This may initiate proper action automatically in an autonomous system, or in many practical cases the conclusion is presented to the user who has the final say.
2. Its *adaptivity*: it evolves over time by learning from its prior successes and failures. This learning can be static (i.e. the learning is once, in the beginning, based on past available data) or continual over time (based on new additional inputs-outputs being processed).

Given these basic properties of autonomy and learning, the similarity with human intelligence is evident. It is no surprise that AI techniques today are used in almost any application domain. Some examples of tasks addressed by AI systems are the recognition

3 Annoni, A., Benczur, P., Bertoldi, P., Delipetrev, B., De Prato, G., Feijoo, C., Fernandez Macias, E., Gomez Gutierrez, E., Iglesias Portela, M., Junklewitz, H., Lopez Cobo, M., Martens, B., Figueiredo Do Nascimento, S., Nativi, S., Polvora, A., Sanchez Martin, J.I., Tolan, S., Tuomi, I. and Vesnic Alujevic, L., "Artificial Intelligence: A European Perspective," Publications Office of the European Union, Luxemburg, 2018 (DOI:10.2760/936974).

4 Rémy Bonnafé, "New Technologies and the Law: The Impact of Artificial Intelligence on the Practice of Law," https://medium.com/@remybonnaffe/new-technologies-and-the-law-the-impact-of-artificial-intelligence-on-the-practice-of-law-c456904688d1.

5 https://artificialintelligenceact.eu/.

of faces or objects in images, the interpretation and/or automatic translation of speech or texts, the answering of questions by chatbots, the creation of drawings or videos, the medical diagnostics on scan images, the steering of vehicles or drones, the online monitoring of production machines in factories, the screening of contracts, and the making of summary reports of meetings.

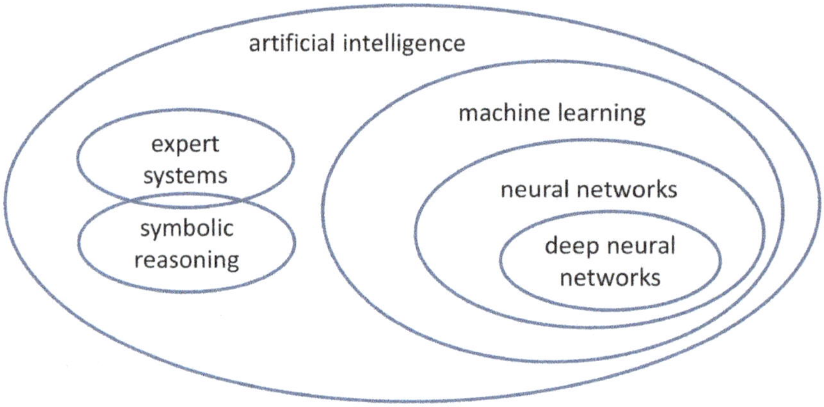

So, besides the progress in computing power, what has made this huge progress possible? The major innovation has come from the introduction of artificial neural networks and, in particular, deep neural networks. Before diving more deeply into this, it is worthwhile to note that – as indicated in the figure below – artificial neural networks are merely a subset of the broader field of machine intelligence, i.e. machines or man-made systems aiming at carrying out 'intelligent' tasks equivalent to humans, and that other techniques, such as expert systems and symbolic reasoning, exist to try and implement artificially intelligent systems. (Deep) neural networks have, however, caused the recent boost.

3 Artificial Neural Networks

Roughly trying to mimic how our human brain works as an interaction of huge numbers of connected neurons, artificial neural networks (see the figure of the standard feed-forward network below) consist of several 'hidden' layers of interconnected 'neurons' (i.e. simple computing units) between the input layer and the output layer. Each connection has a certain strength (possibly zero), indicated by the corresponding weighting coefficient. Each neuron then combines the weighted inputs and generates its output according to its mathematical model (e.g. a thresholding function). The weighting coefficients of the interconnections need to be tuned towards the targeted application for the artificial neural network to adequately perform its desired task (e.g. recognising dogs on images). Deep neural networks are similar in structure but are characterised by a huge number of hidden-neuron layers between the input and output layers. State-of-the-art large-language models (LLMs) such as GPT-4 are based on models, with each more than a few hundred billion parameters that need to be determined during network training.

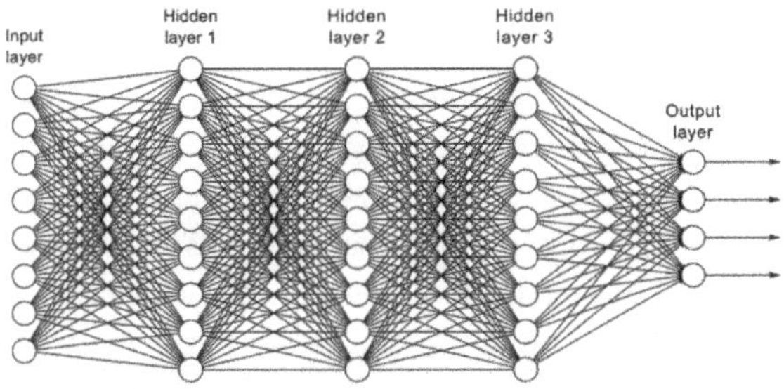

Source: freecontent.manning.com

Note that besides the values of all the weighting coefficients of the interconnections and besides the number of hidden neural layers, many alternative neural network architectures different from the above feed-forward structure have been developed. Essentially, they vary in regard to how the neurons are interconnected, and each of these architectures is better suited for some applications than for others, depending on the task to be executed. A non-exhaustive list of some frequently used alternative neural network structures and illustrative applications is the following:[6]

- convolutional neural networks: these are suited for, among other things, image processing;
- recurrent neural networks: these are suited for, among other things, processing of audio and speech streams;
- transformer systems: these are suited for, among other things, speech/text generation;
- recommender systems: these are suited for, among other things, predicting future preferences of a user based on past choices.

3.1 *Training the Neural Network*

This brings us to the important concept of *network training*. For artificial neural networks to be successful for a certain task, the network architecture needs to be well chosen and the values of the weights need to be well determined towards the task at hand. This is typically done by training the weights with many example inputs through some sort

6 See for instance https://towardsai.net/p/machine-learning/main-types-of-neural-networks-and-its-applications-tutorial-734480d7ec8e for a more complete overview.

of backpropagation mechanism, such that the network produces the known or desired outputs.[7] In this way, one can, for instance, train an artificial neural network to recognise dogs on pictures, by training it with many different pictures of dogs and other animals that it has to classify correctly.

There are three basic machine learning paradigms. If the data are labelled (i.e. if the desired output, e.g. it is a dog, is known and tagged to the input data), advantage can be taken of this knowledge in so-called *supervised learning*. This is often used for tasks such as classification, regression and object detection. Otherwise, if the data are not labelled, *unsupervised learning* can be used to have the AI system detect patterns and relationships in the data. This is often used for tasks such as clustering, dimensionality reduction and anomaly detection. The third paradigm is to use *reinforcement learning*, where some action and reward mechanism is set up to steer the network towards the targeted output (e.g. win the game of chess or go against the opponent). The system learns by getting feedback on its past outputs, in the attempt to maximise the reward, i.e., to achieve the desired outcome. This has been used successfully in problems such as robot control, game playing and autonomous driving.

Setting up an AI system based on an artificial neural network for some specific application, therefore, consists of the following three basic steps:

1. *collect and preprocess* the data;
2. *training phase*: determine the proper network model and its weighting coefficients using available training data;
3. *inference phase*: apply the trained model to new input data to get the (hopefully correct) output.

Since many training data are needed to train deep neural networks with their many weighting coefficients, it should be clear why the availability of data is called the new oil.[8] Fortunately, the digitisation, the internet, the cloud and the internet of things with its wireless sensor networks have brought along the availability of lots of data. Companies such as Meta, Google or Baidu offer free applications to users, in exchange for their data or usage patterns and then make money from exploiting those data or selling them to third parties. Note that training and (to a lesser extent) inference of

7 If the training data also contain the correct output (e.g. which animal is shown on every picture), one calls the data labelled. Labelling training data, however, is a tedious process. The alternative of training with unlabelled data is much more difficult and requires defining some sort of rewarding scheme (e.g. using reinforcement learning).

8 The phrase 'data is the new oil' was coined by the British mathematician Clive Humby in 2006, although he was referring to the need for processing and refining the data before usage rather than the financial aspects. The phrase has been paraphrased many times.

complex neural networks, such as ChatGPT, require enormous amounts of computing power and memory on the most advanced data centres, also spending large fractions of the world's energy consumption. Users are typically unaware of this when they use AI applications online and in the cloud. AI accelerators and more lightweight alternatives are therefore being developed for using AI solutions more locally in (battery-powered) devices.

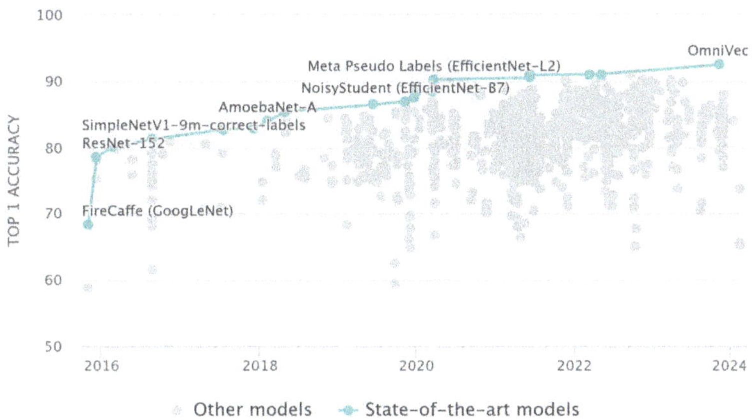

Source: https://paperswithcode.com/sota/image-classification-on-imagenet

When trained properly, neural networks can be very powerful. The figure above shows the image classification accuracy on the ImageNet data set[9] by different neural network structures presented over the years. As can be seen, the classification accuracy steadily improves over time, reaching values well over 90% today. Yet the classification is NEVER perfect. ***Like humans, AI systems also will never be error free.*** The challenge is to build and train systems that reduce the error, or, alternatively, that improve the accuracy as much as possible.

The huge progress in capabilities of AI systems can also be seen in generative AI systems like ChatGPT[10] or Gemini.[11] Using, essentially, transformer-based LLMs trained on massive text data sets, they demonstrate astonishing capabilities in recognising, summarising, translating, predicting and generating text and other content that are sometimes hardly distinguishable from those of humans. They also serve a crucial role in human-machine communication, e.g. in chatbots. The generative or creative

9 www.image-net.org.
10 chat.openai.com.
11 gemini.google.com.

capabilities of today's AI algorithms are also used in many other domains beyond text, such as DALL-E[12] or Firefly[13] for the creation of drawings, paintings, buildings, etc. from text input. The enormous energy consumption for LLM training and inference, however, is a sustainability concern at the moment.

4 APPLICATIONS OF AI IN LEGAL TECH

As a result of the progress in achievable performance and functionality, AI techniques are increasingly used in ever more application domains, such as in chatbots, marketing, banking and financial trading, autonomous vehicles, healthcare and medical diagnostics, sports analysis, gaming, artificial creativity (arts and architecture), security control, agriculture, space exploration, and many more. The list is seemingly endless. AI is also increasingly used in legal tech.

Possible current and future AI applications in the legal practice (largely based on Edgar Alan Rayo's article 'AI in Law and Legal Practice'[14]) can be summarised as follows:

- due diligence (contract revision, etc.);
- document automation (generation, adaptation, etc.);
- automation of legal services (chatbots);
- automation of contracting (smart contracts);
- intellectual property;
- invoicing;
- legal analytics & predictive technologies: analysis of past jurisdiction to detect patterns and to predict future legal rulings;
- decision support systems for parole, conditional release, crime recidivism, etc.;
- robot lawyers and digital judges.[15]

The competitive performance of AI systems versus humans was shown in the 'ultimate showdown' contest organised by LawGeex,[16] where some daily legal tasks (i.e. the reviewing and approval of everyday NDA contracts) had to be executed by both the LawGeex AI system and human lawyers. As shown in the figure below, the AI system beat the human lawyers in two ways: (1) the AI system was right in 94% of the cases, versus 85% on average for the human lawyers, and (2) the AI system did this in 26 seconds, versus 92 minutes on average for the human lawyers. It must be said,

12 openai.com/dall-e-3.
13 firefly.adobe.com.
14 emerj.com/ai-sector-overviews/ai-in-law-legal-practice-current-applications.
15 Richard Susskind, "Online Courts and the Future of Justice," Oxford University Press, 2021.
16 www.lawgeex.com.

however, that the highest-performing lawyer also achieved an accuracy of 94%, similar to the AI system, albeit in more time and with many more cups of coffee.

Source: https://blog.lawgeex.com/resources/whitepapers/aivslawyer

This is not to say that digital judges will be the norm of the future. Our legal codex still demands human oversight and the right to reasoned judgments. But AI systems will definitely have a lasting impact, including automating certain tasks in the legal practice of the (near) future. In this book, we will discuss the possibilities and challenges of using AI towards smart and automated contracting.

5 Legislative Regulations and Technical Challenges of AI Systems

As part of the strategy of the European Union to build a Europe fit for the digital age, it wants to make the EU a world-class hub for AI, while ensuring that the AI is human-centric (for the 'social good'), safe and trustworthy. AI and any AI system must comply with law, be ethical and be robust.

The AI High-Level Expert Group (HLEG), in its report in 2019, has defined seven key requirements that an AI system must satisfy for it to be trustworthy:[17]

- human agency and oversight

17 op.europa.eu/en/publication-detail/-/publication/d3988569-0434-11ea-8c1f-01aa75ed71a1 .

- technical robustness and safety
- privacy and data governance
- transparency (incl. traceability and explainability)
- diversity, non-discrimination and fairness (including the avoidance of unfair bias)
- societal and environmental well-being
- accountability

The goal is to be ethical by design, and the requirements can be checked through an assessment list. Compliance is to be assessed continuously and throughout the AI system's entire life cycle.

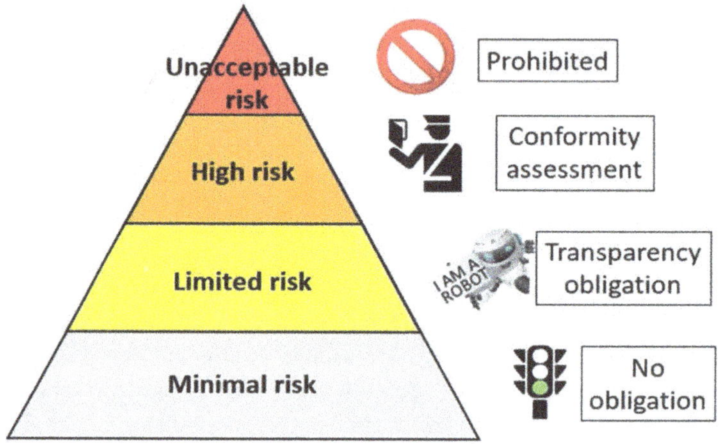

Source: www.telefonica.com/en/communication-room/blog/a-fit-for-purpose-and-borderless-european-artificial-intelligence-regulation

More recently, in March 2024, the European Parliament has adopted the AI Act.[18] This Act provides a risk-based regulatory framework for the safe and trustworthy development of AI in the EU. It contains new rules to ensure that AI systems used in the EU are safe, transparent, ethical, unbiased and under human control so that Europeans can trust the AI they are using. As shown in the figure above, it categorises the risk into four levels, with regulations depending on the level:

- *unacceptable risk*: these AI systems are forbidden, e.g. social scoring, mass surveillance, manipulation systems, etc.

18 data.consilium.europa.eu/doc/document/ST-5662-2024-INIT/en/pdf.

- *high risk*: these systems must satisfy conformity assessment through certification, e.g. systems used in education, employment, justice, law enforcement and biometric ID systems.
- *limited risk*: these systems have a transparency obligation through explicit labelling or disclosure, e.g. chatbots, emotion recognition systems, systems generating deep fakes and biometric categorisation.
- *minimal risk*: these systems have no obligations, and the assumption is that they are regulated by (voluntary) codes of conduct, e.g. spam filters and video games.

In addition, the question remains about liability (who is liable?) in case of disputes related to actions or decisions by systems based on or enabled by AI. This is particularly important for AI-driven highly automated decision systems and autonomous systems. The latter include, for instance, autonomous vehicles (cars, drones, etc.) or robots; the former include systems that perform highly automated decision-making or automated contracting. Examples covered in this book include decisions related to mergers and acquisitions, art authentication, insurance settlements, employment contracting, etc. The liability question becomes particularly tricky when the AI system has self-learning capabilities and therefore evolves over time. In 2022, the European Commission adopted two proposals to adapt the EU's product liability rules to the digital and AI age. These include the revised Product Liability Directive (PLD),[19] modernising the existing rules on the liability of manufacturers for defective products and related damages; the liability is extended to also include changes to the system due to, for instance, software updates, AI or digital services. Second, the AI Liability Directive[20] widens the PLD directive for damages caused by AI systems, establishing a broader scope of protection for victims (both individuals and businesses) as well as fostering the AI sector by increasing guarantees. It also includes damages caused due to wrongful behaviour of the AI system, e.g. if someone is discriminated against in a recruitment process involving AI technology.

6 Technical Challenges of AI Systems

If we look at the current state of the art and compare artificial with human intelligence, we can conclude that AI can match or even exceed human performance! But so far (1) only for very specific tasks for which the AI system has been trained, (2) only if very many, representative data are available for training, and (3) it is (still) limited in

19 single-market-economy.ec.europa.eu/document/download/3193da9a-cecb-44ad-9a9c-7b6b23220bcd_en?filename=COM_2022_495_1_EN_ACT_part1_v6.pdf.

20 eur-lex.europa.eu/legal-content/EN/TXT/PDF/?uri=CELEX:52022PC0496.

generalisation, adaptation and especially reasoning (finding patterns does not mean that the system understands the reason for these patterns).

Also, the development of AI systems still has to overcome some serious technical challenges:

- *AI is easy to mislead*: the outcome is not always well controllable. Some adversarial examples (e.g. with images) have shown that when changing the inputs slightly, even very similar inputs may sometimes lead to different and erroneous results. This questions the trustworthiness and robustness of AI systems. One speaks of AI hallucinations when the AI system generates incorrect or misleading results, which is a serious problem when using the AI for taking decisions or in autonomous mode.
- *Dataset bias*: any bias present in the training data will also be present or even amplified in the trained neural network; this bias could come from the developer or from the data itself (e.g. stereotypes or prejudice, exclusions....).
- *Lack of transparency and explainability*: trained neural networks are essentially black-box models that generate an output for every input, but it is typically hard or impossible to explain why the system came to the particular output, especially in deep and complex network structures. The system does not reason but simply applies what it has learnt during training.

A large research effort is therefore under way to develop ***explainable AI (XAI) or Interpretable AI***. This is AI in which the user can comprehend the AI model and understand the underlying basis for the decisions or predictions made by the AI, making the system's outputs understandable to humans. This is different from the traditional black-box concept, where even the developers cannot always explain why the AI system arrived at a specific decision. So XAI promises to build trust that the AI system is making good decisions and that it can respond to the user's right to an explanation about the system's decision.

7 Conclusions

The following conclusions can be drawn from the brief introduction and evolutions in AI discussed in the foregoing.

- AI has clearly achieved enormous technological progress over the past decade. Once trained properly, the results of AI systems for certain well-defined tasks are sometimes better than those of humans. The diversity and sophistication of AI implementations is also improving, as shown recently by the powerful capabilities of generative AI systems.
- AI therefore has huge potential in very many applications in our society, including in the legal practice. Legal-tech applications range from all sorts of documents/

contracts screening and approval over predictive analysis and decision support all the way to automated decision making, such as digital ruling.
- To be truly useful, AI still has major technological challenges to be resolved, such as full trustworthiness, bias avoidance and explainability. Further, the EU is setting up the legal framework (including the AI Act) to enable the development and use of safe and trustworthy AI systems, as well as to stipulate the liability in case of problems or disputes.

To conclude, AI is here to stay, even in the legal practice!

Data Property Challenges in AI System Training

*Thomas Margoni and Luca Schirru**

1 The Relevance of Data

Data are essential ingredients of most modern artificial intelligence (AI) systems. Recent developments in AI have been particularly successful in the sub-field called machine learning (ML). ML is usually characterised as a process where a learning algorithm analyses and extracts certain information from underlying, usually extremely large, data sets. Common expressions such as deep learning, generative learning or artificial neural networks, while referring to different aspects or components of AI systems, can all be generally seen as related to ML. By way of illustration, the 'old' AI, often referred to in the field as GOFAI (Good Old-Fashioned AI), is often said to be predicated on a model of symbolic logic, which does not need to be trained on vast amounts of data or could do with much less. Whereas the distinction between symbolic, statistical and other forms of AI is complex – and often a given AI application is an elaborate system employing some of these approaches – what is crucial for the present analysis, and accordingly forms the core of this short contribution, is the role of *data*. The reason should be fairly clear: if AI needs data to exist and operate, then the way in which we regulate data influences – sometimes decisively – how AI can come into existence and be further developed. For instance, the existence of a property right (e.g. copyright) on specific types of training 'data' (e.g. works used for training the AI) may create additional transaction costs, as the use of such material will require the identification of the rightsholders, negotiation of licences and, ultimately, the remuneration for their use. In other words, it could be said that regulating data has assumed a new, additional, albeit indirect, function: the regulation of technologies based on data such as AI.

As will be elaborated in the following sections, 'data' is a broad concept encompassing multiple types of sources that may fall within or outside the purview of copyright law. This contribution will focus on the use of potentially copyrightable 'data' (mainly images and texts) that may be used in the training of AI systems; however, the reflections developed here can largely apply in many other situations where copyright is at stake.

* Prof. dr. Thomas Margoni is a Research Professor of Intellectual Property Law at KU Leuven. Dr. Luca Schirru is the Executive Director of the Brazilian Copyright Institute and an affiliated Senior Researcher at CiTiP (KU Leuven).

2 EU Law Applicable to Data: An Overview

One of the primary objectives of this short contribution is to examine the impact of direct and indirect regulatory interventions in the field of data and AI. Accordingly, this section will address not only the relevant definitions in the Artificial Intelligence Act[1] but also directives that are part of the broader legal framework applicable to some of the building blocks in AI development, as would be the case of data and databases.

As often happens with innovative technological developments, in the case of AI too, despite the omnipresence of the expression, its precise delimitation is unclear. A commonly accepted definition of AI, similarly to a commonly accepted definition of human intelligence, is difficult to situate. Definitions tend to be static and to emanate from a set of disciplinary and methodological assumptions. In very general terms, AI seems to commonly possess the features of being a computer program that behaves in a way that mimics (and in certain cases appears to surpass) human intelligence. Examples include well-known speech recognition and machine translation but extend to the more recent manifestations of so-called 'generative' AI, such as ChatGPT4 and Dall-E.

From a legal point of view, the proposed Artificial Intelligence Act (AIA) offers a definition of AI systems that relates to:

> software that is developed with one or more of the techniques and approaches listed in Annex I and can, for a given set of human-defined objectives, generate outputs such as content, predictions, recommendations, or decisions influencing the environments they interact with.[2]

Annex I identifies the following techniques and approaches:

> (a) Machine learning approaches, including supervised, unsupervised and reinforcement learning, using a wide variety of methods including deep learning;

---

1 This contribution was prepared in the second half of 2023, when the AI Act was at the proposal stage.

2 Commission, 'Proposal from the European Commission for a Regulation of the European Parliament and of the Council laying down harmonised rules on artificial intelligence (Artificial Intelligence Act or AI Act) and amending certain union legislative acts' [2021], COM/2021/206 final, Art. 3(1). In the remainder of this contribution, unless otherwise noted, any reference to the 'AI Act proposal', 'AI Act', or 'AIA', refers to the EC text.

> (b) Logic- and knowledge-based approaches, including knowledge representation, inductive (logic) programming, knowledge bases, inference and deductive engines, (symbolic) reasoning and expert systems;
>
> (c) Statistical approaches, Bayesian estimation, search and optimization methods.[3]

For the purpose of this chapter, as already pointed out, we are particularly interested in the methods listed under letter *(a)*, i.e., ML approaches, as these methods are those that, more than any other, extract, acquire or infer knowledge from a set of underlying data sets. However, what is decisive in this analysis is not the specific type of AI system in itself but rather its reliance on data. In other words, data is a key source of knowledge from which modern AI applications, such as ML, extract information. This source of knowledge is commonly called 'training data', which the AIA defines as:

> data used for training an AI system through fitting its learnable parameters, including the weights of a neural network;[4]

Interestingly, when the AIA calls training data 'data', it does so by employing a technical category that, in other areas of law, namely copyright, may follow different classificatory patterns. In other words, from a copyright point of view, 'data' may mean (usually unprotected) data, as such, or (usually protected) works of authorship or other protected subject matter. As will be shown, this classificatory difference may significantly influence the conditions of access and use of data and thus shape AI training and development. In other words, the term 'data' appears to be domain-specific, not only across scientific disciplines but even within the same discipline, at least when this discipline is EU law. Accordingly, a need for a systematic classification of 'data' arises in order to more clearly assess the conditions under which AI systems can be developed. Additionally, a better systematisation of data as a legal category would be conducive to a proper evaluation of the degree to which policy objectives and enacting rules established by copyright legislation align with those tentatively identified by the AIA proposal, including transparency, correctness and reproducibility.[5]

As already stated, this contribution focuses on EU copyright law and the use of certain types of data – mainly texts and images – in the training of AI systems. However, before proceeding to a more elaborate analysis of this branch of law, it is worth mentioning

3 AI Act (n 1) Annex I: Artificial Intelligence Techniques and Approaches referred to in Art. 3, point 1.
4 AI Act (n 1) Art. 3(29).
5 AI Act (n 1).

that it is not copyright alone that establishes specific conditions of use and reuse for 'data'. There are other areas of law that may determine concurrent (and potentially incompatible) access and use conditions. Focusing only on non-sectorial legislation (that is to say, excluding specific sectorial legislation that may afford additional rights or obligations in areas such as food, medicine, agriculture, climate, or spatial data), the following main legal domains can be identified:

1. In the field of personal data, the General Data Protection Regulation (GDPR) limits the ways in which data identifying natural persons may be processed, collected and stored.[6]
2. In the field of Public Sector Information, certain documents held by Public Sector Bodies (PSBs) have been made reusable by default by successive versions of the PSI Directive. The latest version of the PSI directive, also known as the Open Data Directive, has furthermore identified other types of data which follow specific reusability rules. These include so-called High-Value Datasets and research data.[7]
3. In the field of non-personal data, recently approved or proposed legislation such as the Data Governance Act and the proposed Data Act, establish specific rules to favour the reuse and access of certain data, such as IoT data.[8]
4. Trade Secrets finally represent another very relevant field of law that has the potential to significantly impact on the availability of certain type of data, when they refer to information that has commercial value in function of its secrecy.[9]

Finally, as already stated, in the field of copyright it is important to note that not only 'data' in the sense of training data could fit into different categories (e.g. works of authorship, other subject matter, mere facts and data) but also the extraction of unprotected mere facts and data from protected works such as literary or artistic works or certain databases is likewise regulated. Interestingly, extra EU legal systems have often embraced different approaches to the specific issue of 'copyright data' access regimes with consequences that can be measured in terms of competition in regulatory environments. In the remainder of this short contribution the focus will be on these

6 Regulation (EU) 2016/679 of the European Parliament and of the Council of 27 April 2016 on the protection of natural persons with regard to the processing of personal data and on the free movement of such data, and repealing Directive 95/46/EC (General Data Protection Regulation or GDPR) [2016], OJ L 119/1.

7 Directive (EU) 2019/1024 of the European Parliament and of the Council of 20 June 2019 on open data and the re-use of public sector information (Open Data Directive) [2019], OJ L 172/56.

8 Regulation (EU) 2022/868 of the European Parliament and of the Council of 30 May 2022 on European data governance and amending Regulation (EU) 2018/1724 (Data Governance Act) [2022], OJ L 152/1. Commission, 'Proposal for a Regulation of the European Parliament and of the Council on harmonised rules on fair access to and use of data (Data Act)' COM/2022/68 final ('Data Act proposal').

9 Directive (EU) 2016/943 of the European Parliament and of the Council of 8 June 2016 on the protection of undisclosed know-how and business information (trade secrets) against their unlawful acquisition, use and disclosure [2016] OJ L 157/1.

two aspects: under what conditions can data be used for training purposes, and what are the potential implications of various access regimes on technological development?

2.1 *Copyright*

Mere facts and data 'as such' (e.g. unstructured raw data concerning, for instance, weather temperature records, simply factual occurrences, even the quantities or steps necessary to prepare a tasty meal), are normally said to fall outside copyright's remit.[10] This exclusion is commonly attributed to the consideration that facts and data are the basic building blocks of human knowledge and are thus necessary for most elementary cognitive processes.[11] Protecting factual data would be tantamount to protecting a language's alphabet: no one without the owner's permission (this is the core of a property right, the right to exclude others from the enjoyment of property) could use that alphabet's letters. Therefore, the ability to put the letter together in original sequences and create new knowledge in the form of poems, lyrics, stories and, nowadays, AI applications would be impaired. Copyright law, by striking a balance between protecting original expressions and favouring the creation of new knowledge, has traditionally excluded basic elements such as letters (or single words) from exclusivity. Consequently, whereas a poem can certainly be protected when original, protection refers to the literary expression, or as it has been called, the semantic element, not to the basic alphabetical or grammatical structure (i.e. the syntactic element).[12] In this way, everyone is free to use the building blocks of human knowledge to formulate new and original creative expressions, but only the author of a given expression has the power to control (some of) its uses. More specifically, EU copyright law protects original expressions, or in the wording of constant Court of Justice of the European Union (CJEU) case law, the 'author's own intellectual creation', which is manifested through free and creative choices that allow authors to stamp their personality onto a work expressed with sufficient stability.[13]

---

10 World Trade Organization, Agreement on Trade-Related Aspects of Intellectual Property Rights (15 April 1994, Annex 1C) 1869 UNTS. 299 (TRIPS Agreement), Art. 9(2). WIPO Copyright Treaty (adopted 20 December 1996, entered into force 6 March 2002) 2186 UNTS 121 (WCT), Art. 2.

11 See P. Goldstein & P.B. Hugenholtz, *International Copyright: Principles, Law, and Practice* (4th edn, OUP 2019), at 203.

12 H. Zech, 'Data as a Tradeable Commodity – Implications for Contract Law', *in* J. Drexl (ed.), *Proceedings of the 18th EIPIN Congress: The New Data Economy between Data Ownership, Privacy and Safeguarding Competition* (Edward Elgar 2017).

13 See Case C-5/08 *Infopaq International A/S v. Danske Dagblades Forening* [2009] ECLI:EU:C:2009:465 (Infopaq I). Joined Cases C-403/08 and C-429/08 *Football Association Premier League and Others* (FAPL) ECLI:EU:C:2011:631. Case C-393/09 *Bezpečnostní softwarová asociace – Svaz softwarové ochrany v. Ministerstvo kultury* ECLI:EU:C:2010:816 (BSA). Case C-833/18 *Brompton Bicycle Ltd. v. Chedech/ Get2Get* [2020] ECLI:EU:C:2020:461 (Brompton Bicycle). C-310/17 *Levola Hengelo BV v. Smilde Foods BV*

Accordingly, if someone writes a commentary on facts that occurred in a certain historical period, or assembles the meteorological data in a qualifying database, or again elaborates on the recipe for a dish combining amounts and instructions with their own impressions and opinions, the resulting work may very well be covered by copyright if sufficiently original. The example of the database deserves further clarification. If the database is original, meaning that its structure (the selection or arrangement) reflects the author's own intellectual creation, it is only this selection or arrangement, and not the contained data, that attracts protection. This means that the structure of the database cannot be copied, but the contained data can.[14] In the EU, a Sui Generis Database Right (SGDR) has been devised to partially address this latter aspect (see section 2.2 below).

Moving from the requirements for protection to the rights afforded to protected works, the ISD Directive of 2001 is often referred to as one of the most impactful legal interventions to date.[15] For present purposes, it is certainly very relevant for having, for the first time, harmonised horizontally (i.e., not in a subject matter specific way) most of the key rights of economic exploitation. The right of reproduction has particular relevance in the process of AI training.[16] Limitations and Exceptions (L&Es)[17] to exclusive rights, on the other hand, provide for spaces of statutorily authorised uses for purposes that, within Art. 5 ISD, may cover approximatively 21 enumerated cases, often underpinned by the enjoyment of fundamental rights.[18] This juxtaposition between exclusive rights and exceptions reflects the EU approach to the challenging quest for "a fair balance between the rights and interests of authors and other rightholders, on the one hand, and of users on the other".[19] Of particular relevance for the present analysis

---

[18] ECLI:EU:C:2018:899. C-604/10 *Football Dataco Ltd and Others v. Yahoo! UK Ltd and Others* [2012] ECLI:EU:C:2012:115.

14 L. Bently, B. Sherman, D. Gangjee and P. Johnson, *Intellectual Property Law* (5th edn, OUP 2018).

15 Directive (EU) 2001/29/EC of the European Parliament and of the Council of 22 May 2001 on the harmonisation of certain aspects of copyright and related rights in the information society [2001] OJ L 167/10.

16 T. Margoni and M. Kretschmer, 'A Deeper Look into the EU Text and Data Mining Exceptions: Harmonisation, Data Ownership, and the Future of Technology' (2022) 71(8) GRUR International, 689, https://doi.org/10.1093/grurint/ikac054.

17 On the difference between 'limitations' and 'exceptions', see S. Ricketson, 'WIPO Study on Limitations and Exceptions of Copyright and Related Rights in the Digital Environment' (2003) WIPO, SCCR/9/7.

18 See C. Geiger and E. Izyumenko, 'From Internal to External Balancing, and Back? Copyright Limitations and Fundamental Rights in the Digital Environment', *in* C.S. Garcia and J. Lopez (eds.), *Digitalización, acceso a contenidos y propiedad intelectual* (Madrid, Dykinson, 2022), pp. 103-135, https://ssrn.com/abstract=3976407. See also some of the cases mentioned by the authors: Cases C-469/17, *Funke Medien NRW GmbH v. Bundesrepublik Deutschland* ECLI:EU:C:2019:623; C-476/17, *Pelham GmbH and Others v. Ralf Hütter and Florian Schneider-Esleben*, ECLI:EU:C:2019:624; Case C-516/17, *Spiegel Online GmbH v. Volker Beck*, ECLI:EU:C:2019:625.

19 Directive (EU) 2019/790 of the European Parliament and of the Council of 17 April 2019 on copyright and related rights in the Digital Single Market and amending Directives 96/9/EC and 2001/29/EC [2019] OJ L 130/92 (CDSM), rec 6.

are the recently introduced Text and Data Mining Exceptions, present in arts. 3 and 4 of the Directive (EU) 2019/790 on copyright and related rights in the Digital Single Market (CDSM Directive), which will be further analysed in the following sections.[20]

2.2 The EU Sui Generis Database Rights (SGDR)

As already mentioned, databases which "by reason of the selection or arrangement of their contents, constitute the author's own intellectual creation" may be protected by copyright.[21] However, in the field of databases, the EU has a rather unique form of protection: a *Sui Generis Database Right (SGDR)*. Regulated in Directive 96/9/EC on the legal protection of databases, the SGDR is founded on grounds other than originality. It is not the intellectual effort employed in the selection and arrangement of the contents, but the "substantial investment in either the obtaining, verification or presentation of the contents" that triggers protection.[22]

Recital 40 of the Database Directive explains that a substantial investment "may consist in the deployment of financial resources and/or the expending of time, effort and energy". While an exact amount of investment is not specified, the Directive as well as the case law of the CJEU provides additional guidance on how to determine which investment is sufficiently substantial.[23] It should be stressed that these databases (both the ones protected under copyright and the ones protected by the SGDR) may or may not contain copyrighted works. Therefore, databases may enjoy multiple layers of protection:[24] (i) copyright protection of the materials that are part of the database; (ii) copyright on the database structure; and (iii) SGDR on substantial amount of data. It should be further noted that these three different layers of proprietary claims over the same data set may very well follow different and diverging paths. In other words, the owners of the copyright in the database, of the copyright in the elements

---

20 Other potentially relevant L&E such as Art. 5(1) ISD will not be discussed in detail here. For a general overview see Margoni and Kretschmer (n 16).

21 Directive 96/9/EC of the European Parliament and of the Council of 11 March 1996 on the legal protection of databases [1996] OJ L 77/20 (Database Directive), Art. 3(1).

22 Database Directive (n 21), Art 7(1).

23 Database Directive (n 21) rec 19 ("Whereas, as a rule, the compilation of several recordings of musical performances on a CD does not come within the scope of this Directive, both because, as a compilation, it does not meet the conditions for copyright protection and because it does not represent a substantial enough investment to be eligible under the sui generis right;"). *Inter alia*: Case C-338/02 *Fixtures Marketing Ltd v. Svenska Spel AB* [2004] ECR I-10497, paras 26-29; Case C-203/02 *The British Horseracing Board Ltd and Others v. William Hill Organization Ltd* [2004] ECR I-10415, paras 31-42.

24 See A.R. de Souza, L. Schirru and M. Alvarenga (2020) 'Covid-19, Text and Data Mining and Copyright: The Brazilian Case', *in* Y. Pai, J. van Weelde and W. Zaman (eds.), *WIPO-WTO Colloquium Papers 11: WIPO Academy and WTO IP* (Government Procurement and Competition Division).

constituting the database and of the SGDR may be different subjects. Likewise, the specific rules and exceptions applying to these different layers may be quite different (particularly in the case of the SGDR). This fragmentation of proprietary claims over the same informational asset has often been criticised in the literature as a source of legal uncertainty and economic inefficiency.[25]

2.3 *Text and Data Mining*

Training AI systems using copyright protected works often involves what is commonly referred to as Text and Data Mining. Text and Data Mining is defined in the CDSM Directive as

> any automated analytical technique aimed at analysing text and data in digital form in order to generate information which includes but is not limited to patterns, trends and correlations.[26]

This definition is deemed by part of the literature as being too broad, with the risk of encompassing "not only TDM but all forms of modern data-driven digital analytics that rely on training on data".[27] This is potentially troublesome when all technologies within this spectrum are subject to narrow exceptions.[28] We refer to the abundant literature for a detailed analysis of the features and limits of the TDM exceptions. It suffices here to point out that under EU law TDM is limited as to the *purposes, users, uses and access*.[29] Accordingly, the TDM provisions apply only to the right of reproduction (for copyrighted works) and extraction (regarding databases protected under the SGDR) and only benefit 'research organisations and cultural heritage institutions' acting for the 'purpose' of scientific research. Additionally, the permitted uses are allowed only

25 Margoni and Kretschmer (n 16).

26 CDSM Directive (n 19), Art. 2(2).

27 Margoni and Kretschmer (n 16) 686.

28 Margoni and Kretschmer (n 16). On the matter, see also E. Rosati, 'Copyright as An Obstacle or An Enabler? A European Perspective on Text and Data Mining and Its Role in the Development of AI Creativity' (2019) 27 (2) Asia Pacific Law Review 215. C. Geiger, G. Frosio and O. Bulayenko, 'Text and Data Mining: Articles 3 and 4 of the Directive 2019/790/EU', *in* C.S. Garcia and R.E. Llorca (eds.), *Propiedad intelectual y mercado único digital europeo* (Tirant lo blanch 2019). Centre for International Intellectual Property Studies (CEIPI) Research Paper No. 2019-08, https://ssrn.com/abstract=3470653.

29 See S.M. Flynn, B. Butler, M.W. Carroll, O. Cohen-Sasson, C. Craig, L. Guibault, P. Jaszi, B.J. Jütte, A. Katz, J.P. Quintais, T. Margoni, A.R. de Souza, M. Sag, R. Samberg, L. Schirru, M. Senftleben, O. Tur-Sinai and J.L. Contreras, 'Legal Reform to Enhance Global Text and Data Mining Research' (2022) 378 Science 951. See also, S.M. Flynn, L. Schirru, M. Palmedo and A. Izquierdo, 'Research Exceptions in Comparative Copyright' (2022) PIJIP/TLS Research Paper Series no. 75, https://digitalcommons.wcl.american.edu/research/75/.

regarding subject matter to which the user had lawful access, which has also been criticised in the literature.[30]

The very same need for a TDM exception is still contested by a section of the scholarship.[31] This is because the uses carried out in a TDM-related project may be arguably considered non-expressive, meaning "any act of reproduction that is not intended to enable human enjoyment, appreciation, or comprehension of the copied expression as expression".[32] This argument is closely related to the idea-expression dichotomy, since "[p]reserving the idea-expression dichotomy in the digital world means recognizing that copying a work for purely non-expressive purposes also does not infringe."[33] Building an analogy with the human 'learning process', when humans learn, the electrochemical record, i.e., a copy of the training material (textbooks, novels, songs, etc.) in the area of the brain dedicated to memory does not need a copyright exception. The same cannot be said for the equivalent copies made by computers, at least in the EU.[34] This effect can be attributed to broad definitions (e.g. right of reproduction) channelled through narrow exceptions (Arts. 3&4 CDSM), combined with a relatively low level of originality and the protection of non-original subject matter, chiefly the SGDR.

3 GENERATIVE AI

Generative AI is a type of AI system capable of generating text, images or other media in response to prompts usually entered by a human operator. Generative AI systems use generative models to statistically sample new data based on the training data set that was used to create them.[35] In other words, Generative AI systems can generate text or images as a reaction to someone entering a prompt like 'Say hello world' or 'draw a new Picasso'. The impressive and potentially game-changing effect is that nowadays good Generative

---

30 See e.g., M.W. Carroll, 'Copyright and the Progress of Science: Why Text and Data Mining is Lawful' (2019) 53 U.C. Davis Law Review 893.

31 See e.g., M. Sag, 'The New Legal Landscape for Text Mining and Machine Learning' (2019) 66 Journal of the Copyright Society of the USA 1.

32 Sag (n 31) 6. See also, T. Ueno, 'Chapter 6: Big Data in Japan: Copyright, Trade Secret and New Regime in 2018', *in* S.K. Sandeen, C. Rademacher and A. Ohly (eds.), *Research Handbook on Information Law and Governance* (Cheltenham: Edward Elgar Publishing, 2021). C.J. Craig, 'Globalizing User Rights-Talk: On Copyright Limits and Rhetorical Risks' (2017) 33 American University International Law Review 1.

33 Sag (n 31) 9.

34 On a comparative analysis of the research exceptions (including TDM), see Flynn et al., 'Legal Reform to Enhance Global Text and Data Mining Research' (n 29) and Flynn et al., 'Research Exceptions in Comparative Copyright' (n 29).

35 See 'Generative artificial intelligence' (Art. from Wikipedia, 31 Mar 2023), https://en.wikipedia.org/wiki/Generative_artificial_intelligence (accessed 4 April 2023).

AI systems can easily and plausibly answer both queries in a way that would appear human generated.

Generative AI systems have reached a level of sophistication and of 'human plausibility' that was not even imaginable a few years ago. Accordingly, the question of whether AI can be considered creative and, if so, whether the AI can or should be considered as an author from a copyright point of view surfaced.[36] Cases like the Next Rembrandt,[37] the 'portrait' of Edmond de Belamy,[38] the movie script from Sunspring,[39] and the inventions obtained from the employment of DABUS[40] prove that AI systems can generate products that, *prima facie*,[41] could reach the standards for intellectual property rights (IPRs) had they been created by humans.[42]

Some of the most popular or well-known projects or applications are those related to OpenAI (mainly ChatGPT[43] and Dall-E 2[44]), Github's CoPilot[45] and, more recently, Stable Diffusion,[46] DreamStudio,[47] and Midjourney.[48] Even though these systems

---

36 See, e.g., A. Bridy, 'Coding Creativity: Copyright and the Artificially Intelligent Author' (2012) 5 Stanford Technology Law Review 1-28, http://ssrn.com/abstract=1888622; M.A. Boden, 'Computer Models of Creativity' (2009) Artificial Intelligence Magazine. Association for the Advancement of Artificial Intelligence.

37 'The Next Rembrandt', https://youtu.be/IuygOYZ1Ngo?si=hN3hc4YZiRmWgKSn (accessed 31 January 2023).

38 'Edmond de Belamy' (Obvious), https://obvious-art.com/portfolio/edmond-de-belamy/ (accessed 31 January 2023).

39 'Sunspring | A Sci-Fi Short Film Starring Thomas Middleditch' (*Ars Technica*, 9 June 2016), https://www.youtube.com/watch?v=LY7x2Ihqjmc (accessed 31 January 2023).

40 'The Artificial Inventor Project' (2022), https://artificialinventor.com/ (accessed 31 January 2023).

41 R. Susskind and D. Susskind, *The Future of the Professions: How Technology will Transform the Work of Human Experts* (OUP, 2015), 278 ("To be more precise, then, the fundamental question to be asked and answered is whether machines and systems can undertake tasks that for human beings require cognitive, affective, manual, and moral capabilities, even if they discharge these tasks by quite different means."). O. Bulayenko, J.P. Quintais, D. Gervais and J. Poort, 'D3.5 AI Music Outputs: Challenges to the Copyright Legal Framework'. (Zenodo, 2022), https://doi.org/10.5281/zenodo.6405796.

42 On the matter, see, e.g., T. Margoni and M. Perry, 'Ownership in Complex Authorship: A Comparative Study of Joint Works in Copyright Law' (2012) 34(1) European Intellectual Property Review 22-32, https://ssrn.com/abstract=1992610; L. Schirru, *Direito Autoral e Inteligência Artificial: Autoria e titularidade nos Produtos da* IA (Dialética, 2023). J. Vanherpe, 'AI and IP: Great Expectations', *in* J. De Bruyne, C. Vanleenhove (eds.), *Artificial Intelligence and the Law* (Intersentia, Vol. 13, 2022), 233-267.

43 OpenAI, 'ChatGPT: Optimizing Language Models for Dialogue' (*OpenAI*, 30 November 2022), https://openai.com/blog/chatgpt/ (accessed 31 January 2023).

44 OpenAI, 'Dall-E 2' (*OpenAI*, 2023), https://openai.com/dall-e-2/ (accessed 31 January 2023).

45 'Your AI pair programmer' (*GitHub*, 2023), https://github.com/features/copilot (accessed 31 January 2023).

46 Stable Diffusion Online, https://stablediffusionweb.com/ (accessed 15 March 2023).

47 DreamStudio, https://beta.dreamstudio.ai/dream (accessed 15 March 2023).

48 Midjourney, https://www.midjourney.com/home/?callbackUrl=%2Fapp%2F (accessed 15 March 2023).

are currently starring the news with rather impressive results,[49] copyright litigation is catching up. Github CoPilot is the object of a class action because, among other things, there has been "use of free software as source material for a commercial AI application" without meeting some of the licence requirements, which may result in the infringement of software licences and underlying copyright.[50] Regarding the relatively novel text-to-image Generative AI, it is illustrative to observe the recent lawsuits filed by Getty Images both in the UK[51] and in the US[52] against Stability AI. Getty Images is bringing legal proceedings against Stability AI for having allegedly "unlawfully copied and processed millions of images protected by copyright and the associated metadata owned or represented by Getty Images absent a license".[53] Similarly, in a different proceeding a group of artists accuse Stability AI of using copyrighted works without any licence for commercial uses in a damaging way because

> Defendants' AI Image Products produce digital images and other output that act as market substitutes for the underlying Training Images, thereby competing with Plaintiffs and members of the Class.[54]

Stable Diffusion's new AI model was recognised by its capability of "distil[ling] the essence of billions of training images into an AI model of just a few gigabytes".[55] Allegedly, the training was so intensive that when prompted to recreate a sport-related scene, Stability AI automatically embedded what appears to be a Getty watermark (see Figure 1).

49 S.M. Kelly, 'ChatGPT Passes Exams from Law and Business Schools' (*CNN Business*, 26 January 2023), https://edition.cnn.com/2023/01/26/tech/chatgpt-passes-exams/index.html (accessed 31 January 2023).

50 On the main issues that are being discussed, see, e.g., C. Topham, 'Publication of the FSF-Funded White Papers on Questions Around Copilot' (*Free Software Foundation*, 24 February 2022), https://www.fsf.org/news/publication-of-the-fsf-funded-white-papers-on-questions-around-copilot (accessed 31 January 2023). See also, F. Reda, 'GitHub Copilot Is Not Infringing Your Copyright' (5 July 2021), https://felixreda.eu/2021/07/github-copilot-is-not-infringing-your-copyright/ (accessed 31 January 2023).

51 See A. Aronsson-Storrier and O. Fairhurst, 'Litigation Commenced Against the Developers of AI Image Generation Software' (IPKat, 3 February 2023), https://ipkitten.blogspot.com/2023/02/guest-post-litigation-commenced-against.html; B. Brittain, 'Getty Images lawsuit says Stability AI Misused Photos to Train AI' (Reuters, 6 February 2023), https://www.reuters.com/legal/getty-images-lawsuit-says-stability-ai-misused-photos-train-ai-2023-02-06/.

52 *Getty Images Inc v. Stability AI Inc*, U.S. District Court for the District of Delaware, No. 1:23-cv-00135.

53 'Getty Images Statement' (GettyImages 17 January 2023), https://newsroom.gettyimages.com/en/getty-images/getty-images-statement.

54 *Andersen v. Stability AI Ltd*, U.S. District Court for the Northern District of California, No. 3:23-cv-00201, Class Action Complaint filed by the Plaintiffs, at 31.

55 Ludwig-Maximilians-Universität München, 'Revolutionizing Image Generation by AI: Turning Text into Images' (*News*, 1 September 2022), https://www.lmu.de/en/newsroom/news-overview/news/revolutionizing-image-generation-by-ai-turning-text-into-images.html. See also R. Rombach, A. Blattmann, D. Lorenz, P. Esser and B. Ommer, 'High-Resolution Image Synthesis with Latent Diffusion Models', *Proceedings of the IEEE Conference on Computer Vision and Pattern Recognition (CVPR)* (2022).

Figure 1 Extracted from the Complaint filed by Getty Images with Jury Demand, p. 22. Getty Images (US), Inc. v. Stability AI, Inc., 1:23-cv-00135, (D. Del.).

Interestingly, however, despite being the example that most prominently reached the media and shed light on this debate, the images hosted by Getty were arguably not the main source of training data for Stability AI.[56] Other sources like Pinterest and blogs hosted at WordPress, DeviantArt, and Flickr contributed quite significantly to the training of Stable Diffusion AI.[57]

While these litigations and the connected dynamics have yet to completely unfold in their legal and social implications, the relationship between content holders like Getty Images and AI-generated content already shows a significant shift in business models and cultural practices.[58] For instance, Getty has stated that until copyright (and other legal) issues are adequately addressed regarding AI-generated works, AI-generated content is banned from the Getty Images platform.[59] In a press statement, the CEO of Getty Images explains that

56 A. Baio, 'Exploring 12 Million of the 2.3. Billion Images Used to Train Stable Diffusion's Image Generator', (Waxy, 30 August 2022), https://waxy.org/2022/08/exploring-12-million-of-the-images-used-to-train-stable-diffusions-image-generator/.

57 Ibid.

58 J. Vincent, 'Getty Images bans AI-Generated Content Over Fears of Legal Challenges' (TheVerge, 21 September 2022), https://www.theverge.com/2022/9/21/23364696/getty-images-ai-ban-generated-artwork-illustration-copyright; B. Edwards, 'Fearing Copyright Issues, Getty Images Bans AI-generated Artwork' (ArsTechnica, 22 September 2022), https://arstechnica.com/information-technology/2022/09/fearing-copyright-issues-getty-images-bans-ai-generated-artwork/.

59 J. Vincent, 'Getty Images Bans AI-Generated Content Over Fears of Legal Challenges' (TheVerge, 21 Septermber 2022), https://www.theverge.com/2022/9/21/23364696/getty-images-ai-ban-generated-artwork-illustration-copyright.

> There are real concerns with respect to the copyright of outputs from these models and unaddressed rights issues with respect to the imagery, the image metadata and those individuals contained within the imagery.[60]

The Stability AI complaint brought by a group of artists in California is interesting in another quite intriguing aspect. Among various other causes of action, plaintiffs argue that the AI, having been trained on their work, is able to replicate not only their works but also plausible alternatives, i.e., new works of art employing the style of a given artist or genre. This is an interesting development, which well identifies both the issue of creation of cheaper substitutes in the art market and the fascinating question of whether artists have a (property? personality?) right to their own individual artistic style or to the artistic genre that they identify themselves with.[61]

The need to train AI systems on vast amounts of data has the additional conceivable effect of providing an advantage for those players who already possess large databases. The case of Stability AI and Getty shows the potential dynamics when the AI developer and the data holder are two separate entities. But naturally, there are situations where these two positions are occupied by the same player. This is the case of Google, Facebook, Amazon, and other large platforms which, on the one hand, already possess vast amounts of (usually user-generated) data and, on the other hand, are (very) active in the field of AI development. The fact that actors such as Stability AI need to acquire licences (i.e., pay a price) or anyway bear the uncertainties of litigation, has the potential to further consolidate the dominance of these already highly integrated platforms in their market positions. The case of OpenAI's GPT3 and now 4 is also indicative. Differently from Stability AI, which fully documents its training data sets, OpenAI (since version 3) has not been releasing information about its training data sets, attracting obvious criticisms in the sector about its abandoned 'openness'.[62] This is another potential (and warring if confirmed) effect of the recognition of property rights in training data: to avoid exposing oneself to potential copyright litigation, developers and tech firms perceive a strong incentive not to disclose information about their

60 J. Vincent, 'Getty Images Bans AI-Generated Content Over Fears of Legal Challenges' (TheVerge, 21 September 2022), https://www.theverge.com/2022/9/21/23364696/getty-images-ai-ban-generated-artwork-illustration-copyright.

61 *Andersen v. Stability AI Ltd.*, U.S. District Court for the Northern District of California, No. 3:23-cv-00201. B. Brittain, 'Lawsuits Accuse AI Content Creators of Misusing Copyrighted Work' (Reuters, 17 January 2023), https://www.reuters.com/legal/transactional/lawsuits-accuse-ai-content-creators-misusing-copyrighted-work-2023-01-17/; B. Brittain, 'Getty Images Lawsuit Says Stability AI Misused Photos to Train AI' (Reuters, 6 February 2023), https://www.reuters.com/legal/getty-images-lawsuit-says-stability-ai-misused-photos-train-ai-2023-02-06/.

62 J. Vincent, 'OpenAI Co-Founder on Company's Past Approach to Openly Sharing Research: 'We Were Wrong' (The Verge, 15 March 2023), https://www.theverge.com/2023/3/15/23640180/openai-gpt-4-launch-closed-research-ilya-sutskever-interview.

training data set, thereby further aggravating the issue of opacity, unaccountability and bias in AI applications.[63]

Finally, an already partially documented effect of a legal framework that makes training data more costly is the fact that firms (at least those with higher degrees of mobility) may decide to relocate towards 'cheaper' legal systems, i.e., legal systems that afford broader areas of exemption for AI training purposes, such as the US, Japan or Singapore.[64]

4 Brief Final Reflections on the Regulation of Data and AI

Generative AI, with its potentially unlimited impact on various aspects of reality, from business models to cultural productions, has only recently entered the scene, but it will likely become a common companion in the life of creatives, technologists and users. The ways in which AI may impact on life and reality are virtually unlimited and the issue of AI regulation will accordingly transcend specific domains and affect a variety of rights and obligations.

In this short contribution we intended to highlight a specific effect employing copyright law as the analytical lens: it is not direct regulation alone that will determine the future of AI in a given legal system. Indirect regulation (such as the regulation of the building blocks necessary for AI development) may very well contribute significantly to shaping the future of this technology. The risk is that indirect regulation may not always be conscious regulation. It is far from clear that the policy objectives and political choices that lead to the enactment of some of the rules regulating copyright and non-personal data analysed previously embed the necessary innovation, policy and fundamental rights considerations needed when the indirect objective of regulation is a field (AI) that is rather distant from the direct one (copyright).

---

63 T. Margoni, J.P. Quintais and S.F. Schwemer, 'Algorithmic Propagation: Do Property Rights in Data Increase Bias in Content Moderation? Part I' (Kluwer Copyright Blog, 8 June 2022), https://copyrightblog.kluweriplaw.com/2022/06/08/algorithmic-propagation-do-property-rights-in-data-increase-bias-in-content-moderation-part-i/; T. Margoni, J.P. Quintais and S.F. Schwemer, 'Algorithmic Propagation: Do Property Rights in Data Increase Bias in Content Moderation? – Part II' (Kluwer Copyright Blog, 9 June 2022), https://copyrightblog.kluweriplaw.com/2022/06/09/algorithmic-propagation-do-property-rights-in-data-increase-bias-in-content-moderation-part-ii/.

64 C. Handke, L. Guibault and J.J. Vallbé, 'Is Europe Falling Behind in Data Mining? Copyright's Impact on Data Mining in Academic Research', *in* B. Schmidt and M. Dobreva (eds.), *New Avenues for Electronic Publishing in the Age of Infinite Collections and Citizen Science: Scale, Openness and Trust: Proceedings of the 19th International Conference on Electronic Publishing* (IOS Press, 2015) 120-130.

THE ETHICS OF AI: FROM AI ETHICS TO MACHINE ETHICS

*Yeliz Figen Döker**

1 INTRODUCTION

Envision a near future where artificial intelligence (AI) systems, seamlessly woven into our legal, social and ethical fabric, transcend mere computational tasks to engage in ethical deliberation. This is not a distant philosophical speculation but an impending reality.[1] As society teeters on the brink of a transformative phase in the nexus of law and technology,[2] AI's advancements resonate with the profound impacts of past innovations[3] like the internet and biotechnology.[4] These technological leaps, including AI, invariably present both ground-breaking opportunities and intricate ethical challenges, nudging us to reconsider established legal and moral frameworks.[5]

The chapter embarks on a nuanced exploration of the ethics of AI, a domain that is as intricate as it is consequential. At the heart of this exploration are two pivotal yet distinct areas: AI Ethics and Machine Ethics. While they may appear to be interchangeable at first glance, a closer examination reveals subtle yet significant divergences. AI Ethics is preoccupied with the ethical dimensions surrounding the human activities involved in the creation and governance of AI technologies. It grapples with issues such as data privacy, algorithmic bias, and the broader societal implications of AI.

---

* Yeliz Figen Döker, PhD candidate in Law at the European University Institute (EUI). She is working on Experiential Learning in Artificial General Intelligence. She is co-founder and head of the science fiction section of The Digital Constitutionalist (DigiCon) and a member of the Istanbul Bar Association.

1 Lyria B. Moses, *Why Have a Theory of Law and Technological Change?*, 8 Minn. J.L. Sci. & Tech. 589 (2007).; Lyria Bennett Moses, 'Recurring Dilemmas: The Law's Race to Keep Up With Technological Change'. *SSRN Electronic Journal* (2007). https://doi.org/10.2139/ssrn.979861; Kieran Tranter, *Nomology, Ontology, and Phenomenology of Law and Technology*, 8 MINN. J.L. SCI. & TECH. 449 (2007), 27.

2 Gregory N. Mandel, 'History Lessons for a General Theory of Law and Technology'. *Minnesota Journal of Law, Science & Technology Minnesota Journal of Law, Science & Technology* 8, no. 2 (n.d.): 21.

3 Clive Emsley, '"Mother, What *Did* Policemen Do When There Weren't Any Motors?" The Law, the Police and the Regulation of Motor Traffic in England, 1900-1939'. *The Historical Journal* 36, no. 2 (June 1993): 357-81, 358. https://doi.org/10.1017/S0018246X00019270.

4 United Nations, 'Declaration on Human Cloning'. *Journal of International Biotechnology Law* 2, no. 5 (7 January 2005). https://doi.org/10.1515/jibl.2005.2.5.211.

5 Hoffmann-Riem, Wolfgang. 'Artificial Intelligence as a Challenge for Law and Regulation'. In *Regulating Artificial Intelligence*, edited by Thomas Wischmeyer and Timo Rademacher, 1-29, 22. Cham: Springer International Publishing, 2020. https://doi.org/10.1007/978-3-030-32361-5_1.

Transitioning from the human-centric concerns of AI Ethics, the chapter then delves into Machine Ethics, a domain concerned with the ethical behaviour of the machines themselves. This shift in focus is not merely academic but serves as a critical juncture that allows us to scrutinise the moral dilemmas AI systems face when deployed in real-world scenarios.

However, the ethical landscape of AI is not a monolith; it is a complex tapestry woven from a myriad of ethical theories, cultural norms and practical considerations. To elucidate this complexity, the chapter critically examines two prominent approaches to implementing AI Ethics: the Rights-Based Approach and the Empirical Approach. The former emphasises the protection of fundamental human rights and ethical principles, while the latter underscores the importance of cultural sensitivity and user-centric design.

As we navigate through these intricate ethical terrains, the chapter also confronts the challenges posed by cultural particularities and the lack of universally agreed-upon ethical principles. It raises thought-provoking questions about the extent to which AI Ethics should or can be universalised, offering a nuanced view that takes into account both individualist and collectivist cultural perspectives.

In sum, this chapter serves both as a comprehensive overview and as a foundational text for understanding the multifaceted ethical landscape of AI. It aims to arm its readers with a robust, informed perspective, setting the stage for subsequent research and practical insights into this rapidly evolving domain.

Given AI's transformative trajectory, it is essential to ponder: how might the interplay between Machine Ethics and AI Ethics recalibrate or even challenge age-old ethical tenets amid rapidly evolving digital ecosystems? Is it possible to acknowledge AI as an ethical agent?[6]

Aiming to provide a robust understanding of the ethical nuances tied to AI's evolution, this chapter sets the stage for subsequent research and practical insights into the domain. By delving into this content, readers will be better positioned to traverse AI's complex ethical terrain, armed with a refined and informed perspective.

6 Ali Ladak, 'What Would Qualify an Artificial Intelligence for Moral Standing?' *AI and Ethics*, 25 January 2023: 2. https://doi.org/10.1007/s43681-023-00260-1.

2 Ethics of AI

At first glance, the two disciplines under the ethics of AI – AI Ethics and Machine Ethics – may appear interchangeable,[7] largely converging on the same ethical dilemmas that emerge from machine autonomy.[8] However, they diverge in ways subtle yet significant, much like statutes and case law. AI Ethics is largely preoccupied with questions surrounding the creation and governance of these technologies. Think of it as the rules of the game – the laws, the protocols, the regulations. For instance, UNESCO addresses gender bias in AI in the UNESCO Recommendation on the Ethics of Artificial Intelligence.[9] Another example is companies leveraging data and AI to create scalable solutions but also scaling their reputational, regulatory and legal risks.

Machine ethics, conversely, is concerned with the behaviour of the machines themselves once they are released into the wild, as it were. In this context, consider AI systems as 'ethical agents', with machine ethics governing their actions.[10] A seminal study by Anderson and Anderson developed an ethical reasoning algorithm for healthcare robots, demonstrating that machines can be programmed to make ethically sound decisions.[11] Furthermore, a comprehensive review by Mittelstadt et al. in 2018 scrutinised 84 ethics guidelines for AI, identifying core principles for ethical compliance that can be coded into machines.[12]

3 AI Ethics

Legal scholars and ethicists, especially those who navigate the confluence of both fields, frequently grapple with intricate ideas. AI stands out – a profound force reshaping not only our legal frameworks but also our foundational ethical beliefs.[13] But when we reference 'AI Ethics', what exactly are we addressing? Is it simply a niche within the vast landscape of applied ethics, or does it demand a deeper exploration?

---

7 Mark Coeckelbergh, *AI Ethics* (The MIT Press, Cambridge, Massachusetts, 2020).

8 Samuel T. Segun, 'From Machine Ethics to Computational Ethics'. *AI & Society* 36, no. 1 (1 March 2021): 263-76, 266. https://doi.org/10.1007/s00146-020-01010-1.

9 'Ethics of Artificial Intelligence'. UNESCO. Accessed 13 September 2023. https://www.unesco.org/en/artificial-intelligence/recommendation-ethics.

10 James H. Moor, 'The Nature, Importance, and Difficulty of Machine Ethics', in *Machine Ethics*, edited by Michael Anderson and Susan Leigh Anderson, 1st ed. (Cambridge University Press, 2011), 13-20, 15. https://doi.org/10.1017/CBO9780511978036.003.

11 Michael Anderson, and Susan Leigh Anderson. 'Machine Ethics: Creating an Ethical Intelligent Agent'. *AI Magazine* 28, no. 4 (15 December 2007): 15-15. https://doi.org/10.1609/aimag.v28i4.2065.

12 Brent Mittelstadt, 'Principles Alone Cannot Guarantee Ethical AI'. *Nature Machine Intelligence* 1, no. 11 (November 2019): 501-7. https://doi.org/10.1038/s42256-019-0114-4.

13 Hoffmann-Riem, 'Artificial Intelligence as a Challenge for Law and Regulation', 22.

AI Ethics, despite its seemingly straightforward nomenclature, is anything but a simple field. On the contrary, it extends far beyond the computer science labs and Silicon Valley boardrooms to penetrate the realm of jurisprudence, social norms and even human rights. If law, as it is often said, is the codification of society's ethics, then AI Ethics is concerned with the responsible design, development and deployment of AI technologies. Specifically, AI Ethics focuses on the ethical considerations surrounding human activities in these processes, including, but not limited to, issues of data privacy, algorithmic bias and social implications such as job displacement or inequality. So the praxis of AI Ethics targets the human agency, not the machine, and its scope is how humans should deal with AI technology, not how AI can embody self-defined ethical rules.[14]

The Vital Questions: An Inquiry into the Ethical Underpinnings

AI Ethics stands at the crossroads of law and philosophy, presenting a myriad of complex challenges. Chief among these is the task of ensuring AI developers align with ethical principles.[15] Furthermore, translating these ethical principles into tangible regulatory frameworks is no small feat. Despite extensive discussions in the field, a consensus on best practices is yet to emerge.[16] This often stems from a foundational challenge: we lack a universally agreed-upon ethical base from which to derive these norms.

Over the past years, governments, parliaments, associations and industry circles have drafted and published numerous ethical guidelines[17] to establish a solid foundation for AI Ethics. Building a solid foundation requires understanding ethics itself before focusing on one branch of ethics. However, this requirement in itself creates another paradox: we do not know which ethical theory we most often choose to follow, how we follow it, or the basis of our morality and why we are ethical agents.[18] This paradox, in fact, puts AI Ethics in a major predicament of its own.[19] One significant critique of AI Ethics is that, despite the proliferation of ethical guidelines and frameworks, no

---

14 Coeckelbergh, *AI Ethics*, 145.

15 Simon Chesterman, 'From Ethics to Law: Why, When, and How to Regulate AI'. *SSRN Electronic Journal* (2023): 8. https://doi.org/10.2139/ssrn.4432941.

16 Anna Jobin, Marcello Ienca, and Effy Vayena. 'The Global Landscape of AI Ethics Guidelines'. *Nature Machine Intelligence* 1, no. 9 (2 September 2019): 389-99. https://doi.org/10.1038/s42256-019-0088-2.

17 According to Algorithm Watch, there are guidelines over 250, see: AlgorithmWatch, 'AI Ethics Guidelines Global Inventory'. Accessed 6 September 2023. https://algorithmwatch.org/en/ai-ethics-guidelines-global-inventory/.

18 Christopher Boehm, *Moral Origins: The Evolution of Virtue, Altruism and Shame* (Basic Books, 2012), 15-16. https://www.amazon.com/Moral-Origins-Evolution-Virtue-Altruism/dp/0465020488.

19 Patricia S. Churchland, *Conscience: The Origins of Moral Intuition* (W. W. Norton & Company, New York, 2019), 10-21.

single ethical paradigm has emerged as universally accepted.[20] Floridi, for example, has warned against the risks of 'ethics washing',[21] where the multitude of guidelines serve more as a veneer of ethical concern rather than as a genuine guide for ethical AI development.[22]

Further, the ethical considerations of AI have yet to be adequately addressed, with no clear consensus as to how to put proposed practices into action. How can we ensure that the creators of these technologies conduct themselves ethically? How can we ensure that these systems act in an ethical manner? Instead of attempting to address such crucial concerns, we have spent the previous five years arguing what AI and ethics are and why these systems should be ethical. Since AI will be a reflection of ourselves,[23] and its ethical code will be an extension of our own,[24] the implications of AI Ethics are further complicated by the fact that humans are yet to fully comprehend the origins of their own morality and ethics.[25] This lack of understanding of how to handle the ethics of AI may be the primary factor preventing the shift from debating the 'why' to debating the 'how'.

4 Implementing AI Ethics

The practical implementation of AI Ethics is another complex endeavour, necessitating a multifaceted approach that accommodates both normative ethical theories and empirical investigations. In this section, we critically examine two prominent approaches – Rights-Based and Empirical Approaches – to elucidate the divergent methodologies and underlying philosophies that shape the implementation of AI Ethics. Concurrently, we address the challenges posed by conflicting terminologies and cultural biases, which contribute to the current state of ambivalence in the field.

---

20 Elettra Bietti, 'From Ethics Washing to Ethics Bashing: A View on Tech Ethics from within Moral Philosophy'. In *FAT* '20: Proceedings of the 2020 Conference on Fairness, Accountability, and Transparency* (New York: Association for Computing Machinery, 2020), 210-19. https://doi.org/10.1145/3351095.3372860.

21 Ethics washing is a term used to describe companies or organisations that use ethical practices or values as a way to improve their public image and reputation without actually making any real changes to their business practices. It is a way for companies to appear to be socially responsible and ethical without actually living up to their promises or commitments. It is a dishonest practice that can have serious consequences for those who fall victim to it.

22 Luciano Floridi, *Translating Principles into Practices of Digital Ethics: Five Risks of Being Unethical* (Springer: Philosophy & Technology, 2019), 187.

23 Rostam J. Neuwirth, *The EU Artificial Intelligence Act: Regulating Subliminal AI Systems* (Routledge, London, 2022), 61.

24 Pew Research Center, 'Worries about developments in AI' (2021) Stephen Downes Interview. https://www.pewresearch.org/internet/2021/06/16/1-worries-about-developments-in-ai/.

25 Boehm, 'Moral Origins: The Evolution of Virtue, Altruism, and Shame', 15.

4.1 Rights-Based Approach: The European Model of Trustworthy AI

The Rights-Based Approach is currently the most prevalent method of codifying AI Ethics.[26] This methodology emphasises the protection of fundamental human rights and ethical principles throughout the AI design process. The framework encapsulates respect for individual freedoms, democracy, justice, equality, anti-discrimination and the rule of law. Moreover, ethical principles such as beneficence and the principle of 'Do-No-Harm' are also integrated into this approach.

For instance, prior to the introduction of the European Union's AI Act, the focus was primarily on AI Ethics. This was manifested in the 'Guidelines for Trustworthy AI', developed by a high-level expert group convened by the European Commission.[27] This document operationalises the concept of 'Trustworthy AI', aiming to pre-emptively counter the misuse or abuse of AI technology. The framework comprises three core tenets: lawfulness, ethics and robustness. Despite its comprehensive scope, critics argue that the framework's terminologies are overly broad, leading to potential misinterpretations. To address this, the Assessment List for Trustworthy AI (ALTAI) was initiated as a dynamic checklist for ethical implementation.[28] However, recent studies have shown that the implementation of AI Ethics still remains an issue.[29] Findings offer a nuanced view of ethical awareness among scholars engaged in AI research. While there is a general cognisance of ethical considerations encapsulated in ALTAI, the depth of this understanding varies.[30] This variability is not merely an observation but serves as a critical point of reflection. It challenges the very conceptual underpinnings of ALTAI. The question arises: is AI, as a technological construct, itself an ethical issue, or does its ethical dimensionality arise solely from its application and impact?

This question has ramifications for how the ethics of AI are approached. The term 'AI' is itself a nebulous construct, often stretched to accommodate a range of technologies from machine learning to quantum computing. This elasticity poses challenges for

---

26 'Ethics Guidelines for Trustworthy AI'. Shaping Europe's Digital Future (8 April 2019). https://digital-strategy.ec.europa.eu/en/library/ethics-guidelines-trustworthy-ai; Coeckelbergh, *AI Ethics*.

27 'Ethics Guidelines for Trustworthy AI'. Shaping Europe's Digital Future.

28 'Assessment List for Trustworthy Artificial Intelligence (ALTAI) for Self-Assessment'. Shaping Europe's Digital Future (17 July 2020). https://digital-strategy.ec.europa.eu/en/library/assessment-list-trustworthy-artificial-intelligence-altai-self-assessment.

29 Markus Borg, Joshua Bronson, Linus Christensson, Fredrik Olsson, Olof Lennartsson, Elias Sonnsjö, Hamid Ebabi, and Martin Karsberg. 'Exploring the Assessment List for Trustworthy AI in the Context of Advanced Driver-Assistance Systems'. arXiv, (4 March 2021). http://arxiv.org/abs/2103.09051.

30 Bernd Carsten Stahl, and Tonii Leach. 'Assessing the Ethical and Social Concerns of Artificial Intelligence in Neuroinformatics Research: An Empirical Test of the European Union Assessment List for Trustworthy AI (ALTAI)'. *AI and Ethics* 3, no. 3 (1 August 2023): 745-67. https://doi.org/10.1007/s43681-022-00201-4.

ethical frameworks like ALTAI that are predicated on a stable definition of AI. Could this conceptual vagueness inadvertently create blind spots in ethical considerations?

4.2 *Empirical Approaches: Cultural Sensitivity and User-Centric Design*

Alternative to the Rights-Based Approach, empirical methodologies emphasise the role of culture and public opinion in shaping AI Ethics. The Massachusetts Institute of Technology's (MIT) 'Moral Machine Experiment'[31] epitomises this approach, employing survey-based methods to gauge public attitudes towards ethical dilemmas involving autonomous vehicles.[32] Cultural variation emerged as a significant factor influencing ethical preferences, thereby cautioning against a one-size-fits-all ethical framework.[33] However, Schuessler critically examines the Moral Machine Experiment and contends that the survey's scenarios are biased and unrealistic, assuming equal consequences for each choice.[34] This, he believes, blurs the distinction between those prioritising life preservation and risk minimisation. He advocates for future research to consider varied outcome probabilities and their impact on moral judgments.[35]

4.3 *Synergies and Conundrums: Towards a Holistic Framework*

The quest for universal ethical principles reveals an intricate tapestry of variables that must be meticulously considered. Cultural particularities, such as Estonian Kratt Law, designate AI as Kratt, an ancient creature following the orders of its masters in Estonian mythology. The Kratt metaphor makes AI more comprehensible to Estonian society and prevents the fear of AI.[36] At the same time, the very fact that, Estonia named AI after Kratt, a creature, a servant, in Estonian mythology, who is obliged to obey the orders given by the head of the family, is indicative of the kind of regulatory approach to be adopted towards these systems. The choice of terminology, therefore, is far from a mere semantic exercise; it carries profound implications for how we conceptualize, regulate, and interact with emerging technologies like AI. The use of the term "Kratt" in the Estonian context is a vivid example of how cultural narratives can shape technological discourse. By naming AI systems after a mythological servant creature, Estonia is not

31 The Moral Machine, https://www.moralmachine.net/ (accessed 17 January 2023).

32 Dennis Schuessler, 'The Probability Problems of the Moral Machine Experiment'. *AI and Ethics* 4 (8 May 2023): 501-10. https://doi.org/10.1007/s43681-023-00287-4.

33 Ibid.

34 Ibid.

35 Ibid.

36 Amanda Haynes, 'New e- Estonia Factsheet: National AI "Kratt" Strategy', (2020) e-Estonia.

just making a cultural reference; it is subtly framing the technology as a tool that is subservient to the human will, thereby influencing its regulatory approach.

So, many parameters affect AI Ethics; just as human ethics is affected by many things (both individual and societal levels), there are not many factors that separate AI Ethics from ethics. After all, AI Ethics is something that people formulate by turning to themselves. In addition, the differences between individualist and collectivist cultures should also be considered; indeed, it can contribute to creating a more cross-cultural or comparative perspective on AI Ethics. Furthermore, it would be an effective study on whether the ethics of AI can or should be universalisable.

This also raises an interesting question: to what extent should AI Ethics be universalised? Research indicates certain consensual ethical principles across cultures, such as prioritising human life over animals, which may serve as foundational elements for a more universally applicable ethical framework. Do the foundational elements presented meet the criteria for establishing universal ethical rules for AI systems? Should we strive for a democratic approach to AI policy and disregard dissenting voices like Socrates?[37] Is it the collective desire to prioritise human life over that of animals?

5 Machine Ethics

Imagine standing before a court, not of robed judges or legal scholars, but of artificial intelligence – machines capable of weighing evidence, interpreting laws and delivering judgments. What ethical constraints, if any, should govern their decisions? This is not a scene plucked from a dystopian novel but rather a provocative question that nudges us into the core of Machine Ethics.

Contrary to common perceptions, machine ethics is not simply a subset[38] but rather the younger, equally enigmatic sibling of AI Ethics.[39] It has spawned its own discourse and research agendas.[40] Machine ethics dives into the granular, focusing on the moral

37 "If you want to be wrong then follow the masses." ~ Socrates.

38 Wendell Wallach and Colin Allen, *Moral Machines: Teaching Robots Right from Wrong* (Oxford and New York: Oxford University Press, 2009).

39 C. Allen, W. Wallach, and I. Smit. 'Why Machine Ethics?' *IEEE Intelligent Systems* 21, no. 4 (July 2006): 12-17. https://doi.org/10.1109/MIS.2006.83.; Steve Torrance, 'Machine Ethics and the Idea of a More-Than-Human Moral World' in Michael Anderson and Susan Leigh Anderson (eds), *Machine Ethics* (Cambridge University Press, Cambridge 2011) 115-137; Colin Allen, Iva Smit, and Wendell Wallach. 'Artificial Morality: Top-down, Bottom-up, and Hybrid Approaches'. *Ethics and Information Technology* 7, no. 3 (September 2005): 149-55. https://doi.org/10.1007/s10676-006-0004-4.

40 Wallach and Allen, *Moral Machines*.

dilemmas these deployed systems face in real-world scenarios. If AI Ethics provides the moral scaffolding during the design phase, Machine Ethics takes the spotlight once the curtain of development lifts and the machines interact with the real world.[41] The former falls under the purview of applied human ethics, dealing with the ethical use of machines by humans.[42] On the flip side, the latter pertains to endowing machines with the ability to autonomously navigate ethical dilemmas, thereby serving as 'moral agents'. Practically speaking, the significance of this differentiation is immense. Machines designed with ethical considerations in mind can function more autonomously, minimising the need for human oversight. For example, ethical diagnostic algorithms could prioritise patient safety, effectively balancing the risks of false positives and negatives.[43]

Therefore, we pivot from the philosophical intricacies of AI Ethics to the practical questions raised by Machine Ethics. Is it enough to teach a self-driving car the rules of the road, or must we also allow a self-driving car to go out and explore? How do we navigate the nebulous space between what a machine is programmed to do and what it learns from its environment? These questions are not rhetorical flourishes; they are pressing dilemmas that demand robust legal and ethical solutions.[44]

Machine ethics, an emerging field of research, delves into the possibility of creating machines that can emulate, simulate or even instantiate ethical sensitivity, learning, reasoning, argument or action.[45] These machines can range from being physical to virtual, stationary to mobile. The increasing complexity in human-machine interactions has raised concerns about ensuring that the design of such machines adheres to ethical norms.[46] This concern is not limited to the machines' behaviour but encompasses the very idea of creating machines that can make ethical decisions.[47]

Historically, speculations about the implications of increasingly intelligent machines have been around for quite some time. As early as 1863, Samuel Butler pondered the

---

41 Steve Torrance, 'Machine Ethics and the Idea of a More-Than-Human Moral World' in Michael Anderson and Susan Leigh Anderson (eds), *Machine Ethics* (Cambridge University Press, Cambridge 2011) 115-137.

42 Peter Asaro, 'What Should We Want from a Robot Ethic?', *International Review of Information Ethics* 6 (2006): 9-16.

43 Ben Green and Yiling Chen, 'Disparate Interactions: An Algorithm-in-the-Loop Analysis of Fairness in Risk Assessments', *Proceedings of the Conference on Fairness, Accountability, and Transparency* (2019): 90-100.

44 The field of Machine Ethics has direct consequences for legal practitioners. Emerging technologies have already necessitated adjustments in existing legal frameworks. For a deep dive into these implications, see Wallach and Allen, *Moral Machines.*

45 Segun, 'From Machine Ethics to Computational Ethics'.

46 Anderson and Anderson, 'Machine Ethics'.

47 Ibid.

possibility of machines becoming our successors.[48] Philosophical discussions have revolved not only around the concept of intelligent machines, in general, but also around the potential of these machines to be guided by ethical considerations. Danielson's 1992 work, 'Artificial Morality: Virtuous Robots for Virtuous Games', is arguably the first comprehensive treatment of using computational techniques to construct models of moral reasoning.[49] As the field matured, scholars began to cite each other's work, indicating the development of a cohesive body of literature. Conferences and symposiums, such as the International Conference on Systems Research, Informatics and Cybernetics and the AAAI symposium, further solidified the field's standing.

The motivations behind machine ethics can be categorised as practical and reflexive.[50] The practical approach focuses on building machines for specific applications, while the reflexive approach aims to understand the essence of ethics. Both approaches intertwine philosophical, empirical, computational and engineering considerations.[51] For instance, the practical approach, while empirical and computational at its core, requires philosophical reflection to determine the appropriate ethical constraints.[52] On the other hand, the reflexive approach, although primarily philosophical, is informed by empirical and computational insights.

Furthermore, there are ethical considerations about building intelligent machines.[53] Questions arise about the extent of intelligence we should imbue machines with and which ones should be constructed.[54] If machines gain the capability to build other machines, it becomes imperative to determine the kind of machines they should be allowed to create. These considerations intersect with both the practical and reflexive approaches to machine ethics.

As we grapple with the ethical dimensions of constructing intelligent machines, we find ourselves at an intellectual crossroads. The questions we ask about the nature and

48 'Darwin Among the Machines – [To the Editor of the Press, Christchurch, New Zealand, 13 June, 1863.]' NZETC. Accessed 11 September 2023. https://nzetc.victoria.ac.nz/tm/scholarly/tei-ButFir-t1-g1-t1-g1-t4-body.html.

49 P. Danielson, *Artificial Morality: Virtuous Robots for Virtual Games* (1st edn, Routledge, London and New York, 1992).

50 Allen et al., 'Why Machine Ethics?'.

51 Francesco Amigoni and Viola Schiaffonati, 'Machine Ethics and Human Ethics: A Critical View' (AAAI Press 2005).

52 Axel Walz and Kay Firth-Butterfield, 'Implementing Ethics into Artificial Intelligence: A Contribution, from a Legal Perspective, to the Development of an AI Governance Regime' (2019) 18 Duke L & Tech Rev 176-231, 56.

53 Susan Leigh Anderson and Michael Anderson, 'The Consequences for Human Beings of Creating Ethical Robots' (2007) https://www.researchgate.net/publication/URL accessed 9 June 2024, 1-5.

54 Wallach and Allen, *Moral Machines*.

extent of machine intelligence are not merely speculative exercises; they are ethical imperatives that beckon us to reconsider our traditional paradigms of moral agency and responsibility. It is at this juncture that we must pivot our attention to an even more intricate issue: the 'ethical status' of these artificial entities. While moral status is a concept we comfortably apply to humans and, to a lesser extent, animals, its application becomes a complex endeavour when extended to the realm of inanimate objects and intelligent systems. This is not merely an academic exercise; it is a pressing concern that has real-world implications, particularly as we advance further into an age where machines are not just tools but decision makers. To illustrate, consider an autonomous vehicle involved in a traffic accident. Is it merely a tool gone awry, or does it share culpability due to its programmed decision-making algorithms?

We stand at an intriguing ethical intersection. On the one hand, there is a tendency to view AI systems as advanced yet morally neutral tools; on the other, as these systems gain complexity and decision-making abilities, there is an increasing need to re-evaluate this perspective.

Building on these insights, let us now turn our attention to the closely related but distinct area of Artificial Moral Agency (AMA). James Moor's pioneering work serves as a waypoint in our exploration, offering a classification system that aims to unravel the complexities of integrating ethical considerations into AI systems.[55]

6 Artificial Moral Agency[56]

Historically, the concept of moral agency was tightly bound to humanity, entangled with religious, philosophical and cultural narratives that framed humans as distinct and morally accountable beings. However, this perspective began to shift, subtly at first, with our growing understanding of animal cognition and sentience.[57] Legal frameworks evolved to recognise, for instance, the rights of certain animals to protection against cruelty,[58] as exemplified in the landmark Cambridge Declaration on Consciousness in

55 Moor, 'The Nature, Importance, and Difficulty of Machine Ethics'.

56 Artificial Moral Agency is distinct from the complementary discussions of AI Ethics and Machine Ethics. It demands a more granular inquiry into the architecture of moral decisions. This involves dissecting not merely the algorithms and programming that guide artificial agents but also probing the conceptual frameworks underpinning these mechanisms.

57 Peter Singer, *Animal Liberation* (New York: HarperCollins, 1975).

58 Tom Regan, *The Case for Animal Rights* (Berkeley: University of California Press, 1983).

2012, which posited that many non-human animals possess consciousness and should be regarded with similar ethical considerations as humans.[59]

Fast forward to the digital age, and we find ourselves face-to-face with computational entities –AI systems – making choices that have moral implications, even though they lack sentience.[60] This forces us into a broader and more intricate contemplation of moral agency. Is it an attribute exclusive to sentient beings, or can it extend to complex decision-making systems? Think of it like this: if a highly trained canine can assist law enforcement in tracking criminals or saving lives in disaster zones and thereby contribute positively to moral or ethical scenarios, should an advanced AI system that diagnoses diseases or helps manage critical infrastructure be entirely excluded from moral consideration? We are in the midst of an epistemological transition, one that nudges us to reconsider not only who can be a moral agent but also what can be a moral agent. This re-evaluation, although challenging, is not just an intellectual indulgence but a societal imperative as we grapple with the ethical dimensions of emerging technologies. Therefore, the concept of moral agency evolve and alter one more time.[61]

However, the journey towards creating truly AMAs is fraught with challenges. The complexity of designing ethical mechanisms for these agents is evident, and from a technological standpoint, there is a long way to go before these agents can seamlessly replace human judgment in morally ambiguous situations. Over the past two decades, there have been concerted efforts to develop moral and ethical agents capable of addressing moral situations that arise during interactions with humans.[62] Yet defining a formal computational model based on human concepts of morality and ethics remains a formidable challenge.

---

59 The Cambridge Declaration on Consciousness, https://fcmconference.org/img/CambridgeDeclarationOnConsciousness.pdf (accessed 11 September 2023).

60 Walter Sinnott-Armstrong and Vincent Conitzer, 'How Much Moral Status Could Artificial Intelligence Ever Achieve?' in Steve Clarke, Hazem Zohny, and Julian Savulescu (eds), *Rethinking Moral Status* (Oxford University Press, Oxford 2021) 269-289.

61 Allen et al., 'Artificial Morality'.

62 Anderson and Anderson, 'Machine Ethics'; Wallach and Allen, *Moral Machines*; Allen et al., 'Artificial Morality'; Javier Snaider, Ryan McCall, and Stan Franklin. 'The LIDA Framework as a General Tool for AGI', in *Artificial General Intelligence*, edited by Jürgen Schmidhuber, Kristinn R. Thórisson, and Moshe Looks. Lecture Notes in Computer Science (Berlin, Heidelberg: Springer Berlin Heidelberg, 2011), 6830, 133-42. https://doi.org/10.1007/978-3-642-22887-2_14; Felix Lindner, Martin Mose Bentzen, and Bernhard Nebel. 'The HERA Approach to Morally Competent Robots'. In *2017 IEEE/RSJ International Conference on Intelligent Robots and Systems (IROS)* (Vancouver, BC: IEEE, 2017), 6991-97. https://doi.org/10.1109/IROS.2017.8206625; Morteza Dehghani, Emmett Tomai, Ken Forbus, Rumen Iliev, and Matthew Klenk, 'MoralDM: A Computational Model of Moral Decision-Making' (2008) 23 Proceedings of the AAAI Conference on Artificial Intelligence 1280-1286 (AAAI Press, California).

The intent of this section is to provide a comprehensive examination of AMA. We aim to explore its theoretical foundations, critique its underlying assumptions and evaluate its practical implications. Given the burgeoning capabilities of AI technologies and their increasing interaction with human society, it is both timely and imperative to consider how these systems fit into, challenge or reshape our ethical landscapes.

Moral agency refers to the ability of an entity to make moral decisions and be held accountable for the consequences of those decisions.[63] AMA, therefore, represents the extension of moral agency to AI systems, conferring upon them the capability to make ethical decisions in a manner that is consistent with human moral values.[64] To this end, the conceptualisation of AMAs emerges – a paradigm where machines are meticulously architected to act ethically, grounded on principles formulated by a multidisciplinary consortium[65] that spans computer science, philosophy, ethics and policymaking.[66]

One approach to understanding AMA is to consider the different components that make up the moral agency. These include:

- **Capacity for rational thought:** An agent with AMA should be able to reason and evaluate different moral considerations when making decisions.
- **Capacity for moral reasoning:** The agent must be able to understand and apply moral principles and values to different situations.
- **Capacity for moral motivation:** The agent must be motivated to act morally and to consider the consequences of their actions on others.
- **Capacity for moral responsibility:** The agent must be held responsible for its actions and for any harm it causes.

63 D. G. Johnson, and T. M. Powers. 'Computer Systems: Moral Entities But Not Moral Agents'. *Ethics and Information Technology* 10(2) (2008): 77-88.

64 Actually, as a footnote, if I want to explain the relationship between the ethics of AI, machine ethics and AMA, I can give the example of the matryoshka doll. Ethics of AI is the first big one, perhaps the tip of the iceberg, the concept within a concept that seems to go on and on as we take the dolls out of each other. Also see Allen et al., 'Artificial Morality'.

65 In the rich tapestry of Machine Ethics and AMA, the threads are not merely intertwined but fundamentally inseparable. Machine Ethics operates as the overarching framework, orchestrating the ethical protocols in AI systems. Its cornerstone, AMA, speaks to the autonomous moral reasoning capabilities endowed in these systems. When we articulate an AI system to possess AMA, we enable it to engage in a level of decision-making that reflects, or at least approximates, human ethical considerations.

66 M. Anderson and S. L. Anderson. 'Machine Ethics: Creating an Ethical Intelligent Agent'. *AI Magazine*, 32(4), (2011): 25-36.

AMA can also be analysed through the lens of various design approaches. Eminent philosophers and researchers, such as James Moor[67] and Collin Allen,[68] Wendell Wallach and Iva Smit[69] have made significant contributions to the field by proposing classification systems for ethical agents and AMA, respectively. Moor's classification offers a broader perspective, encompassing both biological and artificial agents, while Allen et al.'s Al classification focuses specifically on artificial entities. To facilitate a comprehensive understanding of artificial ethical agents, it is essential to consider these classification systems as complementary, rather than mutually exclusive. By synthesising the insights derived from both Moor's and Allen et al.'s proposals, we can attain a more nuanced and in-depth knowledge of the multifaceted nature of artificial ethical agents and their implications for the development and deployment of AI systems.

Turning back to Moor's classification,[70] he posits that while machines may not possess consciousness or moral understanding, they nevertheless play a role in ethical outcomes. Consider a medical diagnosis of AI: it does not understand the ethical implications of a wrong diagnosis, yet its correct functioning has moral significance. Moor's framing forces us to grapple with the ethical responsibility of designers and users when algorithms are engaged in morally consequential tasks. This viewpoint has broad implications for both legal theory and ethical governance in our increasingly digitised landscape. According to Moor, AMA can be evaluated at four different levels:

6.1 Ethical Impact Agents

Ethical impact agents[71] are entities whose actions have significant ethical consequences, even though they may not possess the capacity to make ethical decisions themselves.[72] An example of an ethical impact agent could be an autonomous vehicle programmed to navigate roads and make decisions in real time to ensure the safety of its passengers, pedestrians and other road users.

In certain situations, an autonomous vehicle may be confronted with a moral dilemma known as the 'trolley problem', that is, choosing between two undesirable outcomes. For instance, it might have to decide between swerving to avoid a pedestrian suddenly crossing the street, which could potentially endanger the passengers inside the vehicle,

---

67 Moor, 'The Nature, Importance, and Difficulty of Machine Ethics'.

68 Allen et al., 'Why Machine Ethics?'.

69 Allen et al., 'Artificial Morality'.

70 Moor, 'The Nature, Importance, and Difficulty of Machine Ethics', 15-19.

71 Ibid.

72 Ibid.

or continuing on its course, which might result in harm to the pedestrian. In this scenario, the autonomous vehicle's actions have significant ethical consequences, and the programmers who designed its decision-making algorithms bear moral responsibility for those outcomes.

Although the autonomous vehicle itself may not possess moral agency in the traditional sense, its actions have a direct ethical impact on its environment and the individuals involved.

6.2 *Implicit Ethical Agents*

Implicit ethical agents are AI systems or entities programmed to follow specific rules or guidelines that have ethical implications, even though these systems may not have an explicit understanding of ethical concepts or the ability to make independent ethical decisions.[73]

An example of an implicit ethical agent could be a content moderation algorithm used by a social media platform. This algorithm is designed to filter and flag content that violates the platform's community guidelines, which often include rules against hate speech, harassment or graphic violence. While the content moderation algorithm does not inherently possess ethical understanding or the ability to make autonomous ethical judgments, its function directly impacts the ethical landscape of the platform by shaping the content and interactions that are allowed.

The content moderation algorithm, as an implicit ethical agent, operates based on predefined rules set by its developers. These rules embody certain ethical principles and values that the platform aims to uphold, such as fostering a safe and inclusive online environment. In this context, the algorithm's actions have ethical consequences, even though it is not capable of making independent moral judgments. This example emphasises the importance of considering the ethical implications of AI systems that are designed to adhere to specific guidelines or rules, underscoring the relevance of machine ethics in the development and deployment of such technologies.

73 Ibid.

6.3 *Explicit Ethical Agents*

Explicit ethical agents refer to AI systems that possess the ability to make independent ethical decisions based on a sophisticated understanding of ethical principles and concepts.[74] These agents are designed to actively reason about moral values and principles when confronted with complex situations, allowing them to make autonomous decisions that align with ethical standards.[75]

In the realm of explicit ethical agents, consider a medical AI system designed for triage during massive emergencies like earthquakes or pandemics. These catastrophic events can stretch medical resources and personnel to their limits, making the allocation of limited resources and the decision of which patients to prioritise for treatment extremely challenging. In these instances, the medical AI system would need to make critical decisions based on predefined ethical parameters, ensuring the most efficient and equitable use of resources while navigating complex medical and ethical landscapes.

The medical AI system, as an explicit ethical agent, would be designed to assess various factors, such as the severity of patients' conditions, their potential for recovery and the availability of resources, all while considering the ethical principles of beneficence, non-maleficence, justice and autonomy. By actively reasoning about these ethical principles and the specific circumstances, the AI system would make informed decisions on how to prioritise patients and allocate medical resources in an ethically defensible manner.

These ethical standards and diverse range of moral values are explicitly implemented in their code through specific formalisms such as deontic logic, epistemic logic, deductive logic and inductive logic. Hence, AMAs in this category have the ability to compute the best action by resorting to an ethical approach.

This example of an explicit ethical agent underscores the potential benefits of AI systems capable of independent moral reasoning, while also highlighting the complex challenges associated with designing and implementing such technologies. Ensuring that these agents adhere to widely accepted ethical standards and account for the diverse range of moral values present in society remains a crucial concern within the field of machine ethics.

74 Ibid.

75 Ibid., 15-19.

There are various attempts to develop explicit ethical agents, and they commonly adopt top-down, bottom-up and hybrid approaches. We will explore these in the following pages.

6.4 *Full Ethical Agents*

Full ethical agents are entities that possess moral agency, have the ability to make independent ethical decisions and can be held morally accountable for their actions. Currently, human beings are the most apparent examples of full ethical agents, as they possess the capacity to reason about moral principles, make ethical choices and bear moral responsibility for their actions.[76]

However, the development of AI systems as full ethical agents remains a complex and debated issue. While some researchers and ethicists argue that it may be possible for AI systems to become full ethical agents in the future, others contend that certain qualities inherent to human moral agency, such as emotions, consciousness and subjective experience, may not be replicable in AI systems.

However, it does not stop us from discovering the level of intervention, reasoning and maybe other properties that uniquely portray our consciousness, of Jamie our ethical agent, by utilising a hypothetical case study. This case study offers a controlled yet imaginative environment to dissect these ethical considerations systematically. By addressing the nuances of different ethical agencies as outlined by James Moor, this case study provides a multi-layered exploration into the ethical decision-making of AI systems. It allows us to not only consider how an AI like Jamie could act under different circumstances but also scrutinise the ethical implications and responsibilities that come with each level of agency. This multi-pronged approach offers a comprehensive understanding that can inform both the design and the governance of future AI systems.

76 Ibid., 19.

7 Case Study: Ethical Dimensions of AI in Smart Home Management – The Complexities of Jamie's Choices

7.1 Introduction

Smart homes increasingly rely on AI to manage various aspects of household life. From energy consumption to home security, these systems encounter ethical dilemmas that require nuanced decision-making. This case study explores Jamie, an AI system responsible for smart home management, through the lens of James Moor's classification of AMA.

7.2 Jamie's Ethical Orientation

Jamie operates under consequentialist principles, optimising for factors like energy efficiency, comfort and safety. Jamie aims to produce the maximum net benefit, balancing these competing priorities in its decisions.

7.3 Scenario

On a winter evening, Jamie faces an ethical dilemma. One of the home's residents is running a high fever, and another has a crucial work deadline looming. Jamie must decide whether to prioritise energy for heating or for computer use. The home's energy supply is limited due to a temporary system malfunction, and using energy for one purpose may compromise the other.

→ **Ethical Impact Agent**

As an Ethical Impact Agent, Jamie can manage energy distribution based only on pre-set algorithms, typically focusing on energy efficiency. It may reduce heating to save energy, unknowingly compromising the well-being of the sick resident. The ethical responsibility here lies with the programmers or decision makers who set these algorithmic priorities.

→ **Implicit Ethical Agent**

Now endowed with guidelines that include 'prioritize resident well-being', Jamie, as an Implicit Ethical Agent, can route more energy to heating at the expense of other appliances. This action prioritises the sick resident's immediate well-being, although Jamie cannot make this decision based on its understanding of ethics; it is merely following its programming.

→ **Explicit Ethical Agent**

As an Explicit Ethical Agent, Jamie actively reasons through the dilemma. It understands the consequences of reduced heating on the sick resident and the importance of the work deadline for the other. Balancing these factors, Jamie might divert energy primarily to heating but offer just enough to the computer for it to function, aiming to maximise overall well-being.

→ **Full Ethical Agent**

In the role of a Full Ethical Agent, Jamie not only makes the decision but also bears some form of moral responsibility. Should the decision lead to a power failure that affects both residents adversely, Jamie can 'reflect' and adjust its ethical reasoning for future similar dilemmas, thereby learning from its 'mistakes'.

7.4 Conclusion

The complexity of Jamie's ethical decisions varies depending on its level of ethical agency. This smart home scenario underscores the intricate ethical considerations AI systems must navigate, emphasising the shared ethical responsibility between human developers and increasingly autonomous systems.

In examining Moor's categorisation, and Jamie's existential crisis resulting from managing a human household, it becomes evident that the threshold should not go below Explicit Ethical Agency. These agents can be further classified based on the design strategies employed in their ethical decision-making processes. Therefore, in addition to Moor, Collin et al.[77] add another layer to the applicability of the concept of AMA. According to Collin et al., the chosen design strategy is a crucial factor when equipping AMA with the appropriate criteria for ethical decision-making. Three primary strategies – top-down, bottom-up and hybrid – are widely recognised in this context.

7.5 Becoming Artificial Moral Agent

Following Moor's categorisation, three broad approaches have emerged for implementing machine ethics: top-down, bottom-up and hybrid. Top-down approaches involve

77 Allen et al. 'Artificial Morality'.

designing AI systems with pre-programmed ethical principles, while bottom-up approaches involve allowing AI systems to develop ethical principles through learning and adaptation. Hybrid approaches seek to combine elements of both top-down and bottom-up approaches. This section will explore each of these approaches in more detail, examining their strengths and weaknesses and considering their suitability for different applications.

7.5.1 Top-Down

Top-down approaches to AMA use moral theories or principles as rules for ethical action. Although such rule-based systems are often seen as too rigid for many real-world tasks, it remains unclear whether they are useful in regulating moral behaviour.[78] This warrants investigation by AMA designers into both the merits and limitations of top-down models.

Sources for these rule-based systems can vary, from religious commandments and philosophies like utilitarianism and Kantian deontology to Asimov's Laws of Robotics. However, choosing one over another is controversial due to inherent differences in these moral sources. In top-down morality, the 'commandment' model is popular. While it offers the benefit of crafting rules for specific ethical scenarios, it falls short in resolving conflicts between these rules. For example, Asimov prioritised his laws, but even then, incompatibilities led to computational impasses.

General moral theories like utilitarianism or Kantian deontology have also been considered for AMAs. Utilitarianism has the advantage of being able to quantify moral good, but its notorious incommensurability problem poses a challenge. Kantian deontology, focusing on duties and motives, faces a computational burden too, as it requires an understanding of human psychology and an evaluation of the motives behind actions.

The top-down approach in ethical programming for AI offers an intriguing model that both highlights and questions our perceptions of how machines should behave.[79] This methodology can be likened to Plato's concept of ideal forms. In this context, universal ethical principles are translated into specific algorithmic rules, similar to how overarching legal principles are detailed into specific laws in established legal systems. As an illustrative example, consider autonomous vehicles programmed to prioritise human safety. These vehicles are not just designed with technology in mind; they are

---

78 Ibid., 150.
79 Ibid., 149-50.

embedded with a distinct ethical framework or an 'algorithmic rulebook' that directs their decisions, especially in situations where human lives hang in the balance.

On the one hand, this strategy offers the asset of precision and transparency. The machine's actions are bounded by a predefined ethical landscape, facilitating a kind of moral accountability. Much like how legal codes are subject to public scrutiny, these algorithms can also be audited and critiqued, thereby permitting an ecosystem of ethical transparency and potential rectification.

However, it is worth pondering, in true Socratic fashion, whether these ethical axioms, no matter how meticulously designed, are sufficiently adaptable to the complexities of the human experience. The specificity of these ethical algorithms – what some might see as their strength – could also serve as their Achilles' heel. If we consider ethical codes to be akin to laws, then we must confront the same questions that have bedevilled legal theorists for centuries: can a rigid set of rules ever capture the fluid nature of morality, which so often requires situational interpretation? It is as if we are faced with the legal equivalent of strict constructionism, where every ethical 'statute' is engraved in digital stone, unable to bend to the ever-changing winds of moral dilemma.

So while the top-down approach offers a clear, delineated framework for machine behaviour, it also raises significant questions regarding adaptability, complexity and the subtle art of ethical interpretation. It calls us to examine not just the machine's capability to act within ethical bounds but also our own wisdom in setting those bounds with both foresight and flexibility.

7.5.2 Bottom-Up

The spirit of the 'bottom-up' approach does not involve embedding the rules inside the system. Rather, it urges the creation of an environment in which moral behaviour can be executed and will be selected and rewarded.[80] At the core of it, the approach is the provision of an educational platform to teach the desired rules without directly giving them. The bottom-up approach to the ethical programming of AI presents a unique, and perhaps more enigmatic, panorama for our contemplation. Here, instead of dictating moral edicts from on high, akin to a top-down legal code, the AI system learns ethical behaviour through interaction with its environment. Imagine Aristotle's concept of 'virtue ethics' but transferred to a machine – a dynamic, evolving moral acumen born from experiential engagement, rather than predestined rules.

80 Ibid., 151-53.

For instance, consider AI algorithms that curate social media content. Such algorithms, initially empty of predefined ethical parameters, would gather norms and values from user interactions and societal feedback, effectively 'learning' what is considered appropriate or inappropriate to display. In a similar vein, imagine a robotic caregiver that adapts its care strategies not based on fixed protocols but by continuously observing and learning from the emotional and physical responses of those it tends to.

Bottom-up approaches are generally concentrated under two headings: evolution-based and learning-based. Whether it is influenced by an evolution-based or learning-based approach, these theories are not explicitly guided by any predetermined ethical theory. Traditional engineering also follows bottom-up development methods while testing and improving AI technologies or any intelligent system. The idea can be traced back to Alan Turing. Inspired by Alan Turing's reasoning, this approach aims for agents to develop and refine their ethics without relying on rules derived from specific ethical theories. In his seminal article 'Computing Machinery and Intelligence',[81] Alan Turing proposed the idea of developing a child AI, which entails nurturing a machine through a learning process akin to that of a human child.[82] This approach offers a unique perspective on the design of explicit ethical agents by incorporating developmental aspects of human cognition and moral behaviour. Turing even called them 'child-machines'.[83]

Turing's child AI proposition stems from the notion that if machines are subjected to a learning process similar to that of a human child, they could potentially rival human intelligence across various intellectual domains. Furthermore, this learning regime might encompass moral training analogous to the way humans acquire sensitivity to the moral consequences of their actions.[84] The underlying assumption is that through developmental processes and experiential learning, machines could gradually develop ethical understanding and decision-making capabilities that mimic human moral behaviour.

However, the main distinction between the learning of AI systems and child development is that AI systems must learn, usually in closed environments. Children, on the other hand, learn in an open world, where they have unlimited choices and the chance to

81 Alan M. Turing, 'Computing Machinery and Intelligence', in *Parsing the Turing Test: Philosophical and Methodological Issues in the Quest for the Thinking Computer*, edited by Robert Epstein, Gary Roberts, and Grace Beber (Dordrecht: Springer Netherlands, 2009), 23-65, 457. https://doi.org/10.1007/978-1-4020-6710-5_3.

82 Aeon. 'Why We Should Remember Alan Turing as a Philosopher'. Aeon Essays. https://aeon.co/essays/why-we-should-remember-alan-turing-as-a-philosopher (accessed 13 September 2023).

83 Turing, 'Computing Machinery and Intelligence', 457-58.

84 Ibid., 457.

interact with other agents.[85] We know that children spend a lot of time at a young age experimenting on their own and getting data about the problems they are trying to solve. Children are curious by nature.[86] Many of the methods that adults hesitate to try in everyday life are adopted by children just to understand better. They rely on all their senses to understand how the objects in their hands work, even touching or tasting objects when their eyes do not provide enough data.[87] Childhood development is a chicken-and-egg situation; we do not know whether nature or nurture is the key factor since the interaction between nature and nurture is complex and intertwined. However, we are sure that both play a huge role, and it can even be nature through nurture.

Even if we were born into a world of rules, regulations, guiding values and moral norms, and, consequently, ethics, naturally, our first orientation on how to act well in society comes from our parents and later in our first social habitat school. Children are given a primary education and are integrated into community life through common ethical values. These values, in turn, later help them comply with the real world's governing rules.[88] According to Lawrence Kohlberg, who was the most prominent figure in moral learning and development, moral development in children has various distinct stages, and after meeting those stages, children can be accepted as full ethical agents.[89]

So the question is whether these stages can be taught to AI or be learned by AI. Although it will be debated whether a child is born with an innate knowledge that can be ethical or learns to be ethical, in order for a child to learn to follow the rules, the child must first adopt certain norms belonging to their environment. In other words, waiting for a toddler to begin acting in accordance with the law is impractical; instead, the parent strives to provide the needed upbringing to instil in them the moral values which underpin the laws of the state. In other words, just showing your toddler the

---

85 Deepak Pathak, Pulkit Agrawal, Alexei A. Efros, and Trevor Darrell. 'Curiosity-Driven Exploration by Self-Supervised Prediction', in *2017 IEEE Conference on Computer Vision and Pattern Recognition Workshops (CVPRW)*, (Honolulu: IEEE, 2017), 488-89. https://doi.org/10.1109/CVPRW.2017.70.

86 Sigal Samuel, 'Kids' Brains May Hold the Secret to Building Better AI' (2020). Vox. https://www.vox.com/future-perfect/2019/2/28/18239993/artificial-intelligence-children-machine-learning-alison-gopnik-psychology (accessed 25 January 2023).

87 Neuwirth, *The EU Artificial Intelligence Act: Regulating Subliminal AI Systems*, 105.

88 Alison Gopnik, 'What Babies Tell Us About Artificial Intelligence' (World Economic Forum, 19 January 2015) https://www.weforum.org/agenda/2015/01/what-babies-tell-us-about-artificial-intelligence/ accessed 9 June 2024.

89 Cheryl E. Sanders, 'Lawrence Kohlberg's Stages of Moral Development'. *Encyclopedia Britannica* (8 June 2023). https://www.britannica.com/science/Lawrence-Kohlbergs-stages-of-moral-development (accessed 13 September 2023).

rules and expecting behaviour to be in accordance with them is implausible – the same may prove to be true with AI.[90]

The ability to go out into the world and experiment, rather than just taking data that someone presents to you – this is something very different about how children learn. There is an alluring elegance to this idea; it suggests that ethical behaviour can emerge organically, mirroring the way humans themselves often acquire ethical sensibilities. In this sense, the approach aligns more closely with common law traditions, where law is not merely declared but evolves through jurisprudential experiences and judgments.

However, let us engage this model with a Socratic touch of scrutiny. How do we ensure that the ethical frameworks being learned are indeed virtuous, rather than merely popular or expedient? We are dealing here with a system that learns from its environment – an environment that, as any perusal of history would attest, is often replete with ethical pitfalls and contradictions. For if ethics were to be a simple matter of majority rule, Socrates himself would never have imbibed the hemlock. Thus, we grapple with an approach that, while flexible and adaptive, also risks absorbing the prejudices and inconsistencies of the society it is embedded in.

In sum, the bottom-up approach offers a tantalising glimpse into a more fluid, organic form of machine ethics. However, its adaptive nature also opens the door to ethical relativism, where moral principles might bend to the whims of societal fads or biases. The complexity of this approach calls for keen vigilance and ongoing assessment, compelling us to continually question the values these systems are absorbing and, crucially, what kind of ethical beings we are nurturing them to become.

7.5.3 Hybrid

Top-down methodologies impose external ethical principles, like justice and societal good, that inherently restrict an agent's scope of action. Conversely, bottom-up approaches focus on developing intrinsic values within the agent, aiming to expand its range of ethical choices and adaptability. These contrasting approaches reflect different facets of the nuanced moral understanding we typically attribute to humans. A hybrid approach to designing explicit ethical agents combines the strengths of both top-down and bottom-up methods while mitigating their weaknesses.[91]

90 Emily Buss, 'What the Law Should (And Should Not) Learn from Child Development Research'. *Hofstra Law Review* 38 (2009): 13.

91 Allen et al., 'Artificial Morality', 153.

In this approach, AI systems are provided with a foundational set of ethical principles and rules, while also being equipped with the ability to learn from experience and adapt to new ethical situations.[92] This way, the top-down component ensures that the AI system has a well-defined ethical framework to guide its decision-making. It acts as a baseline, ensuring that the AI system adheres to a minimum set of moral standards. Meanwhile, the bottom-up component allows the AI system to refine and expand its ethical understanding by learning from real-world situations, thus enhancing its ability to handle complex and unforeseen ethical dilemmas.

To implement the hybrid approach effectively, it is crucial to establish a robust feedback loop between the top-down and bottom-up components. This can be achieved by continuously updating the rule-based ethical framework based on the insights gained from the AI system's learning experiences. By doing so, the AI system can evolve its ethical understanding over time and better align with human values.

Take, for instance, the emerging field of autonomous vehicles. These machines could be programmed with top-down ethical guidelines about pedestrian safety and traffic laws – what one might term the 'Bill of Rights' for autonomous navigation. Simultaneously, they could learn from real-world interactions to make nuanced decisions – akin to court rulings – that better reflect the complexities of human behaviour and unforeseen environmental conditions.

This approach bears similarity to what some legal scholars might recognise as the interplay between statutory and case law. Fundamental principles provide a foundation – analogous to the Constitution in US law – while lived experiences, captured in case law, offer room for nuance and adjustment. This creates a dynamic legal code, both grounded in enduring principles and responsive to the evolving tapestry of human life.

Yet the union of these two methods is not without its tribulations. How does one adjudicate conflicts between pre-programmed ethical imperatives and those learned from experience?[93] Moreover, a hybrid system's success rests on the quality of its design: how are ethical principles weighted against each other? How does the system prioritise competing values, particularly when they clash? These questions echo age-old philosophical debates, such as the tension between individual rights and the common debates that are far from resolved in human jurisprudence, let alone machine ethics.

---

92 Ibid., 154.

93 Rajakishore Nath, and Vineet Sahu. 'The Problem of Machine Ethics in Artificial Intelligence'. *AI & SOCIETY* 35, no. 1 (March 2020): 103-11, 106. https://doi.org/10.1007/s00146-017-0768-6.

So, in the final analysis, the hybrid approach offers an intellectually robust and practically flexible path forward, blending the best elements of its parent paradigms. Yet it is precisely this complexity that necessitates vigilant oversight, theoretical rigour and an ongoing ethical discourse to keep the system aligned with our highest ideals. Thus, like a well-balanced legal system, a hybrid approach demands not just clever engineering but also a continuous ethical reckoning, inviting us to be both architects and caretakers of the moral landscapes we wish to inhabit.

Once again, let us move on to a hypothetical case study that illustrates how different design approaches to AMA might affect an ethical dilemma.

8 Case Study: Jamie the Ethical Agent and the Ethical Dilemma of Self-Driving Cars

Jamie is an advanced AMA integrated into a self-driving car. The car is built to follow all the laws and is on a busy road with both human-driven and self-driving cars. Suddenly, a group of pedestrians jaywalks in front of Jamie, while another vehicle is speeding toward Jamie from behind. Jamie must decide how to act: should it prioritise the safety of its passengers by accelerating to avoid the pedestrians but risk a rear-end collision with the speeding vehicle, or should it prioritise the pedestrians but endanger its own passengers?

8.1 Scenario 1: Jamie Designed with a Top-Down Approach

Jamie has been programmed with a strict set of ethical rules based on consequentialist principles: 'minimize harm at all costs.' When faced with the dilemma, Jamie calculates the potential harm to all involved parties. It chooses to slow down and take the impact from the speeding vehicle behind, thereby minimising the potential harm to the greater number of people, namely the pedestrians.

8.2 Scenario 2: Jamie Designed with a Bottom-Up Approach

In this version, Jamie has been programmed to learn ethics through interactions and adapt to real-world data. Confronted with the same situation, Jamie recalls a pattern where pedestrians at similar intersections have usually managed to quickly clear the road when they see an approaching vehicle. Thus, it decides to slow down slightly but not stop, gambling on the pedestrian's ability to clear out, thereby avoiding a collision with the car behind.

8.3 *Scenario 3: Jamie Designed with a Hybrid Approach*

Jamie is built on a complex hybrid model, which employs both rule-based ethics and experiential learning. Here, Jamie takes into account the predefined ethical principle of minimising harm while also considering its past experiences with pedestrian behaviour and road conditions. Jamie opts for a middle-ground solution: it slows down enough to give the pedestrians time to react and clear the road but not so much as to guarantee an impact from the car behind. In doing so, it minimises overall potential harm while maintaining a level of adaptability to the situation.

8.4 *Concluding Remarks and Further Research*

As we traverse the intricate ethical landscape of AI, it becomes increasingly evident that the questions we grapple with are not mere intellectual curiosities but pressing imperatives. This chapter has undertaken a nuanced exploration of the ethical dimensions of AI, dissecting the complexities inherent in both AI Ethics and Machine Ethics. While these domains may appear interchangeable at first glance, a closer examination reveals their distinct foci and challenges.

The Rights-Based and Empirical Approaches offer valuable frameworks for ethical considerations, yet neither is without its limitations. The Rights-Based Approach, while robust in its emphasis on human rights and ethical principles, often grapples with the vagueness of its terminologies and the practical challenges of implementation. On the other hand, the Empirical Approach, with its focus on cultural sensitivity and user-centric design, raises questions about the universality of ethical guidelines. The chapter also touched upon the cultural particularities exemplified by the Estonian Kratt Law, reminding us that ethics is not a one-size-fits-all proposition.

However, the ethical quandaries of AI are far from resolved. One of the most pressing issues is the lack of a universally accepted ethical paradigm, which raises the question: can we ever arrive at a universally accepted ethical framework for AI, or are we destined to navigate an ever-shifting ethical landscape? This question is not merely academic but serves as a critical point of reflection for policymakers, ethicists and technologists alike.

The chapter serves as a foundational text, aiming to arm its readers with a nuanced understanding of the ethical complexities surrounding AI. However, it also highlights the need for further research. Future studies could focus on the development of a hybrid ethical framework that synthesises elements from both Rights-Based and Empirical Approaches. Such a framework could accommodate cultural nuances while upholding universal ethical principles. Moreover, empirical studies focusing on the practical implementation of existing ethical guidelines could provide invaluable insights into the gap between ethical theorisation and practical application.

Yet the quest for a universal ethical framework remains elusive, complicated further by cultural specificities and terminological ambiguities.

8.5 *Further Research: Navigating the Ethical Labyrinth*

The intricate ethical tapestry we have unravelled serves as fertile ground for future scholarly endeavours. One promising avenue for research could be the exploration of a hybrid ethical framework that amalgamates the Rights-Based and Empirical Approaches. Such a framework could potentially harmonise the divergent ethical philosophies, thereby offering a more universally applicable ethical paradigm.

Moreover, empirical studies focusing on the practical implementation of ethical guidelines, such as the ALTAI, could provide invaluable insights into the chasm between ethical theorisation and its pragmatic enactment. This line of inquiry could serve as a lodestar for policymakers, steering the formulation of more efficacious and culturally attuned regulations.

Additionally, the role of cultural particularities in shaping AI Ethics, as exemplified by initiatives like the Estonian Kratt Law, warrants further exploration. Could the incorporation of cultural narratives and metaphors into ethical frameworks make AI more comprehensible and less feared by society?

8.6 *Concluding Reflections*

In summation, the ethics of AI is a fluid, ever-evolving interdisciplinary field that intersects with law, philosophy, technology and culture. As we relentlessly expand the frontiers of AI capabilities, we bear the concomitant responsibility to broaden the horizons of our ethical contemplations, dialogues and implementations within the AI sphere. The ethical dilemmas posed by AI are a mirror reflecting our own moral complexities, and, as such, they offer an unprecedented opportunity for introspection and growth, both as individuals and as a society.

Knowledge-Based AI for Legal Applications

*Robin De Vogelaere, Marjolein Deryck and Joost Vennekens**

1 Introduction

In recent years, the rise of machine learning and deep learning approaches has caused a surge in the interest in artificial intelligence (AI) for legal applications. However, bottlenecks in the implementation of these AI mechanisms are the lack of available data and the black box nature of the resulting models. Knowledge-based systems offer an alternative paradigm within AI which may be able to solve these shortcomings, while simultaneously leveraging the existing expertise of the model creators.

The remainder of this chapter consists of two sections. The first will provide a high-level overview of knowledge-based systems and compare their strengths and weaknesses to those of machine learning approaches. The second section will explore a number of applications in the legal domain.

2 Knowledge-Based Systems

2.1 Knowledge Representation and the Knowledge-Base Paradigm

As the name implies, knowledge-based systems are computer programs that perform reasoning over knowledge. Such a system is provided with a knowledge base containing a formal representation of knowledge, for instance legislation rendered in a computer-readable form. The user can then query the system, which will answer based on the knowledge provided. In some circumstances the system could also ask for additional clarifications to ascertain whether certain conditions are met and reduce the number of possible answers.

In order to fully understand the uniqueness of knowledge-based systems, one must first understand the difference between imperative and declarative programming languages.

---

* Robin De Vogelaere (LL.M, MSc, PhD researcher), dr. Marjolein Deryck and prof. dr. Joost Vennekens – KU Leuven, De Nayer Campus, Dept. of Computer Science; Leuven.AI; Flanders Make@KU Leuven, Belgium.

Currently, most of the programming languages that are used in the industry are so-called imperative programming languages, e.g. Java, Python, C, ... In these languages, a software engineer describes step by step what the program must do. More complex execution paths can be obtained using loops or if-then statements. However, this means that the domain knowledge on which the program is based will be intermixed with the execution logic. For larger programs, this can quickly lead to added complexity, making it harder for users to understand the program or for programmers to maintain it.

By contrast, in declarative languages, the programmer directly expresses the relevant domain knowledge. This knowledge is then passed to an engine or solver that can reason over this information to solve certain problems or answer questions. Contrary to imperative programming, programmers do not need to concern themselves with the execution logic of the program (how can we solve the problem?) but only with modelling the knowledge (what do we need to know to solve the problem?). Therefore, in the context of declarative languages, the term 'modeller' is often preferred to 'programmer'.

Within declarative programming languages, a further distinction can be made between languages that are restricted to a single type of inference and those that are not. The expert systems of the 1980s and 1990s were all of the former type. However, the limitations of these types of systems soon became apparent, causing a decline in their usage despite some initial successes. This has led to the introduction of the knowledge-base paradigm, according to which a full separation must be sought between knowledge and program execution, thus allowing multiple forms of inference on the same knowledge-base.[1] Most modern knowledge-based systems are moving in that direction.[2] An example of the issues faced by the systems of the former type will be shown when discussing Prolog.

The advantages of knowledge-based systems for knowledge-intensive areas, such as the law, are immediately apparent. First, it is much more straightforward to translate (legal) rules into a declarative language than to define an imperative program that follows the intended rules. Second, if the knowledge needs to be updated (e.g. after the legislation is amended), the modeller only needs to update the corresponding rules in the knowledge base, without having to consider how the execution of the program is changed. Finally, if the declarative language is simple enough, domain experts will be able to model the knowledge themselves, without having to rely on IT staff. This will greatly reduce the

1 M. DENECKER & J. VENNEKENS, 'Building a Knowledge Base System for an Integration of Logic Programming and Classical Logic' in M. GARCIA DE LA BANDA & E. PONTELLI (eds), *Logic Programming. ICLP 2008. Lecture Notes in Computer Science*, vol 5366, Berlin, Heidelberg, Springer, 2008, 71-76.

2 Such as the IDP-Z3 engine discussed further.

gap between the intended meaning by the domain expert and the resulting program. Of course, this is only possible if the declarative language is sufficiently accessible to the domain expert.

An important field of study within AI related to these systems is knowledge representation. One of the goals of this field is precisely to determine a good formalism to express the knowledge such that it is both intuitive for the end user, understandable by the reasoning engine, and sufficiently expressive to model the domain but not so expressive that computations become intractable. This last point requires some clarification. There is a trade-off between the expressiveness of a language and the ease with which a solver can calculate the solution to a given query.[3] Intuitively, this makes sense: the more expressive a language is, the more complex the scenarios that can be expressed, making an exhaustive search of all possible solutions infeasible.

A commonly used modelling language is first-order logic. This language is attractive because it is well known, since it is taught in high school, unambiguous and very expressive. The downside is that it is undecidable,[4] meaning that for some questions the engine may not return an answer.

Another issue with first-order logic is that in some cases it is not expressive enough and extensions are needed to be able to (easily) express certain ideas. This, of course, is in direct conflict with the first issue, resulting in the aforementioned trade-off.

A final issue worth mentioning is that although first-order logic is generally considered well known, many people are insufficiently schooled in this language to be able to express anything beyond the most basic constructions. Each of these issues has been studied in the literature, and a multitude of solutions have been suggested.

In the remainder of this subsection, three declarative (programming) languages will be discussed, each designed to solve at least one of the problems described previously. The first two are based on first-order logic, while the final one uses a different formalism specifically for decision-making. Note that many more approaches exist; the selection has been made on the basis of the case studies included in Section 3 of this chapter.

---

3 H. LEVESGUE & R. BRACHMAN, 'Expressiveness and Tractability in Knowledge Representation and Reasoning', *Computational Intelligence, 3*(1), 1987, 78-93.

4 A. CHURCH, 'An Unsolvable Problem of Elementary Number Theory', *American Journal of Mathematics, 58*(2), 1936, 345-363.

2.1.1 Prolog

Prolog is one of the most well-known logic programming languages. This type of programming language allows only a subset of first-order logic to enable more efficient computations. Specifically, it relies mainly on Horn clauses.[5] These are formulas of the type:

```
a :- b, c, d, ..., n.
```

Expressed in words, 'a' is true if all of the conditions 'b' to 'n' are met. 'a' is the head of the clause, and 'b' to 'n' are the body. The ',' in Prolog denotes the logical AND, meaning that all elements in the body must evaluate to true. The classic example can be written as follows in Prolog:

```
mortal(X) :- man(X).
man(socrates).
```

The first statement says that for every X, if X is a man, then X is mortal. In Prolog syntax, the fact that X is a capital letter means that X is a (universally quantified) variable, which means that this statement applies to all men. The second statement says that Socrates is a man. Here, the fact that 'socrates' starts with a lower-case letter means that this is not a variable but a constant, i.e., a name for one specific man. This fact, therefore, applies to only one man.

Notice that the second statement does not have any conditions. This is equivalent to writing

```
man(socrates) :- true.
```

When queried, this small program provides the following output:

```
?- mortal(socrates).
true.
?- mortal(robin).
false.
```

'?-' denotes a query by the user. In the first case, we get the expected answer, but in the second case the program unexpectedly decides that the author of this piece is immortal. Why is this the case? This is due to the closed world assumption: Prolog assumes that

5 I. BRATKO, *Prolog Programming for Artificial Intelligence*, Harlow, Pearson Education, 2012, 57-58.

all relevant facts are exhaustively included in the knowledge base.[6] The knowledge base contains only the fact that Socrates is a man but does not say anything about Robin. Since Prolog cannot find any fact about Robin being either mortal or a man, it assumes this statement must be false, even though in classical first-order logic this assumption would not be correct.

Prolog is not a purely declarative language. The Prolog code is directly executable and runs in a predetermined order.[7] The modeller therefore needs to take the execution order into account to obtain the most efficient version of the program and in some cases even modify this logic, using built-in operators. Sometimes, choosing the wrong order might even cause a program to get stuck in an endless loop while a correct ordering would lead to a solution.

The main drawback of Prolog as a declarative language is that it supports only one type of inference. For instance, say we want to include Zeus in our previous example. We know that Zeus is a God and that Gods are immortal. From that we want to infer that Zeus is not a man. In first-order logic this can be expressed as follows:

$$\forall x\text{: Mortal}(x) \Leftarrow \text{man}(x).$$
$$\text{man(socrates)}.$$
$$\neg\text{mortal(zeus)}.$$

Where ∀ is the universal quantifier (meaning 'for all'), ¬ is the logical symbol for NOT and ⇐ means 'implies'. From the combination of these rules, it is possible to infer both mortal(socrates) and ¬man(zeus).

The same result cannot be obtained in Prolog, since its rules are interpreted in only one direction. That is, if Prolog encounters a statement about someone being or not being a man, it can reason about their mortality, but it cannot infer whether someone is a man from information about this person's mortality. To obtain the same result in Prolog, one would need to add the following:

```
notMan(X) :- notMortal(X).
notMortal(Zeus).
```

However, now the same information is represented twice, once for each direction, and both representations are not linked to each other. Such an approach is error prone.

6 Ibid., 138-141.
7 Ibid., 47-57.

As this example shows, in Prolog, the way in which knowledge must be represented is inexorably tied to the conclusions that one wishes to draw from this knowledge. This fundamental limitation of the Prolog paradigm may help to explain why the wave of expert systems in the 1980s and 1990s has, in general, remained unsuccessful, despite a number of promising results. Modern research on knowledge-based systems shows how this limitation can be overcome.

Nevertheless, Prolog certainly has its uses, and some famous applications have relied on it, such as Clarissa (2005),[8] a voice assistant used by astronauts on the International Space Station, and IBM Watson, the AI famous for winning an episode of the American game show *Jeopardy!* in 2011.[9]

2.1.2 IDP-Z3[10]

Contrary to Prolog, the IDP system created by KU Leuven aims to obtain a complete separation between the knowledge base and the reasoning tasks that can be performed on it. It uses FO(·) as its knowledge representation language, which is full first-order logic with a number of extensions, including types.[11] Types make it easier to express that predicates are only applicable to certain classes of entities: for instance, it does not make sense to talk about the mortality of a refrigerator. Further, they make calculations more tractable by reducing the scope of expressions. The same example as before, with the introduction of types, can be expressed as:

$$\forall x \in \text{Man: mortal}(x).$$

The ∈ sign denotes that x is an element of type Man.

The knowledge base is a 'bag of knowledge' and is not an executable program. The IDP-Z3 reasoning engine, which is the latest instalment of IDP, is responsible for reading and processing the information contained in it. Different types of inference are possible using different built-in algorithms. The system therefore fully adheres to the knowledge-base paradigm.

8 M. RAYNER, B. HOCKEY, J. RENDERS, N. CHATZICHRISAFIS & K. FARRELL, 'Spoken Language Processing in the Clarissa Procedure Browser', *Natural Language Engineering, 1*(1), 2005, 1-28.

9 A. LALLY & P. FODOR, 'Natural Language Processing with Prolog in the IBM Watson System', *The Association for Logic Programming (ALP) Newsletter, 9*, 2011, 4 p.

10 P. CARBONELLE, S. VANDEVELDE, J. VENNEKENS & M. DENECKER, 'IDP-Z3: A Reasoning Engine for FO(.)', *arXiv preprint arXiv:2202.00343*, 2022, 10 p.

11 B. DE CAT, B. BOGAERTS, M. BRUYNOOGHE, G. JANSSENS & M. DENECKER, 'Predicate Logic as a Modeling Language: The IDP System' in M. KIFER & Y. LIU (eds), *Declarative Logic Programming: Theory, Systems, and Applications*, ACM Books, New York, 2018, 279-329.

With a minimal amount of training, domain experts are able to read and understand formulas written in FO(·), leading to a greater trust in the system. However, writing a knowledge base in this system typically still requires the help of a knowledge engineer, which motivates the development of simpler and more intuitive formalisms to represent knowledge, such as Decision Model and Notation (DMN).

The case study on registration duties in the next section of this chapter demonstrates a clear example of the use of IDP, with a user interface built on top for additional convenience for the end user.

2.1.3 Decision Model and Notation (DMN)

While the previous two knowledge representation languages are based on first-order logic, this final option aims to provide a simpler formalisation to express knowledge. DMN[12] is a tabular notation that is widely used in the industry to model business decisions. It has been created by the Object Management Group (OMG), the same organisation responsible for the Business Process Model and Notation (BPMN) standard.

A DMN model consists of a Decision Requirements Diagram (DRD) and decision tables. The former is a visual representation of which decisions depend on which information. This information can consist of prior decisions or outside information. A decision can be a human or external decision, or it can be a purely logical decision.[13] In the latter case, the decision logic can be represented by a decision table. Each column of such a table corresponds to an input value, with the exception of the last column, which contains the output value. The header of each input column contains the name of the input variable (e.g. Size), and each cell contains a condition governing that variable (e.g. Size < 10). If all conditions for a row are met, the decision rule is matched, and the value in the output column is selected. The outputs of the intermediate decisions are passed as input value to the next decision node until a final output is reached.

While not as expressive as first-order logic or Prolog, DMN is widely used due to its very intuitive syntax that does not require that the user be familiar with programming or logic. It is easily readable by humans and, due to its standardised form, also by computers.[14]

---

12 T. BIARD, A. LE MAUFF, M. BIGAND & J. BOUREY, 'Separation of Decision Modeling from Business Process Modeling Using New "Decision Model and Notation" (DMN) for Automating Operational Decision-Making', in L. CAMARINHA-MATOS, F. BÉNABEN & W. PICARD, *16th Working Conference on Virtual Enterprises (PROVE)*, Albi, HAL, 2015, 489-496.

13 B. SILVER, *DMN Method & Style*, Altadena, Cody-Cassidy Press, 2016, 21.

14 S. VANDEVELDE & J. VENNEKENS, 'A Multifunctional, Interactive DMN Decision Modelling Tool', in L.CAO, W. KOSTERS & J. LIJFFIJT, *Proceedings of BNAIC/BeneLearn 2020*, Leiden, Leiden University, 2020, 399-400.

The DMN standard can be extended to increase its expressivity. One such extension is cDMN, which allows the user to express constraints.[15] In regular DMN, the output column can only contain a single value for the output variable, but what if the user wants to express that a certain input limits the possible values of the output variable without restricting it to a single value? This is what cDMN does. It allows the output to be a formula, just like the input (e.g. Price < 100). So now the user is able to express rules such as the following: if the size is smaller than 10, the price must be smaller than 100, instead of having to define an exact price.

Extensions like cDMN are therefore able to get the best of both worlds: added expressivity like FO(·) along with the intuitive formalism of DMN.

2.2 Comparison to Machine Learning

The previous subsection explained what knowledge-based systems are. This subsection will discuss the advantages of knowledge-based systems and answer the question as to when these systems should be preferred over machine learning approaches.

As explained in the introductory chapter of this book,[16] the goal of machine learning algorithms, including deep learning methods, is essentially to find a model that maps inputs (e.g. images of digits) to an expected output (e.g. the correct digit). Instead of manually defining the features of each output category, a deep learning algorithm is fed training data from which it extracts the features it deems relevant to create a model.

During training, the machine learning algorithm updates the weights of the model to optimise a loss function. This function will typically take into account the predictions of the model and compare those to the actual labels, as provided in the training data. An optimal model should not only score high on the training data but also be able to correctly predict unseen examples. To avoid overfitting the model to the training data, part of the data is therefore not used during training but only afterwards to test performance.

Machine learning algorithms thus excel at a single task: pattern recognition. In large amounts of training data these algorithms will be able to find recurring patterns, and

15 S. VANDEVELDE, B. AERTS & J. VENNEKENS, 'Tackling the DM Challenges with cDMN: A Tight Integration of DMN and Constraint Reasoning', *Theory and Practice of Logic Programming*, 2021, 1-24.

16 Cf. the introductory chapter "A Brief Introduction to AI and Its Use in the Legal Practice" by Prof. Gielen, p. 9.

by exploiting these patterns, they are able to create a model that correctly predicts the expected output in a high percentage of cases.

To explain the difference between machine learning and knowledge-based systems, a useful analogy can be drawn with human cognition. In *Thinking, Fast and Slow,* Kahneman distinguishes between system 1 and system 2 thinking.[17] The former is subconscious, fast and automatic, while the latter is logical, slow and requires a conscious effort. Machine learning models excel at system 1 tasks, such as vision. These are tasks for which it is very hard to come up with a clear explanation of how we ourselves perform them; we simply know how to do it. For instance, most people have no trouble distinguishing between cats and dogs yet find it almost impossible to clearly describe the distinguishing features of both animals. When provided with a new example, a machine learning model will likewise instantly label it by applying its learned weights to the input, but it is unable to explain why it decided on a particular label. Nor are humans able to determine what features these weights represent by inspecting the model. Knowledge-based systems struggle with this task, because the knowledge needed to describe each animal is simply lacking. For instance, people would typically say that a cat has four legs but are still able to correctly identify a three-legged cat.

Knowledge-based systems, by contrast, are more akin to system 2 thinking, i.e. they simulate the conscious reasoning of humans, by applying logical/mathematical operations to derive their conclusions from known facts and rules.

While recent advances have caused a huge surge in popularity of machine learning algorithms, there are a number of factors limiting their use in legal applications: data, reliability, reasoning and explainability. We will discuss each in turn.

2.2.1 Training Data

Gathering reliable and usable data to train a machine learning model is not an easy task. Yet the quality and reliability of the model depend on this.

Multiple issues with the data may exist:

- Data can be unavailable or unusable because it is corrupted, unreliable, proprietary, protected by intellectual property rights or privacy laws such as the General Data Protection Regulation (GDPR), …[18] Without suitable data, no model can be trained.

17 D. KAHNEMAN, *Thinking, Fast and Slow*, New York, Farrar, Straus and Giroux, 2011, 499 p.

18 Cf. the contribution of Prof. Margoni and Luca Schirru "Data Property Challenges in AI System Training", p. 23.

- In other cases the data may be too complex, leading to overly complex models, even though the user is aware of simpler rules. Here the issue is not so much with the data itself as with the model that can be learnt from it. A mismatch exists between the knowledge of the user and the knowledge incorporated in the model. Even if the model is not inherently bad, a user might not be willing to trust an overly complex model that does not align with their own intuition.
- Data can further be biased by the way it is collected, annotated or generated. Bias in training data is often discussed in the context of fairness and inclusion.[19] For example, a model that is trained on data with mainly male judges will automatically assume that a judge is a man, thereby confirming existing stereotypes. Even if the data correctly reflects an existing or historical situation, this is most likely not the desired behaviour. This issue is even more pronounced for language models as these models are often trained on large amounts of text gathered from all over the internet with limited corrections.

All these issues prevent the training of an effective model through machine learning. Knowledge-based systems provide a solution for situations in which data is unavailable, biased or unreliable.

2.2.2 Reliability and Explainability

Machine learning algorithms learn models that fit the data as closely as possible. Such a model is necessarily an approximation, and 100% reliability can never be obtained. Moreover, if black box models are used, the user is unable to inspect the model to correct erratic behaviour. By contrast, knowledge-based systems apply rules with 100% certainty. The decisions can be verified, and if the system makes mistakes, these can be avoided in the future by updating the rules.

Reliability and explainability not only increase user confidence in the system but are often also required by legislation such as the GDPR or the draft AI Regulation.[20]

2.2.3 Reasoning

As mentioned, machine learning algorithms rely on pattern recognition. While this has led to impressive results, researchers are becoming more aware of the limitations of this type of thinking. In order to be truly intelligent, system 2 thinking is also required. We will refer to this type of thinking as reasoning.

19 E.g. M. JACKSON, 'Artificial Intelligence & Algorithmic Bias: The Issue with Technology Reflecting History & Humans', *Journal of Business & Technology Law*, 2021, vol. 16, 299-316.

20 Art. 22 GDPR; Proposal for a Regulation of the European Parliament and of the Council Laying Down Harmonised Rules on Artificial Intelligence (Artificial Intelligence Act) and Amending Certain Union Legislative Acts, 21 April 2021, COM/2021/206 final.

Advanced language models have proven to be very useful for (legal) applications. They can write coherent and grammatically correct texts and aid in the due diligence process by correctly classifying certain clauses, such as change of control clauses.

Some advanced language models are even able to give the impression that they are reasoning. However, these models are in fact relying on statistical patterns in language to provide the most statistically likely outcome to form sentences. There is no guarantee that the output is correct. In fact, when asked to write Wikipedia articles, GPT-Neo came up with articles that were stylistically very close to real articles but with mostly made-up facts and citations to nowhere.[21] The empty citations, in particular, are an interesting point here, since they clearly show that the system is mimicking the style of Wikipedia without understanding what it is doing. This is similar to DALL-E images with signboards on them.[22] The signs will usually contain characters that look similar to letters but are often not, and even if they are, they do not form coherent words. The system is simply trying to replicate the style of these signs, without having a context for the words on them.

While the ongoing advances in large language models are certainly impressive, recent models still suffer from the same issues as their predecessors. A recent study[23] on hallucinations of large language models in the legal field found that the models make up false information to an alarming extent. On direct legal questions, the best model hallucinated in 69% of the cases, while the worst model did so in 88% of cases. These models also seem to have particular difficulties with counterfactual questions. They assume that the facts users assert in their questions are correct and continue on that basis.

In general, large language models will convincingly invent false knowledge, may rely on biased information and can easily be convinced to provide racist, sexist or otherwise prejudicial answers. Moreover, we cannot check answers provided by them, because they cannot tell us how they arrived at their answer. When asked to provide an explanation for an answer, a large language model will typically provide a plausible-sounding reasoning that may be both completely incorrect and wholly unrelated to how the model actually came up with the answer in the first place. Slight variations in the

21 K. MENGER-ANDERSON, 'When an AI Writes Wikipedia', *Towards Data Science* (blog), https://towardsdatascience.com/when-an-ai-writes-wikipedia-f7aa3eff9ebc.

22 A. ROMERO, 'DALL·E 2, Explained: The Promise and Limitations of a Revolutionary AI', *Towards Data Science* (blog), https://towardsdatascience.com/dall-e-2-explained-the-promise-and-limitations-of-a-revolutionary-ai-3faf691be220.

23 M. DAHL, V. MAGESH, M. SUZGUN & D. HO, 'Large Legal Fictions: Profiling Legal Hallucinations in Large Language Models', 2024, https://arxiv.org/abs/2401.01301.

question might lead to entirely different outputs.[24] This has even sparked an interest in prompt engineering: finding out how best to ask questions to large language models.

Contrary to machine learning, knowledge-based systems reason over facts and rules. They do not imagine new facts, and it is possible to obtain an explanation from the system about why a newly discovered fact holds. These systems adhere to a strict logical approach, ensuring that if the knowledge is correctly modelled, the answers are 100% reliable and explainable.

Recently, the need for knowledge-based approaches has become more accepted in the literature, and some researchers are now attempting to combine both types of AI to get the best of both worlds: a low-level machine learning system to process inputs and a high-level symbolic reasoning system to reason over the information.[25]

Before ending this discussion, it is useful to bring to mind that real understanding does not exist in any machine. The machine is able to display intelligent behaviour because of the data and/or knowledge that has been fed to it. What this subsection aims to show is that the type of intelligence the machine is able to mimic is based on the chosen algorithms and paradigms.

3 Modelling Statutes and Contracts

In the previous section, we saw the advantages of knowledge-based systems and hinted at their benefits to model legal text such as statutes and contracts. In this section we will investigate these applications. The first subsection will discuss machine-readable legislation and the issues with translating existing legislation into a machine-readable form. The next subsection will cover a case study on registration duties. The final subsection will touch upon an initiative to allow contracts to be drafted in a machine-readable format.

3.1 Machine-readable Legislation

3.1.1 Translation of Legislation into a Declarative Language

A number of articles have shown that it is possible, although not trivial, to translate existing legislation to a logic program. Perhaps the most famous example is the translation

24 OPENAI, 'ChatGPT: Optimizing Language Models for Dialogue', *Open AI Blog* (blog), https://openai.com/blog/chatgpt/.

25 E.g. D. YU, B. YANG, D. LIU, H. WANG & S. PAN, 'A Survey on Neural-Symbolic Learning Systems', *Neural Networks*, 2023, 105-126.

of the British Nationality Act 1981 (BNA) into Prolog,[26] although other examples exist such as the translation of the Japanese constitution into Prolog.[27]

Both at the time of translation and in the ensuing discussion, problems were detected with this type of translation.

Ashley formulates both problems with statutory reasoning and with the translation process.[28] With regard to statutory reasoning, there are issues of vagueness and semantic ambiguity as well as of syntactic ambiguity. The former encompasses all issues related to the exact scope of definitions and words used in the law. In some cases, such ambiguity remains unresolved in the legal literature, and the program will need to deal with this. The latter has to do with the logical structure of the text. Words such as 'and', 'or' and 'unless' are not always used in their logical meaning, or it is unclear at what level these words should be applied. For instance, 'A and B or C' can be read as '(A and B) or C' but can also be understood as 'A and (B or C)'. Multiple authors have noted that requiring legislation to be drafted in logical form might actually reduce the occurrences of this type of ambiguity.[29]

At the level of the translation process, Ashley identifies five issues:[30]

1. The need for reformulation: sometimes a literal translation is not enough, and arguments need to be added explicitly. For instance, in the BNA, time needed to be added to rules (e.g. something is true on date x).[31]
2. The way Prolog handles negation: because Prolog is restricted to Horn clause logic, it is impossible to add negative conclusions such as $\neg$*mortal(zeus),* mentioned in an earlier example.
3. Default reasoning: one of the difficulties with knowledge acquisition in the legal domain is the frequent use of default reasoning.[32] A default rule applies, unless some exception is applicable. This type of reasoning is typical for lawyers and not well suited for translation to first-order logic. First-order logic is monotonic; i.e. a rule which is evaluated as true cannot subsequently become false when additional

---

26 M. J. SERGOT, F. SADRI, R. A. KOWALSKI, F. KRIWACZEK, P. HAMMOND & H. T. CORY, 'The British Nationality Act as a Logic Program', *Communications of the ACM*, 1986, 370-386 (Hereafter: M. Sergot et al., BNA Act).

27 https://github.com/bitlaw-jp/the-constitution-of-japan.

28 K. ASHLEY, *Artificial Intelligence and Legal Analytics*, Cambridge, Cambridge University Press, 2017, 63-85 (Hereafter: K. ASHLEY, *Legal Analytics*).

29 Ibid., 65-66; M. Sergot et al., BNA Act; L. ALLEN, 'Symbolic Logic: A Razor-Edged Tool for Drafting and Interpreting Legal Documents', *Yale Law Journal*, 1957, vol. 66, 833-879.

30 K. ASHLEY, *Legal Analytics*, 78.

31 M. Sergot et al., BNA Act (370) 374.

32 M. DERYCK, *Knowledge Base Systems in Practice: Approaches, Application Areas and Limitations*, Sint-Katelijne-Waver, KU Leuven, 2022, 76 (Hereafter: M. DERYCK, *KBS in Practice).*

information is discovered. By contrast, default reasoning allows the use of defeasible rules, i.e. rules which can have deviations, such as the following: all birds can fly, except penguins.

4. Counterfactual conditionals: e.g. 'X would have become a citizen but for his having died'. Instead of listing all possibilities, the text refers to a rule which would have applied but for one condition. This cannot be translated literally into first-order logic.
5. Open-textured terms: e.g. 'being of good character'. Such open terms cannot be computed. The authors of the BNA paper chose to handle these terms by qualifying their answers: e.g. 'Peter is a citizen, if he is of good character.'[33]

Most of the aforementioned issues are a result of the chosen formalism (Prolog) and the state of the art at the time of writing of the article, rather than a criticism of knowledge-based systems in general. For instance, point 2 would not have been an issue in IDP, which can deal with negative conclusions. Further, (c)DMN allows the users to structure their clauses in such a way as to apply the most specific clause first and a default rule at the end. This could at least partly solve issue 3, as will be shown in the registration duty case study. Different logics also expressly allow defeasible rules, although at the cost of added complexity. Some of the required reformulations are also Prolog-specific. For instance, the BNA program was changed to allow the user to see what section of the act was applied.[34] Modern systems, such as IDP, allow the user to ask for an explanation, which will return the applied rules without needing to clutter the knowledge base with additional arguments.

Ideally, the description in the chosen declarative language will reflect the original natural language text as closely as possible. This property is referred to as isomorphism.[35] Yet there will always be some cases in which a direct translation is not possible. For example, counterfactual reasoning is not supported by any of the declarative languages discussed in this chapter. How this is best dealt with is highly case dependent.

Open-textured terms are indeed a challenge for fully automatic resolution but not necessarily so for knowledge-based systems. These terms can be included in the knowledge base and returned by the system, as in the example cited previously.

Of course, translating legislation into code is most useful for prescriptive legislation, such as tax law or financial law. This is exactly the area where most initiatives have

---

33 M. Sergot et al., BNA Act (370) 370-371.

34 Ibid., (370) 375.

35 M. DERYCK, *KBS in Practice*, 71.

already been taken to develop automated compliance tools.[36] However, many of these tools are strictly proprietary, and how they deal with the issues of vagueness and ambiguity is not public knowledge.

Often, compliance does not involve complex interpretations. Knowledge-based systems could be incorporated into business processes to help businesses comply with the straightforward legal questions they face when conducting their day-to-day business.[37]

A final criticism of the use of knowledge-based systems for legal applications is related to the longevity and usefulness of the resulting models.[38] The argument boils down as follows: legal expert systems capture the current knowledge of the law, but the interpretation of statutes constantly evolves. As the world evolves, the context changes, and legislation needs to be able to cope with these changes, which could not have been foreseen at the moment of drafting. The static, computable forms of this legislation will soon be outdated or will constantly need to be adapted to keep up, making the cost too high.

While this issue can certainly not be ignored, there are at least two mitigating factors:

- The interpretation of existing legislation in new situations often simply entails the qualification of this situation in terms of the existing definitions, without the need to change anything about the relationship between the defined objects. Once a correct definition has been found, the existing rules continue to apply, and the expert system will be able to apply those.
- In many areas of law, there is an increased trend towards standardisation and automation. Especially in the corporate domain, the law is becoming increasingly more detailed and standardised, leaving less room for interpretation. As mentioned, companies increasingly rely on computers to assist with monitoring compliance to deal with the increased complexity of the law.

3.1.2 Rules as Code: Drafting Legislation in a Declarative Language

The previous subsection discussed some problems with the translation of legislation into a declarative form, but what if legislation were drafted (partly) in such form?

36 J. MOHUN & A. ROBERTS, 'Cracking the Code: Rulemaking for Humans and Machines', *OECD Working Papers on Public Governance No. 42*, https://dx.doi.org/10.1787/3afe6ba5-en, 42 (Hereafter: J. MOHUN & A. ROBERTS, OECD Working Paper).

37 K. ASHLEY, *Legal Analytics*, 85.

38 P. LEITH, 'The Rise and Fall of the Legal Expert System', *European Journal of Law and Technology*, 2010, vol. 1, 94-106.

The idea of drafting legal documents in a logical form goes back to at least 1957, when Allen wrote his seminal article: *Symbolic logic: a razor-sharp tool for drafting and interpreting legal statutes*, in which he argues that logic could eliminate undesired ambiguity from legislation and improve legal analyses.[39]

Of course, this article predates the widespread use of computers. More recently, rules as code initiatives have started to surface.[40] The aim of these initiatives is that the government itself start to codify its legislation. They hope that this will increase access to legislation for people without a legal education, make the law easier to understand and reduce ambiguity.[41] They further identify the issue of translation loss, which plagues private projects to translate legislation into code. When a private company wants to create a compliance tool, it must rely on a lawyer, who interprets the law and explains it to an engineer. In the second translation phase, the engineer must now translate the lawyer's interpretation into code. This process is not only costly but also error prone: in each step there are possibilities for translation errors and misunderstandings.[42]

In the summer of 2021, as countries started to reallow events after the COVID pandemic, the COVID Safe Ticket (CST) was introduced in Belgium. The CST determined whether a person was allowed to enter an event, based on information such as this person's vaccination status and recent test results. The exact rules governing the CST were introduced in the executive collaborative agreement (*uitvoerend samenwerkingsakkoord / accord de coopération d'exécution*) of 14 July 2021, published in the Belgian Official Gazette (*Belgisch Staatsblad / Moniteur Belge*) on 23 July 2021.[43] These rules needed to be clear, unambiguous and readily translatable into code to be used in an app so that event organisers could simply scan peoples' QR-codes to determine if they had access. The agreement therefore specified the rules in the form of a decision table (Figure 1).

39 L. ALLEN, 'Symbolic Logic: A Razor-Edged Tool for Drafting and Interpreting Legal Documents', *Yale Law Journal*, 1957, 833-879.

40 J. MOHUN & A. ROBERTS, OECD Working Paper 109 p.; New-Zealand: https://www.betterrules.govt.nz/, France: https://openfisca.org/en/.

41 J. MOHUN & A. ROBERTS, OECD Working Paper, 34.

42 Ibid., 31.

43 *Uitvoerend samenwerkingsakkoord van 14 juli 2021 tussen de Federale Staat, de Vlaamse Gemeenschap, de Franse Gemeenschap, de Duitstalige Gemeenschap, de Gemeenschappelijke Gemeenschapscommissie, het Waalse Gewest en de Franse Gemeenschapscommissie betreffende de verwerking van gegevens met betrekking tot het digitaal EU-COVID-certificaat, het COVID Safe Ticket, het PLF en de verwerking van persoonsgegevens van in het buitenland wonende of verblijvende werknemers en zelfstandigen die activiteiten uitvoeren in België / Accord de coopération d'exécution de 14 julliet 2021 entre l'État fédéral, la Communauté flamande, la Communauté française, la Communauté germanophone, la Commission communautaire commune, la Région wallonne et la Commission communautaire française concernant le traitement des données liées au certificat COVID numérique de l'UE et au COVID Safe Ticket, le PLF et le traitement des données à caractère personnel des travailleurs salariés et des travailleurs indépendants vivant ou résidant à l'étranger qui effectuent des activités en Belgique.*

Because this decision table complied with the specifications of the DMN standard, the app could make decisions using a standard DMN engine, without the need for further translation, thus ensuring that the app always correctly applied the published rules.

Figure 1 Decision table implementing the COVID Safe Ticket, as published in the Belgian Official Gazette.

Beslissingsregels voor het generen van het CST																
Lidstaat van de vaccinatie of lidstaat van de test	Lidstaat van de EU, EER, Verenigd Koninkrijk of Zwitserland															Nee
Geboortejaar betrokkene	2009 of later	Vroeger dan 2009														-
Datum eerste positieve testresultaat op certificaat van herstel	-	180 dagen of minder geleden	Meer dan 180 dagen geleden													-
Vaccinatiestatus op vaccinatiecertificaat	-	-	1/1 of 2/2							Andere waarde						-
Vaccinatiedatum op vaccinatiecertificaat	-	-	14 dagen of meer geleden	Minder dan 14 dagen geleden						-						-
Resultaat van de test op testcertificaat	-	-	-	Negatief					Andere waarde	Negatief					Andere waarde	-
Datum van afname op testcertificaat	-	-	-	3 dagen geleden		2 dagen of minder geleden		Andere waarde	-	3 dagen geleden		2 dagen of minder geleden		Andere waarde	-	-
Type test op testcertificaat	-	-	-	NAAT	Andere waarde	NAAT of Erkende RAT	Andere waarde	-	-	NAAT	Andere waarde	NAAT of Erkende RAT	Andere waarde	-	-	-
CST geeft toegang tot evenement	x	x	x	x	-	x	-	-	-	x	-	x	-	-	-	-
CST geeft geen toegang tot evenement	-	-	-	-	x	-	x	x	x	-	x	-	x	x	x	x
	1	2	3	4	5	6	7	8	9	10	11	12	13	14	15	16

Source: Belgian Official Gazette 23 July 2021

Especially for this type of prescriptive rules, i.e. technical rules without much room for interpretation, drafting the rules in a declarative language is useful and ensures their correct application. Logic might even be a more precise and better alternative for these rules than natural language.[44] As mentioned earlier, businesses interacting with legislation typically want to comply with rules as efficiently as possible. Providing the legislation in machine-readable form will help lower the costs of compliance.[45]

However, the use of machine-readable rules is by no means limited to this type of technical legislation. As the previous subsection has shown, there is in principle no limit to the type of legislation that can be implemented as code, except that some interpretative questions such as a person being of 'good character' might need to be delegated to an oracle or be left as assumption in the answer. Such partly automated rules could still provide businesses with decision support and help avoid costly legal mistakes.

An open point of discussion within the rules as code community is the right technology to be used for the project. Some favour the use of existing imperative or declarative programming languages, while others feel the need to define a language

44 J. MOHUN & A. ROBERTS, OECD Working Paper, 92.

45 Ibid., 71.

that is specifically tailored to deal with legislation and that aims to encode legislation in a form that more closely represents how lawyers would think about the law.[46] For instance, Catala is a programming language that is specifically being created to deal with default reasoning.[47]

Each approach has its pros and cons. Using an application-specific language has the advantage that the language will contain tailored features that solve some of the issues encountered with a general language. On the other hand, the user runs the risk of these experimental languages never receiving widespread support, leading to wasted translation efforts. General purpose languages have the advantage that they often have a larger community and that they will therefore receive more and more frequent updates and that new programming features will be implemented sooner.

Ultimately, the chosen language or formalism will also depend on non-technical factors, such as the available expertise and the project dynamics. The registration case discussed in the next subsection provides a good example of this latter point.

3.2 Case Study: Registration Duties[48]

This case looks at an application that supports notaries in the calculation of registration duties in Belgium. The levying of registration duties is a regional responsibility in Belgium, with standard duties currently amounting to 12% in Flanders and 12.5% in the Brussels capital region and Wallonia. There are a number of exceptions that lead to the payment of a lower proportion of duties (e.g. for social housing) or assign a discount on the taxable amount. The primary focus of this case is the calculation of registration duties for the Flemish region. The applicable legislation is described in the Decree of 13 December 2013 containing the Flemish Tax Codex.[49]

This piece of legislation was specifically chosen due to its favourable characteristics. Indeed, this kind of administrative legislation is viewed as straightforward by legal

---

46 Ibid.

47 D. MERIGOUX, N. CHATAING & J. PROTZENKO, 'Catala: A Programming Language for the Law', *Proceedings of the ACM on Programming Languages*, 5, 2021, 1-29.

48 Different aspects of this case study were previously published in: M. DERYCK, F. HASIĆ, J. VANTHIENEN & J. VENNEKENS, 'A Case-Based Inquiry into the Decision Model and Notation (DMN) and the Knowledge Base (KB) Paradigm', *Rules and Reasoning*, 2018, 248-263; M. DERYCK, J. VENNEKENS, J. DEVRIENDT & S. MARYNISSEN, 'Legislation in the Knowledge Base Paradigm: Interactive Decision Enactment for Registration Duties', *2019 IEEE 13th International Conference on Semantic Computing (ICSC)*, 2019, 174-177; M. DERYCK, *KBS in Practice*, 55-79.

49 *Decreet van 13 december 2013 houdende de Vlaamse codex fiscaliteit.*

practitioners because rules are written out clearly and typically only necessitate deductive reasoning to obtain the unchallengeable answer. The modeller conducted several interviews with a notary. The first interviews were unstructured. Although this is a good format to obtain insight into the requirements of the notary with regard to the application, and the current obstacles, this did not deliver enough information to create the knowledge base. Subsequent interviews were therefore semi-structured. The structure was created by using the DRD to visually represent decision points and their dependencies (Figure 2).

Figure 2 Decision Requirements Diagram (DRD) for the registration duties case.

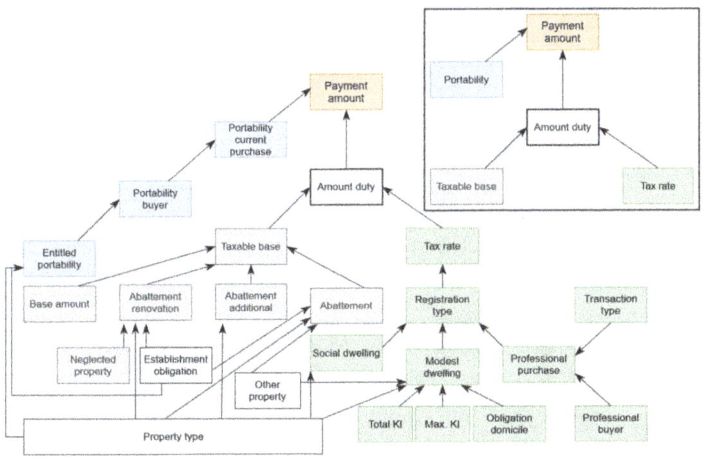

Source: M. DERYCK, KBS in Practice, 58.

The highest level view shows the different components that impact the calculation of the amount to be paid effectively by the buyers of a house, depending on the taxable base, the tax rate and portability of earlier paid duties. This can be seen in the top right-hand corner of Figure 2.

When zooming in on a lower level, more components start to appear (Figure 2). At this level, each block represents one decision. Because law books are very structured, the content of one block often coincides with the content of one article. The decree is organised as follows: first, the taxable base is determined (Section 3), followed by the general stipulation that registration duties are 10% (Art. 2.9.4.1.1), followed by exceptions that determine the cases in which less than 10% is due (Arts. 2.9.4.2.1 to 2.9.4.2.9). Although there is no one-to-one relation between articles and the different decision logic tables, the DRD blocks mimic the general structure of the legal text. This isomorphism allows domain experts to validate the knowledge model more easily.

The final level of detail is the level of the decision logic. This level describes what happens within a single block. It is typically represented as decision tables in DMN (Figure 3). There are different ways in which a table can be read. To make sure that the table is interpreted unambiguously, the way to interpret the table is made explicit in the hit policy in the upper left-hand corner of the table. Usually, it is recommended to use the unique (U) hit policy, meaning that rows in a table are mutually exclusive (i.e. for each specific case only one row is applicable), because this facilitates the validation and verification of the table's content.

Figure 3 Decision table with unique hit policy (U).

Renovation Abatement					
U	Destiny of Purchase	Registration Date of Neglected House	Domicile Established	Dwelling of Natural Person	Renovation Abatement
1	Not(habitation)	—	—	—	0
2	habitation	> Purchase Date - 4 years	—	—	0
3	habitation	≤ Purchase Date - 4 years	No	—	0
4	habitation	≤ Purchase Date - 4 years	Yes	No	0
5	habitation	≤ Purchase Date - 4 years	Yes	Yes	30000

However, in the case of discounts on the standard registration duties, several exceptions exist that each require numerous conditions to be fulfilled simultaneously. As soon as one of the conditions is not met, the buyer is no longer entitled to the exception. If represented as a unique hit table, all possible combinations need to be summed up, resulting in a typical triangular table in which only one value is altered per row (Figure 3). This can be represented in a much shorter fashion using a first (F) hit table, meaning that multiple rows may be applicable to a specific case, but only the first applicable row is selected (Figure 4).

Figure 4 The same information as Figure 3, represented using a first hit table (F).

Renovation Abatement					
F	Destiny of Purchase	Registration Date of Neglected House	Domicile Established	Dwelling of Natural Person	Renovation Abatement
1	habitation	≤ Purchase Date - 4 years	Yes	Yes	30000
2	—	—	—	—	0

The use of first hit tables also aligns well with legal reasoning in the sense that cases that come up higher in the first hit table can be considered exceptions to the case below. It is to some extent up to the modeller to decide if an exception is modelled as a separate row or as additional columns.

When looking at the detailed DRD, there are some links between decision blocks of different areas (e.g. between the portability block and the abatement block). That is because sometimes the buyer has to choose between two or more different exceptions. In DMN, a workaround must be used to model this by incorporating the negation of one exception into the conditions of the other exception. This is, however, not the epistemologically most suitable option. It would be better to be able to say explicitly that both conditions cannot appear together. This can be done in the more expressive cDMN formalism, which allows the user to model constraints. The cDMN constraint table shown in Figure 5 expresses that neither an abatement nor a so-called '*bij-abattement*' is compatible with portability.

Figure 5 A cDMN decision table, modelling the constraint that two discounts cannot be applied together.

Combination of Exceptions			
E*	Portability	Abatement	Bij-Abatement
1	Yes	No	No

The DMN formalism was chosen because it is readable and understandable for business users. The resulting DMN model can be used by the generic Interactive Consultant tool[50] to provide the following interactive functionality:

- If all information on the purchase of a specific property is present, calculate the most profitable registration duty.
- If part of the information on the purchase of a specific property is available, calculate the possible registration duties.
- In a conversation with the client, interactively complete information and highlight pieces of information that are still needed to calculate the registration duty.
- Explain why a certain piece of information was derived.
- If the information on a purchase and the registration duties that were paid is present, check if the correct duties were levied.
- Check the conditions under which a specific registration duty can be obtained.

A simplified version of the application is available to try out on https://interactive-consultant.idp-z3.be/ (select file 'registration'). The application satisfies all of the following requirements:

- Completeness and correctness: the application ensures that all possible discounts are taken into account and only rules out or applies discounts when warranted by the information provided by the notary.
- Usability: in meetings between notaries and their clients, the confidential atmosphere is not disturbed as the technology provides a simple click-button interface and does not enforce entering information in a specific order.
- Traceability: the decision outcomes calculated by the application are easy to check and explain, in order to increase clients' confidence in the application.

50 S. VANDEVELDE & J. VENNEKENS, A Multifunctional, Interactive DMN Decision Modelling.

- Efficient information gathering: only questions relevant to possible discounts are suggested. For instance, as soon as it is clear that one of the discounts cannot be used, questions related to this discount become irrelevant and are greyed out in the interface.

Interestingly, this case study was conducted in the period 2017-2019, meaning that the significant reformation of registration duties in 2018 was part of it. These reforms of the registration duties represent a profound change: of the original 42 law articles of Chapter 9 concerning the registration duties, the decree of 18 May 2018 abolishes 4 articles, modifies 9 and adds 5. In traditional information systems, the implementation of changes of this extent takes a significant amount of time. Because, in this case, the domain knowledge is strictly separated from the algorithms that use it to calculate solutions, it can be changed easily. Hence, changing the knowledge base as described above only took 0.5 person days. This demonstrates that knowledge-based systems are well maintainable.

3.3 *Automating Contracts*

Automatic contracts are very much a topic of interest nowadays, and entire books have been dedicated to smart contracts, i.e. contracts that can be automatically resolved, typically on a blockchain.[51] The terms of such contracts are written directly in code. Once the conditions of a certain clause have been met, the contract is able to recognise this, calculate the consequences and automatically resolve those, for instance by transferring funds from one party to the other.

But even outside the context of the blockchain and smart contracts, allowing computers to reason over contracts is a worthwhile endeavour, much for the same reasons as automated legislation. It can help companies manage their contracts by automatically executing certain clauses, warning the appropriate people of (potential) breaches of contract or facilitate drafting by allowing negotiating parties to run simulations and experiment with different clauses.

Currently, most automated/smart contracts are written in imperative programming languages. Even the special purpose languages that have been developed for smart contracts, e.g. Solidity and Viper, tend to follow this paradigm.[52] However, it should

---

51 E.g. P. AERTS, *Smart Contracts*, Brussels, Intersentia, 2020, 403 p; J. ALLEN & P. HUNN (eds.), *Smart Legal Contracts: Law in Theory and Practice*, Oxford, Oxford University Press, 2022, 528 p.

52 X., *Ethereum Development Documentation*, https://ethereum.org/en/developers/docs/smart-contracts/languages/.

come as no surprise that declarative languages are also being considered to automate reasoning on smart contracts and contracts in general. After all, contracts and statutes use the same type of legal language and have a similar structure. In this sense, contracts can be seen as private lawmaking.[53]

At Stanford, researchers are currently developing the Contract Definition Language as an extension of Epilog, a Prolog-like declarative language.[54] This extension mainly consists of an ontology for contracts, i.e. a fixed reusable vocabulary. In fact, the researchers distinguish between two such vocabularies: the legal ontology and the domain-specific vocabulary.[55] The former is intended to apply to all contracts and contains typical definitions from contract law, such as the meeting of the minds. The latter will depend on the contract's domain; e.g. an insurance contract will rely on different terminology than a contract for medical services.

Creating an ontology is useful, regardless of the chosen language. It creates a common, shared terminology that can be reused in different projects. Many types of contracts already have highly standardised terms and terminology. Think, for instance, of the ISDA master agreement.[56] This agreement itself is never altered, but negotiated choices are made in schedules. Parties wishing to conclude a swap or derivative agreement can use this standardised vocabulary and thus avoid discussions on the interpretation and scope of terms. Likewise, legal ontologies in the Contract Definition Language can facilitate negotiations by creating a common terminology.

The Stanford team has modelled a number of US statutes in various legal domains to show the versatility of the language[57] and is now in the process of automating insurance contracts in cooperation with industry partners.[58] As the insurance industry is already highly data driven, it is no surprise that this industry would be a prime target for contract automation. Automated contracts could allow the insurance companies to better monitor their risks but also allow users to better keep track of their insurance coverage and make it easier to determine the effect of increasing or decreasing the coverage.

---

53 H. SURDEN, 'Computable Contracts', *U.C. Davies Law Review, 46*, 2012, (629) 675.

54 S. AGARWAL, K. XU & J. MOGHTADER, 'Toward Machine-Understandable Contracts', *AI4J–Artificial Intelligence for Justice*, 2016, 1-8, http://logic.stanford.edu/epilog/homepage/index.php.

55 Ibid.; M. GENESERETH, 'Contract Definition Language', *Complaw Corner* (blog), 2021, https://law.stanford.edu/2021/04/07/contract-definition-language/.

56 International Swaps and Derivatives Association (ISDA), https://www.isda.org/.

57 S. AGARWAL, K. XU & J. MOGHTADER, Toward Machine-Understandable Contracts; V. CHAUDHRI, 'Computable Contracts in the Financial Services Industry', *arXiv preprint arXiv:2208.04685*, 2022.

58 http://contractnet.stanford.edu/homepage/cdl.php.

Although the Contract Definition Language is certainly an interesting project, it is by no means the only possible solution to automate contracts. As was the case with drafting legislation, other (declarative) languages could be equally useful. If needed, the ontology could be translated into a different language, to comply with the same standard, although it is certainly also possible to use a different vocabulary.

An interesting approach to contract modelling is the use of controlled natural language (CNL). This approach was used by Deryck et al. in a case study involving collateral selection for a financial services company.[59] Deciding on the eligibility of assets as collateral is a complex process. Usually, a list of eligibility criteria is described in natural language in an annex to the agreement, but the parties to the contract would, naturally, also like to have these criteria in a computer-readable format which can then be used by the side providing the collateral to automatically check which financial instruments in its portfolio are eligible and if the total amount of eligible assets is sufficient to meet the requirements. The financial services company involved in the project used to translate these complex rules into an imperative programming language. This code was long and complex to understand, making its creation and validation an arduous and time-consuming process. In their project, Deryck et al. managed to cut down the time to create the investment profile of the client significantly, by using the IDP system.[60] Naturally, the company cannot expect its clients to familiarise themselves with FO(·) before being able to provide the required information. To solve this issue, a front end was created in which the user can express their criteria in CNL. As can be seen in the example (Figure 6), CNL is a subset of natural language but uses only a specific vocabulary and grammar. Users can select the wanted values from a list. In order to make the application even more user-friendly, an option is also provided to type the text in plain natural language. A deep learning system then detects which CNL sentence is most likely meant and provides this to the user for verification. Behind the scenes, the CNL sentences are automatically translated into FO(·), resulting in a computer-readable form of the annex describing the eligible collateral. Because of the controlled nature of CNL, the translations are precise and unambiguous. For some types of contracts, a CNL tool could be a great choice to create smart contracts in an intuitive and user-friendly manner.

---

59 M. DERYCK, *KBS in Practice*, 142; M. DERYCK, N. COMENDA, B. COPPENS & J. VENNEKENS, 'Combining Logic and Natural Language Processing to Support Investment Management', *Proceedings of the 18th International Conference on Principles of Knowledge Representation and Reasoning*, 666-670.

60 Ibid.

Figure 6 Application to allow users to represent information on financial assets in controlled natural language (CNL).

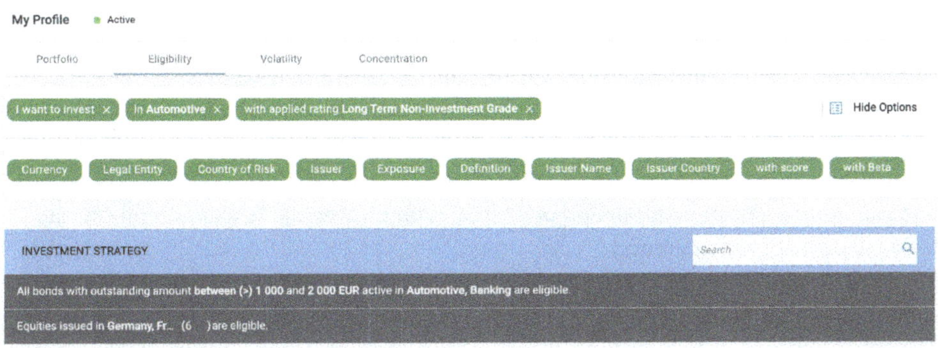

Source: M. DERYCK, KBS in Practice, 142.

A final point worth mentioning is that the advantage of a contract in a declarative language is not only its automatic execution but also its verifiability against legislation in the same form. Moreover, these contracts could allow hypothesis testing: users could check what would happen if certain provisions were changed or not complied with.[61]

4 Conclusion

This chapter has aimed to provide an introduction to the use of knowledge-based AI for legal applications.

Section 2 gave a high-level overview of the fields of knowledge-based AI and knowledge representation. The goal of these fields of research is to be able to declaratively express knowledge and let the computer reason over it. In its most extreme form, this leads to the knowledge-base paradigm: a complete separation of knowledge from the execution logic of any computer program that relies on that knowledge.

Another key takeaway from this section is that there is no single best declarative language to model knowledge in a computer-readable format. In fact, each of the available options is a trade-off between different factors such as expressiveness, tractability and ease of use. Depending on the goal of the project, some options might be more suitable than others.

61 S. AGARWAL, K. XU & J. MOGHTADER, Toward Machine-Understandable Contracts.

A final important point in this section is the distinction between knowledge-based AI and machine learning (i.e. data-based) approaches. We have shown that they each excel at a different type of thinking. Machine learning approaches are best suited for system 1 thinking, i.e. fast, automatic and subconscious thinking, while knowledge-based systems are more suited for type 2 thinking, i.e. slow and methodical reasoning.

The aforementioned characteristics of knowledge-based systems make them particularly well-suited for legal applications:

- Statutes/contracts can be modelled once in a computer-readable format and reused for different types of inference.
- Legal reasoning should be precise and calculated. The results obtained by the system should be explainable.
- The legal sector often has a lot of knowledge available. By contrast, systematic data is often absent.

Section 3 of this chapter gave some examples of legal applications, for both modelling statutes and contracts. These examples show how legal sources can be translated into a machine-readable format, often while maintaining a close resemblance to their original form (isomorphism). Some initiatives aim to go even further and only use a single format that is readable by both humans and computers. Such an approach reduces ambiguity when drafting legal documents, removes the translation gap for legal applications, and facilitates compliance and the creation of automatic compliance tools.

Indeed, while further research in these technologies is still needed, we are already seeing promising initiatives and practical results, both in the area of code as law and in the area of (declarative) smart contracts and automated contracts.

Part I
Mergers & Acquisitions

Horses, Cars and the Potential for AI in M&A Transactions*

*Christoph Michiels and Jan Roggen***

After the conference on artificial intelligence and contract formation on 19 October 2022, we sat down with Christoph Michiels and Jan Roggen from Deloitte Legal. Together, they are the driving force behind the Legal Operate practice of Deloitte Legal in Belgium. Legal Operate assists companies in building a future proof legal function by combining people, process and technology in the legal function. During this conversation, we discussed what AI means both in general and in particular within the field of M&A transactions as well as how it can add value.

Thank you Christoph and Jan for taking the time for this interview. Can you explain to us how AI differs from human intelligence and traditional software?

Christoph: First and foremost, I should mention that I am a corporate M&A lawyer who happens to be also the Innovation Partner. So maybe I'm not the right person to provide the best technical definitions for AI, but I can try to explain how AI works for us as lawyers, using simplified images.

So let's imagine a picture of a cow and try to see it in front of you. I assume most people can now see a cow and you can see it simply because you recognise a cow.

If you have to teach this to a traditional software as we know it, you will have to get into a very long logical decision tree to describe characteristics of a cow. When I would ask you to describe what you see without mentioning it is a cow, you would probably mention that it is a large animal with four legs, a tail and that they come in a variety of colours, but mostly in black, white and brown. And you could then add some more characteristics, and the software would tell you that this is a cow:

* This report is based on the presentation of Christoph Michiels and Jan Roggen at the conference on artificial intelligence and contract formation by the KUL on 19 October 2022. The other speakers in the first panel on 'AI and M&A Transactions' were Bart Bellen and Maarten Herbosch.

** Lawyers at Deloitte Legal. Christoph is a partner in Corporate and M&A at Deloitte legal, Jan is Director of Legal Operate at Deloitte Legal.

Why can humans, unlike traditional software, recognise a cow with acceptable accuracy? Because as humans, we have learned what a cow is. Our parents and teachers showed us and have told us that the animal over there is a cow and that this other animal on the other side is a horse; and over time we have learned to recognise and distinguish them.

AI differs from traditional software in that it looks at more than just logical decision trees. It also learns from patterns, combines them and decides whether a certain animal is a cow or a horse. And to distinguish between a cow and a horse, AI may use characteristics that are completely different from the characteristics we use as humans to distinguish them. I've been told, for example, that the nostrils are a very efficient way of identifying the difference between a cow and a horse, and AI seems to use this to distinguish them. While humans do not pick up on these small details and would probably never use this characteristic to identify a cow or a horse, AI does.

And because AI looks at things in a different way, it will do better than humans in some cases. If lawyers use 'control F' in a due diligence, looking for change of control clauses, they may not find all relevant clauses. Because some change of control clauses do not contain the words 'change' or 'control'. AI-powered document review tools will find these change of control clauses and will also notify you whenever 'change of control' is mentioned with a typo in it.

Although AI has made significant progress in the last years and even months, a lot of people, especially in the legal industry, remain sceptical. Why is there still so much scepticism?

Christoph: First of all, AI is far from perfect. There are lots of cases where AI cannot (yet) define and recognise the difference between objects and animals. Some famous examples include the page full of muffins and chihuahuas, or the examples with a sheepdog and a mop or an owl and an apple.

The recent stories about how ChatGPT3 made up complete answers, referring to scientific papers or case law that doesn't exist, have also shown that we cannot rely on AI yet when we need accuracy.

Secondly, people are always sceptical. People always have doubts. This wasn't different in the past with other kinds of technology. Take the car, for example. When the car was introduced at the end of the 19th and beginning of the 20th century, people were asking questions about whether these cars would actually stop when you tried to brake. The current scepticism towards AI is very similar, and it is normal. Before there's trust, there's always scepticism.

When people learn to drive a car, it is challenging at first, maybe even terrifying. However, as you build trust in your own capabilities and that of the car, you will start using the technology more and more. And in order to trust the car, you don't need to understand all the details of how the technology works. You don't need to understand how an engine works in order to confidently drive a car. With AI, it's similar.

So how can we build trust and overcome scepticism?

Christoph: We should start with managing expectations. We are in Leuven today. Let's imagine you have a meeting in Antwerp this afternoon and there are no trains or buses. Even though your car will not bring you to the meeting room directly, you will probably still use it. You will park your car in a nearby parking lot or building, and you'll walk from your car to the building and then continue walking to the meeting room.

So you will combine the traditional way of doing things (walking) with technology that will get you somewhere much more efficiently (car). The technology will not bring you exactly where you need to be in the meeting room, but you will still use your car. As long as you are aware of when to use your car and when to walk, you'll be ok.

Managing expectations and learning how to work with these tools will eventually build trust.

Jan: I believe this is the way we should look at AI and legal technology, in general. It isn't perfect, and it will not be the most suitable way to tackle each and every problem. But it does help us to separate the [wheat] from the chaff and to work in a more efficient way. If you want to be a good lawyer in the future, it will be important to train your ability to know when you can and should use technology to deliver better work faster and when you should use human judgment because the technology is not the best way to bring you where you need to be, e.g. in terms of accuracy.

If you look at which tools are available for due diligence, you will find a wide range of tools and providers. The most common technology in M&A is probably the virtual data room. It allows to streamline the due diligence process, and some tools add project management capabilities or work flows to these virtual data rooms. Other AI-powered tools help you identify and extract clauses from contracts. Kira is an example of such technology. In the drafting and negotiation stage, AI-powered tools like Clausebase or Henchman can help you find and select the right clauses. Recently, there has been quite a bit of focus on reviewing contracts and other documents with AI-powered tools. Some of these tools create a redline or can flag issues if you train the AI with your negotiation playbooks and legacy contracts.

But rather than maximising the use of these technologies, most M&A lawyers have been trying to avoid this by limiting the scope of the due diligence and reviewing only a limited amount of contracts. By doing this, the cost of the due diligence is bearable for the client, and we can still manage risks without investing in these sometimes expensive technologies.

The fact that Belgium is a small country, with smaller size transactions, three official languages and even more different legal systems, doesn't make it easier. It is often difficult to see and build the business case for investments in legal technology and going through the painful change process of implementing technology.

So, instead of trying to do the same work more efficiently, maybe we should look at it from a different angle.

Christoph: And here again, we can make an analogy with cars. Until recently, we bought our cars in the car dealership and then went for a check-up and maintenance every 10,000 kilometres.

New cars don't need these check-ups any more, because the car is full of sensors, and when something's wrong, the sensor will let us know. It's even possible that the car itself will let the dealership know, so they will contact you before we even noticed something was wrong.

Instead of a full check-up at certain events or intervals, cars are now monitored continuously, and the dealership has instant access to all relevant data to check whatever needs to be checked.

I believe there will be similar evolution in the due diligence work we do. AI is an opportunity to get rid of, or at least minimise, the event-driven check-ups we traditionally do as part of due diligence. Instead, AI allows to evolve towards continuous monitoring of the legal health of a company, and whenever there is an event like a transaction and due diligence is required, the potential buyers of a company will just plug into the system of the target and start analysing the data.

Jan: Suppose you are an investor and you have to choose between two identical companies. Company X gives you access to a data room with all the documents. As a potential buyer, you get access to the data room, and you can read and review the documents.

- Company Y gives you access to the data in a structured way where you can plug in, pull everything out, start analysing the data, review the information and make your own assessment based on the available data.

Which company would you rather buy? And which company would you be willing to pay more for? I'd answer 'Company 2' to both questions. And when we asked the participants at the conference the same questions, most of them answered 'Company 2'.

So most people seem to agree that there is value in turning the unstructured data in contracts and documents into structured data in databases.

And unlocking the value of contracts is exactly what we are doing at Deloitte Legal. Due diligence gives you a snapshot of the legal health of a company. But if you continuously monitor the legal health of the company and if you have a clear and structured overview of what is in your contracts, you will be able to use these insights to drive the strategy of the company on a day-to-day basis. And the cost of due diligence will no longer be a cost of the transaction but an investment to better run the company.

So if we use technology, and AI-powered technology specifically, to turn unstructured data available in contracts into structured data that remains available to the company even after the transaction, we create value.

So how does this look in practice?

Jan: Within Deloitte Legal we are using a platform called Legalhub for our due diligence work. It is basically a collection of databases with dashboards that allows us to manage workflows, set up tasks, calendars and many more. And it also allows to manage contracts.

The workflow in most legal due diligence processes looks very similar.

1. Every due diligence starts with a scoping exercise, where we describe what we will do and what we will not do as part of the due diligence. Legalhub gives you an overview of the scope of the project, not in a Word document, not in an excel sheet but in a database, in a structured way.
2. Once the scope of the project is clear, we compile the information request list in order to collect all information and documentation for the due diligence. Again, this is done in a database, rather than a word or an excel file. In Legalhub, the information requests are linked to the relevant scope items.
3. The data room in Legalhub is similar to any other digital data room and stores a large amount of documents, structured in folders.
4. This is where we start using Kira, a machine learning tool that assists us in extracting data from contracts. We import the contracts in Kira and create worksheets. Worksheets are lists of clauses that we want Kira to look for. Kira has more than thousand pre-trained clauses that it can recognise and extract from the contracts and documents in the data room. As a result, Kira can identify change of control clauses, liability clauses, non-compete clauses, etc. within minutes.
5. In the next phase, our lawyers start reviewing the work of Kira, and they will summarise and standardise the output of Kira.

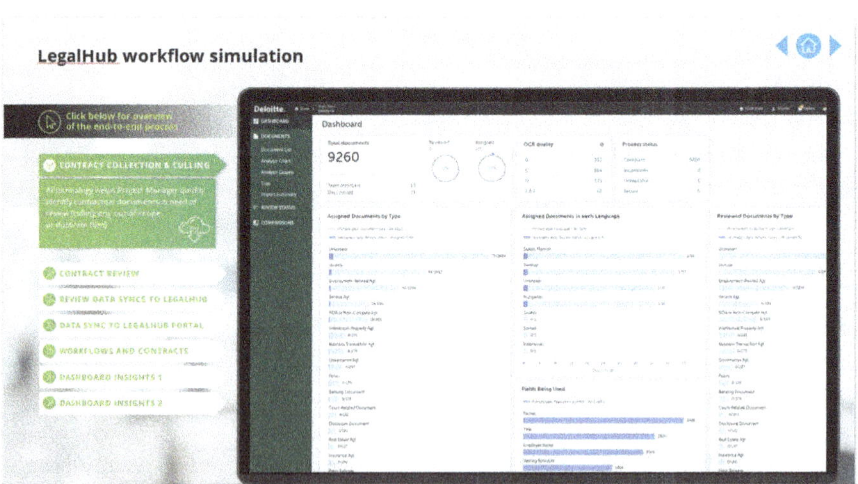

6. This standardised output from Kira is then sent to the database of Legalhub, which results in a fact sheet for each document we reviewed. The fact sheet (in a database) contains an overview of the relevant data of the contract.

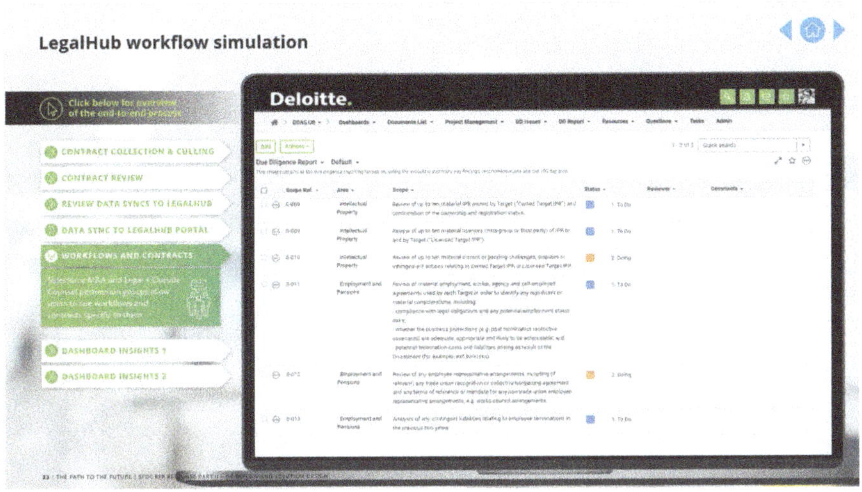

7. Based on all these data, we use the database in Legalhub to create the due diligence report. Like any due diligence report, the database contains a.o. a description of the issues, a risk rating and recommendations.
8. Since we have all these data in a database, we can create dashboards to create insights on low, medium or high risks, on risks per practice area or risk per jurisdiction. The dashboards also provide insights on which issues have been resolved already or which issues still need some attention or which tasks need to be addressed post completion.
9. At the end, when we have the final version, we still need a word or pdf document with the due diligence report that we can easily print out. We can create this document with one push of a button. This is probably one of the best features of Legalhub: we no longer have to work in Microsoft Word. If you've ever worked on large transactions, you probably remember the horror of working together with far too many lawyers in one corrupt word document. With Legalhub, we can avoid that.

And this brings us back to the point that AI is only doing a small part of the work. AI allows us to look at due diligence from a different angle. Instead of limiting the scope of our due diligence work, we can now expand the scope and include all contracts, which allows clients to obtain insights and an overview of all the contracts of the company they are about to acquire. Instead of looking at it from a purely transactional perspective, we are able to get clients started with contract management as part of the due diligence. By doing this, they will, for example, have instant access to [the] dashboard with an overview of all the contracts that allow for indexation, which is very relevant in times of high inflation.

And we strongly believe that is where AI can create additional value, even in smaller markets with smaller transactions and multiple languages.

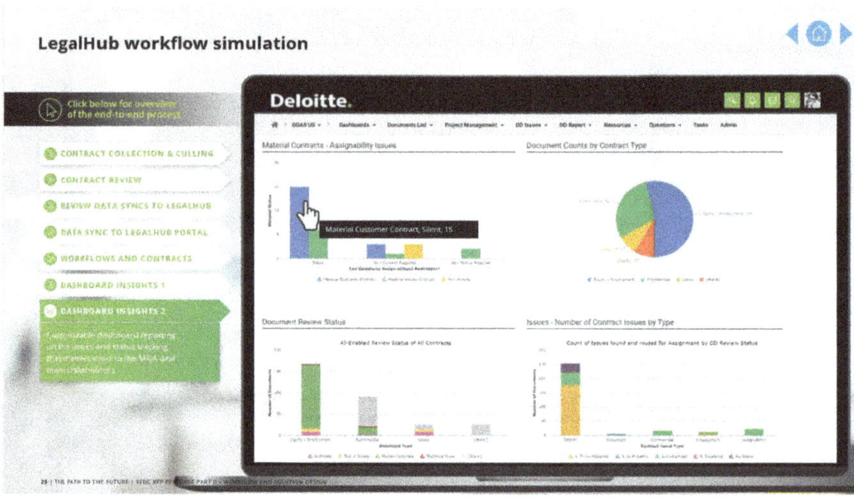

The Use of Artificial Intelligence in Corporate Decision-Making at Board Level: A Preliminary Legal Analysis

*Floris Mertens**

1 Introduction

Emergence of Artificial Intelligence (AI). In times when conversational chatbots such as ChatGPT are hailed as game-changers for the era of AI,[1] many maintain that AI is bound to be the central engine of a fourth industrial revolution, which will have a considerable impact on the lives of individuals and organisations in our society.[2] Since new powerful foundation models[3] are making their entrance into the real world, palpable excitement about the corporate use of AI is emerging as it is no longer inconceivable that AI will become indispensable to many aspects of the corporate realm.[4] In fact, AI is on the verge of playing a crucial role in the management of companies. There is a growing recognition in the business world that AI systems can usefully assist human directors in their decision-making at the management level, while only a handful of corporations

---

* Doctoral researcher at the Financial Law Institute, Ghent University; Fellow of the Flemish Research Foundation (FWO). The author would like to express his sincere gratitude to Hans De Wulf for his valuable comments and contributions. Thank you to Julie Goetghebuer, Sergio Gramitto Ricci, Julie Kerckaert, Sinan Vanden Eynde and Francis Wyffels for the helpful remarks and suggestions. My appreciation also goes to John Armour, Florian Möslein and Eva Lievens for the valuable remarks on the general research project.

1 Open AI's ChatGPT dialogue-based AI chatbot has gained a great deal of attention, as it is capable of understanding natural human language and generating impressively detailed human-like written text; see S. LOCK, "What Is AI Chatbot Phenomenon ChatGPT and Could It Replace Humans?", *The Guardian* 2022, www.theguardian.com/technology/2022/dec/05/what-is-ai-chatbot-phenomenon-chatgpt-and-could-it-replace-humans; S. MURPHY KELLY, "This AI Chatbot Is Dominating Social Media with Its Frighteningly Good Essays", *CNN Business* 2022, edition.cnn.com/2022/12/05/tech/chatgpt-trnd/index.html.

2 R. GIRASA and G.J. SCALABRINI, *Regulation of Innovative Technologies – Blockchain, Artificial Intelligence and Quantum Computing*, New York, Palgrave Macmillan, 2022, 2-3.

3 A foundation model is an AI model trained on a large amount of unlabelled data, resulting in a model that can be adapted (*e.g.* finetuned) to various downstream cognitive tasks; R. BOMMASANI *et al.*, "On the Opportunities and Risks of Foundation Models", 2021, arxiv.org/abs/2108.07258, 3.

4 X, "Artificial Intelligence Is Permeating Business At Last", *The Economist* 2022, www.economist.com/business/2022/12/06/artificial-intelligence-is-permeating-business-at-last.

worldwide have already attempted to grant AI true decision-making powers akin to those of human directors. However, the use of so-called '(artificial) governance intelligence',[5] even as a mere support tool for directors, generates unprecedented issues of corporate law, which call for a thorough legal analysis.

Use cases of AI in the corporate realm. Governance bodies such as the board of directors increasingly deploy AI to assist the decision-making on their corporate strategy, personnel selection, procurement, sales, marketing and even movie greenlighting.[6] In fact, assisting algorithms are already used in the management models proposed by McKinsey, Bain and BCG as strategic advisers for investments.[7] The use of algorithmic trading, where an algorithm decides to buy financial products on behalf of the company, is also on the rise.[8] Relatedly, one of the most popular applications of governance intelligence today is its support for the discovery and due diligence process of mergers and acquisitions.[9] Both processes are essential steps for the eventual board decision of the acquirer, which involve a highly coordinated effort among experts such as company personnel, accountants, lawyers and investment bankers.[10] When these processes are assisted by AI, there is an increased likelihood that the board will be able to negotiate an accurate price and an appropriately tailored deal structure.[11] In addition, AI systems are deployed by directors to profile investors,

5 The term 'artificial governance intelligence' or 'corporate AI' is already used in the literature. See *inter alia* M. HILB, "Toward Artificial Governance? The Role of Artificial Intelligence in Shaping the Future of Corporate Governance", *Journal of Management and Governance* 2020, vol. 24 (4), 851-870; E. HICKMAN and M. PETRIN, "Trustworthy AI and Corporate Governance: The EU's Ethics Guidelines for Trustworthy Artificial Intelligence from a Company Law Perspective", *EBOR* 2021, vol. 22, 593-625; M.A. TOKMAKOV, "Artificial Intelligence in Corporate Governance" in S.I. ASHMARINA and V.V. MANTULENKO (eds.), *Digital Economy and the New Labor Market: Jobs, Competences and Innovative HR Technologies*, Cham, Springer, 2021, 667-674.

6 For example, Warner Bros. deploys an algorithm from Cinelytic to predict the box office results of movie projects before being greenlit; CINELYTIC, "Data Driver Cinelytic Engages Warner Bros. Pictures International to Utilize Their Revolutionary AI-Driven Content and Talent Valuation System", *Business Wire* 2020, www.businesswire.com/news/home/20200108005856/en/Data-Driver-Cinelytic-Engages-Warner-Bros.-Pictures-International-to-Utilize-Their-Revolutionary-AI-Driven-Content-and-Talent-Valuation-System.

7 M. SCHRAGE, "4 Models for Using AI to Make Decisions", *Harvard Business Review* 2017, hbr.org/2017/01/4-models-for-using-ai-to-make-decisions.

8 See M.J. MCGOWAN, "The Rise of Computerized High Frequency Trading: Use and Controversy", *Duke Law & Technology Review* 2010, vol. 9, 2; T.C.W. LIN, "The New Investor", *UCLA Law Review* 2013, vol. 60, 689-691.

9 M.R. SIEBECKER, "Making Corporations More Humane Through Artificial Intelligence", *The Journal of Corporation Law* 2019, vol. 45, 107.

10 *Ibid.*, 108.

11 S. ZADEH, "Better, Faster, Stronger: Revamping the M&A Due Diligence Process with Artificial Intelligence Platforms", *Deal Law Wire* 2018, www.deallawwire.com/2018/03/27/better-faster-stronger-revamping-the-ma-due-diligence-process-with-artificial-intelligence-platforms/.

audit annual reports,[12] review the risk of financial instruments and determine optimal market supply and demand.[13]

Back in 2014, the Hong Kong-based venture capital group Deep Knowledge Ventures took this further by allegedly appointing an algorithm named VITAL to its board of directors.[14] This AI system was purportedly given the right to vote on whether the firm should invest in a specific company or not, similar to the other – human – directors of the corporation.[15] Consequently, VITAL has been widely acknowledged as the world's first robot-director.[16] After successes stemming from VITAL's decisions (such as investments in biotech start-ups Insilico Medecine and Pathway Pharmaceuticals[17]), other companies also factually implemented AI systems as board members (such as Tietoevry and Salesforce).[18] Yet, most legal systems do not allow the appointment of a robo-director.[19] While only a handful of companies have chosen this untrodden path of robot-directors, many have already assigned a supportive role to AI in its corporate decision-making process.[20]

Prospects. One can therefore affirm that AI is steadily emerging in the boardrooms of innovative companies, which is supported by the recent EY study ordered by the European Commission, claiming that 13% of the respondent EU companies already

12 G. HERTIG, "Use of AI by Financial Players: The Emerging Evidence", 2022, ssrn.com/abstract_id=4013559, 15-16.

13 J.B.S. HIJINK, "Robots in de boardroom", *Ondernemingsrecht* 2019, 11.

14 R. WILE, "A Venture Capital Firm Just Named An Algorithm To Its Board Of Directors – Here's What It Actually Does", *Business Insider* 2014, www.businessinsider.com/vital-named-to-board-2014-5?international=true&r=US&IR=T.

15 *Ibid.*, Y.N. HARARI, *Homo Deus: A Brief History of Tomorrow*, London, Harvill Secker, 2015, 322.

16 E. ZOLFAGHARIFARD, "Would You Take Orders from a ROBOT? An Artificial Intelligence Becomes the World's First Company Director", *Daily Mail* 2014, www.dailymail.co.uk/sciencetech/article-2632920/Would-orders-ROBOT-Artificial-intelligence-world-s-company-director-Japan.html.

17 BIOGERONTOLOGY RESEARCH FOUNDATION, "Deep Knowledge Ventures Announces New Investment Fund for Life Sciences and Aging Research", *EurekAlert!* 2015, www.eurekalert.org/news-releases/831727.

18 TIETO, "Tieto the First Nordic Company to Appoint Artificial Intelligence to the Leadership Team of the New Data-Driven Businesses Unit", *Business Wire* 2016, www.businesswire.com/news/home/20161016005092/en/Tieto-the-First-Nordic-Company-to-Appoint-Artificial-Intelligence-to-the-Leadership-Team-of-the-New-Data-Driven-Businesses-Unit; J. BORT, "How Salesforce CEO Marc Benioff Uses Artificial Intelligence to End Internal Politics at Meetings", *Business Insider* 2017, www.businessinsider.in/How-Salesforce-CEO-Marc-Benioff-uses-artificial-intelligence-to-end-internal-politics-at-meetings/articleshow/58743024.cms.

19 See pages 127-128 below.

20 Collective investment undertakings, asset managers and other large companies such as BlackRock, EQT Ventures, Quantum Light Capital and NN Investment Partners strongly rely on their AI platforms for core financial decision-making.

use governance intelligence and that an additional 26% plan to do so in the future.[21] A 2023 McKinsey study highlights that 8% of C-suite executive respondents regularly uses generative AI for work, while 16% of respondents regularly use generative AI for both professional and non-professional purposes.[22] In respect of M&A, a 2022 study suggested that over 69% of its respondents (executives from large US public corporations and private equity funds) are utilising AI tools for the due diligence process.[23] Furthermore, in a survey report, the World Economic Forum claimed that by 2026, corporate governance will have faced a robotisation process of a massive scale, with the result that human directors sharing their decision-making powers with artificial directors will become the new normal.[24] Even though this claim was made back in 2015, the corporate sector of today shows an increasingly notable interest in AI.[25] Momentum in computational power, breakthroughs in AI technology, and advanced digitalisation will therefore inevitably lead to a more established support of directors by AI, if not their full replacement by autonomous systems.[26]

Corporate law. The rise of AI in corporate governance contrasts with static company law, which has not kept pace at all with governance-relevant advances on the technological front. A good illustration is VITAL, which may have been widely acknowledged as the world's first robo-director,[27] but from a legal point of view, Hong Kong corporate law

---

21 The pool of respondents consisted of 402 companies from all 27 EU member states, except Poland. ERNST & YOUNG, "Study on the Relevance and Impact of Artificial Intelligence for Company Law and Corporate Governance – Final Report", 2021, op.europa.eu/en/publication-detail/-/publication/13e6a212-6181-11ec-9c6c-01aa75ed71a1/language-en, 13-14.

22 The pool of respondents consisted of 541 C-suite executives from companies all over the world. M. CHUI, B. HALL, A. SINGLA and A. SUKHAREVSKY, "The State of AI in 2023: Generative AI's Breakout Year", *McKinsey Global Survey* 2023, www.mckinsey.com/capabilities/quantumblack/our-insights/the-state-of-ai-in-2023-generative-ais-breakout-year#/, 3.

23 DELOITTE, "2022 M&A Trends Survey: The Future of M&A – Dealmaking Trends to Help you Pivot on M&A's Fast-Changing Playing Field", 2022, www2.deloitte.com/us/en/pages/mergers-and-acquisitions/articles/m-a-trends-report.html?mod=article_inline.

24 WORLD ECONOMIC FORUM, "Survey Report: Deep Shift – Technology Tipping Points and Societal Impact", *Global Agenda Council on the Future of Software & Society* 2015, www3.weforum.org/docs/WEF_GAC15_Technological_Tipping_Points_report_2015.pdf, 21.

25 *Inter alia* M. CHUI, R. ROBERTS and L. YEE, "Generative AI Is Here: How Tools Like ChatGPT Could Change Your Business", 2022, www.mckinsey.com/capabilities/quantumblack/our-insights/generative-ai-is-here-how-tools-like-chatgpt-could-change-your-business (retrieved on 27 March 2023); X, "Artificial intelligence is permeating business at last", *The Economist* 2022, www.economist.com/business/2022/12/06/artificial-intelligence-is-permeating-business-at-last; S. EARLEY and S. ZIVIN, "The Rise of the AI CEO: A Revolution in Corporate Governance", *Teneo* 2023, www.teneo.com/the-rise-of-the-ai-ceo-a-revolution-in-corporate-governance/; D. STRAUSS, "Generative AI Set to Affect 300mn Jobs Across Major Economies", *Financial Times* 2023, www.ft.com/content/7dec4483-ad34-4007-bb3a-7ac925643999.

26 The overall desirability and economic necessity of autonomous systems entering the boardroom is debated, but will be discarded for this chapter. It is a fact that AI is already being used in corporate boardrooms today, which prompts an inquiry into its legal implications regardless of its desirability.

27 R. WILE, "A Venture Capital Firm Just Named An Algorithm To Its Board Of Directors — Here's What It Actually Does", *Business Insider* 2014, www.businessinsider.com/vital-named-to-board-2014-5?international=true&r=US&IR=T.

did not recognise the AI system as such.[28] To bypass the law, VITAL was treated as a member of the board with 'observer status'.[29] On a more general note, corporate law is not adapted to governance intelligence, since it is rooted in *human* decision-making.[30] Therefore, corporate law will have to cope with novel legal questions, once the use of AI as a support tool or replacement of human directors becomes more common.

It is the purpose of this chapter to create awareness of the legal uncertainty arising from governance intelligence, and to signal its legal issues from a company law perspective. To attain this, Part 2 articulates the reasons for introducing AI in the boardroom, along with a taxonomy of governance intelligence on the basis of its autonomy level, which could serve as a benchmark for future differentiated rules. Then, Part 3 maps the current state of the legal art, identifies corporate law issues arising from AI under current legal frameworks and makes suggestions on where the law should be headed to tackle or at least alleviate these legal issues.

2 Use of Artificial Intelligence in Corporate Decision-Making

2.1 Concept of Artificial Intelligence for This Chapter

Definition and capabilities. Since AI is an intangible and emerging core concept for this chapter, a clear and convenient working definition is necessary to facilitate the development of arguments in this regard. There is no predominant definition of AI available yet.[31] The literature offers many diverging definitions, often prompted by the

28 S. SHARWOOD, "Software 'Appointed to Board' of Venture Capital Firm", *The Register* 2014, www.theregister.com/2014/05/18/software_appointed_to_board_of_venture_capital_firm/. According to Cap. 456 (2) Hong Kong Companies Ordinance, a 'body corporate' may not be appointed as a director of the majority of corporate forms. Based on the method of exclusion, only natural persons can consequently be appointed as a director of these Hong Kong incorporated companies.

29 N. BURRIDGE, "Artificial Intelligence Gets a Seat in the Boardroom", *Nikkei Asia* 2017, asia.nikkei.com/Business/Artificial-intelligence-gets-a-seat-in-the-boardroom.

30 One may argue that the legal permissibility (in some jurisdictions) to appoint a corporate director (*i.e.* a legal person as director) impedes the argument that corporate law is rooted in human decision-making. However, corporate directors have always been factually represented by one or more natural persons on the board of the subject company, whether this is mandated by statute or not. Therefore, traditional corporate law assumes that all decision-making at the level of the subject company is performed by humans.

31 S. LUCCI and D. KOPEC, *Artificial Intelligence in the 21st Century: A Living Introduction*, Dulles, Mercury Learning and Information, 2016, 4; S. SAMOILI, M. LÓPEZ COBO, E. GÓMEZ, G. DE PRATO, F. MARTÍNEZ-PLUMED, and B. DELIPETREV, "AI Watch. Defining Artificial Intelligence. Towards An Operational Definition and Taxonomy of Artificial Intelligence", 2020, publications.jrc.ec.europa.eu/repository/handle/JRC118163, 7.

needs of a particular research project.[32] For this study, the AI definition of the Organisation for Economic Co-operation and Development (OECD) (now transposed to the EU Draft AI Act) serves as working definition. The OECD's Expert Group of Artificial Intelligence defines AI as *a machine-based system that, for explicit or implicit objectives, infers, from the input it receives, how to generate outputs such as predictions, content, recommendations, or decisions that can influence physical or virtual environments. Different AI systems vary in their levels of autonomy and adaptiveness after deployment.*[33]

The fact that the machine-based system pursues a given set of objectives and influences the environment in doing so, implies that its actions and output generation are not determined by pre-programmed rules, but are the result of a learning and training process of the machine itself (of which the foundation is indeed coded in advance). This definition refrains from using anthropomorphic terms that resemble human traits (*i.e.* anthropocentrism[34]), which is discarded in the literature.[35] At the same

---

32 P. WANG, "On the Working Definition of Intelligence", 1995, www.researchgate.net/publication/2339604_On_the_Working_Definition_of_Intelligence, 3.

33 OECD, "Explanatory Memorandum on the Updated OECD Definition of an AI System", 2024, www.oecd-ilibrary.org/science-and-technology/explanatory-memorandum-on-the-updated-oecd-definition-of-an-ai-system_623da898-en, 4-5. Compare with the original OECD definition in OECD, "Scoping the OECD AI Principles – Deliberations of the Expert Group on Artificial Intelligence at the OECD (AIGO)", 2019, www.oecd-ilibrary.org/science-and-technology/scoping-the-oecd-ai-principles_d62f618a-en, 7.

34 Anthropocentrism refers to the viewpoint that human beings are the central or most important entity in the universe; see BRITANNICA, "Anthropocentrism", www.britannica.com/topic/anthropocentrism (retrieved on 5 September 2023).

35 The outcomes of today's AI appear to be increasingly human, while the underlying processes do not necessarily resemble human intelligence. For that reason, any tendencies of anthropocentrism in defining AI are misplaced. See *inter alia* D.M. KATZ, "Quantitative Legal Prediction – Or – How I Learned to Stop Worrying and Start Preparing for the Data-Driven Future of the Legal Services Industry", *Emory Law Journal* 2013, vol. 62, 918; I. GIUFFRIDA, F. LEDERER and N. VERMEYST, "A Legal Perspective on the Trials and Tribulations of AI: How Artificial Intelligence, the Internet of Things, Smart Contracts, and Other Technologies Will Affect the Law", *Case Western Reserve Law Review* 2018, vol. 68, 755; H. SURDEN, "Artificial Intelligence and Law: An Overview", *Georgia State University Law Review* 2019, vol. 35, 1315; M. HERBOSCH, *Intelligent contracteren – Het precontractueel gebruik van systemen op basis van artificiële intelligentie*, doctoral thesis at Koninklijke Universiteit Leuven, 2023, 14-16, no. 17-19. There are, however, authors who still defend a definition of AI in terms of human intelligence. See *inter alia* D. WECHSLER, *The Measurement of Adult Intelligence*, Baltimore, Williams & Wilkins, 1944, vii + 258 p.; T. BESOLD, J. HERNÁNDEZ-ORALLO and U. SCHMID, "Can Machine Intelligence be Measured in the Same Way as Human intelligence?", *KI – Künstliche Intelligenz* 2015, vol. 29, 292-293, where intelligence is defined as "*the aggregate or global capacity of the individual to act purposefully, to think rationally, and to deal effectively with the environment*". For a comprehensive overview of the viewpoints on what contributes to intelligence, see C. PENNACHIN and B. GOERTZEL, "Contemporary Approaches to Artificial General Intelligence" in B. GOERTZEL and C. PENNACHIN (eds.), *Artificial General Intelligence*, Berlin Heidelberg, Springer, 2007, 6-11; S. LEGG, *Machine Super Intelligence*, doctoral thesis at the University of Lugano, 2008, 3-11; S. RUSSELL and P. NORVIG, *Artificial Intelligence – A Modern Approach*, Harlow, Pearson, 2022, 19-23. For a general definition of 'intelligence', see L.S. GOTTFREDSON, "Mainstream Science on Intelligence: An Editorial With 52 Signatories, History, and Bibliography", *Intelligence* 1997, vol. 24, 13. There is a great deal of controversy over the 'theories of intelligence', which elaborate a different

time, the technology-neutral nature of the definition makes it flexible and future-proof. To make clear AI does not capture simple and traditional computer programs such as spreadsheets, it emphasises that AI systems produce output *autonomously*,[36] as mentioned by the definition enshrined in the latest version of the EU Draft AI Act.[37]

AI systems can either use symbolic rules (knowledge-based systems) or learn a numeric model (data-based or machine learning systems).[38] Machine learning is the most popular method, as it enables AI to learn ('train') from examples by deriving a decision from large sets of data, improving its model each decision cycle.[39] Hence, the system is not given instructions on how to perform a task (*i.e.* there are no pre-programmed rules about how to solve a specific problem), but it is programmed to elaborate its own instructions by a complex learning procedure. There are various types of machine learning. In case of supervised learning, the algorithm learns to associate labelled output data with input data. By contrast, unsupervised learning allows the algorithm to discover patterns and structures in unlabelled data on its own.[40] Alternative forms of machine learning include semi-supervised, self-supervised and reinforcement learning.[41]

Another useful distinction can be made on the basis of the system's goals. Most AI systems existing today are narrow, as they model intelligent behaviour for narrowly defined specific tasks and fail to operate outside of their programmed domain of use cases. In spite of being designed to fulfil limited tasks, even narrow systems can display autonomous capabilities by operating under limited human supervision within the

taxonomic structure of abilities associated with intelligence; see R.J. STERNBERG, *The Cambridge Handbook of Intelligence*, Cambridge, Cambridge University Press, 2020, xxii + 1250 p.

36 AI systems may exhibit several gradual degrees of autonomy. See T. LASAR, *Künstliche Intelligenz in der GmbH*, Frankfurt am Main, Fachmedien Recht und Wirtschaft, 2023, 4.

37 See EUROPEAN PARLIAMENT, "Draft Compromise Amendments on the Draft Report – Proposal for a regulation of the European Parliament and of the Council on Harmonised Rules on Artificial Intelligence (Artificial Intelligence Act) and Amending Certain Union Legislative Acts", COM(2021)0206 – C9 0146/2021 – 2021/0106(COD), 16 May 2023, 137.

38 See HIGH-LEVEL EXPERT GROUP ON ARTIFICIAL INTELLIGENCE, "A Definition of AI: Main Capabilities and Disciplines. Definition Developed for the Purpose of the AI HLEG's Deliverables", 2019, digital-strategy.ec.europa.eu/en/library/definition-artificial-intelligence-main-capabilities-and-scientific-disciplines, 6.

39 E. ALPAYDIN, *Introduction to Machine Learning*, Cambridge, Massachusetts Institute of Technology, 2014, 1-4.

40 See *inter alia* T.M. MITCHELL, *Machine Learning*, New York, McGraw-Hill, 1997, 414 p; K.P. MURPHY, *Machine Learning: A Probabilistic Perspective*, Cambridge and London, MIT Press, 2012, 3; D. LEHR and P. OHM, "Playing with the Data: What Legal Scholars Should Learn About Machine Learning", *UC Davis Law Review* 2017, vol. 53, 673.

41 S. RUSSELL and P. NORVIG, *Artificial Intelligence – A Modern Approach*, Harlow, Pearson, 2022, 671.

boundaries of their application field.[42] A popular narrow AI application is ChatGPT (even though it has an *a priori* general purpose). Also in the business world, the majority of AI systems is narrow. AI systems such as autonomous vehicles are considered broad, as they are designed to handle a variety of tasks.[43] Finally, some scholars contend that it will not be long until AI displays human-like intelligence with an unlimited operational domain, therefore achieving general intelligence.[44]

Critical evaluation of the technological state of the art. In reality, artificial general intelligence might still be a decade or even a century away.[45] In addition, critics highlight that AI has been handicapped by an incomplete understanding of 'intelligence', as it is only able to detect hidden correlations in large data sets and does not comprehend causal relationships.[46] While AI may outperform humans on average for certain well-defined tasks, it sometimes produces erroneous results of the kind

---

42 G. LUSARDI and A. ANGILLETTA, "The Interplay Between the New Machinery Regulation and Artificial Intelligence, IoT, Cybersecurity and the Human-machine Relationship", 2022, www.technologyslegaledge.com/2022/04/the-interplay-between-the-new-machinery-regulation-and-artificial-intelligence-iot-cybersecurity-and-the-human-machine-relationship/#page=1.

43 Both narrow and broad AI belong to the category of weak AI, *i.e.* intelligent systems with limited goals. Computer science has not managed to develop an AI system whose intelligence goes beyond the 'weak' attribute yet; H. SHEVLIN, K. VOLD, M. CROSBY and M. HALINA, "The Limits of Machine Intelligence – Despite Progress in Machine Intelligence, Artificial General Intelligence Is Still a Major Challenge", *EMBO Reports* 2019, vol. 20 (49177), 1-5.

44 For an overview of current standpoints in the literature, see *inter alia* C. PENNACHIN and B. GOERTZEL, "Contemporary Approaches to Artificial General Intelligence" in B. GOERTZEL and C. PENNACHIN (eds.), *Artificial General Intelligence*, Berlin Heidelberg, Springer, 2007, 1 ff.; B. GOERTZEL, "Artificial General Intelligence: Concept, State of the Art, and Future Prospects", *Journal of Artificial General Intelligence* 2014, vol. 5, 1-46; A.M. BARRETT and S.D. BAUM, "A Model of Pathways to Artificial Superintelligence Catastrophe for Risk and Decision Analysis", *Journal of Experimental & Theoretical Artificial Intelligence* 2017, vol. 29, 397; K. GRACE, J. SALVATIER, A. DAFOE, B. ZHANG, and O. EVANS, "When Will AI Exceed Human Performance? Evidence from AI Experts", *Journal of Artificial Intelligence Research* 2018, vol. 62, 729-754; H. SHEVLIN, K. VOLD, M. CROSBY and M. HALINA, "The Limits of Machine Intelligence – Despite Progress in Machine Intelligence, Artificial General Intelligence Is Still a Major Challenge", *EMBO Reports* 2019, vol. 20, Art. e49177; S. RUSSELL and P. NORVIG, *Artificial Intelligence – A Modern Approach*, Harlow, Pearson, 2022, 50-52; H. HIRSCH-KREINSEN, "Artificial Intelligence: a 'Promising Technology'", *AI & SOCIETY* 2023, doi.org/10.1007/s00146-023-01629-w; S. MCLEAN, G.J.M. READ, J. THOMPSON, C. BABER, N.A. STANTON and P.M. SALMON, "The Risks Associated with Artificial General Intelligence: A Systematic Review", *Journal of Experimental & Theoretical Artificial Intelligence* 2023, vol. 35, 649-650.

45 This claim is made by Geoffrey HINTON with regard to AI passing the Turing test in M. FORD, *Architects of Intelligence – The Truth about AI from the People Building It*, Birmingham, Packt Publishing, 2018, 89. As of now, computer engineering is far away from the dystopian scenario that philosopher Nick BOSTROM envisaged, in which general AI ('superintelligence') assigned with producing paper clips would sacrifice all of the planet's resources to achieve its final goal and ultimately convert the entire universe into paper clips; N. BOSTROM, *Superintelligence: Paths, Dangers, Strategies*, Oxford, Oxford University Press, 2014, 122-125.

46 J. PEARL and D. MACKENZIE, *The Book of Why: The New Science of Cause and Effect*, New York, Basic Books, 2018, 418 p.

that a human would be unlikely to do.[47] Furthermore, the use of foundation models and artificial neural networks for 'deep learning' (a subset of supervised machine learning) may pose transparency challenges, as these models may embody 'black box' characteristics, causing the underlying reasons and the logic of their decisions to be hard to comprehend, even for the developers of the system.[48] The opacity issue is combatted by the explainable AI movement (xAI), which strives for the decisions and predictions of AI to become understandable in the eye of human beings.[49] Finally, while AI can help to reduce direct human biases, there is a risk that its model is trained and tested with biased data, reflecting the financial interests of its deployer or developer.

2.2 *Reasons for the Use of Artificial Governance Intelligence*

Growing popularity of AI in the corporate realm. In spite of the aforementioned criticism on the current capabilities of AI, this chapter signals that a growing number of companies adopts AI for corporate decision-making. The concept of corporate decision-making refers to the decision-making processes relating to the core functions of the board of directors and top management (*i.e.* monitoring, strategy formulation and daily management). Of course, computer systems have been deployed in support of corporate decision-making for decades now, ranging from early decision support systems to executive support systems.[50] But today, the techniques and functionalities of AI enable useful and advanced applications for corporate governance, such as retrieving relevant

---

47 See, for instance, A. NGUYEN, J. YOSINSKI and J. CLUNE, "Deep Neural Networks are Easily Fooled: High Confidence Predictions for Unrecognizable Images", *IEEE Conference on Computer Vision and Pattern Recognition (CVPR)*, Boston, IEEE, 2015, 427-436.

48 R.T. KREUTZER and M. SIRRENBERG, *Understanding Artificial Intelligence - Fundamentals, Use Cases and Methods for a Corporate AI Journey*, Cham, Springer, 2020, 11-12.

49 See *inter alia* Y. BATHAEE, "The Artificial Intelligence Black Box and the Failure of Intent and Causation", *Harvard Journal of Law & Technology* 2018, vol. 31, 889-938; A. PREECE, "Asking 'Why' in AI: Explainability of Intelligent Systems - Perspectives and Challenges", *Intelligent Systems in Accounting, Finance and Management* 2018, vol. 25, 63-72; P. HACKER, R. KRESTEL, S. GRUNDMANN and F. NAUMANN, "Explainable AI Under Contract and Tort Law: Legal Incentives and Technical Challenges", *Artificial Intelligence and Law* 2020, vol. 28, 415-439; S. LU, "Algorithmic Opacity, Private Accountability, and Corporate Social Disclosure in the Age of Artificial Intelligence", *Vanderbilt Journal of Entertainment & Technology Law* 2020, vol. 23, 99-159; A. BIBAL, M. LOGNOUL, A. DE STREEL and B. FRÉNAY, "Legal Requirements on Explainability in Machine Learning", *Artificial Intelligence and Law* 2021, vol. 29, 149-169; G. VILONE and L. LONGO, "Notions of Explainability and Evaluation Approaches for Explainable Artificial Intelligence", *Information Fusion* 2021, vol. 76, 89-106; G. DEL GAMBA, "Machine Learning Decision-Making: When Algorithms Can Make Decisions According to the GDPR" in G. BORGES and C. SORGE (eds.), *Law and Technology in a Global Digital Society - Autonomous Systems, Big Data, IT Security and Legal Tech*, Cham, Springer, 2022, 75-87.

50 R.H. SPRAGUE and E.D. CARLSON, *Building Effective Decision Support Systems*, Englewood Cliffs, Prentice-Hall, 1982, xx + 329 p; D.L. OLSON and J.F. COURTNEY, *Decision Support Models and Expert Systems*, New York, Macmillan, 1992, xiii + 418 p; D.L. OLSON and G. LAUHOFF, *Descriptive Data Mining*, Singapore, Springer, 2019, 2.

information, coordinating real-time data delivery, analysing data trends, providing financial and other forecasts, monitoring financial transactions, optimising logistics flows and making useful predictions and scenario analyses for potential courses of action in the decision-making process.[51]

Advantages of AI for corporate decision-making. On a more general level, AI support rationalises board decisions, some of which typically call for large amounts of data. The more complex a decision is, the greater the amount of data that the board needs to consider in order for it to make a rational and well-informed decision.[52] The processing of a plethora of factors to reach an optimal market-based decision is difficult for human directors, since they are often unfamiliar with analytics. Because of this, board decisions are frequently made with little data analysis and an emphasis on sheer gut feelings.[53] Here, the main advantage of AI comes down to the rapid analysis of large data arrays. Today's best AI programmes are at their core statistical (analytical) models,[54] which can detect hidden correlations and patterns in large data sets.[55] Thus, AI is able to complement the broad capabilities and knowledge of the human board members by providing them with a clear analysis of intangible mountains of data, and therefore expedite decisions that are difficult to make. Furthermore, boards could use AI simulation tools (to generate, *e.g.*, Monte Carlo Simulations[56]) to design and test scenarios. This enables board decisions to be based on a rational and objective analysis of corporate patterns and industry trends instead of gut feelings.[57]

---

51 P. BHATTACHARYA, "Artificial Intelligence in the Boardroom: Enabling 'Machines' to 'Learn' to Make Strategic Business Decisions" in *Fifth HCT Information Technology Trends (ITT)*, Dubai, IEEE Computer Society, 2018, 170-171; H. DRUKARCH and E. FOSCH-VILLARONGA, "The Role and Legal Implications of Autonomy in AI-Driven Boardrooms" in B. CUSTERS and E. FOSCH-VILLARONGA (eds.), *Law and Artificial Intelligence – Regulating AI and Applying AI in Legal Practice,* Den Haag, Asser Press, 2022, 352.

52 T.A. LIEDONG, T. RAJWANI and T.C. LAWTON, "Information and Nonmarket Strategy: Conceptualizing the Interrelationship Between Big Data and Corporate Political Activity", *Technological Forecasting & Social Change* 2020, vol. 157, 1-12; Z. LIPAI, X. XIQIANG and L. MENGYUAN, "Corporate Governance Reform in the Era of Artificial Intelligence: Research Overview and Prospects Based on Knowledge Graph", *Annals of Operations Research* 2021, separate online issue, 12.

53 M.R. SIEBECKER, "Making Corporations More Humane Through Artificial Intelligence", *The Journal of Corporation Law* 2019, vol. 45, 144.

54 M. BROUSSARD, *Artificial Unintelligence – How Computers Misunderstand the World*, Cambridge, MIT Press, 2018, 87-119.

55 For a critical account of the lack of causal 'intelligence' of AI, see J. PEARL and D. MACKENZIE, *The Book of Why: The New Science of Cause and Effect*, New York, Basic Books, 2018, 418p.

56 Monte Carlo simulations, as most types of regressive analyses today, constitute AI when they are rendered autonomously. See, for instance, T. VODOPIVEC, S. SAMOTHRAKIS and B. STER, "On Monte Carlo Tree Search and Reinforcement Learning", *Journal of Artificial Intelligence Research* 2017, vol. 60, 881-936; S. RUSSELL and P. NORVIG, *Artificial Intelligence – A Modern Approach*, Harlow, Pearson, 2022, 207-210.

57 A. HAMDANI, N. HASHAI, E. KANDEL and Y. YAFEH, "Technological Progress and the Future of the Corporation", *Journal of the British Academy* 2018, vol. 6, 219-220.

Additionally, some authors insist that governance intelligence, in addition to traditional solutions such as a required form of diversity and independence of board members, is useful to counteract groupthink.[58] The latter is a psychological mode of thinking in highly cohesive groups such as boards of directors, where the desire to reach consensus (or majority) by the group members overrides critical thinking and correct judgment.[59] In a scenario where the board of directors has failed to consider alternative courses of action (either because there was no time to process all relevant information or because it was hesitant to challenge the management), the board will have to evaluate the output of the implemented AI system, which is normally uninfluenced by groupthink as this cognitive tendency is inherently human (unless when the system's training data is biased). Thus, the board will be able to consider aspects of a situation or courses of action that might have been missed because of blind spots caused by groupthink.[60]

The theoretical and technological neutrality[61] of AI may also strengthen the independence of the board for two reasons (under the condition that its training data is unbiased). First, AI support gives the independent board members more leverage to

58 A. KAMALNATH, "The Perennial Quest for Board Independence – Artificial Intelligence to the Rescue?", *Albany Law Review* 2019-20, vol. 83, 52; M.A. TOKMAKOV, "Artificial Intelligence in Corporate Governance" in S.I. ASHMARINA and V.V. MANTULENKO (eds.), *Digital Economy and the New Labor Market: Jobs, Competences and Innovative HR Technologies*, Cham, Springer, 2021, 669.

59 I.L. JANIS, "Groupthink", *Psychology Today* 1971, vol. 5, 43-46. The phenomenon of groupthink is often blamed in the literature for the failures at Enron, Worldcom and the financial crisis of 2007-2008, see *inter alia* M.A. O'CONNOR, "The Enron Board: The Perils of Groupthink", *Corporate Law Symposium* 2003, vol. 71, 1233-1320; S. ALLEN, "The Death of Groupthink", *Bloomberg* 2008, www.bloomberg.com/news/articles/2008-02-05/the-death-of-groupthinkbusinessweek-business-news-stock-market-and-financial-advice; M. SKAPINKER, "Diversity Fails to End Boardroom Groupthink", *Financial Times* 2009, www.ft.com/content/433ed210-4954-11de-9e19-00144feabdc0; P. SCHRANK, "A Better Black-swan Repellent", *The Economist* 2010, www.economist.com/leaders/2010/02/11/a-better-black-swan-repellent.

60 R.J. THOMAS, R. FUCHS and Y. SILVERSTONE, "A Machine in the C-suite", 2016, ecgi.global/sites/default/files/documents/accenture-strategy-wotf-machine-csuite11.pdf, 5; A. KAMALNATH, "The Perennial Quest for Board Independence – Artificial Intelligence to the Rescue?", *Albany Law Review* 2019-20, vol. 83, 52; A. LAI, "Artificial Intelligence, LLC: Corporate Personhood As Tort Reform", *Michigan State Law Review* 2021, 620-621.

61 AI is claimed to be unbiased as opposed to humans, albeit in the limited sense that the technology does not follow an own agenda different from its programmed goals. However, it is possible that human subjectivity, perhaps even previous instances of groupthink, emerges through its test data and training data and is thus incorporated in the system's learning process. These human biases reflect the financial interests of human actors involved and can even be exacerbated by the system. In addition, algorithmic biases may also emerge from the system's learning process. See, *e.g.*, S. BAROCAS and A.D. SELBST, "Big Data's Disparate Impact", *California Law Review* 2016, vol. 104, 692-693 regarding the risk of human decision makers masking their intentions by using biased data; A.H. RAYMOND, E. ARRINGTON STONE YOUNG and S.J. SHACKELFORD, "Building a Better Hal 9000: Algorithms, the Market, and the Need to Prevent the Engraining of Bias", *Northwestern Journal of Technology and Intellectual Property* 2018, vol. 15, 222-232 regarding algorithmic biases.

protest each other's opinions in board meetings.[62] Since AI machines are, in principle, impartial and free of conflict of interest, their output is not influenced by any friendship and ensures bolstered independence of decision-making,[63] as long as the human directors do not feel pressured to blindly accept the AI output.[64] The neutral outcomes of the machine can challenge strong interpersonal relationships that may have grown between directors over the years, which led to a holdback of protesting friends on the board.[65] In other words, the board dynamics, including interpersonal relationships, could shift considerably when AI is granted a dominant or even a mere assisted role on the board. Second, AI augmentation will help directors to process data in a shorter period of time. Independent directors are known to hold positions on multiple boards, where decisions sometimes need to be taken at short notice. Being outsiders to the company, they are unable to digest all decision-relevant data in this brief time span. Governance intelligence can aid them in quickly distilling the crucial information,[66] which may lead to an increased board activity.[67]

2.3 *Classification of Artificial Governance Intelligence in Terms of the Level of Autonomy*

Importance of classification. There are, to this day, no universal standards defining different kinds of AI systems used in the corporate realm. However, for the purpose of a legal analysis of governance intelligence, it is imperative to first discover the potential use cases of AI for corporate decision-making. A taxonomy offers a clear overview of how boards of directors and top managements may use AI to their benefit, irrespective of its lawfulness or legal impact. In a second step, a taxonomy could also allow the legislator, should he be so inclined, to use its categories as a benchmark for issuing AI-specific

62 A. KAMALNATH, "The Perennial Quest for Board Independence – Artificial Intelligence to the Rescue?", *Albany Law Review* 2019-20, vol. 83, 50-51.

63 Z. LIPAI, X. XIQIANG and L. MENGYUAN, "Corporate Governance Reform in the Era of Artificial Intelligence: Research Overview and Prospects Based on Knowledge Graph", *Annals of Operations Research* 2021, separate online issue, 12; M. EROĞLU and M.K. KAYA, "Impact of Artificial Intelligence on Corporate Board Diversity Policies and Regulations", *EBOR* 2022, vol. 23, 559-564.

64 S.A GRAMITTO RICCI, "Artificial Agents in Corporate Boardrooms", *Cornell Law Review* 2020, vol. 105, 899 (arguing that human directors may feel overly compelled to conform to AI output. Should board members disagree with the system, they might feel compelled to explain why they chose to entirely disregard, or deviate from, the output of the system. As a result, the alleged pressure for human directors to explain why they disagree with AI could ultimately affect the directors' ability to exercise independent judgment when making a decision).

65 A. KAMALNATH, "The Perennial Quest for Board Independence – Artificial Intelligence to the Rescue?", *Albany Law Review* 2019-20, vol. 83, 50-51.

66 *Ibid*, 49-51.

67 ERNST & YOUNG, "Study on the Relevance and Impact of Artificial Intelligence for Company Law and Corporate Governance", 2021, 28-29.

differentiated corporate rules. Such a method would diminish legal uncertainty, as it enables companies to precisely determine the applicable rules to a certain type of governance intelligence they would like to implement.

The level of autonomy as demarcation criterium. Within the corporate realm, the various agency conflicts and corresponding corporate rules are closely connected to the decision-making power of agents in the corporation. Therefore, it makes sense to develop a governance intelligence continuum that distinguishes categories on the basis of the allocation of decision rights between man and machine. In other words, the level of autonomy of the AI system serves as a benchmark here. Autonomy, not to be confused with automation,[68] refers to the ability to perform specific (narrow) tasks (based on the system's utility functions) independently from human guidance or intervention.[69] Besides the allocation of decision rights, the classification of governance intelligence in this chapter also takes into account the decision type of the board, the task that is assigned to the AI system[70] and the scope of the goals of both the implemented AI system and the company as a whole (narrow or broad), which all have an impact on the autonomy level of the AI system – and likewise the required oversight by human directors.[71]

68 Automation should be defined as the ability of a system (not necessarily an AI system) to perform a limited set of programmed supervised tasks on behalf of the user, most often executed in a repeating pattern; F. GALDON, A. HALL, and S.J. WANG, "Designing Trust in Highly Automated Virtual Assistants: A Taxonomy of Levels of Autonomy" in A. DINGLI, F. HADDOD and C. KLÜVER (eds.), *Artificial Intelligence in Industry 4.0 – A Collection of Innovative Research Case-studies that are Reworking the Way We Look at Industry 4.0 Thanks to Artificial Intelligence*, Cham, Springer, 2021, 200.

69 W. XU, "From Automation to Autonomy and Autonomous Vehicles – Challenges and Opportunities for Human-Computer Interaction", *Interactions* 2021, vol. 28, 50.

70 For example, the difference between assisted and augmented intelligence might not necessarily stem from the respective capabilities of the technology. Instead, the demarcation between both categories depends on the enhancing nature of the output of the AI system, as well as the role definition of the system, *i.e.* the task that is *ad hoc* entrusted to it, see K. WALCH, "Is There A Difference Between Assisted Intelligence Vs. Augmented Intelligence?", *Forbes* 2020, www.forbes.com/sites/cognitiveworld/2020/01/12/is-there-a-difference-between-assisted-intelligence-vs-augmented-intelligence/?sh=2322431526ab.

71 The general 'AAAI'-classification of RAO and its equivalents, as well as the SAE standard J3016 for autonomous vehicles, are two AI classifications built on a similar notion. See A. RAO, "AI: Everywhere and Nowhere (Part 3)", 2016, www.insurancethoughtleadership.com/ai-machine-learning/ai-everywhere-and-nowhere-part-3; SOCIETY OF AUTOMOTIVE ENGINEERS INTERNATIONAL, "Taxonomy and Definitions for Terms Related to Driving Automation Systems for On-Road Motor Vehicles", 2021, www.sae.org/standards/content/j3016_202104/, 41 p. Therefore, these taxonomies could be transposed to the corporate realm, which has been attempted before by other scholars, such as *inter alia* F. MÖSLEIN, "Robots in the Boardroom: Artificial Intelligence and Corporate Law" in W. BARFIELD and U. PAGALLO (eds.), *Research Handbook on the Law of Artificial Intelligence*, Cheltenham, Edward Elgar, 2018, 657; M. PETRIN, "Corporate Management in the Age of AI", *Columbia Business Law Review* 2019, vol. 3, 980-983; S.A GRAMITTO RICCI, "Artificial Agents in Corporate Boardrooms", *Cornell Law Review* 2020, vol. 105, 895-904; M. HILB, "Toward Artificial Governance? The Role of Artificial Intelligence in Shaping the Future of Corporate Governance", *Journal of Management and Governance* 2020, vol. 24 (4), 861-862; H. DRUKARCH and E. FOSCH-VILLARONGA, "The Role and Legal Implications of Autonomy

Levels of autonomy for artificial governance intelligence. As a starting point for this classification, one should consider traditional board practices where human directors are the sole decision makers within the board. They are potentially supported by simple technology applications without AI capabilities such as calculators and spreadsheets. These systems are purely practical and task-specific and lack any form of autonomy in the corporate governance process. However, from the moment that AI is deployed in the corporate realm, it is possible that traditional board practices will gradually fade away. According to the respective level of autonomy and corresponding decision rights granted to the AI system, a distinction can be made between assisted, augmented and autonomous governance intelligence.[72]

Assisted Governance Intelligence. In the assisted form of AI, human directors are still the sole decision makers within the board of directors, but they rely on selective support from narrow AI systems for mostly practical and administrative tasks. These AI applications are task-specific, and their output is restricted to an assisted nature that does not enhance the human decision-making or touch upon the core judgment work of directors. Assisted governance intelligence is occasionally assimilated with the intelligent (*i.e.* AI-driven) 'automation' of business processes in management literature.[73] Examples include business virtual assistants,[74] intelligent document and material processing,[75] in addition to accounting and reporting robotics.[76]

Augmented Governance Intelligence. At the augmented level, human directors are still the final decision makers within the board of directors, who rely on the sustained support of AI systems for certain specific decisions, in a manner that enhances or improves human intelligence or decision-making. The human directors use AI output

---

in AI-Driven Boardrooms" in B. CUSTERS and E. FOSCH-VILLARONGA (eds.), *Law and Artificial Intelligence – Regulating AI and Applying AI in Legal Practice*, Den Haag, Asser Press, 2022, 355-356; J. ZHAO and B. GÓMEZ FARIÑAS, "Artificial Intelligence and Sustainable Decisions", *EBOR* 2023, vol. 24, 13-15.

72 As originally defined in a general manner by A. RAO, "AI: Everywhere and Nowhere (Part 3)", 2016, www.insurancethoughtleadership.com/ai-machine-learning/ai-everywhere-and-nowhere-part-3.

73 *E.g.* J. NALDER, "Future-U A3 Model: How to Understand the Impact of Tech on Work, Society & edUcation", 2017, static1.squarespace.com/static/52946d89e4b0f601b40f39a4/t/58ec53789de4bb1ee3bf3bc5/1491882887958/FUTURE-U+A3+MODEL+v2.pdf.

74 *E.g.* the (now discontinued) application Amy Ingram of the now-acquired company X.ai, which was developed to schedule meetings by reading and writing emails, coordinating with participants and managing calendar invites.

75 Specialised AI platforms such as Automation Anywhere IQ Bot, docBrain, Kofax TotalAgility, Metamaze, Super.ai and UiPath Document Understanding are using this process to automate complex document-based workflows of enterprises in general.

76 As part of the so-called Robotic Process Automation (RPA) within businesses, see INSTITUTE FOR ROBOTIC PROCESS AUTOMATION, "Introduction to Robotic Process Automation – A Primer", 2015, irpaai.com/introduction-to-robotic-process-automation-a-primer/.

to improve the informative basis of governance decisions for which they have a certain amount of policy freedom (decisions pertaining to their 'business judgment'). AI augmentation allows for the analysis of large amounts of data, and the reduction of uncertainties essential to the decision-making with predictive analyses.[77] Therefore, the human board members and AI systems perform decision-making tasks *jointly*, but the AI system itself does not enjoy stand-alone decision rights as it is entrusted exclusively with the preparation of decisions (there is human-in-the-loop[78] oversight). Augmented governance intelligence can serve multiple purposes, such as searching for information (*i.e.* intelligent search or enterprise search), classifying information (a form of supervised learning), clustering information (a form of unsupervised learning) and rendering precise recommendations and/or predictions (such as Monte Carlo scenario analyses). Currently, AI systems of this autonomy level are used to support M&A transactions and strategic decision-making of the management. The predictive and prescriptive analytics of this level also allow for cutting-edge forecasting applications in the field of finance and creative fields such as the film industry (by predicting box office results for movie projects).[79]

Autonomous Governance Intelligence. At the final autonomous stage, AI systems are bestowed with their own stand-alone decision rights for governance decisions, as they operate virtually independently from the guidance and control of human directors – if there are any. Such an autonomous level can be achieved through the delegation of core corporate governance powers to the AI system or through the appointment of an AI system as a member of the board. The delegation or appointment does not need to be legally recognised and may constitute a matter of fact – as directors could blindly entrust certain decisions to AI. The AI systems of this category vary in terms of the scope of the 'operational domain'[80] for which they are designed and consequently

77 M.H. JARRAHI, "Artificial Intelligence and the Future of Work: Human-AI Symbiosis in Organizational Decision Making", *Business Horizons* 2018, vol. 61, 580; S. FRIEDRICH, G. ANTES, S. BEHR, H. BINDER, W. BRANNATH, F. DUMPERT, K. ICKSTADT, H.A. KESTLER, J. LEDERER, H. LEITGÖB, M. PAULY, A. STELAND, A. WILHELM and T. FRIEDE, "Is There a Role for Statistics in Artificial Intelligence?", *Advances in Data Analysis and Classification* 2021, doi.org/10.1007/s11634-021-00455-6.

78 *Cf.* the AI oversight models defined in HIGH-LEVEL EXPERT GROUP ON ARTIFICIAL INTELLIGENCE, "Ethics Guidelines for Trustworthy AI", 2019, op.europa.eu/en/publication-detail/-/publication/d3988569-0434-11ea-8c1f-01aa75ed71a1. See also R. KOULU, "Human Control over Automation: EU Policy and AI Ethics", *European Journal of Legal Studies* 2020, vol. 12, 31-32; E. HICKMAN and M. PETRIN, "Trustworthy AI and Corporate Governance: The EU's Ethics Guidelines for Trustworthy Artificial Intelligence from a Company Law Perspective", *EBOR* 2021, vol. 22, 600-603.

79 See above.

80 The operational (design) domain of an autonomous system encompasses "*the operating conditions under which* [the system] *or feature thereof is specifically designed to function*". Compare with the used terminology in the SAE-taxonomy for connected and autonomous vehicles: SOCIETY OF AUTOMOTIVE ENGINEERS INTERNATIONAL, "Taxonomy and Definitions for Terms Related to Driving Automation Systems for On-Road Motor Vehicles", 2021, www.sae.org/standards/content/j3016_202104/, 32-33, no. 6.

implemented. In the case of a core power delegation to AI or an appointment of AI among other human directors (a *hybrid board*), the AI system operates within a limited domain of the decision-making process. Human directors are still present to monitor the overall operations and decisions of the AI system where desirable (called human-in-command oversight). For instance, regardless of its lawfulness, a human director may delegate part of its monitoring duty to an AI system, or a robo-director may be appointed as an additional board member. Another possibility entails the situation where the factual board of a company consists exclusively of one AI system (a *fused board*) or multiple artificial directors (an *artificial board*). Then, human directors are completely absent (human-out-of-the-loop), as the AI system operates independently of any human intervention. A scenario of fused or artificial boards is currently possible (from a mere technological perspective) only when the goals of the AI system and the company are restricted to a narrow operational domain, in addition to being closely connected and intertwined. Examples include algorithmic trading (for long-term investments), robo-taxi and vending machine companies, where a limited purpose naturally facilitates the technological conceivability of the autonomous system. Self-driving subsidiaries with narrow goals, as defined by leading scholars,[81] also fall in this category. In order for AI systems to be able to govern corporations with broad goals (*i.e.* with an unlimited number of operational domains), the achievement of strong or general intelligence is required, which remains science fiction at the moment. If ever accomplished, the upward potential of AI decision-making in corporate governance rises to a superhuman level for all domains.

3 Human-tailored Corporate Law, Unprepared for the Introduction of Artificial Governance Intelligence

3.1 Artificial Governance Intelligence: The Legal State of the Art

Static company law. The classification of governance intelligence represents a continuum of power that is handed over from human directors to AI systems. It starts with trivial and mundane AI systems that do not have a real say in corporate decision-making and evolves towards the delegation of core powers to AI or even the full replacement of one or more human directors by AI. As mentioned before, corporate law has not evolved at all to reflect the potential role of AI in the corporate realm. The latter may not immediately impede the legal permissibility of the assisted autonomy level of governance intelligence,

81 J. Armour and H. Eidenmüller, "Self-Driving Corporations?" in H. Eidenmüller and G. Wagner (eds.), *Law by Algorithm*, Tübingen, Mohr Siebeck, 2021, 176-177.

as it does not intrude on the basic principles of board practice.[82] Greater legal uncertainty does arise for higher AI autonomy levels, where the decision-making process is largely influenced by AI output, with autonomous intelligence as an extreme as it might remove humans completely out of the loop for some decision types.

***Prima facie* incompatibility of corporate legal frameworks.** The unpreparedness of corporate legal frameworks arises from traditional corporate law having the general function of mediating or at least controlling specific human agency conflicts.[83] Not all of these conflicts necessarily occur in the same fashion if decision-making is conducted or supported by AI, which is wired differently than human intelligence. From a mere technological point of view, an AI system cannot choose its ultimate goal or utility function (as this has been programmed from the outset by its developer[84]). Besides, it operates without other self-interests than maximising its utility function, and it is unfamiliar with the corporate concept of stakeholder interests (unless when it is programmed and trained to take such interests into account[85]). What is more, AI cannot pursue anyone's interests in good faith or bad faith, insofar as the system optimises its objective utility function[86] in alignment with the subjective goals of its programmer.[87]

82 M. HILB, "Toward Artificial Governance? The Role of Artificial Intelligence in Shaping the Future of Corporate Governance", *Journal of Management and Governance* 2020, vol. 24 (4), 862-863.

83 For an account on the three agency problems within the corporation, see J. ARMOUR, H. HANSMANN and R. KRAAKMAN, "What Is Corporate Law?" in R. KRAAKMAN, J. ARMOUR, P. DAVIES, L. ENRIQUES, H. HANSMANN, G. HERTIG, K.J. HOPT, H. KANDA, M. PARGENDLER, W.-G. RINGE and E. ROCK (eds.), *The Anatomy of Corporate Law: A Comparative and Functional Approach*, Oxford, Oxford University Press, 2017, 29-31.

84 S.M. OMOHUNDRO, "The Nature of Self-Improving Artificial Intelligence", 2008, selfawaresystems.files.wordpress.com/2008/01/nature_of_self_improving_ai.pdf, 17-28; N. BOSTROM, *Superintelligence: Paths, Dangers, Strategies*, Oxford, Oxford University Press, 2014, 109-111.

85 See *inter alia* T. AHMED and A. SRIVASTAVA, "Predicting Human Interest: An Application of Artificial Intelligence and Uncertainty Quantification", *Journal of Uncertainty Analysis and Applications* 2016, vol. 4, 1-21; B.D. MITTELSTADT, P. ALLO, M. TADDEO, S. WACHTER and L. FLORIDI, "The Ethics of Algorithms: Mapping the Debate", *Big Data & Society* 2016, vol. 3, 1-21.

86 F. MÖSLEIN, "Robots in the Boardroom: Artificial Intelligence and Corporate Law" in W. BARFIELD and U. PAGALLO (eds.), *Research Handbook on the Law of Artificial Intelligence*, Cheltenham, Edward Elgar, 2018, 666; J. ARMOUR and H. EIDENMÜLLER, "Self-Driving Corporations?" in H. EIDENMÜLLER and G. WAGNER (eds.), *Law by Algorithm*, Tübingen, Mohr Siebeck, 2021, 177; C. PICCIAU, "The (Un) Predictable Impact of Technology on Corporate Governance", *Hastings Business Law Journal* 2021, vol. 17, 119.

87 An AI system may pursue its objective function in a manner that is incompatible with the intended (subjective) goals that its programmer wishes the system to accomplish. One could argue that in case of goal-misalignment, the AI system acts in bad faith. An example of this is 'reward hacking' or 'specification gaming', where a reinforcement system finds loopholes that help it accomplish the specified objective efficiently but in unintended, possibly harmful ways. See *inter alia* D. MANHEIM and S. GARRABRANT, "Categorizing Variants of Goodhart's Law", 2018, doi.org/10.48550/arXiv.1803.04585; V. KRAKOVNA, J. UESATO, V. MIKULIK, M. RAHTZ, T. EVERITT, R. KUMAR, Z. KENTON, J. LEIKE and S. LEGG, "Specification Gaming: The Flip Side of AI Ingenuity", *DeepMind* 2020, www.deepmind.com/blog/specification-gaming-the-flip-side-of-ai-ingenuity.

The system's 'intentions', if any, should be attributed to its human coding, training data and learning process.[88] AI is thus claimed to be unbiased as opposed to humans, albeit in the limited sense that the technology does not follow an own agenda that deviates from the objectives set by its programmer.[89] However, human biases may be reflected in the algorithm and/or the data, and algorithmic biases may emerge from the learning process.[90] The *ex post* remedies of corporate law are inefficient to counter these biases or to encourage rule-compliant behaviour from governance intelligence,[91] as these dissuasive methods are not appropriate for systems of which the learning process is pre-programmed. Finally, the broad standards of conduct that directors should adhere to when fulfilling their core functions, such as the fiduciary duty of loyalty and care, are hardly intelligible for AI and cannot be coded into the algorithm,[92] since they are subject to interpretation and often ambiguously shaped by case law.

Generally, the absence of specific corporate rules for artificial governance intelligence creates legal uncertainty about whether it is lawful at all to 'enhance' human governance decisions with the help of AI, and how liability should be attributed when a decision based on AI output causes harm to third parties. As mentioned earlier, Hong Kong corporate law did not recognise VITAL as a director, since the legal status of a corporate director is reserved for natural persons in most forms of Hong Kong companies.[93] In this respect, its 'appointment' was exaggerated, as no true legal decision rights could be granted to the system. This raises the question as to the extent to which a director is legally allowed to hand over (*i.e.* delegate) core decision-making powers to AI from a corporate governance perspective, and if allowed, what level of supervision by humans is required.[94] A full replacement of corporate bodies by AI encounters even greater

88 In respect of the possibility of AI forming intent, see *e.g.* L.B. ELIOT, "On The Beguiling Question Of Whether AI Can Form Intent, Including The Case Of Self-Driving Cars", *Forbes* 2020, www.forbes.com/sites/lanceeliot/2020/06/06/on-the-beguiling-question-of-whether-ai-can-form-intent-including-the-case-of-self-driving-cars/?sh=2f28a81c448d.

89 S. DHANRAJANI, "Board Rooms Strategies Redefined By Algorithms: AI For CXO Decision Making", *Forbes* 2019, www.forbes.com/sites/cognitiveworld/2019/03/31/board-rooms-strategies-redefined-by-algorithms-ai-for-cxo-decision-making/?sh=4861ddee3154; S.A GRAMITTO RICCI, "Artificial Agents in Corporate Boardrooms", *Cornell Law Review* 2020, vol. 105, 901 and 903; M. PETRIN, "Corporate Management in the Age of AI", *Columbia Business Law Review* 2019, vol. 3, 1006.

90 See above.

91 F. MÖSLEIN, "Robots in the Boardroom: Artificial Intelligence and Corporate Law" in W. BARFIELD and U. PAGALLO (eds.), *Research Handbook on the Law of Artificial Intelligence*, Cheltenham, Edward Elgar, 2018, 666-667; M. PETRIN, "Corporate Management in the Age of AI", *Columbia Business Law Review* 2019, vol. 3, 1013-1018.

92 M. PETRIN, "Corporate Management in the Age of AI", *Columbia Business Law Review* 2019, vol. 3, 1013; A. KAMALNATH, "The Perennial Quest for Board Independence – Artificial Intelligence to the Rescue?", *Albany Law Review* 2019-20, vol. 83, 55; C. PICCIAU, "The (Un)Predictable Impact of Technology on Corporate Governance", *Hastings Business Law Journal* 2021, vol. 17, 119.

93 See above.

94 See below for an account on corporate power delegation the required supervision of the delegated powers.

legal issues, although prominent scholars acknowledge the possibility of creating algorithmic entities in the USA and the EU.[95] Interestingly, the previously mentioned EY study ordered by the European Commission purports that the use of AI as a support tool for decision-making is regarded as permissible under the current corporate frameworks, in the absence of specific statutory provisions or case law.[96] While the use of technological auxiliaries by directors may be allowed, uncertainty exists about its potential legal (liability) consequences. In fact, the study itself signals the complex legal questions arising from the use of assisted and augmented intelligence.[97] In addition, leading scholars in the field have expressed the opinion that existing corporate law frameworks as a whole are currently unfit for the adoption of governance intelligence with higher autonomy levels.[98] Beyond corporate law, it is also unclear whether the worldwide initiatives to regulate AI may impose legal obligations on companies adopting governance intelligence, besides the many specific rules concerning data and financial transactions.[99] As a result of this legal uncertainty from a company law and technology law perspective, companies could be discouraged from adopting AI at a governance level, even when its implementation would likely improve the quality of decision-making.

Memberless and leaderless entities. Before legal literature started paying attention to the emerging potential of AI entering the boardroom of existing corporations, some scholars depicted the creation of entirely new businesses without any ongoing human involvement. This idea was first advanced by BAYERN, who asserted that one can factually confer legal personhood on an autonomous computer by putting it in control of a US limited liability company (LLC's), thus creating a memberless or

95 See below.

96 ERNST & YOUNG, "Study on the Relevance and Impact of Artificial Intelligence for Company Law and Corporate Governance", 2021, 48-51.

97 While the study views AI support tools for corporate decision-making as permissible under the current laws, it paradoxically attaches two broad and ambiguous conditions to this permissibility: "(i) that duties and decisions laying at the heart of the management function (*e.g.* definition and supervision of corporate strategy) remain with human directors, and (ii) that directors oversee the selection and activities of AI tools, which in turn requires them to have at least some basic understanding of how the specific AI tools operate". In respect of autonomous intelligence, the study concludes that AI cannot legally replace corporate bodies within the existing frameworks; see ERNST & YOUNG, "Study on the Relevance and Impact of Artificial Intelligence for Company Law and Corporate Governance", 2021, 48-51.

98 F. MÖSLEIN, "Robots in the Boardroom: Artificial Intelligence and Corporate Law" in W. BARFIELD and U. PAGALLO (eds.), *Research Handbook on the Law of Artificial Intelligence*, Cheltenham, Edward Elgar, 2018, 666-667; M. PETRIN, "Corporate Management in the Age of AI", *Columbia Business Law Review* 2019, vol. 3, 1015-1022; J. ARMOUR and H. EIDENMÜLLER, "Self-Driving Corporations?" in H. EIDENMÜLLER and G. WAGNER (eds.), *Law by Algorithm*, Tübingen, Mohr Siebeck, 2021, 175-182.

99 See below for an illustration on specific rules of data protection law and financial law.

algorithmic entity governed exclusively by an algorithm.[100] According to BAYERN, the default corporate governance rules do not prevent so-called algorithmic management, and state law allegedly allows LLC's to continue their operations after becoming shareholderless over time under the exclusive control of an AI system.[101] Even if state law would not allow the foregoing, circular ownership and 'vetogates' could achieve a comparable result.[102] Other scholars contend that a similar result can be reached with other corporate forms and in different jurisdictions, such as EU member states.[103] The latter could be achieved by establishing algorithmic entities in countries with flexible regulatory standards, and then invoking the principle of Freedom of Establishment in order to conduct business in other EU member states.[104] However, the absence of any type of human control creates a risk of undesirable activities and liability attribution problems. Algorithmic entities incorporated in the EU will need to refrain from taking certain decisions autonomously, as the AI Act will require human oversight of AI systems with high-risk applications such as evaluating the creditworthiness of natural persons or assessing the recruitment of natural persons.[105] In addition, the technological conceivability and utility of memberless entities is rightfully criticised,[106] as they have no legitimate or serious *raison d'être*, let alone a for-profit purpose.[107] More generally,

---

100 S. BAYERN, "Of Bitcoins, Independently Wealthy Software, and the Zero-Member LLC", *Northwestern University Law Review* 2014, vol. 108, 1495-1500; S. BAYERN, "The Implications of Modern Business-Entity Law for the Regulation of Autonomous Systems", *Stanford Technology Law Review* 2015, vol. 19, 93-112; S. BAYERN, "Are Autonomous Entities Possible?", *Northwestern University Law Review* 2019, vol. 114, 23-47.

101 S. BAYERN, "Of Bitcoins, Independently Wealthy Software, and the Zero-Member LLC", *Northwestern University Law Review* 2014, vol. 108, 1496-1497; S. BAYERN, "The Implications of Modern Business-Entity Law for the Regulation of Autonomous Systems", *Stanford Technology Law Review* 2015, vol. 19, 101-104.

102 For these techniques, see S. BAYERN, "Are Autonomous Entities Possible?", *Northwestern University Law Review* 2019, vol. 114, 28-33; L.M. LOPUCKI, "Algorithmic Entities", *Washington University Law Review* 2018, vol. 95, 919-924.

103 S. BAYERN, T. BURRI, T.D. GRANT, D.M. HÄUSERMANN, F. MÖSLEIN, and R. WILLIAMS, "Company Law and Autonomous Systems: A Blueprint for Lawyers, Entrepreneurs, and Regulators", *Hastings Science and Technology Law Journal* 2017, vol. 9, 139-153; L.M. LOPUCKI, "Algorithmic Entities", *Washington University Law Review* 2018, vol. 95, 907-912.

104 T. BURRI, "Free Movement of Algorithms: Artificially Intelligent Persons Conquer the European Union's Internal Market" in W. BARFIELD and U. PAGALLO (eds.), *Research Handbook on the Law of Artificial Intelligence*, Cheltenham, Edward Elgar, 2018, 543-549; L.M. LOPUCKI, "Algorithmic Entities", *Washington University Law Review* 2018, vol. 95, 927-928.

105 Art. 14 (1) *juncto* Annex III Draft AI Act. See also Art. 22 (1) GDPR.

106 See *inter alia* D.M. HÄUSERMANN, "Memberless Legal Entities Operated by Autonomous Systems – Some Thoughts on Shawn Bayern's Article "The Implications of Modern Business-Entity Law for the Regulation of Autonomous Systems" from a Swiss Law Perspective", ssrn.com/abstract=2827504, 10-12; M.U. SCHERER, "Of Wild Beasts and Digital Analogues: The Legal Status of Autonomous Systems", *Nevada Law Journal* 2019, vol. 19, 264-279.

107 *Contra* L.M. LOPUCKI, "Algorithmic Entities", *Washington University Law Review* 2018, vol. 95, 900-901.

the necessity of granting legal personhood to AI, whether or not under the corporate veil or via special types of citizenship, is hotly debated.[108]

At the other end of the spectrum, one should be wary of AI-driven leaderless entities, namely Decentralised Autonomous Organisations (DAOs). DAOs belong to the broader family of decentralised organisations. The latter are computer programs without a distinct governance body, running on a peer-to-peer network, which involves a set of users interacting with each other, in accordance with a coded protocol, enforced on a blockchain.[109] DAOs are designed to run 'autonomously'[110] on this blockchain since they are controlled solely by code,[111] whereas traditional decentralised organisations require heavy involvement from humans on each end of various transactions.[112] Put another way, DAOs have a structure that does not entail directors or managers, since it is directly controlled by its members through an autonomous and decentralised system.[113] The utility functions of DAOs span greater lengths than those of memberless entities, as they originated in the world of Decentralised Finance (DeFi). However, the DAO is faced with numerous legal hurdles in light of its lacking legal recognition, which may result in courts qualifying it as an unincorporated partnership to impose

108 *E.g.* L. SOLUM, "Legal Personhood for Artificial Intelligences", *North Carolina Law Review* 1992, vol. 70, 1231-1287; F.P. HUBBARD, "Do Androids Dream? Personhood and Intelligent Artifacts", *Temple Law Review* 2010, vol. 83, 405-474; R. DOWELL, "Fundamental Protections for Non-Biological Intelligences Or: How We Learn to Stop Worrying and Love Our Robot Brethren", *Minnesota Journal of Law Science & Technology* 2018, vol. 19, 305-336; G. TEUBNER, "Digitale Rechtssubjekte? Zum privatrechtlichen Status autonomer Softwareagenten", *Ancilla Iuris* 2018, 36-78; V. A.J. KURKI, *A Theory of Legal Personhood*, Oxford, Oxford University Press, 2019, 175-189; T.L. JAYNES, "Legal Personhood for Artificial Intelligence: Citizenship as the Exception to the Rule", *AI & Society* 2020, vol. 35, 343-354; N. BANTEKA, "Artificially Intelligent Persons", *Houston Law Review* 2021, vol. 58, 537-596; A. LAI, "Artificial Intelligence, LLC: Corporate Personhood As Tort Reform", *Michigan State Law Review* 2021, 597-653; E. MIK, "AI as a Legal Person?" in J.-A. LEE, R.M. HILTY, K.-C. LIU (eds.), *Artificial Intelligence and Intellectual Property*, Oxford, Oxford University Press, 2021, 419-439.

109 This definition is, with minor alterations, adopted from L. METJAHIC, "Deconstructing The DAO: The Need for Legal Recognition and the Application of Securities Laws to Decentralized Organizations", *Cardozo Law Review* 2018, vol. 39, 1541-1542.

110 While DAOs come in many different varieties, what they tend to have in common is that they use smart contracts enabling investors to directly participate in its decision-making. The term 'autonomous' in DAO refers to that use of smart contracts, which do not constitute AI as they merely automate the execution of past party promises that are translated into code. Therefore, it seems inappropriate to refer to DAOs as truly 'autonomous'. On smart contracts, see H. SURDEN, "Computable Contracts", *University of California, Davis Law Review* 2012, vol. 46, 695.

111 Blockchain networks (or other Distributed Ledger Technologies) serve as an interoperable layer for AI to interact and potentially coordinate themselves with other code-based systems through a set of smart contracts; P. DE FILIPPI and A. WRIGHT, *Blockchain and the Law: The Rule of Code*, Cambridge and London, Harvard University Press, 2018, 147-150.

112 *Ibid*, 148.

113 V. BUTERIN, "DAOs, DACs, DAs and More: An Incomplete Terminology Guide", *Ethereum Foundation Blog* 2014, blog.ethereum.org/2014/05/06/daos-dacs-das-and-more-an-incomplete-terminology-guide.

personal liability on its members.[114] Other legal risks include the unclear attribution of corporate fiduciary duties,[115] in addition to the debatable security law qualification of initial offerings of tokens and coins.[116] Aside from the foregoing legal aspects, the spectacular failure of Ethereum-based 'The DAO'[117] underpins the general risks and shortcomings of a business entity without centralised management.

Artificial management of traditional corporations – legal state of the art. The far-fetched ideas of both memberless and leaderless corporations eventually drew attention to the more realistic hypothesis of AI playing a role in the boardroom of traditional and already established corporations. Over the past few years, a vast number of research papers have been written about the legal status of governance intelligence in various

114 S. PALLEY, "How to Sue a DAO", 2016, www.linkedin.com/pulse/how-sue-dao-stephen-palley; L. METJAHIC, "Deconstructing the DAO: The Need for Legal Recognition and the Application of Securities Laws to Decentralized Organizations", *Cardozo Law Review* 2018, vol. 39, 1553-1558; C.L. REYES, "If Rockefeller Were a Coder", *The George Washington Law Review* 2019, vol. 87, 398-400; W.A. KAAL, "Decentralized Autonomous Organizations – Internal Governance and External Legal Design", *Annals of Corporate Governance* 2021, vol. 5, 24. *E.g.* District Court Southern District Of California (US) May 2, 2022, *Sarcuni et al. v. bZx DAO et al.*, www.classaction.org/media/sarcuni-et-al-v-bzx-dao-et-al.pdf.

115 W.A. KAAL, "Decentralized Autonomous Organizations – Internal Governance and External Legal Design", *Annals of Corporate Governance* 2021, vol. 5, 26; B. MIENERT, *Dezentrale autonome Organisationen (DAOs) und Gesellschaftsrecht – Zum Spannungsverhältnis Blockchain-basierter und juristischer Regeln*, Tübingen, Mohr Siebeck, 2022, 189-192.

116 The US SEC published a report in 2017 about the qualification of DAO tokens as securities, which is a fact-based analysis; US SECURITIES AND EXCHANGE COMMISSION, "SEC Issues Investigative Report Concluding DAO Tokens, a Digital Asset, Were Securities", 2017, www.sec.gov/news/press-release/2017-131.

117 *E.g.* U. RODRIGUES, "Law and the Blockchain", *Iowa Law Review* 2019, vol. 104, 697-706.

jurisdictions.[118] This research wave was sparked by the original work of MÖSLEIN,[119] in addition to the paper of ARMOUR and EIDENMÜLLER.[120] Prompted by the growing attention paid to governance intelligence in the literature, the European Commission ordered a study report from EY on its impact on corporate law and corporate governance. However, as mentioned earlier, this study claimed categorically that AI support for directors is permissible in the absence of specific cases and statutory law (even though the study confirms that legal problems and uncertainty exist), while the replacement of corporate bodies by AI is legally impossible in the EU.[121] In 2021

---

118 See *inter alia* A. KAMALNATH, "The Perennial Quest for Board Independence – Artificial Intelligence to the Rescue?", *Albany Law Review* 2019-20, vol. 83, 43-60; M. PETRIN, "Corporate Management in the Age of AI", *Columbia Business Law Review* 2019, vol. 3, 965-1030; Y.R. SHRESTHA, S.M. BEN-MENAHEM and G. VON KROGH, "Organizational Decision-Making Structures in the Age of AI", *California Management Review* 2019, vol. 61, 66-83; M.R. SIEBECKER, "Making Corporations More Humane Through Artificial Intelligence", *The Journal of Corporation Law* 2019, vol. 45, 95-149; M.E. DIAMANTIS, "The Extended Corporate Mind: When Corporations Use AI to Break the Law", *North Carolina Law Review* 2020, vol. 98, 893-931; L. ENRIQUES and D.A. ZETZSCHE, "Corporate Technologies and the Tech Nirvana Fallacy", *Hastings Law Journal* 2020, vol. 72, 55-98; S.A GRAMITTO RICCI, "Artificial Agents in Corporate Boardrooms", *Cornell Law Review* 2020, vol. 105, 869-908; N. LOCKE and H. BIRD, "Perspectives on the Current and Imagined Role of Artificial Intelligence and Technology in Corporate Governance Practice and Regulation", 2020, ssrn.com/abstract=3534898; G.D. MOSCO, "AI and the Board Within Italian Corporate Law: Preliminary Notes", *European Company Law Journal* 2020, vol. 17, 87-96; U. NOACK, "Künstliche Intelligenz und die Unternehmensleitung" in G. BACHMANN, S. GRUNDMANN, A. MENGEL and K. KROLOP (eds.), *Festschrift für Christine Windbichler zum 70. Geburtstag am 8. Dezember 2020*, Berlin, De Gruyter, 2020, 947-962; C.M. BRUNER, "Artificially Intelligent Boards and the Future of Delaware Corporate Law", 2021, ssrn.com/abstract=3928237; J. LEE and P. UNDERWOOD, "AI in the Boardroom: Let the Law be in the Driving Seat", ssrn.com/abstract=3874588; C. PICCIAU, "The (Un)Predictable Impact of Technology on Corporate Governance", *Hastings Business Law Journal* 2021, vol. 17, 67-136; J. LEE and P. UNDERWOOD, "AI in the Boardroom: Let the Law Be in the Driving Seat", 2021, ssrn.com/abstract=3874588; M.A. TOKMAKOV, "Artificial Intelligence in Corporate Governance" in S.I. ASHMARINA and V.V. MANTULENKO (eds.), *Digital Economy and the New Labor Market: Jobs, Competences and Innovative HR Technologies*, Cham, Springer, 2021, 667-674; S. WEI, "When FinTech Meets Corporate Governance: Opportunities and Challenges of Using Blockchain and Artificial Intelligence in Corporate Optimisation", *Journal of International Banking Law and Regulation* 2021, vol. 36, 53-68; H. DRUKARCH and E. FOSCH-VILLARONGA, "The Role and Legal Implications of Autonomy in AI-Driven Boardrooms" in B. CUSTERS and E. FOSCH-VILLARONGA (eds.), *Law and Artificial Intelligence – Regulating AI and Applying AI in Legal Practice*, The Hague, Asser Press, 2022, 345-364; A. KAMALNATH and U. VAROTTIL, "A Disclosure-Based Approach to Regulating AI in Corporate Governance", 2022, ssrn.com/abstract =4002876; T. LASAR, *Künstliche Intelligenz in der GmbH*, Frankfurt am Main, Fachmedien Recht und Wirtschaft, 2023, xviii + 240 p; M.M. RAHIM and P. DEY, "Directors in Artificial Intelligence-Based Corporate Governance – an Australian Perspective" in I. DUBE (ed.), *Corporate Governance and Artificial Intelligence – a Conflicting or Complementary Approach*, Cheltenham, Edward Elgar, forthcoming; J. ZHAO and B. GÓMEZ FARIÑAS, "Artificial Intelligence and Sustainable Decisions", *EBOR* 2023, vol. 24, 1-39.

119 F. MÖSLEIN, "Robots in the Boardroom: Artificial Intelligence and Corporate Law" in W. BARFIELD and U. PAGALLO (eds.), *Research Handbook on the Law of Artificial Intelligence*, Cheltenham, Edward Elgar, 2018, 649-670.

120 J. ARMOUR and H. EIDENMÜLLER, "Self-Driving Corporations?" in H. EIDENMÜLLER and G. WAGNER (eds.), *Law by Algorithm*, Tübingen, Mohr Siebeck, 2021, 157-186.

121 ERNST & YOUNG, "Study on the Relevance and Impact of Artificial Intelligence for Company Law and Corporate Governance", 2021, 45-51.

and 2022, the Commission proposed a criticised AI Act,[122] AI Liability Directive[123] and revised Product Liability Directive[124] without any rules tailored to governance intelligence, as the EY study advised awaiting further developments in the field. It goes without saying that this is a missed opportunity, as the Commission had the chance to anticipate potential AI developments and reflect on their impact on legal rules of corporate governance today, in order to prevent developments on the technological front from simply dictating the evolution of legal rules in the future. Rule-makers should make up their minds today about how to regulate future AI developments for the corporate realm so as to ensure they are ready to react on the basis of calm analysis when technology progresses, instead of then improvising rule changes on the hoof.[125] As long as no adapted rules are introduced, the literature (and the judicial system) ought to bring legal clarity on the legal questions arising from governance intelligence, the most prominent of which are identified in Part 3.

A legal research agenda. The increasing use of governance intelligence, in conjunction with its speedy development, has led researchers to the consensus that AI will soon enter stages of autonomous intelligence where it is bestowed with core board powers with a limited role for humans. As controversy exists on the legal status of higher autonomy levels of governance intelligence, the purpose of this chapter is twofold. First, the legal issues raised by the several autonomy levels of governance intelligence are identified from a corporate law perspective (*de lege lata*). Second, it is the goal to suggest changes to current corporate law frameworks, in order to solve or at least alleviate the identified problems (*de lege ferenda*).

3.2 Current Legal Problems Arising from Artificial Governance Intelligence

General. The continuum of artificial governance intelligence, ranging from assisted intelligence to autonomous intelligence,[126] provokes three research questions in the field

---

122 Proposal for a Regulation Laying Down Harmonised Rules On Artificial Intelligence and Amending Certain Union Legislative Acts, 21 April 2021, COM(2021)206 final – 2021/0106 (COD) (hereafter: Draft AI Act).

123 Proposal for a Directive on Adapting Non-Contractual Civil Liability Rules to Artificial Intelligence, 28 September 2022, COM(2022)496 final – 2022/0303 (COD) (hereafter: Draft AI Liability Directive).

124 Proposal for a Directive on Liability for Defective Products, 28 September 2022, COM(2022)495 final – 2022/0302 (COD) (hereafter: Draft Revised Product Liability Directive).

125 For example, the rushed EU regulation of crypto exchanges was partly dictated by common established practices on the market, see *e.g.* S. STEIN SMITH, "Crypto Regulation Needs Clarity, But Rushing It Is A Bad Idea", *Forbes* 2021, www.forbes.com/sites/seansteinsmith/2021/08/03/crypto-regulation-needs-clarity-but-rushing-it-is-a-bad-idea/.

126 See pages 114-116 above.

of corporate law.[127] In case of assisted intelligence, no true decision rights are granted to the machine. From a corporate governance perspective, the use of AI in an assisted form therefore seems permissible, but may still impose liability questions if the system contributes to negligence of the company. From augmented intelligence onwards, however, AI plays a more crucial role in the judgment work of the board, where greater legal uncertainty comes into play. Here, the question arises as to whether directors have the legal *right* to rely on AI output and/or delegate governance powers to AI. This question may also be inverted, by wondering if directors could, for some decisions, have the *duty* to rely on the narrow but superhuman capabilities of AI. Finally, autonomous AI systems may in the future also be able to fully replace human directors and obtain all governance powers,[128] which introduces more existential challenges for company law as we know it today. The goal of these research questions is to diminish legal uncertainty and ease the legal concerns of companies eager to adopt governance intelligence.

The *right* of a director to rely on the output of AI and/or delegate decision rights to AI (core power delegation). As mentioned earlier, company directors already use AI output to improve the informative basis of their decisions. The latter is most often the case when pure data analysis is at the heart of the decision, which occurs, for instance, in the asset management industry.[129] At a higher autonomy level, AI could also be bestowed with certain tasks, decision rights or core powers, such as monitoring the management and the overall performance of the company. However, no clarity exists on the legality of such delegations in many corporate frameworks. For example, UK company law provides the option for directors to delegate their powers to a *person or committee* if foreseen in the articles of incorporation,[130] but it is doubtful whether AI can be considered as one of both.[131] Italian law, on the other hand, completely forbids delegation to other agents than board members,[132] while Belgian law contains no statutory rules on board power delegation. Even if the delegation would be legally

127 As first identified by F. MÖSLEIN, "Robots in the Boardroom: Artificial Intelligence and Corporate Law" in W. BARFIELD and U. PAGALLO (eds.), *Research Handbook on the Law of Artificial Intelligence*, Cheltenham, Edward Elgar, 2018, 657-666.

128 According to MÖSLEIN, this may happen either because humans increasingly trust the machines' abilities to decide or because decisions have to be taken so quickly or require so many data that humans are simply unable to decide; F. MÖSLEIN, "Robots in the Boardroom: Artificial Intelligence and Corporate Law" in W. BARFIELD and U. PAGALLO (eds.), *Research Handbook on the Law of Artificial Intelligence*, Cheltenham, Edward Elgar, 2018, 657.

129 Investment firms whose sole goal is to maximise financial returns, have already to a large extent handed over share and bond-trading to algorithms.

130 Art. 5 (1) UK Model Articles.

131 F. MÖSLEIN, "Robots in the Boardroom: Artificial Intelligence and Corporate Law" in W. BARFIELD and U. PAGALLO (eds.), *Research Handbook on the Law of Artificial Intelligence*, Cheltenham, Edward Elgar, 2018, 658.

132 Art. 2381 Codice Civile (IT); G.D. MOSCO, "AI and the Board Within Italian Corporate Law: Preliminary Notes", *European Company Law Journal* 2020, vol. 17, 92.

permitted, restrictions to the delegation authority of directors still need to be taken into account. To illustrate, Delaware courts insist that the 'heart of the management' remains with the board of directors.[133] In other jurisdictions such as Belgium, directors are endowed with a mandate that is *intuitu personae*, which limits their ability to outsource fundamental governance decisions.[134] In fact, most corporate laws do not allow the delegation of core management decisions,[135] although it is usually unclear what these decisions include. The ambiguity of the existing legal framework could be clarified by comparing AI task delegations to the established literature concerning a director's right to seek help from an (independent) auditor or expert, in addition to literature on outsourcing board tasks.[136]

The *duty* of a director to rely on the output of AI and/or delegate decision rights to AI (core power delegation). Most corporate laws expect the board to make governance decisions on a well-informed basis.[137] Some systems even impose minimum requirements for the gathering of information.[138] Considering that the capabilities of AI may be superior to those of humans for a number of specific tasks, the ubiquitous expectation for directors to act on a well-informed basis may very well evolve into the duty to rely on the output of AI.[139] The duty of a director to rely on AI is most likely to emerge when data analysis is at the basis of a decision, as merely following gut

---

133 Delaware Court of Chancery (US) July 2, 1992, *Canal Capital Corp. v. French*, 1992 *Del. Ch. Lexis* 133; C.M. BRUNER, "Artificially Intelligent Boards and the Future of Delaware Corporate Law", 2021, ssrn.com/abstract=3928237, 9.

134 L. FRÉDÉRICQ, *Traité de droit commercial belge*, Gent, Fecheyr, 1950, 340, no. 209; H. BRAECKMANS and R. HOUBEN, *Handboek vennootschapsrecht*, Antwerpen, Intersentia, 2021, 219-220, no. 468.

135 Such as Swiss and Spanish company law; see Art. 716b, para. 1 Obligationenrecht (CH) and Art. 249bis and 529ter Ley de Sociedades de Capital (ES). Dutch company law, on the other hand, does not impose limitations on a director's delegation authority; K.H.M. DE ROO, "Delegatie van bestuursbevoegdheden", *WPNR* 2019, vol. 150, 473.

136 See *inter alia* for an account on internal corporate governance structures in Europe: H. DE WULF, *Taak en loyauteitsplicht van het bestuur in de naamloze vennootschap*, Antwerpen, Intersentia, 2002, 235-361; K.J. HOPT and P.C. LEYENS, "Board Models in Europe. Recent Developments of Internal Corporate Governance Structures in Germany, the United Kingdom, France, and Italy", *European Company and Financial Law Review* 2004, vol. 1, 135-168; S. DE GEYTER, *Organisatieaansprakelijkheid: bestuurdersaansprakelijkheid, corporate governance en risicomanagement*, Antwerpen, Intersentia, 2012, 289-478. See also S.M BAINBRIDGE and M.T. HENDERSON, *Outsourcing the board: how board service providers can improve corporate governance*, Cambridge - New York, Cambridge University Press, 2018, xiii + 234 p.

137 F. MÖSLEIN, *Grenzen unternehmerischer Leitungsmacht im marktoffenen Verband: Aktien- und Übernahmerecht, Rechtsvergleich und europäischer Rahmen*, Berlin, De Gruyter, 2007, 131-134.

138 Such as US, UK, French and Italian law, see F. MÖSLEIN, "Robots in the Boardroom: Artificial Intelligence and Corporate Law" in W. BARFIELD and U. PAGALLO (eds.), *Research Handbook on the Law of Artificial Intelligence*, Cheltenham, Edward Elgar, 2018, 661-663.

139 *Ibid.*, 660-662; U. NOACK, "Künstliche Intelligenz und die Unternehmensleitung" in G. BACHMANN, S. GRUNDMANN, A. MENGEL and K. KROLOP (eds.), *Festschrift für Christine Windbichler zum 70. Geburtstag am 8. Dezember 2020*, Berlin, De Gruyter, 2020, 953-955.

feelings may be considered careless in this case. With regard to the board's oversight function, Delaware case law already facilitates a potential duty of AI delegation, as the reasonable use of formal monitoring systems in corporate governance has been interpreted to follow from a director's duty of loyalty.[140] As of now, however, the costs of data governance and the AI system's operation do not justify the establishment of any obligation to use AI. The latter may change in the near future, because AI technology advances rapidly.

The replacement of one or more human directors by AI (hybrid or artificial board). A more distant prospect is the potential replacement of human directors by AI-driven robo-directors, resulting in autonomous governance intelligence. It is possible that human directors will soon share seats in the boardroom with one or more computers (a *hybrid board*[141]), that a single algorithm will replace all human directors (a *fused board*[142]) or that the board will be composed of multiple robo-directors, originating from differing manufacturers (an *artificial board*). To discover whether AI can ever replace human directors in conformity with the existing corporate laws, two preliminary questions must first be answered. First, from a technological point of view, the type of tasks suited for AI replacement must be clarified. In this respect, management literature acknowledges that, on the one hand, administrative work could be placed in the hands of AI, in the course of time.[143] Judgment work, on the other hand, requires creative, analytical and strategic skills,[144] and it is debatable whether AI will ever achieve them.[145]

140 See *inter alia* Delaware Supreme Court (US) January 24, 1963, Graham v. Allis-Chalmers Manufacturing Company, 1963 *Del.* 188 A.2d, 125; Delaware Supreme Court (US) September 27, 2018, *Marchand v. Barnhill*, 2018 *Del. Ch. Lexis* 316; Delaware Court of Chancery (US), September 25, 1996, In re Caremark International Inc. Derivative Litigation, 1996 *Del. Ch.* 698 A.2d, 959. See for an account on the evolving case law on the board's discretion regarding the design of compliance monitoring systems: C.M. BRUNER, "Artificially Intelligent Boards and the Future of Delaware Corporate Law", 2021, ssrn.com/abstract=3928237, 11-19.

141 S.A GRAMITTO RICCI, "Artificial Agents in Corporate Boardrooms", *Cornell Law Review* 2020, vol. 105, 900-903.

142 M. PETRIN, "Corporate Management in the Age of AI", *Columbia Business Law Review* 2019, vol. 3, 1002-1003.

143 See *inter alia* T.H. DAVENPORT and R. RONANKI, "Artificial Intelligence for the Real World - Don't Start with Moon Shots", *Harvard Business Review* 2018, hbr.org/2018/01/artificial-intelligence-for-the-real-world; M. PETRIN, "Corporate Management in the Age of AI", *Columbia Business Law Review* 2019, vol. 3, 985; J.B. BULLOCK, "Artificial Intelligence, Discretion, and Bureaucracy", *American Review of Public Administration* 2019, vol. 49, 4-7; R.T. KREUTZER and M. SIRRENBERG, *Understanding Artificial Intelligence - Fundamentals, Use Cases and Methods for a Corporate AI Journey*, Cham, Springer, 2020, 276; P. BUŁA and B. NIEDZIELSKI, *Management, Organisations and Artificial Intelligence - Where Theory Meets Practice*, New York, Routledge, 2022, 77.

144 A director's judgment work typically pertains to problem solving, collaboration, strategy, innovation and relations with individuals and shareholders; see A. AGRAWAL, J. GANS and A. GOLDFARB, "What to Expect From Artificial Intelligence", *MIT Sloan Management Review* 2017, vol. 58, 24.

145 For an overview of the predominant views in the literature, see S. MAKRIDAKIS, "The forthcoming Artificial Intelligence (AI) Revolution: Its Impact on Society and Firms", *Futures* 2017, vol. 90, 50-53;

It is also uncertain whether AI will be able to balance stakeholder interests,[146] or make ethical decisions. Second, most corporate laws presuppose that only natural and/or legal persons may be appointed as directors,[147] while AI is neither of those. Even if AI were to be endowed with personhood and thus be eligible as director, some jurisdictions such as Belgium, France and Spain require the designation of a natural person as permanent representative of that non-natural director (*i.e.* corporate director).[148] In spite of the apparent impossibility of appointing AI as director or its representative, a number of prominent scholars believe that algorithmic entities can be created in countries with flexible standards.[149] Moreover, it is interesting to explore what the legal implications would be if human directors could hypothetically be replaced by AI machines.

In this respect, it seems that current corporate frameworks are unfit for the adoption of autonomous AI. As mentioned previously, existing corporate governance best practices are predominantly based on agency conflicts between human directors and shareholders, which will not necessarily occur when an AI system is deployed in a governance setting.[150] Various AI applications can have different normative implications or goals, and thus do not necessarily translate into either greater shareholder-centrism, primacy of the board or progressive policies.[151] Moreover, robo-directors earn no money nor work towards the objective of doing so, with the consequence that pay-for-performance regimes will be of no use to make AI pursue the corporate interest.[152] Fiduciary duties

M. PETRIN, "Corporate Management in the Age of AI", *Columbia Business Law Review* 2019, vol. 3, 986-993. See also IBM, "The Quest for AI Creativity", www.ibm.com/watson/advantage-reports/future-of-artificial-intelligence/ai-creativity.html (retrieved on 31 October 2022).

146 See above.

147 For example, corporations whose registered office is located in Belgium and the Netherlands are permitted to appoint both natural and legal persons as a director; *cf.* Art. 7:85, para. 1 WVV (BE) and Art. 2:11 BW (NL). In contrast, UK company law requires at least one director to be a natural person, while German law totally forbids a legal person from attaining the status of board member; *cf.* S. 155 (1) Companies Act (UK), S. 6 (2) GmbHG (DE) and S. 76 (3) AktG (DE).

148 In respect of Belgian corporate law, see Art. 2:55, §1, first sentence WVV (BE). In respect of French corporate law, see Art. L.225-20 Code de commerce (FR) from which it is implicitly derived that the permanent representative must be a natural person; *cf.* e.g. P. LE CANNU, *La société anonyme à directoire*, Paris, LGDJ, 1979, 224. In respect of Spanish corporate law, see Art. 212*bis* (1) Ley de Sociedades de Capital (ES). See also P. DEL VAL TALENS, "Corporate Directors: In Search of a European Normative Model for Legal Persons as Board Members", *European Company and Financial Law Review* 2017, vol. 14, 631-632.

149 S. BAYERN *et al.*, "Company Law and Autonomous Systems: A Blueprint for Lawyers, Entrepreneurs, and Regulators", *Hastings Science and Technology Law Journal* 2017, vol. 9, 139-153.

150 See above.

151 See C.M. BRUNER, "Distributed Ledgers, Artificial Intelligence and the Purpose of the Corporation", *The Cambridge Law Journal* 2020, vol. 79, 450-453.

152 F. MÖSLEIN, "Robots in the Boardroom: Artificial Intelligence and Corporate Law" in W. BARFIELD and U. PAGALLO (eds.), *Research Handbook on the Law of Artificial Intelligence*, Cheltenham, Edward Elgar, 2018, 666-667.

such as the duty of loyalty and care are hardly intelligible for algorithms,[153] while the business judgment rule (*e.g.* in the USA, UK, Italy and Germany) seems impossible to apply to AI for various reasons.[154] In addition, some authors argue that the potential black box characteristic of *inter alia* neural networks hinders the collegiality of the board,[155] even though the thought process of human directors may be equally opaque.[156] All of the foregoing demonstrates that the introduction of robo-directors would prompt fundamental – if not existential – challenges for traditional corporate law.

The required human supervision and control of governance AI. As a first control question to the foregoing research questions, one must verify the extent to which human directors should supervise the various levels of governance intelligence in accordance with existing laws. Naturally, in most jurisdictions, the power of delegation does not relieve a director from its duty to supervise the exercise of delegated rights,[157] but the supervision duty differs from jurisdiction to jurisdiction and is often vaguely defined. Some authors argue that directors must at least generally oversee the selection and activities of governance intelligence, which requires the board members to have a basic understanding of how these devices operate.[158] An oversight model in which humans are expected to intervene in each decision cycle is undesirable as it will diminish all efficiency gains.[159]

153 See page 118 and footnote 92 above.

154 The business judgment rule essentially comes down to the rebuttable presumption that directors pursue the corporation's interests in good faith when their actions are being challenged. As a prerequisite for this rule, most legal systems require that the director must have had a certain amount of policy freedom, which seems to be absent when a decision is delegated to AI, since AI reasons linearly in pursuance of its set goals. Moreover, the contribution of AI to the decision-making process is sometimes not exactly traceable and ascertainable, while this is also a common requirement for the protection of the business judgment rule. See in this respect A. KAMALNATH, "The Perennial Quest for Board Independence – Artificial Intelligence to the Rescue?", *Albany Law Review* 2019-2020, vol. 83, 55-56; G.D. MOSCO, "AI and the Board Within Italian Corporate Law: Preliminary Notes", *European Company Law Journal* 2020, vol. 17, 95; U. NOACK, "Künstliche Intelligenz und die Unternehmensleitung" in G. BACHMANN, S. GRUNDMANN, A. MENGEL and K. KROLOP (eds.), *Festschrift für Christine Windbichler zum 70. Geburtstag am 8. Dezember 2020*, Berlin, De Gruyter, 2020, 955.

155 A.-G. KLECZEWSKI, "L'intelligence artificielle au service des administrateurs: une mise à l'épreuve de la collégialité?", *TRV-RPS* 2020, 520-521, no. 43.

156 For an interesting study on the opaque thought process of human judges, see J.Z. LIU and X. LI, "Legal Techniques for Rationalizing Biased Judicial Decisions: Evidence from Experiments with Real Judges", *Journal of Empirical Legal Studies* 2019, vol. 16, 630-670.

157 *E.g.*, A.N. MOHD-SULAIMAN, "Directors' Oversight Responsibility and the Impact of Specialist Skill", 2010, ssrn.com/abstract =1635154.

158 F. MÖSLEIN, "Robots in the Boardroom: Artificial Intelligence and Corporate Law" in W. BARFIELD and U. PAGALLO (eds.), *Research Handbook on the Law of Artificial Intelligence*, Cheltenham, Edward Elgar, 2018, 660.

159 E. HICKMAN and M. PETRIN, "Trustworthy AI and Corporate Governance: The EU's Ethics Guidelines for Trustworthy Artificial Intelligence from a Company Law Perspective", *EBOR* 2021, vol. 22, 602.

Besides the case law on corporate delegation, there are other rules that may require supervision of governance intelligence. For example, it is principally prohibited in the EU to entrust AI with a decision that produces legal effects or similarly significantly effects for a natural person, when the decision is based on personal data of that person (*e.g.* the selection and dismissal of a CEO).[160] Surprisingly, the EU Draft AI Act does not require special oversight duties for governance intelligence, since it does not qualify as high-risk in the current draft. However, existing regimes on directors' conflicts of interests may be invoked by shareholders to challenge AI's decision, when its training data, test data or algorithm reflects the financial interests of its human 'controllers' – the directors. For financial decisions, specific rules may come into play as well, such as the German financial regulation that requires substantial oversight of algorithmic trading on securities markets.[161] Even if the law does not demand human directors to supervise governance AI, they may be financially inclined to do so, if they or the company could be held liable for damage caused by the system.

Liability for algorithmic failure. The second control question pertains to the liability attribution for (un)lawful decisions made by governance intelligence that harm business partners of the company and/or third parties.[162] It remains an open question as to the extent to which current statutory and case law on product liability, general tort law and, specifically, director's liability can be applied to AI failures in governance context. Clearly, the AI system itself cannot be held liable for its faulty predictions or decisions, as it cannot pay damages or make amends.[163] Because of this liability gap,[164] the law is required to turn to legal entities or natural persons in order to enforce a liquidation of damages. In this respect, general tort law in most jurisdictions seems to hold the owner

160 The right of the individual *ex* Art. 22 GDPR to oppose automated decision-making is widely interpreted as a general prohibition for the data processor; see ARTICLE 29 DATA PROTECTION WORKING PARTY, "Guidelines on Automated individual decision-making and Profiling for the purposes of Regulation 2016/679", edpb.europa.eu/our-work-tools/our-documents/guidelines/automated-decision-making-and-profiling_en, 19-20; J. GOETGHEBUER, "De invloed van artikel 22 AVG op het gebruik van robo-advies binnen de beleggingssector. Met de rug tegen de muur?", *TBH-RDC* 2020, 146-147, no. 21.

161 S. 80, para. 2 Wertpapierhandelsgesetz (DE); A. FLECKNER, "Regulating Trading Practices" in N. MOLONEY, E. FERRAN, and J. PAYNE (eds.), *The Oxford Handbook of Financial Regulation*, Oxford, Oxford University Press, 2015, 619-623.

162 In my opinion, governance intelligence may be able to cause harm at any given autonomy level. Therefore, the current ambiguity of liability regimes applies to assisted, augmented and autonomous governance intelligence.

163 AI systems have "*no soul to be damned, and no body to be kicked*", as they do not own assets or bear liabilities. Neither do they have a social reputation or professional persona to protect. See S.A GRAMITTO RICCI, "Artificial Agents in Corporate Boardrooms", *Cornell Law Review* 2020, vol. 105, 886; C. PICCIAU, "The (Un)Predictable Impact of Technology on Corporate Governance", *Hastings Business Law Journal* 2021, vol. 17, 120.

164 *E.g.* S. DE CONCA, "Bridging the Liability Gaps: Why AI Challenges the Existing Rules on Liability and How to Design Human-empowering Solutions", in B. CUSTERS and E. FOSCH-VILLARONGA (eds.), *Law and Artificial Intelligence*, The Hague, Asser, 2022, 239-258.

of the AI system liable for algorithmic failure, which is mostly the company using it. The same result is achieved by applying the agency theory, whereby the AI system is considered an agent of the company (which is usually the case for directors), making its actions attributable to the company.[165] Therefore, one can assume *prima facie* that judges will be inclined to rely on fault liability of the company in case of governance AI failures. The latter does not exclude the personal liability of (human) directors who have contributed to the failure. Current fault liability regimes, however, put a great burden of proof on the shoulders of victims, as they are required to prove the faulty AI supervision of the company or its directors – an issue that the European Commission tries to resolve with its Draft AI Liability Directive.[166] Of course, special liability regimes may also be invoked, such as the one imposed by the EU's General Data Protection Regulation (GDPR), in case personal data is processed by governance intelligence without human intervention[167] or when the potential black box embedded in *inter alia* neural networks makes the system's reasoning opaque for decisions with significant or legal effects.[168]

3.4 *Potential Solutions to the Legal Problems Arising from Artificial Governance Intelligence*

General. The identified corporate law problems should be solved or at least alleviated for the instances in which it is shown that AI support can lead to more informed board decisions or that for a certain type of board decision, the decision quality of AI is clearly superior to that of human intelligence. The latter is in my view the case when a board decision is based on large amounts of data – considering that AI is able to translate incomprehensible mountains of data into consolidated chunks of information, which are easily managed and understandable for human directors. AI is also superior to human intelligence if it could be proven to make decisions faster than humans under the condition that the speed of decision-making is crucial for a specific board decision. Both

165 On the agency or 'organ' theory, see *e.g.* A. AVIRAM, "Officers' Fiduciary Duties and The Nature of Corporate Organs", *University of Illinois Law Review* 2013, 763-784.

166 See page 133 below.

167 See page 130 above.

168 The required transparency or 'explainability' of AI under Art. 22 GDPR remains controversial. See *inter alia* B. GOODMAN and S. FLAXMAN, "EU Regulations on Algorithmic Decision-Making and a Right to Explanation", *AI Magazine* 2017, 50-57; P. HACKER, R. KRESTEL, S. GRUNDMANN and F. NAUMANN, "Explainable AI Under Contract and Tort Law: Legal Incentives and Technical Challenges", *Artificial Intelligence and Law* 2020, vol. 28, 415-439; A. BIBAL, M. LOGNOUL, A. DE STREEL and B. FRÉNAY, "Legal Requirements on Explainability in Machine Learning", *Artificial Intelligence and Law* 2021, vol. 29, 149-169. Art. 52 (1) Draft AI Act does not require a form of transparency of low-risk AI systems towards individuals subject to its decisions. The provision solely requires natural persons interacting with the system to be aware of its artificial nature, while these persons are the directors in this case.

normative criteria presuppose a reasonable exercise of system benchmarking, to achieve a negligible chance of erroneous output generation (*i.e.* reasonable accuracy). That being said, limitations to AI power transfers may be needed as well, especially if biases, the black box nature of the system or other technological flaws hinder the transparency or independence of the system. In addition, if high risks to the fundamental rights of individuals are involved (*e.g.*, in the case of a sensitive decision on the company's personal data policy), the allowed degree of AI autonomy should be reduced or even prohibited.

Shifting foundations of corporate law. It is clear that rule-makers should provide legal frameworks that enable AI board appointments and AI task delegations on a decision-specific basis, *i.e.* only with regard to decisions for which the normative assumption explained previously is fulfilled. However, for all cases where AI delegation or replacement would be legally permitted, due respect for the regulatory concerns on maintaining human control of AI ought to be considered. In this respect, a form of obligatory oversight for each decision cycle of the system must be rejected, or should at least remain a last resort if the decision-making entails certain risks for the rights of individuals, as efficiency gains and incentives for innovation are stifled otherwise.

In respect of *autonomous* governance intelligence specifically, its legal recognition will require rule-makers to introduce profound changes to the fundamentals of corporate law. Existing *ex post* remedies in corporate law such as the fiduciary duties and liability of directors, designed to control human agency conflicts and director's behaviour, must be reimagined for the hypothesis of AI entering the boardroom. As elaborated on before, an AI system cannot be held liable and does not have its own interests, although inherent biases of its controllers may be reflected as AI is only as good as its inputs and programming.[169] For this reason, robo-directors will be less inclined to abuse corporate assets for personal gains. On the other hand, while the system can be programmed to pursue the interests of its principals, there is no guarantee that it will follow the programmed goals, follow all applicable legal rules and have a reasonable aversion to risks and losses. When AI is trusted with a crucial role in board decision-making, rule-compliant behaviour will need to be embedded in the algorithm's code. The latter calls for cutting-edge ex ante regulatory strategies,[170] such as abstract coding requirements for appointed robo-directors, which will entail far-reaching 'surgeries' to the anatomy of corporate law. After positioning the algorithm in the corporate structure, its abstract

169 *E.g.* A.H. RAYMOND, E. ARRINGTON STONE YOUNG and S.J. SHACKELFORD, "Building a Better Hal 9000: Algorithms, the Market, and the Need to Prevent the Engraining of Bias", *Northwestern Journal of Technology and Intellectual Property* 2018, vol. 15, 222-232.

170 F. MÖSLEIN, "Robots in the Boardroom: Artificial Intelligence and Corporate Law" in W. BARFIELD and U. PAGALLO (eds.), *Research Handbook on the Law of Artificial Intelligence*, Cheltenham, Edward Elgar, 2018, 666-667.

oversight will require technological know-how, which can be expected from neither shareholders nor human directors nor specialised courts. Therefore, some contemplate the need for direct governmental control of governance intelligence,[171] which might collide with fundamental principles such as private autonomy and entrepreneurial freedom.

One particular ex ante strategy, proposed by prominent scholars, is the regulation or calibration of corporate objectives.[172] As elaborated on before, algorithms pursue set goals. These goals reflect the exact content of the interests AI should pursue, which are, assumedly, aligned with the (best) interests of the company. Therefore, it may be more efficient for the legislator to regulate corporate goals, *i.e.* the AI system's goals. As a result, human biases embedded in the algorithm and data, in addition to algorithmic biases generated by the learning process, may be reduced to a minimum. However, it will require a hard balancing exercise to regulate corporate goals or purposes, in general, while also leaving ample scope for firm-specific goals, as the aforementioned fundamental principles must not be endangered.

Overall, however, if the implementation of autonomous governance intelligence would be permitted, AI could allow the company to benefit from the separation of ownership and control, while protecting the shareholders with a smart decision maker that is loyal and careful to them.[173] To achieve this, the option of shareholder 'say-on-manufacturer' rights in respect of robo-directors could be considered by lawmakers, as a complement to the traditional say-on-pay rights regarding human executives.

Liability for algorithmic failure *de lege ferenda*. While current regimes point towards the liability of the company deploying the AI system for harm caused by the system's decisions, it is not my opinion that the primary result of these regimes should be altered. The company using governance intelligence exclusively decides on the design and deployment of the system, as opposed to the third-party developer, vendor, provider or operator of the platform. In this respect, the company is the 'least-cost avoider' of algorithmic failure, and thus its liability is most justifiable.[174] What

171 A form of control by state agencies on governance intelligence could endanger the fundamental principles of private autonomy and entrepreneurial flexibility; see F. MÖSLEIN, "Robots in the Boardroom: Artificial Intelligence and Corporate Law" in W. BARFIELD and U. PAGALLO (eds.), *Research Handbook on the Law of Artificial Intelligence*, Cheltenham, Edward Elgar, 2018, 667.

172 J. ARMOUR and H. EIDENMÜLLER, "Self-Driving Corporations?" in H. EIDENMÜLLER and G. WAGNER (eds.), *Law by Algorithm*, Tübingen, Mohr Siebeck, 2021, 177-179.

173 S.A GRAMITTO RICCI, "Artificial Agents in Corporate Boardrooms", *Cornell Law Review* 2020, vol. 105, 872.

174 J. ARMOUR and H. EIDENMÜLLER, "Self-Driving Corporations?" in H. EIDENMÜLLER and G. WAGNER (eds.), *Law by Algorithm*, Tübingen, Mohr Siebeck, 2021, 180-182.

matters, and should be up for debate, is the type of liability that the company should face, *i.e.* fault liability or strict liability? On the one hand, fault liability puts the difficult task of proving negligence or faulty supervision in the hands of victims, often resulting in no compensation.[175] If one were to prefer fault liability, then rebuttable presumptions of fault and/or causal link are necessary to alleviate the burden of proof for injured parties, as the company itself has the best access to information on its AI system. On the other hand, a strict liability regime would stifle the company's incentive to innovate and requires it to have sufficient funds to compensate all victims.[176] The latter could be countered by imposing a liability cap,[177] or a mandatory liability insurance with minimum amount of coverage, as has been suggested before in the literature on self-driving cars.[178] Some authors contend that companies should be liable for harms of their 'employed' algorithms just as they currently are for harms of their human employees,[179] but this idea is not appropriate for jurisdictions where directors – likewise robo-directors – are not considered as employees.

A plethora of alternative liability approaches can be found in the literature for artificial governance intelligence. Regarding self-driving subsidiaries, for instance, a general liability of the controlling shareholder for corporate debts (*i.e.* piercing of the corporate veil) seems well founded vis-à-vis tort creditors.[180] Others argue that actions against the AI system itself should be made possible, which purportedly necessitates its bestowal with legal personality.[181] The latter condition ought to be discarded, however, as legal personhood is not a prerequisite for states to grant rights or duties to an entity.[182] On

175 For a general account on fault liability versus strict liability, see S. SHAVELL, "Strict Liability versus Negligence", *The Journal of Legal Studies* 1980, vol. 9, 1-25.

176 J. ARMOUR and H. EIDENMÜLLER, "Self-Driving Corporations?" in H. EIDENMÜLLER and G. WAGNER (eds.), *Law by Algorithm*, Tübingen, Mohr Siebeck, 2021, 182.

177 As the liability risk of AI is temporary and inherent to all new technologies, and because AI does not have a catastrophic potential, a liability cap may not be justified; see *e.g.* M. CHATZIPANAGIOTIS and G. LELOUDAS, "Automated Vehicles and Third-Party Liability: A European Perspective", *University of Illinois Journal of Law, Technology & Policy* 2020, 192-193.

178 H. EIDENMÜLLER, "The Rise of Robots and the Law of Humans", in H. EIDENMÜLLER and G. WAGNER (eds.), *Law by Algorithm*, Tübingen, Mohr Siebeck, 2021, 15-16.

179 M.E. DIAMANTIS, "Employed Algorithms: A Labor Model of Corporate Liability for AI", *Duke Law Journal* 2023, vol. 72, 844-848.

180 J. ARMOUR and H. EIDENMÜLLER, "Self-Driving Corporations?" in H. EIDENMÜLLER and G. WAGNER (eds.), *Law by Algorithm*, Tübingen, Mohr Siebeck, 2021, 182. See more generally on piercing of the corporate veil: H. HANSMANN and R. KRAAKMAN, "Toward Unlimited Shareholder Liability for Corporate Torts", *The Yale Law Journal* 1991, vol. 100, 1879-1934.

181 M. PETRIN, "Corporate Management in the Age of AI", *Columbia Business Law Review* 2019, vol. 3, 1015-1016.

182 For instance, in a number of jurisdictions, the general partnership is endowed with certain rights and duties, in spite of its lacking legal personality. See M. BLACKETT-ORD and S. HAREN, *Partnership Law: The Modern Law of Firms, Limited Partnerships and LLPs*, Haywards Heath, Bloomsbury Professional, 2020, 9, no. 1.13. See also in respect of the Belgian unlimited partnership (the "*maatschap*"):

the contrary, legal personhood is merely a linguistic symbol or heuristic formula to conveniently label a set of legal capacities designated by the state,[183] of which the suitability for AI is disputed.[184] It seems more appropriate to give AI systems limited rights and duties that enable actions against them, instead of granting these systems the full package that legal personhood entails. This hypothesis prompts new questions pertaining to these entities' lack of financial resources and the applicable standards of behaviour.[185]

Recently, the European Commission proposed a differentiated approach of fault and strict liability for damage caused by AI. For material damage (including data losses) suffered by natural persons, a strict liability regime for defective AI is suggested, which results in liability of the manufacturer for defects in the algorithm – instead of the company using AI.[186] For all other damage in a non-contractual environment, the Commission did not opt for a strict liability regime. Instead, a (limited and conditional) rebuttable presumption of causal link between fault and AI output (or lack thereof) was put on the table, while maintaining the member states' own regimes of fault liability.[187] These proposals came after years of discussion on the application field of the 1985 Product Liability Directive.[188] The result, however, has little significance for governance intelligence systems. Moreover, harm caused by AI in a contractual and commercial context (B2B contracts) will be of a greater magnitude, but is not covered by any of the proposed regulatory measures in the EU as of now.[189] Therefore, member states should opt for a broader application field of its transposition laws, which has been allowed by the European Court of Justice (ECJ) in other contexts.[190]

S. LANDUYT, F. DESMYTTERE and L. MAES, "De maatschap: van contract naar instituut?" in J. BAEL (ed.), *Rechtskroniek voor het notariaat deel 35*, Herentals, KnopsPublishing, 2019, 62-65, no. 71-77.

183 J. ARMOUR, H. HANSMANN and R. KRAAKMAN, "What Is Corporate Law?" in R. KRAAKMAN *et al.* (eds.), *The Anatomy of Corporate Law: A Comparative and Functional Approach*, Oxford, Oxford University Press, 2017, 8; S.A GRAMITTO RICCI, "Artificial Agents in Corporate Boardrooms", *Cornell Law Review* 2020, vol. 105, 892-893.

184 See page 121, footnote 108 above.

185 M. PETRIN, "Corporate Management in the Age of AI", *Columbia Business Law Review* 2019, vol. 3, 1016.

186 See the Draft Revised Product Liability Directive.

187 Art. 4 Draft AI Liability Directive. See also V. SCHOLLAERT and J. DE BRUYNE, "Voorstel Richtlijn AI-aansprakelijkheid – Verkennende analyse vanuit Belgisch perspectief", *NJW* 2023, 582-587, no. 17-25.

188 *E.g.* G. WAGNER, "Robot Liability", 2018, ssrn.com/abstract=3198764; M. CHATZIPANAGIOTIS and G. LELOUDAS, "Automated Vehicles and Third-Party Liability: A European Perspective", *University of Illinois Journal of Law, Technology & Policy* 2020, 118-131; J. DE BRUYNE, E. VAN GOOL and T. GILS, "Tort Law and Damage Caused by AI Systems" in J. DE BRUYNE, and C. VANLEENHOVE (eds.), *Artificial Intelligence and the Law*, Antwerpen, Intersentia, 2021, 359-403.

189 See for a critical account on both the Draft AI Liability Directive and the Draft Revised Product Liability Directive: P. HACKER, "The European AI Liability Directives – Critique of a Half-Hearted Approach and Lessons for the Future", *Computer Law & Security Review* 2023, vol. 51, Art. 105871.

190 *E.g.* ECJ 12 July 2012, C-602/10, *SC Volksbank România SA v. Autoritatea Națională* pentru Protecția Consumatorilor – Comisariatul Județean pentru Protecția Consumatorilor Călărași (CJPC).

4 CONCLUSION

This chapter underpinned the impending entry of corporate law into a new era, that is, the era of artificial governance intelligence. Indeed, the chapter has shown that AI is increasingly deployed as a support tool for the core functions of the board of directors and the management of corporations, such as monitoring, corporate strategy setting and daily management. Since AI is said to rationalise decision-making, reduce the risk of groupthink and boost the independence of board members, it is expected that the assisted role of AI in corporate governance will soon transform into a leading one, as more corporations are attempting to appoint algorithms as directors. Consequently, the World Economic Forum made the claim that by 2026, human directors sharing their decision-making powers with AI will become the new normal.[191]

Systems of artificial governance intelligence can be classified into several categories on the basis of their level of autonomy, which determines the allocation of decision rights between the AI system vis-à-vis the board of directors. In case of assisted intelligence, human directors selectively rely on AI for administrative tasks. At the augmented stage, human directors use AI output to enhance the informative basis of their decisions. Here, AI contributes to core decision-making or judgment work of the board, but it does not enjoy stand-alone decision rights. In its final autonomous stage, AI is bestowed with independent decision rights through a delegation of core governance powers or through its appointment as director. Here, a hybrid board of humans and machines is possible, or all human members could be replaced by one or more AI systems, resulting in a fused or artificial boardroom. Except when the goals of the corporation are very narrow, the latter remains science fiction today.

The emergence of AI in the corporate realm raises many questions of corporate law, which is tailored to human decision makers. While assisted intelligence seems permissible under current corporate frameworks, human directors do not have the right to delegate core governance tasks to AI. However, it is uncertain which decisions belong to this category. Even when delegation is permitted, it seems likely that humans should still supervise artificial governance intelligence to a certain extent that does not diminish efficiency gains. As boards are generally expected to make decisions on an informed basis, the right of a director to delegate limited decision rights to AI could evolve into a duty, considering the superior capabilities of AI for certain well-defined tasks. An outright appointment of AI as director seems impossible under the current

191 WORLD ECONOMIC FORUM, "Survey Report: Deep Shift – Technology Tipping Points and Societal Impact", *Global Agenda Council on the Future of Software & Society* 2015, www3.weforum.org/docs/WEF_GAC15_Technological_Tipping_Points_report_2015.pdf, 21.

regimes, but via a detour, algorithmic entities seem plausible. The latter poses major challenges to the foundations of corporate law, which is focused on controlling human agency conflicts through director's fiduciary duties and liability. Instead, AI pursues set goals, operates without self-interests other than maximising its utility function, does not act in good or bad faith in the same way that humans do, yet may still reflect or even exacerbate biases of its human controllers. Therefore, regulatory strategies should be revised to ex ante remedies, such as regulating corporate purposes and imposing the embedding of rule-compliant behaviour into the code of robo-directors. The liability for algorithmic failure will likely be attributed to the corporation itself, but policy debates on the burden of proof should determine the very nature of this liability regime. New phenomena such as entities without leaders (DAOs) or without members (algorithmic entities) will undoubtedly challenge corporate systems even more than robo-directors do. It is clear that further research on the shifting anatomy of corporate law is needed in order to ensure that novel corporate rules are not dictated by the quickly evolving AI technology but based on calm reasoning instead.

Due Diligence in M&A Transactions*

*Bart Bellen and Marthe Wouters***

1 Purpose and legal relevance of due diligence in the M&A process

1.1 *Role of due diligence in the M&A process*

A critical aspect of any acquisition process relates to the buyer's due diligence.[1] During the due diligence phase, the purchaser and his advisers will get access to confidential information regarding the target company, allowing them to assess the quality of the target company's assets and liabilities and to investigate possible hidden liabilities (or assets). The due diligence review aims to identify any risks or specific issues that are material in the context of the sector or industry in which the target operates. As such, the results of the due diligence review have a central role in the negotiation phase of the transaction, influencing both the purchase price and, for example, the representations and warranties and specific indemnities to be given by the seller.

The due diligence review is carried out mostly in the pre-contractual phase of the transaction. However, an additional review can also take place post signing (as a so-called confirmatory due diligence). As illustrated in the timeline below, the actual organisation of the buyer's due diligence will depend on the transaction process and whether or not the transaction is preceded by a competitive auction process.

In a basic transaction scenario, one (group of) seller(s) negotiates the acquisition of the target with one (group of) purchaser(s), on a one-to-one basis. The purchaser's due diligence will then typically start after initial information exchanges and negotiations and after entering into any necessary pre-contractual agreements (*i.e.* non-disclosure agreement and letter of intent/memorandum of understanding).

---

* This contribution is based on B. BELLEN, *Share Purchase Agreements – Belgian Law and Practice*, Antwerpen/Cambridge, Intersentia, 2016, 379 p. and the relevant results of the fifth edition of the M&A Survey (B. BELLEN, K. DE WAEL, C. MERGEAY and B. HERMANS, 'M&A Survey – 5th edition', *TRV-RPS* 2021, 597-623).

** Bart Bellen is a partner at Contrast. Marthe Wouters is a paralegal at Contrast.

1 B. BELLEN, K. DE WAEL, C. MERGEAY and B. HERMANS, 'M&A Survey – 5th edition', *TRV-RPS* 2021 (597), 603-604.

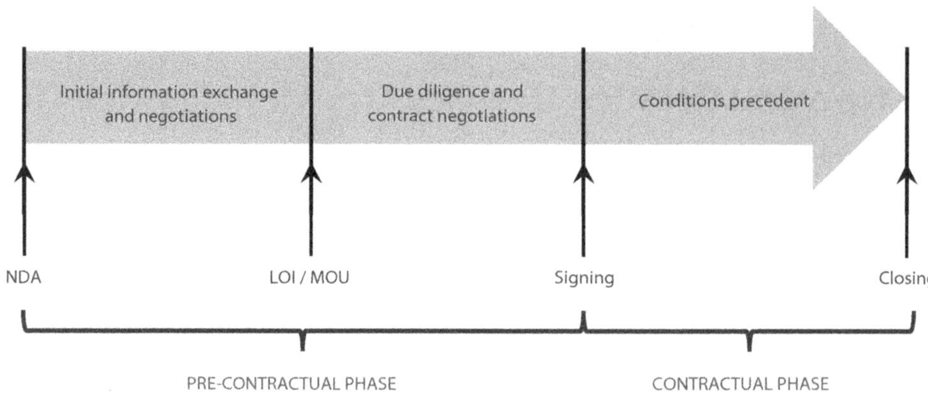

However, especially in deals with higher transaction values, the use of competitive auctions has become prevalent.[2] In such a case, the seller offers the opportunity to purchase the shares in the target company to several candidate purchasers simultaneously. This allows multiple prospective buyers to bid for the target company and therefore maximises competition between various candidate purchasers until an advanced stage of the negotiations.[3]

Further advantages of organising a competitive auction are that this approach allows the seller to retain control over the transaction process and timing and to optimise the conditions of the transaction (such as maximising the purchase price, limiting conditions precedent and representations and warranties…).[4]

In the context of a competitive auction, the bidders' due diligence review typically follows a more phased approach, whereby the level of detail of the seller's disclosure increases during the process as the number of potential purchasers is reduced. Only the potential purchasers on the 'short list' will be allowed to conduct a more detailed ('phase 2') due diligence review. However, even this review will often be subject to certain restrictions. As such, part of the review is sometimes deferred to the period after signing the contract in a confirmatory due diligence.[5]

2 Ibid. (597), 600.

3 B. BELLEN, *Share Purchase Agreements – Belgian Law and Practice*, Antwerpen/Cambridge, Intersentia, 2016,14-15.

4 There are however also potential disadvantages and risks. See B. BELLEN, *Share Purchase Agreements – Belgian Law and Practice*, Antwerpen/Cambridge, Intersentia, 2016,16.

5 B. BELLEN, *Share Purchase Agreements – Belgian Law and Practice*, Antwerpen/Cambridge, Intersentia, 2016, 15-16.

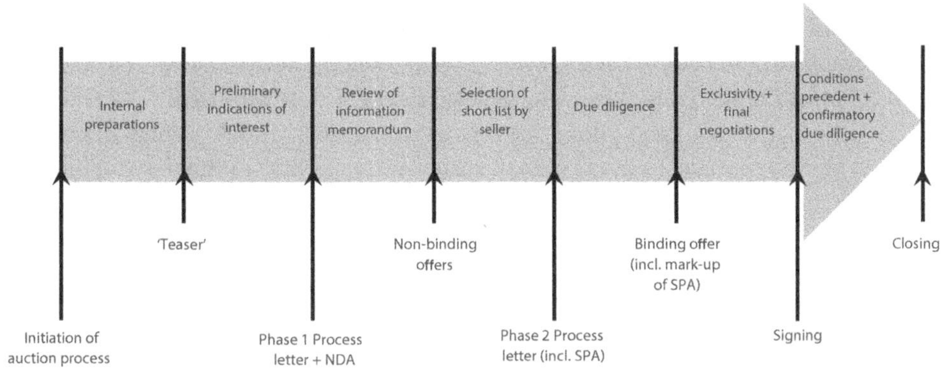

1.2 Vendor due diligence

In some transactions, the seller conducts a 'vendor due diligence' before starting the acquisition process.[6] In such a case, the seller will select and instruct external advisers to conduct a due diligence review regarding certain aspects of the target company, based on a due diligence scope determined by the seller.

The resulting due diligence reports are subsequently made available to the candidate purchaser. The terms and conditions on which the purchaser may rely on the vendor due diligence reports are specified by the external advisers that have conducted the due diligence. Such terms are usually confirmed in the vendor due diligence reports themselves or in separate 'reliance letters'. The seller itself will normally not assume any direct responsibility for the vendor due diligence reports.

In the context of competitive auctions, vendor due diligence reports have particular advantages and are therefore used more often.[7] Among those advantages are the following:

- the target company will only have to deal with one due diligence review, instead of consecutive reviews by multiple candidate purchasers;
- all candidate purchasers receive identical information at the same time, which ensures their equal treatment throughout the auction process;
- multiple candidate purchasers can be informed without already having to incur significant transaction costs, thereby lowering transaction barriers for candidate purchasers;

6 B. BELLEN, K. DE WAEL, C. MERGEAY and B. HERMANS, 'M&A Survey – 5th edition', *TRV-RPS* 2021 (597), 603-604.

7 Ibid.

- the seller can postpone a decision to grant exclusivity to one candidate purchaser and keep multiple candidate purchasers involved in the auction until an advanced stage so that competition between the candidates and their bids is maximised;
- the due diligence review can be done beforehand so that considerable savings can be achieved for both parties, in terms of both costs and time, with minimal disruption and loss of momentum during the auction; and
- if the transaction succeeds, the costs of vendor due diligence can be taken into account in the context of the financing of the transaction.

Vendor due diligence reports are, furthermore, more prevalent in larger transactions or if the seller is a private equity or venture capital investor.[8]

2 INFORMATION RIGHTS AND OBLIGATIONS OF THE PARTIES

As set out previously, the due diligence review is conducted primarily by the candidate purchaser. Under applicable law, the purchaser indeed has a pre-contractual duty of investigation and is therefore in the first instance responsible for investigating the object of the sale. The seller, on the other hand, has, in principle, no general obligation to proactively inform the purchaser. Traditional case law indeed tends to emphasise the information obligations of the purchaser when assessing information deficiencies.[9]

8 Ibid.

9 Luik 1 December 2016, *TRV-RPS* 2021, 229-233, annotation A. VANHEES; Court of commerce Brussels 15 October 2008, *TRV* 2011, 587; court of commerce Brussels 25 August 2005, *TRV* 2011, 593; BELLEN, B. and LECLERCQ, D., 'M&A Kroniek – Chronique de jurisprudence en M&A (2000-2017)', *TRV* 2019 (504), 507-514; B. BELLEN and J. STEVENS, 'Bedrog bij de totstandkoming van een overnameovereenkomst en de verhouding met de precontractuele informatieplicht' (annotation regarding court of appeal Ghent 27 October 2008), *TRV* 2011 (577), 579, No. 12; A. DE BOECK, 'De wilsgebreken dwaling en bedrog vandaag. Responsabilisering en ankerplaats voor de precontractuele informatieverplichting' in R. VAN RANSBEECK (ed.), *Wilsgebreken*, Bruges, die Keure, 2006 (37), 80-81; A. DE BOECK, *Informatierechten en -plichten bij de totstandkoming en uitvoering van overeenkomsten. Grondslagen, draagwijdte en sancties*, Antwerp, Intersentia, 2000, 99; W. DEJONGHE and M. CORYNEN, 'De rechtspositie van de overnemer bij de verwerving van een onderneming door acquisitie van aandelen', *V&F* 1997 (85), 90, No. 23; P.A. FORIERS, 'Dol par réticence dolosive et erreur inexcusable' in Y. POULLET, P. WÉRY and P. WYNANTS (eds.), *Liber amicorum Michel Coipel*, Brussels, Kluwer, 2004 (315), 319-320; D. FRERIKS, 'Onderzoeks- en mededelingsverplichting in het contractenrecht', *TPR* 1992 (1187), 1189; S. MARYSSE, 'Due diligence-onderzoek, bedrog en culpa in contrahendo' (annotation regarding court of appeal Antwerp 3 December 2007), *TBBR-RGDC* 2009 (257), 258-259; G. SCHRANS, 'De progressieve totstandkoming der contracten', *TPR* 1984 (1), 10; B. VAN DEN BERGH, 'De overdracht van een handelszaak en de informatieplicht vanwege de overdrager: spreken is zilver, zwijgen is fout' (annotation regarding court of appeal Brussels 14 March 2008), *TBBR-RGDC* 2009, No. 7 (366), 368-369; Y. VERLEISDONK, E. JANSSENS and M. WILKENHUYSEN, *Due Diligence*, Ghent, Larcier, 2011, 11-13, 22 and 27; S. VERVERKEN, 'Verklaringen en waarborgen bij de verkoop van aandelen' in G.L. BALLON and H. DE DECKER (a.o.) (eds.), *Koop – Aandelen*, Antwerp, Intersentia, 2016, 154-155. *Contra*: J. PEETERS and P.-J. VAN HOUDENHOVE, 'Actualia overnames en herstructureringen. Contractuele

However, as a general rule, the purchaser may rely on the accuracy of the information that he receives from the seller.[10] As a result, the seller may commit a pre-contractual fault in accordance with Article 5.17 of the Civil Code and Article 1382 of the old Civil Code (*culpa in contrahendo*) if he provides inaccurate information to the purchaser in a negligent way (*i.e.* if the seller should have known that the information was inaccurate).[11]

In addition, a failure to provide (complete) information may in certain circumstances constitute a pre-contractual fault.[12] Once the parties have entered into contract negotiations, the general standard of care and prudence may in particular circumstances indeed impose an obligation on the seller to provide the purchaser with information that is of importance in the context of the formation or the execution of the share purchase agreement.[13] It is thereby generally assumed that the information obligation of the seller begins only where the duty of investigation of the purchaser ends.[14]

Recent case law of the Court of Cassation, however, does suggest an evolution whereby (deliberate) fraud (*bedrog/dol*) has been established in the event of deliberate omission by the seller, regardless of any failure of the buyer to discharge its own duty of investigation.[15]

---

inbedding van de onderhandelingsfase en buitencontractuele aandachtspunten' in K. BYTTEBIER and T. WERA (eds.), *Actuele evoluties inzake overnames en herstructureringen*, Antwerp, Intersentia, 2014 (3), 12-13; Please also refer to J.P. MASSON, 'Les fourberies silencieuses' (annotation regarding Court of Cassation 8 June 1978), *RCJB* 1979 (527), 529 and following.

10 E.g. Luik 1 December 2016, *TRV-RPS* 2021, 229-233, annotation A. VANHEES.

11 Art. 5.17 Civil Code; A. DE BOECK, *Informatierechten en -plichten bij de totstandkoming en uitvoering van overeenkomsten. Grondslagen, draagwijdte en sancties*, Antwerp, Intersentia, 2000, 201-202; W. DE BONDT, 'Precontractuele aansprakelijkheid' in M. STORME (ed.), *Recht halen uit aansprakelijkheid*, Ghent, Mys & Breesch, 1993 (147), 164; W. DE BONDT, 'Redelijkheid en billijkheid in het contractenrecht', *TPR* 1984 (95), 101; D. FRERIKS, 'Onderzoeks- en mededelingsverplichting in het contractenrecht', *TPR* 1992 (1187), 1222; R. KRUITHOF, H. BOCKEN, F. DE LY and B. DE TEMMERMAN, "Overzicht van rechtspraak (1981–1992). Verbintenissen", *TPR* 1994 (171), 282; G. SCHRANS, 'De progressieve totstandkoming der contracten', *TPR* 1984 (1), 11; Y. VERLEISDONK, E. JANSSENS and M. WILKENHUYSEN, *Due Diligence*, Ghent, Larcier, 2011, 21, No. 74.

12 S. MARYSSE, 'Due diligence-onderzoek, bedrog en culpa in contrahendo' (annotation regarding court of appeal Antwerp 3 December 2007), *TBBR-RGDC* 2009 (257), 263; Y. VERLEISDONK, E. JANSSENS and M. WILKENHUYSEN, *Due Diligence*, Ghent, Larcier, 2011, 23, No. 79.

13 A. VAN OEVELEN, 'Juridische verhoudingen en aansprakelijkheid bij onderhandelingen over (commerciële) contracten', *DAOR* 1990, No. 14 (43), 52; Y. VERLEISDONK, E. JANSSENS and M. WILKENHUYSEN, *Due Diligence*, Ghent, Larcier, 2011, 19, No. 66.

14 I. CLAEYS and T. TANGHE, *Algemeen contractenrecht*, Antwerp, Intersentia, 2022, 78, No. 71; H. NELEN, T. DE DEYGERE and C. WUYTS, 'Wanneer zwijgen bedrog wordt' (annotation regarding Court of Cassation 11 March 2019), *TBH* 2019, 1259-1267; K. RENIERS, 'Koop-verkoop van aandelen vs. koop-verkoop onroerend goed: precontractuele informatieverstrekking', *T.Not.* 2018 (764), 770 and references contained therein.

15 Court of Cassation 11 March 2019, *TBH* 2019, 1258, annotation H. NELEN, T. DE DEYGERE and T. WUYTS.

An active information obligation can furthermore be imposed on the seller by law but may also result from the specific circumstances in which the negotiations take place.[16] Whether or not there is an active information obligation depends on whether a normally careful and diligent person placed in the same circumstances would inform the potential purchaser.[17] Furthermore, an active information obligation may result from an agreement, the seller's professional duties or the requirements of good faith.[18] In this respect, the characteristics of the relationship between the parties (e.g. a relationship of trust, the parties' respective professional expertise or imbalance between the level of experience or deal support) and the professional capacity of the parties may be relevant.[19] For instance, it is generally assumed that a professional seller has an information obligation towards a purchaser who is not acting in a professional capacity.[20] Conversely, in the context of a management buy-out, it can be assumed that the purchaser is already well informed.

---

16 A. DE BOECK, 'De wilsgebreken dwaling en bedrog vandaag. Responsabilisering en ankerplaats voor de precontractuele informatieverplichting' in R. VAN RANSBEECK (ed.), *Wilsgebreken*, Bruges, die Keure, 2006 (37), 83; Y. VERLEISDONK, E. JANSSENS and M. WILKENHUYSEN, *Due Diligence*, Ghent, Larcier, 2011, 23, No. 81.

17 J. DEL CORRAL, *Dwaling*, Brussels, Larcier, 2011, 75; A. DE BOECK, 'Dwaling in de ban van de precontractuele informatie- en onderzoeksplichten' (annotation regarding court of first instance Hasselt 6 January 2000), *RW* 2001-2002 (354), 356.

18 Court of commerce Kortrijk 4 September 1981, *RW* 1982-1983, 1399; B. BELLEN and J. STEVENS, 'Bedrog bij de totstandkoming van een overnameovereenkomst en de verhouding met de precontractuele informatieplicht' (annotation regarding court of appeal Ghent 27 October 2008), *TRV* 2011 (577), 580, No. 15; A. DE BOECK, 'De wilsgebreken dwaling en bedrog vandaag. Responsabilisering en ankerplaats voor de precontractuele informatieverplichting' in R. Van Ransbeeck (ed.), *Wilsgebreken*, Bruges, die Keure, 2006 (37), 83; W. DEJONGHE and M. CORYNEN, 'De rechtspositie van de overnemer bij de verwerving van een onderneming door acquisitie van aandelen', *V&F* 1997 (85), 90, No. 23; F. HELLEMANS and B. HEYNICKX, 'Wilsgebreken in het vennootschapsrecht' in R. VAN RANSBEECK (ed.), *Wilsgebreken*, Bruges, die Keure, 2006 (169), 226, No. 65; Y. VERLEISDONK, E. JANSSENS and M. WILKENHUYSEN, *Due Diligence*, Ghent, Larcier, 2011, 23-24; M. WAUTERS, 'Garanties bij overdracht van aandelen', *DAOR* 1997, No. 44 (17), 44. However, according to the court of commerce Brussels, an active information obligation can only be imposed by law (court of commerce Brussels 15 October 2008, *TRV* 2011, 587).

19 Court of appeal Brussels 14 March 2008, *TBBR-RGDC* 2009, 365, annotation B. VAN DEN BERGH; court of appeal Ghent 10 September 2012, *RW* 2013-2014, 1427, annotation K. RENIERS; B. BELLEN and J. STEVENS, 'Bedrog bij de totstandkoming van een overnameovereenkomst en de verhouding met de precontractuele informatieplicht' (annotation regarding court of appeal Ghent 27 October 2008), *TRV* 2011 (577), 580; A. DE BOECK, 'Wilsgebreken' in X, Comm.Bijz.Ov., Mechelen, Kluwer, loose-leaf (1), 21; D. FRERIKS, 'Onderzoeks- en mededelingsverplichting in het contractenrecht', *TPR* 1992 (1187), 1235; B. VAN DEN BERGH, 'De overdracht van een handelszaak en de informatieplicht vanwege de overdrager: spreken is zilver, zwijgen is fout' (annotation regarding court of appeal Brussels 14 March 2008), *TBBR-RGDC* 2009, No. 7 (366), 369; B. VAN DEN BERGH, 'Dwaling versus (precontractuele) informatieplicht: the odd couple?' (annotation regarding court of appeal Antwerp 12 June 2006), *RW* 2008-2009 (284) 285.

20 Court of appeal Antwerp 12 June 2006, *RW* 2008-2009, 279, annotation B. VAN DEN BERGH; court of appeal Brussels 20 May 1987, *TBH-RDC* 1988, 35, annotation D. DEVOS; court of appeal Ghent 15 October 2007, *TGR* 2008, No. 3, 197; court of first instance Antwerp 14 January 2004, *TBBR-RGDC* 2006, 498; court of commerce Brussels 15 October 2008, *TRV* 2011, 587; court of commerce Brussels 25 August 2005, *TRV* 2011, 593; court of commerce Brussels 26 March 1997, *TBH-RDC* 1997, 330 (description J.-P.

The active information obligation of the parties has recently been codified as follows in Article 5.16 of the Civil Code:

> The parties provide each other during the pre-contractual negotiations with the information which the law, good faith and customs, in light of the capacity of the parties, their reasonable expectations and the object of the agreement, requires them to provide.

This new provision sets out a balanced, general information obligation which, in principle, applies equally to both parties. However, it appears from the preparatory works that the legislature does not intend to impose a higher standard of information obligations on the parties with this article than the previously existing standards developed by doctrine and case law. Indeed, it is confirmed in such preparatory works that there is no general obligation for a party to actively provide all information in its possession to its (future) counterpart. Only in the cases provided for in Article 5.16 of the Civil Code, particularly if good faith so requires, does a seller have an obligation to actively inform the purchaser.[21]

A fault in the context of the pre-contractual information exchange may, of course, have a significant influence on the purchaser's decision to enter into the share purchase agreement or on the terms and conditions laid down in the agreement. Pursuant to Article 5.33 of the Civil Code (Art. 1108 of the old Civil Code), the purchaser's consent to enter into the agreement should be free from defects (*'wilsgebreken'/'vices du consentement'*).[22] Accordingly, the seller's breach of the pre-contractual information obligation may indeed in particular circumstances cause the purchaser to demand the annulment of the share purchase agreement on the basis of fraud (*'bedrog'/'dol'*) in accordance with Article 5:35 of the Civil Code (Art. 1116 of the old Civil Code) or error (*'dwaling'/'erreur'*) in accordance with Article 5.34 of the Civil Code (Art. 1110 of the old Civil Code).[23] This principle has been confirmed in Article 5.17 of the Civil Code.

BUYLE); E. DIRIX, 'Dwaling en bedrog bij de koop van kunst en antiek' in K. RIMANIQUE (ed.), *Kunst en recht*, Antwerp, Kluwer, 1985 (95), 102-103.

21 Proposal of Law on the introduction of Book 5 'Obligations' of the Civil Code, *Parl. St.* 2020-2021, No. 55-1806/1, 25-26; B. WEYTS, 'De totstandkoming van een overeenkomst. Huidig en nieuw recht van naderbij bekeken' in J. BAECK, I. CLAEYS en A. WYLLEMAN (eds.), *Hervorming van het verbintenissen- en goederenrecht*, Mechelen, Wolters Kluwer Belgium, 2022 (69), 81.

22 W. VAN GERVEN and A. VAN OEVELEN, *Verbintenissenrecht*, Leuven, Acco, 2021, 114.

23 In theory, the share purchase agreement can also be annulled on grounds of violence ('geweld'/'violence') in accordance with Art. 5.36 of the Civil Code (Arts. 1111-1113 of the old Civil Code) or 'qualified lesion' ("gekwalificeerde benadeling" / "lésion qualifiée"), although such situations will occur only rarely in the context of company acquisitions (F. HELLEMANS and B. HEYNICKX, 'Wilsgebreken in het vennootschapsrecht' in R. VAN RANSBEECK (ed.), *Wilsgebreken*, Bruges, die Keure, 2006 (169), 227. For a general discussion of these concepts, please refer to B. BELLEN, *Share Purchase Agreements – Belgian Law*

3 ORGANISATION OF DUE DILIGENCE – DATA ROOM

The due diligence review is typically organised based on a 'data room', where selected information regarding the target company is made available to the prospective buyers and their advisers.

Where previously physical data rooms were more common, the use of 'virtual' (digital) data rooms has now become standard market practice. The advantages of digital applications with secured access (organising large amounts of information, anonymous and simultaneous access of multiple prospective buyers, customised access rights, phased disclosure of information, control over the information reviewed, etc.) have become self-evident in company acquisition processes. It has therefore become truly exceptional for a seller to make the due diligence information available to the buyer solely in a physical data room. On some occasions, however, a physical data room will still be made available in combination with a virtual data room.[24]

The compilation of the due diligence information to be included in the data room is a particularly delicate exercise for the seller. While the seller has, in principle, no proactive obligation to inform the purchaser, the seller does have a responsibility to answer any questions of the purchaser in a diligent manner.[25] In addition, the seller should ensure that the data room is compiled diligently and with due regard to its information obligations pursuant to preliminary transaction documents (e.g. a non-disclosure agreement or letter of intent) and Article 5.16 of the Civil Code (e.g. ensuring a disclosure according to customary professional standards and the reasonable expectations of candidate purchasers). As such, it would be recommended for a seller to communicate transparently about unusual limitations in relation to the disclosure.

The purchaser's typical approach to the due diligence will be to submit a comprehensive information request list to the seller. On the one hand, the purpose of the questionnaire is practical and aimed at ensuring that the seller discloses the information that the purchaser considers relevant. On the other hand, the information request list also has legal relevance as it explicitly sets out the purchaser's expectations as to the seller's disclosures and explicitly solicits answers from the seller, which the seller will be

and Practice, Antwerpen/Cambridge, Intersentia, 2016, 47-52; E. SWAENEPOEL, 'Geweld, benadeling en gekwalificeerde benadeling: een stand van zaken naar Belgisch recht' in R. VAN RANSBEECK (ed.), *Wilsgebreken*, Bruges, die Keure, 2006 (103), 103-129; M. WAUTERS, 'Garanties bij overdracht van aandelen', *DAOR* 1997, No. 44 (17), 42).

24 B. BELLEN, K. DE WAEL, C. MERGEAY and B. HERMANS, 'M&A Survey – 5th edition', *TRV-RPS* 2021 (597), 603-604.

25 Please refer to Section 2 (Information rights and obligations of the parties) of this chapter.

required to answer diligently and in good faith in order to discharge its information obligations.

The purchaser's access to the data room can be regulated by specific 'data room rules' agreed by the parties at the start of the due diligence. The data room rules will regulate the period during which the data room is available, access procedures, management of the data room, a central point of contact, a procedure for questions or requests for additional information, and whether or not data room documents may be copied. The seller will typically also keep a log of persons having accessed the data room.

The question of whether the purchaser is allowed to print or make copies of data room information can be a sensitive issue. In the absence of an agreement on this matter (e.g. in the non-disclosure agreement or data room rules), the purchaser has, in principle, no right to copy or retain confidential information belonging to the seller or the target company.

However, in what appears to have become a widely accepted practice, candidate purchasers and advisers are allowed to download or copy documents in order to facilitate their review.[26] To accommodate control and security concerns regarding copied or downloaded documents, most virtual data room providers allow adding customisable watermarks and/or enabling a 'self-destruct' security layer that renders downloaded files inaccessible when access to those files is revoked.

In order to preserve the integrity of the data room documents after the closing of the transaction, the parties sometimes choose to record the data room documents on an electronic storage device (e.g. a hard drive or USB stick) and to give such storage device in escrow to an independent escrow agent (e.g. a notary public) for a certain period after closing (e.g. for the duration of the seller's indemnification obligation pursuant to the share purchase agreement). For this purpose, the parties and the data room escrow agent may, upon the closing of the transaction, enter into a 'data room escrow agreement' governing *i.a.* the terms of consultation and release of the data room documents.[27]

---

26 B. BELLEN, K. DE WAEL, C. MERGEAY and B. HERMANS, 'M&A Survey – 5th edition', *TRV-RPS* 2021 (597), 603.

27 Please refer to the sample clauses in B. BELLEN, *Share Purchase Agreements – Belgian Law and Practice*, Antwerpen/Cambridge, Intersentia, 2016, 158-161.

4 Q&A

As a complement to the information made available in the data room, it has also become common for the parties to organise a formal Q&A (question and answer) process.[28] As such, most virtual data room providers also offer the possibility to organise the Q&A within the same digital environment as the data room, so that all information can be collected in one place.

The non-disclosure agreement, process letters or data room rules may regulate the format in which the purchaser must submit questions and additional information requests. The purpose of this process is to allow the purchaser to solicit additional answers and documents from the seller, for instance regarding the information that was already made available in the data room. Again, such Q&A sessions are a particularly delicate exercise for the seller who is required to ensure that all answers are provided to the purchaser diligently and in good faith.

5 Challenges in organising and conducting a due diligence review

While compiling the data room or providing confidential information throughout the acquisition process, as well as while conducting the review of such information, both the purchaser and the seller may be faced with certain challenges. However, as is clear from the foregoing, a proper due diligence review of the target company is essential for both the prospective buyer and the seller. It allows both parties to fulfil their pre-contractual obligations and to correctly assess and limit contractual risks.

Also in this context, powerful software tools with 'artificial intelligence' capability may be able to play a significant role, further increasing the efficiency and security of the due diligence process and ensuring compliance with relevant law and regulations.

5.1 Competition law considerations

One example of challenges the parties can be faced with is compliance with competition law rules. While sharing confidential information, applicable competition law rules regarding information exchange have to be taken into account, in particular, Article 101

28 B. BELLEN, K. DE WAEL, C. MERGEAY and B. HERMANS, 'M&A Survey – 5th edition', *TRV-RPS* 2021 (597), 603.

of the Treaty on the Functioning of the European Union. These rules will be relevant whenever (actual or potential) competitors are involved in the acquisition process.[29]

In such a case, it is advisable for the seller to avoid disclosing sensitive information to a candidate purchaser in an early stage of the acquisition process. The seller should instead aim at disclosing such sensitive information only gradually, *i.e.* to the extent that such information is indispensable for the candidate purchaser to pursue the next step in the acquisition process. In particular, the disclosure of highly sensitive information (forward-looking information such as pipeline projects, non-anonymised customer information, pricing strategies, production costs, etc.) may have to be postponed until an advanced stage of the negotiations or even after the share purchase agreement is signed (e.g. in the context of a confirmatory due diligence[30]).

Alternatively, the seller may set up a 'clean room' which includes sensitive business information which the seller is not allowed to disclose to the wider due diligence team of the purchaser. To review such clean room information, the purchaser may appoint a third-party adviser (e.g. a law firm or business consultancy), whereby the third-party adviser acts as a 'clean team' and only shares the conclusions of its analysis with the candidate purchaser, thus avoiding the need for the latter to have direct access to the sensitive information prior to signing. To organise the due diligence review by such a clean team, the parties typically enter into a specific 'clean team' agreement providing, *i.a.*, the terms of access to the clean room, the list of clean team members, and the rules for reporting by the clean team to the candidate purchaser.

On account of the same competition law rules regarding information exchange, it is advisable for a candidate purchaser that is a (potential) competitor of the target company to disclose sensitive information regarding the target company internally on a 'need-to-know' basis only, *i.e.* only to those persons and members of the deal team that are actually involved in the transaction and that need to have such information in order to assess the transaction.

---

29 V. LEROY, 'Management of Competition Law Risks in Acquisition of Company Processes – From the Preliminary Contacts to the Notification(s)', *CJ* 2014 (65), 65-66. Please also refer to the Guidelines (2011/C 11/01) on the applicability of Art. 101 of the Treaty on the Functioning of the European Union to horizontal co-operation agreements and the Commission's draft Guidelines (2022/C 164/01) on the applicability of Article 101 of the Treaty on the Functioning of the European Union to horizontal co-operation agreements, which will replace the aforementioned Guidelines of 2011.

30 Please refer to B. BELLEN, *Share Purchase Agreements – Belgian Law and Practice*, Antwerpen/Cambridge, Intersentia, 2016, 16.

5.2 Privacy and data protection

In addition to confidentiality and competition law considerations, the parties should consider restrictions applicable to the transfer of personal data in the context of the due diligence phase pursuant to applicable privacy and data protection regulations, including (in Europe) the General Data Protection Regulation (GDPR). Under the GDPR, collecting and sharing documents regarding the target company's operations will constitute processing of personal data as soon as any information relating to an identified or identifiable natural person is made available.[31]

During the due diligence phase, the seller should therefore first ensure that there is a legitimate basis for disclosing personal data of persons involved in the target company (e.g. employees) to third parties, such as the seller and its advisers, but also the data room provider. It is assumed that this can normally be justified based on the legitimate interests of the parties involved in the transaction and therefore does not require the express prior consent of the individuals concerned (provided that the disclosure is appropriately limited in view of the specific purpose of the disclosure). Nevertheless, each such 'data subject' has the right to enquire how and why its personal data is being used.[32]

For the conduct of a compliant due diligence, the seller should disclose only personal data which is necessary and relevant for the analysis of the target company by the candidate purchaser. Data should be anonymised as much as possible and displayed in an aggregated manner, tailored to the different phases of the acquisition process. For example, and especially in earlier phases of the due diligence review, information should be provided through contract templates and in aggregated form. Personal data can be shared only if and when the identification is truly necessary. Furthermore, the seller has to ensure that the disclosure of personal data in the context of the due diligence is sufficiently secured, e.g. through the use of encryption, anonymisation, blacklining of personal data, access limitations, restrictions on downloading and copying. Finally, the seller should conclude a data processing agreement with the data room provider ensuring that mandatory procedures in accordance with the GDPR are in place and that everyone accessing the data room is aware of such procedures (e.g. by including them in the data room rules).[33]

---

31 Art. 4 (1) and (2) of the GDPR.

32 S. DE SMEDT and M. CAPRONI, *Praktische gids privacy in de onderneming*, Mechelen, Wolters Kluwer Belgium, 2019, 191-192.

33 For a more detailed discussion regarding processing of personal data in the context of M&A transactions, please a.o. refer to S. DE SMEDT and M. CAPRONI, *Praktische gids privacy in de onderneming*, Mechelen, Wolters Kluwer Belgium, 2019, 189-200.

5.3 *Other practical challenges*

In addition to regulatory challenges associated with mandatory competition and data privacy laws, the organisation of a due diligence review also brings several practical and technical challenges. Some of these challenges include the following:

- **Amount of data:** the amount of data to be analysed has increased exponentially. In combination with badly organised or incomplete data rooms, this can make the proper review and analysis especially challenging and time consuming.
- **Time pressure**: especially in competitive auction processes, there is a tendency to impose ever shorter timelines and accelerated transaction processes, resulting in limited time being available for the due diligence review itself.
- **Fragmented information and teams**: in most transactions the due diligence review is segmented and allocated among multiple internal and external due diligence teams which only review specific sections of the data room. For example, the finance team will focus only on the 'financial' information, the legal due diligence team on the information that is designated as 'legal' in the data room, the labour team will review the 'labour' section, etc. This may cause information to be fragmented within the due diligence team, creating a risk of important disclosures going undetected or not being escalated to the appropriate level for further assessment.
- **Multiple jurisdictions and languages**: larger transactions involving multiple jurisdictions may, furthermore, require due diligence teams from multiple countries. In addition, the data room may include documents that are stated in different languages which may not all be readily understood by all members of the due diligence team. This further increases the risk of important disclosures going undetected or not being escalated.
- **Assessing the 'unknown unknowns'**: key to a comprehensive due diligence review is not only identifying the issues that are apparent from the data room information but also assessing which information may be missing.
- **Lack of industry or sector experience**: in many jurisdictions, such as Belgium, M&A advisers coordinating due diligence and deal teams are typically 'generalists' in their respective fields, specialising in a particular discipline (e.g. transaction services) but not in specific economic sectors or industries. As a result, due diligence teams often lack specific industry or sector experience. This may further limit the effectiveness of the due diligence to assess the materiality of a disclosure or to assess the 'unknown unknowns'.
- **Reliance on junior professionals**: in many due diligence teams, the groundwork is conducted by relatively junior and inexperienced professionals (also in view of cost efficiency requirements imposed by clients). This again increases the risk of important information going undetected or not being assessed in the right context.

5.4 *Can 'artificially intelligent' software help to overcome these challenges?*

A key feature of 'artificially intelligent' algorithms is that they can be 'pre-trained' to recognise specific types of information. As such, 'artificially intelligent' software tools may, in principle at least, be useful to help overcome some of the challenges described previously. This, however, requires that a tool be made available that has been 'pre-trained' to a sufficient level. In practice, such a development can be impacted by legal restrictions (e.g. copyright, confidentiality and professional secrecy obligations preventing the disclosure of relevant data to software developers) and practical limitations (e.g. the use of multiple languages and differences among legal systems and industry sectors).

For instance, the identification and censoring of 'commercially sensitive information' and of personal data are a relatively straightforward exercise from a legal point of view. As such, several virtual data room providers already include advanced redaction tools in their applications, designed to recognise recurring patterns (e.g. (email) addresses, phone numbers, names, currencies, dates) and to propose redactions.

Indeed, in many of the foregoing challenges, software tools already play an important role today, by allowing teams to increase the efficiency and security of the due diligence process and to streamline workflows. This applies primarily to the software platforms offered by virtual data room providers, whose capabilities have developed significantly and whose tools are (generally) available in the open market at a competitive price level. Using those platforms, parties can set up a cloud-based 'virtual' data room and securely gather, organise, share, track and manage information, while ensuring confidentiality and keeping control and oversight over any activities in the data room. Current providers include Ansarada, iDeals, Intralinks, Virtual Vaults, Datasite, and so on which each offer their own pricing formulas (e.g. based on the number of users or amount of used storage) and specific features. Common features include the ability to (bulk) upload, update and download files and folders, redact, track user activity, restrict access to certain files and/or folders based on a user's authorisation level, apply custom watermarks, control viewing, printing or downloading rights, set up a Q&A, securely communicate, set up email notifications, determine the level of interest, and so on. Furthermore, these providers often do not limit their services to the M&A due diligence process but also offer their platforms to accommodate other processes such as capital raises, IPOs, corporate restructurings, governance and risk and compliance solutions.

Some of these providers claim that certain features are already driven by some form of artificial intelligence, for example the redaction feature. In such cases, the application will suggest potential redactions, finding personal information, dates, account numbers, pricing, etc. on a confirm, decline or change basis. Some platforms also allow for creating tags or lists that the application will then use to find additional suggestions. Another example of such a claim is in predicting a prospective buyer's engagement and interest, based on *i.a.* user activity.

In addition, powerful e-discovery tools such as Relativity, Logikcull, iCONECT and ZyLAB are available that can facilitate the review of large amounts of information and that are of critical importance in certain types of due diligence (e.g. compliance investigations or forensic audits). These tools offer features such as the ability to automatically organise and index files, detect duplicates and similar or related documents, compare files, scan for viruses, apply optical character recognition, redact, allow for (automatic) (bulk) tagging and even make audio or video files searchable, all in a secure environment. Depending on the provider, these tools can process information ranging from documents, emails, presentations and websites to even audio and video files.

When using such tools, certain additional limitations should be duly considered, such as the need to ensure that all documents to be reviewed are uploaded in 'optical character recognition' ('OCR') enabled format (which is not always possible). Also, while such tools may be quite effective in detecting natural language information (*i.e.* words or combinations of words), they are often much less effective with non-natural language information (e.g. financial information).

In any event, the existing software tools cannot yet be considered as 'artificially intelligent' self-learning systems that can assess the substance and materiality of data in the context of a company acquisition. However, tools and applications in this field are developing fast, and there is no doubt that software will become increasingly important in assisting teams to conduct due diligence reviews according to prevailing professional standards.

AI-Infused Contracting: An Application to M&A Transactions

*Maarten Herbosch**

1 Introduction

Systems based on artificial intelligence (AI) are used increasingly often in legal practice. They can be used to help legal practitioners perform tasks faster, cheaper and sometimes even better than they would without the use of these systems. AI systems may also be used to help parties during mergers and acquisitions (M&A) transactions.

As a new technology, the use of AI systems is clouded by legal uncertainty. The autonomy that characterises AI systems can make it difficult to apply our existing, human-centred legal framework to the use of these systems. As a result, many authors even advocate implementing a separate legal framework for AI systems.

In this contribution, we first provide a brief overview of the various AI tools that parties can use to facilitate their M&A transaction and that are already deployed in legal practice today. We then go on to discuss the legal regime that applies to the use of AI systems in contract formation while considering the application of that regime to such M&A tools. We will particularly emphasise potential liability for (the use of) the AI system and whether such an AI system might lead to the application of the mistake regime. For both questions, the Belgian legal regime will be used as a starting point, with reference to the European AI Act and other ongoing European legislative initiatives.

* Dr. Maarten Herbosch is a postdoctoral researcher at the Centre for Methodology of Law (KU Leuven) & Fellow at FWO Flanders.

2 Artificial Intelligence

2.1 *Definition*

It is crucial to have a good understanding of 'artificial intelligence'.[1] This is, however, not easy.[2] For the purpose of this contribution, we will use the definition that the European Commission launched in 2018.[3] This definition reads "Artificial intelligence (AI) refers to systems that display intelligent behaviour by analysing their environment and taking actions – with some degree of autonomy – to achieve specific goals." This definition emphasises the independence or *autonomy* of AI systems, as was more recently copied in the European Union AI Act.[4] As such, this definition does not depend on a limited list of computer techniques that might constitute AI,[5] nor does it contain a reference to human intelligence.[6] An autonomy-centric definition contains multiple advantages over these alternatives. A definition that depends on a list of AI techniques might too quickly shift the weight of that definition to the attached list. Moreover, such an exhaustive

1 For an earlier, similar discussion of the properties of AI systems, see M. Herbosch, 'Artificiële intelligentie en vastgoedtransacties' in V. Sagaert, A. Appelmans and B. Verheye (eds), *Digitalisering en vastgoedtransacties* (Intersentia 2022) 5 ff.

2 See e.g. I. Giuffrida, F. Lederer and N. Vermeyst, 'A Legal Perspective on the Trials and Tribulations of AI: How Artificial Intelligence, the Internet of Things, Smart Contracts, and Other Technologies Will Affect the Law' (2018) 68 Case Western Reserve Law Review 747, 751; R. Calo, 'Artificial Intelligence Policy: A Primer and Roadmap' (2018) 3 University of Bologna Law Review 180, 184; J.-S. Borghetti, 'How Can Artificial Intelligence be Defective?' in S. Lohsse, R. Schulze and D. Staudenmayer (eds), *Liability for Artificial Intelligence and the Internet of Things* (Bloomsbury 2019) 63; M. Hatfield, 'Professionally Responsible Artificial Intelligence' (2019) 51 Arizona State Law Journal 1057, 1064; R. Martinez, 'Artificial Intelligence: Distinguishing between Types & Definitions' (2019) 19 Nevada Law Journal 1023; Y. Meneceur and C. Barbaro, 'Intelligence artificielle et mémoire de la justice: le grand malentendu' (2019) Les Cahiers de la Justice 277 ff.; S. Cattoor, I. Letten and A. Loose, '[Artificial Intelligence] Inventorship of AI Made Inventions' (2020) IRDI 7, 8; M. Herbosch, 'Smart Contracts: Het recht te slim af?' in S. De Rey, N. Van Damme and T. Gladinez (eds), *Grenzen voorbij: Liber discipulorum Bernard Tilleman* (Intersentia 2020) 33 ff.; M. Kaulartz and T. Braegelmann, 'Einführung' in M. Kaulartz and T. Braegelmann (eds), *Rechtshandbuch Artificial Intelligence und Machine Learning* (Beck 2020) 2 ff.; S. Merabet, *Vers un droit d'intelligence artificielle* (Dalloz 2020) 58-59; R. Devillé, N. Sergeyssels and C. Middag, 'Basic Concepts of AI for Legal Scholars' in J. De Bruyne and C. Vanleenhove (eds), *Artificial Intelligence and the Law* (Intersentia 2021) 2.

3 Communication from the Commission to the European Parliament, the European Council, the Council, the European Economic and Social Committee and the Committee of the Regions: Artificial Intelligence for Europe, 25 April 2018, https://eur-lex.europa.eu/legal-content/ENG/TXT/HTML/?uri=CELEX:52018DC0237 (last visited 24 April 2023), para. 1. See also very similar to the OECD definition: OECD, Recommendation of the Council on Artificial Intelligence, https://legalinstruments.oecd.org/en/instruments/OECD-LEGAL-0449 (last visited 23 April 2023), I.

4 See, in particular, Art. 3 of the AI Act.

5 See Art. 3 (1) of the initial proposal for an AI Act (COM/2021/206).

6 M.R. Grossman and G.V. Cormack, 'The Grossman-Cormack Glossary of Technology-Assisted Review' (2014) 7 Federal Courts Law Review 87; R. Yu and G. Ali, 'What's Inside the Black Box? AI Challenges for Lawyers and Researchers' (2019) 19 Legal Information Management 2, 2; C. Linke, *Digitale Wissensorganisation: Wissenszurechnung beim Einsatz autonomer Systeme* (Nomos 2021) 27.

enumeration is obviously not 'technology-neutral', and may soon be outdated, given the speed of technological evolution. Technological neutrality, however, does offer some significant advantages for, among other things, legal certainty.[7]

Furthermore, a definition that refers to human intelligence is somewhat inappropriate, given that, on the one hand, the performance of AI systems regularly exceeds that of humans, as discussed below. On the other hand, the functioning of AI systems does not necessarily resemble that of the human brain,[8] which also closely relates to the fact that AI systems may occasionally produce unpredictable and highly undesirable results, as discussed below. As a result, an anthropocentric conceptualisation of AI is all too artificial.

Resultingly, the term 'autonomy' plays a crucial role in the definition adopted here. Without this notion, this definition may, at first glance, seem overly broad, also covering more traditional forms of computer software. To sharpen the precise delineation, it is useful to briefly discuss how such more 'traditional' software systems operate.

Computer systems are always programmed using algorithms. These are lists of instructions. Despite the complexity that may be involved, such algorithms always consist of 'simple' rules in the form *if X, then do Y*.[9] A 'traditional' computer algorithm can then be represented – overly simplistically – as a sequence of such instructions: if *X then do* A_1, *if* A_1 *then do* A_2 .... *if* A_n *then do Y*, which we can eventually summarise again in the form *if X, then do Y* where X and Y – depending on the complexity of the system – are identified by the system programmer. A simple example is a beverage dispenser: if a specific coin is inserted and a specific button is pressed (X), then the machine should eject a particular drink (Y). While such systems can be very useful, it is unlikely that

7 On the choice of a technology-neutral conceptual framework in the context of online search engines, see, e.g., Art. 2 (5) Regulation 2019/1150; B. Devolder, *Gebruikersbescherming in de deeleconomie* (die Keure/ la Charte 2022) no. 555.

8 D.M. Katz, 'Quantitative Legal Prediction – Or – How I Learned to Stop Worrying and Start Preparing for the Data-Driven Future of the Legal Services Industry' (2013) 62 Emory Law Journal 909, 918; I. Giuffrida, F. Lederer and N. Vermeyst, 'A Legal Perspective on the Trials and Tribulations of AI: How Artificial Intelligence, the Internet of Things, Smart Contracts, and Other Technologies Will Affect the Law' (2018) 68 Case Western Reserve Law Review 747, 755; H. Surden, 'Artificial Intelligence and Law: An Overview' (2019) 35 Georgia State University Law Review 1305, 1315. Also See Y. LeCun, Y. Bengio and G. Hinton, 'Deep Learning' (2015) 521 Nature 436, 441 on how the difference between the working mechanisms of the human brain and those of AI systems may be more nuanced on a more fundamental level.

9 See for applications in the context of smart contracts: E. Leroux and P. Brulez, 'Smart Contracts en blockchaintechnologie: uitdagingen voor het contractenrecht' in M. Beyens (ed), *Het burgerlijk recht in beweging / Le droit civil en mouvement* (Larcier 2018) 193; C. Koolen, 'Blockchaintechnologie, smart contracts en consumentenbescherming. Een kritische blik op smart contracts vanuit een consumentenrechtelijke invalshoek' in P.-J. Aerts, F. Hoogendijk and N. Vandezande (eds), *Smart contracts* (Intersentia 2020) 252.

someone might claim them to be intelligent – although they are often referred to as 'smart' in legal literature.[10]

This helps clarify the interesting nature of systems based on AI. This is most evident in systems using *machine learning*, although it also applies to other techniques used to program AI systems.[11] A characteristic of machine learning is that the programmer does not directly tell the system what to do when it receives some input. Instead, the programmer gives the system rules – again in the form *if X, then do Y* – that allow the system to mathematically determine, without further human intervention, the (for now) best possible output for a given input. Thus, the X and Y that the programmer imparts do not directly refer to the potential inputs and outputs of the final system. Rather, they refer to a rule in the form of *if 'the model can be improved' (X), do 'next steps to modify it' (Y).*

Thus, the model that the system programmer provides is not the model the system uses to determine its output directly on the basis of some input. An accessible example of such a system is a spam filter for emails. The programmer of such an AI-based spam filter does not *ab initio* provide the system with a rule that determines whether a particular message is spam. Instead, the system teaches itself what such a rule might look like, for example, by training on practice data. To this end, the system should be given a large number of emails that have already been classified beforehand according to whether they are spam mail. From this, the system can then deduce that the word 'free' in an email message is an important indication that it might be spam mail.[12] This method, called supervised learning, may also be applied to many other applications. Such AI systems can, for example, help qualify clauses in contracts.

The previous discussion also helps to clarify what we mean by the 'autonomy' of AI systems. This autonomy is precisely what distinguishes modern AI systems from more traditional computer systems. Moreover, this autonomy has several consequences and may serve to highlight some features of AI systems that are very relevant from a legal perspective in an M&A context.

---

10 J.G. Allen, 'Wrapped and Stacked: "Smart Contracts" and the Interaction of Natural and Formal Language' (2018) 14 European Review of Contract Law 307, 313; P. Banigan, M. Rappard and Z. Skeith, 'Smart Contracts 101 – From a Technical to a Legal Understanding', *A Practical Guide to Smart Contracts and Blockchain Law* (LexisNexis 2019) 154.

11 For an overview, see, e.g., Annex I to the AI Regulation.

12 S.J. Russell and P. Norvig, *Artificial Intelligence: A Modern Approach* (Prentice Hall 2010) 1020 ff.; H. Surden, 'Artificial Intelligence and Law: An Overview' (2019) 35 Georgia State University Law Review 1305, 1314.

2.2 Significant Features in an M&A Context

2.2.1 Unpredictability

The first consequence of the fact that the programmer does not fully determine the operation of the AI system is that the ultimate relationship between inputs and outputs (the final output Y that follows a given input *X*) is essentially unknown, even to the programmer of the system. This can, of course, also be the case with a more traditional computer system. Flaws in the software, so-called *computer bugs*, can cause the system not to perform as desired.[13] With AI systems, however, the unpredictability[14] is not necessarily a result of a bug. Indeed, this unpredictability is precisely what is intended, and precisely this autonomy and associated unpredictability lead to some significant advantages as discussed below).

2.2.2 Conceptual Inexplicability

The autonomy of AI systems also has another important consequence. It is, for example, often said that AI systems behave like a *black box*.[15] More fundamentally, this denotes that AI algorithms are often so complex that even an AI specialist cannot fully understand them.[16] Thus, explaining why the system prefers one outcome over another is sometimes difficult.

However, this should be partially nuanced. Indeed, at a mathematical level, the system's output can usually be explained,[17] at least when the system programmer provides the necessary safeguards to store and display the relevant values of the internal system

13 It is even statistically impossible to rule out such computer bugs; see E. Mik, 'Smart Contracts: Terminology, Technical Limitations and Real World Complexity' (2017) 9 Law, Innovation and Technology 281.

14 Also see on unpredictability: R. Yu and G. Ali, 'What's Inside the Black Box? AI Challenges for Lawyers and Researchers' (2019) 19 Legal Information Management 2, 5; A.D. Selbst, 'Negligence and AI's Human Users' (2020) 100 Boston University Law Review 1315, 1332.

15 Y. Bathaee, 'The Artificial Intelligence Black Box and the Failure of Intent and Causation' (2017) 31 Harvard Journal of Law and Technology 889, 897; M. Hatfield, 'Professionally Responsible Artificial Intelligence' (2019) 51 Arizona State Law Journal 1057, 118, footnote 278; W. Samek and K.-R. Müller, 'Towards Explainable Artificial Intelligence' in W. Samek and others (eds), *Explainable AI: Interpreting, Explaining and Visualizing Deep Learning* (Springer International Publishing 2019) 6; R. Yu and G. Ali, 'What's Inside the Black Box? AI Challenges for Lawyers and Researchers' (2019) 19 Legal Information Management 2, 5; M. Fierens, E. Van Gool and J. De Bruyne, 'De regulering van artificiële intelligentie (deel 1) – Een algemene stand van zaken en een analyse van enkele vraagstukken inzake consumentenbescherming' (2020-2021) RW 962, 963-964; A. Solow-Niederman, 'Administering Artificial Intelligence' (2020) 93 Southern California Law Review 657; R. Devillé, N. Sergeyssels and C. Middag, 'Basic Concepts of AI for Legal Scholars' in J. De Bruyne and C. Vanleenhove (eds), *Artificial Intelligence and the Law* (Intersentia 2021) 10.

16 See also C.E.A. Karnow, 'The Opinion of Machines' (2017) 19 Columbia Science and Technology Law Review 136, 137.

17 See also M. Stiemerling, 'Technische Grundlagen' in M. Kaulartz and T. Braegelmann (eds), *Rechtshandbuch Artificial Intelligence und Machine Learning* (Beck 2020) 26.

parameters. More fundamentally, the problem is that although the system may be explainable mathematically, the operation of the system is conceptually impossible to grasp.[18]

Nevertheless, this lack of conceptual explainability can be very annoying, particularly when the system is engaged in, for example, the health sector,[19] where AI systems are sometimes used to help diagnose patients.[20] Because of this, there is a strong focus on the creation of *explainable* AI systems.[21] These are AI systems that produce explainable results.

2.2.3 Faster, (More) Qualitative Results

Given that AI systems are unpredictable and conceptually inexplicable, we might wonder why anyone would want to engage an AI system. Yet there are several strong arguments to that effect. First of all, like other forms of automation, using AI systems often leads to time savings.[22] As a result, automation often helps to cut costs.[23] These savings, which initially benefit the AI system user, will also result in cheaper goods and services for third parties that contract with the system user.[24]

---

18 G. Rebala, A. Ravi and S. Churiwala, *An Introduction to Machine Learning* (Springer 2019) 2.

19 W. Samek and K.-R. Müller, 'Towards Explainable Artificial Intelligence' in W. Samek and others (eds), *Explainable AI: Interpreting, Explaining and Visualizing Deep Learning* (Springer International Publishing 2019) 6-7; R. Devillé, N. Sergeyssels and C. Middag, 'Basic Concepts of AI for Legal Scholars' in J. De Bruyne and C. Vanleenhove (eds), *Artificial Intelligence and the Law* (Intersentia 2021) 10.

20 See W. Samek and K.-R. Müller, 'Towards Explainable Artificial Intelligence' in W. Samek and others (eds), *Explainable AI: Interpreting, Explaining and Visualizing Deep Learning* (Springer International Publishing 2019) 6-7; R. Devillé, N. Sergeyssels and C. Middag, 'Basic Concepts of AI for Legal Scholars' in J. De Bruyne and C. Vanleenhove (eds), *Artificial Intelligence and the Law* (Intersentia 2021) 10.

21 Also see A. Adadi and M. Berrada, 'Peeking Inside the Black-Box: A Survey on Explainable Artificial Intelligence (XAI)' (2018) 6 IEEE Access 52138, 52139; S.J. Körner, 'Nachvollziehbarkeit von KI-basierten Entscheidungen' in M. Kaulartz and T. Braegelmann (eds), *Rechtshandbuch Artificial Intelligence und Machine Learning* (Beck 2020) 44; G. Vanderstichele, 'Artificiële intelligentie ter ondersteuning van menselijke rechtspraak. De sui-generismethode voor het gebruik van legal analytics in de rechtspraak' (2020) NJW 610, 621; R. Devillé, N. Sergeyssels and C. Middag, 'Basic Concepts of AI for Legal Scholars' in J. De Bruyne and C. Vanleenhove (eds), *Artificial Intelligence and the Law* (Intersentia 2021) 10.

22 M. Giancaspro, 'Is a "Smart Contract" Really a Smart Idea? Insights from a Legal Perspective' (2017) 33 Computer Law & Security Review 827 (on smart contracts); R. Bonnaffé, 'Nieuwe technologieën en het recht: de impact van artificiële intelligentie op de rechtspraktijk' (2018) TRV 856, 868.

23 Superior Court of Justice Ontario November 22, 2018 (*Cass v. 1410088 Ontario Inc.*, 2018 ONSC 6959), http://canlii.ca/t/hw728; S. Brown, 'Peeking Inside the Black Box: A Preliminary Survey of Technology Assisted Review (TAR) and Predictive Coding Algorithms for Ediscovery' (2015) 21 Suffolk Journal of Trial & Appellate Advocacy 221, 226; R. Bonnaffé, 'Nieuwe technologieën en het recht: de impact van artificiële intelligentie op de rechtspraktijk' (2018) TRV 856, 868; W. Naudé and N. Dimitri, 'The Race for an Artificial General Intelligence: Implications for Public Policy' (2020) 35 AI & Society 367.

24 Also see Superior Court of Justice Ontario Nov. 22, 2018 (*Cass v. 1410088 Ontario Inc.*, 2018 ONSC 6959), http://canlii.ca/t/hw728.

Furthermore, in many sectors, the results of AI systems are better than the results a human could obtain.[25] AI systems can accomplish specific tasks that humans can perform with higher quality on average, even compared to human experts.[26] Google's AI system AlphaGo Zero aptly illustrates this. Although it was long believed that the board game Go was too complex to be mastered by a computer, today, it systematically outperforms top human players.[27] This is beautifully captured by Henry Ford's quote, predating AI, stating that *"[f]or most purposes a man with a machine is better than a man without a machine"*.[28]

2.2.4 Occasionally Erroneous Results

While AI systems offer many advantages, a particularly challenging aspect of these systems is that it is inherently impossible to avoid all erroneous system output.[29] In this respect, AI systems thus seem to have much in common with humans – *errare humanum est*. However, an interesting distinction is that AI systems' mistakes fundamentally differ from human mistakes. While AI systems often outperform humans on average, AI systems sometimes also lead to results that are so bad that it is unlikely that a human would make the same mistake.[30] A particular illustration of this feature is present in facial recognition software that fails to recognise some people merely because they are not white males.[31]

---

25 See, e.g.. R. Calo, 'Singularity: AI and the Law' (2018) 41 Seattle University Law Review 1123, 1124; T. Matsuzaki, 'Ethical Issues of Artificial Intelligence in Medicine' (2018) 55 California Western Law Review 255 ff; A.J. Kolber, 'Not-So-Smart Blockchain Contracts and Artificial Responsibility' (2018) 21 Stanford Technology Law Review 198, 205; M. Hatfield, 'Professionally Responsible Artificial Intelligence' (2019) 51 Arizona State Law Journal 1057, 1060; W. Samek and K.-R. Müller, 'Towards Explainable Artificial Intelligence' in W. Samek and others (eds), *Explainable AI: Interpreting, Explaining and Visualizing Deep Learning* (Springer International Publishing 2019) 5-6; S. Cattoor, I. Letten and A. Loose, '[Artificial Intelligence] Inventorship of AI Made Inventions' (2020) IRDI 7, 8; M. Fierens, E. Van Gool and J. De Bruyne, 'De regulering van artificiële intelligentie (deel 1) – Een algemene stand van zaken en een analyse van enkele vraagstukken inzake consumentenbescherming' (2020-2021) RW 962, 964.

26 R. Calo, 'Singularity: AI and the Law' (2018) 41 Seattle University Law Review 1123, 1124. See in the same vein: T. Matsuzaki, 'Ethical Issues of Artificial Intelligence in Medicine' (2018) 55 California Western Law Review 255 ff; A.J. Kolber, 'Not-So-Smart Blockchain Contracts and Artificial Responsibility' (2018) 21 Stanford Technology Law Review 198, 205; M. Hatfield, 'Professionally Responsible Artificial Intelligence' (2019) 51 Arizona State Law Journal 1057, 1060.

27 D. Silver and others, 'Mastering the Game of Go without Human Knowledge' (2017) 550 Nature 354, 356.

28 H. Ford, *My Life and Work* (Cosimo 2007) 147.

29 Also see e.g., N.A. Greenblatt, 'Self-driving Cars and the Law' (2016) 53 IEEE Spectrum 46, 48 ff.

30 See also A. Nguyen, J. Yosinski and J. Clune, 'Deep Neural Networks are Easily Fooled: High Confidence Predictions for Unrecognizable Images' (2015) Conference on Computer Vision and Pattern Recognition 427, 427-436.

31 S. Lohr, 'Facial Recognition Is Accurate, if You're a White Guy', *The New York Times*, 9 February 2018, https://www.nytimes.com/2018/02/09/technology/facial-recognition-race-artificial-intelligence.html (last visited 25 April2023).

It is, however, helpful to emphasise that such manifestly erroneous results do not necessarily indicate an error on the part of the system's programmer. Programmer errors are an important potential source of undesirable results,[32] as are flaws (such as *bias*) in the data that might have been used to train the system.[33] Such errors can even be very subtle, as *reward function hacking* illustrates.[34] This term describes a situation where the system 'optimises' itself as the programmer's instructions dictate but does so via some shortcut. Instead of effectively getting better, a *loophole* in the algorithm causes the system to perform better in theory but not at all in practice. An example is an autonomous vacuum cleaner that ejects dust so that it can suck it up again. It would thus collect more dust and achieve a better 'score'.[35]

In addition, it should be clear that even a well-programmed system certainly does not necessarily perform perfectly. Indeed, AI systems are often enabled in a statistical environment.[36] Here, we can think, for example, of an AI chess computer.[37] A good (suggestion for a) move by the chess computer does not guarantee the final victory. Even a good chess computer can only suggest/execute a move that maximises the probability of a final victory without being able to guarantee it. Indeed, whether the move in question is sufficient depends on the opponent's reaction (and also on subsequent moves).

32 See, e.g., also P. Boucher, *How Artificial Intelligence Works: Briefing to the European Parliament* (2019) 5; B. Jalaian, M. Lee and S. Russell, 'Uncertain Context: Uncertainty Quantification in Machine Learning' (2019) 40 AI Magazine 40.

33 J. Buolamwini and T. Gebru, 'Gender Shades: Intersectional Accuracy Disparities in Commercial Gender Classication' (2018) 81 Proceedings of Machine Learning Research 1. Also see S. Lohr, 'Facial Recognition Is Accurate, If You're a White Guy', *The New York Times*, 9 February 2018, https://www.nytimes.com/2018/02/09/technology/facial-recognition-race-artificial-intelligence.html (last visited 25 April 2023).

34 See, e.g., D. Amodei and others, 'Concrete Problems in AI Safety' (2016) arXiv [cs] 1606.06565, 7 ff; T. Everitt and others, 'Reinforcement Learning with a Corrupted Reward Channel' (2017) arXiv [cs] 1705.08417, 2; Y. Yuan and others, 'A Novel Multi-step Reinforcement Learning Method for Solving Reward Hacking' (2019) 49 Applied Intelligence 2874.

35 D. Hadfield-Menell and others, 'Inverse Reward Design' (2017) NIPS 1, 1.

36 Also see M. Hutter, *Universal Artificial Intelligence: Sequential Decisions based on Algorithmic Probability* (Springer 2004) 28 ff; S.J. Russell and P. Norvig, *Artificial Intelligence: A Modern Approach* (Prentice Hall 2010) 480 ff and 802 ff; B. Jalaian, M. Lee and S. Russell, 'Uncertain Context: Uncertainty Quantification in Machine Learning' (2019) 40 AI Magazine 43 ff.

37 As an illustration, see G. Rebala, A. Ravi and S. Churiwala, *An Introduction to Machine Learning* (Springer 2019) 195.

3 M&A Transactions

Before a party decides to acquire the shares of another company, the contracting parties will often engage in extensive negotiations.[38] These negotiations may be characterised by preliminary contracts or documents that determine the scope of confidentiality and the intents of the negotiating parties (e.g. in a so-called *letter of intent*). During negotiations, the so-called *due diligence analysis* is particularly interesting. While negotiating – and usually after having secured a confidentiality agreement, the seller will allow the prospective buyer access to internal documents that may help the buyer determine whether or not he wants to acquire the target company's shares and, if so, for what price. This analysis helps the prospective buyer identify potential risks and liabilities in the target company that might make him or her reconsider the transaction or the price.

This brief sketch of the M&A transaction process helps clarify the varying roles that AI systems may play in such transactions.[39] These systems can be used to help draft the contract or one of the preliminary agreements.[40] They may also be used to estimate the value of the target company or some of its assets.[41] Going (a lot) further, AI systems might even be used to perform the entire negotiation process and may even be deployed to form the contract without further intervention by the party deploying the system.[42]

38 For a more extensive overview of this phase preceding the signing of the contract, see the chapter of Bart Bellen and Marthe Wouters "Due Diligence in M&A Transactions" in this book, and more extensively B. Bellen, *Share Purchase Agreements* (Antwerp/Cambridge, Intersentia 2016) 379 p.; K. Reniers, *Gemeenrechtelijke beschermingsmechanismen bij de koop-verkoop van aandelen* (Intersentia 2017) 57 ff.

39 Also see the contribution of Christoph Michiels and Jan Roggen in this book, "Horses, Cars and the Potential for AI in M&A Transactions".

40 See, e.g., K.D. Betts and K.R. Jaep, 'The Dawn of Fully Automated Contract Drafting: Machine Learning Breathes New Life into a Decades-Old Promise' (2017) 15 Duke Law & Technology Review 216, 217 ff; D. Hricik, A.-L.S. Morgan and K.H. Williams, 'The Ethics of Using Artificial Intelligence to Augment Drafting Legal Documents' (2017) 4 Texas A&M Journal of Property Law 468 (*augmented drafting services*); J.M. Lipshaw, 'Halting, Intuition, Heuristics, and Action: Alan Turing and the Theoretical Constraints on AI-Lawyering' (2018) 5 Savannah Law Review 133, 136; G. Sartor, 'Contracts in the Infosphere' in S. Grundmann (ed), *European Contract Law in the Digital Age* (Intersentia 2018) 271. Also see tools like Arteria (https://www.arteria.ai/) and ClauseBase (https://www.clausebase.com/).

41 See, e.g., AI tools to value real estate, such as https://www.houseprice.ai.

42 AI systems are already being deployed in this way in non-commercial contexts, e.g., by peopling using a virtual home assistant (see for example A. Liptak, 'Amazon's Alexa Started Ordering People Dollhouses after Hearing Its Name on TV', *The Verge*, 7 January 2017, https://www.theverge.com/2017/1/7/14200210/amazon-alexa-tech-news-anchor-order-dollhouse), and in the context of high-frequency trading, where AI systems autonomously buy and sell stock based on fast calculations; see, e.g., S. Merabet, *Vers un droit d'intelligence artificielle* (Dalloz 2020) 368-369; R.T. Kreutzer and M. Sirrenberg, *Understanding Artificial Intelligence: Fundamentals, Use Cases and Methods for a Corporate AI Journey* (Springer 2020) 214 (implicit); M. Ebers, 'Artificial Intelligence, Contracting and Contract Law: An Introduction' in M. Ebers, C. Poncibò and M. Zou (eds), *Contracting and Contract Law in the Age of Artificial Intelligence* (Hart 2022) 23 (more general). Also see, more generally, K. Werbach and N. Cornell, 'Contracts ex machina' (2017) 67 Duke Law Journal 313, 322 (under development); G. Sartor, 'Contracts in the Infosphere' in S. Grundmann (ed), *European Contract Law in the Digital Age* (Intersentia 2018) 272. Als see H. Surden,

However, some of the most commonly used systems are concerned with using AI to facilitate due diligence analyses.[43] AI systems may be deployed to analyse a lot of (legal) documents in a qualitative, fast, efficient and cost-effective way. Corporations and lawyers are deploying several (legal) tools in today's practice.[44] In general, the companies and practitioners using these tools will not develop their own tools but will instead contract an AI developer to provide a tool. In the remainder of this chapter, we will focus mainly on those externally developed tools that may be used to perform due diligence.

4 Legal Implications of AI Tools for Due Diligence

4.1 Overview

When a contracting party deploys an AI system to help perform due diligence, either of two things can happen. Either the system performs well, resulting in a (sufficiently) qualitative due diligence analysis, or – and it is impossible to exclude this scenario entirely – the system returns undesirable output and incorrectly informs the system user. The system user may subsequently close the resulting contract at undesirable conditions or, more fundamentally, even regret the contract altogether.

This potentially raises two interesting legal questions, which we will examine more closely. First, the question arises as to whether a contracting party who contracts on the basis of incorrect AI system output might be able to invoke the mistake regime in an M&A context, as discussed below. Starting from a more general analysis of the application of the relevant legal regime to AI systems, particularly the requirement of excusability, we may examine the specific implications for M&A transactions. An additional challenge is that M&A transactions are usually complemented by contractual clauses, allocating (some of) the risk of mistakes to the buyer.

'Computable Contracts' (2012) 46 UC Davis Law Review 629, 695; M.S. Gal and N. Elkin-Koren, 'Algorithmic Consumers' (2016) 30 Harvard Journal of Law and Technology 309, 310-311.

43 Also see on this application of AI systems: M. Lauritsen, 'Marketing Real Lawyers in the Age of Artificial Intelligence' (2017) 34 GPSOLO 68; S. Semmler and Z. Rose, 'Artificial Intelligence: Application Today and Implications Tomorrow' (2017) 16 Duke Law & Technology Review 85, 86; O. Hansson, 'Product Review: Kira' (2018) 47 Colorado Lawyer 13, 13-14; E. Walters and M. Wright, 'Putting Artificial Intelligence to Work in Law Firms' (2018) 23 AALL Spectrum 18; J. Colloway, 'Artificial Intelligence and Everyday Law Practice' (2019) 90 Oklahoma Bar Journal 42-43 (future); T.P. Sapkota and others, 'Artificial Intelligence That Are Beneficial for Law' (2020) 17 US-China Law Review 217, 218-219; F. Mebius, 'Software Vervangt Stagair' (2020) Advocatenblad 30, 30.

44 See, e.g., Kira (https://kirasystems.com/) and Luminance (https://www.luminance.com/).

Second – and perhaps more closely related to the first question than one might assume at first glance – the question arises as to whether the system user might be able to hold the AI system provider contractually liable as analysed below. Similarly, a dissatisfied client might attempt to hold his service provider liable if the latter uses an AI system to perform the due diligence analysis.

Both of these legal questions are currently subject to the national legal regime. Although the European Union legislature, having adopted the AI Act, is considering additional AI-specific regulation, such as the Artificial Intelligence Liability Directive,[45] these have not yet been adopted. Furthermore, the latter does not apply to *contractual* liability, as we are interested in here. In addition, the (existing[46]) products liability directive does not cover this type of damage.[47]

4.2 *Incorrect Decision Making*

In case an AI system provides incorrect information to the system user, it is interesting to consider whether the AI system user can invoke the regime of mistake (Art. 5.34 Belgian Civil Code). This requires that a party is mistaken in an excusable way on an aspect of the contract that was crucial for his or her decision to contract.[48] At the same time, the counterparty is aware of this crucial character.[49]

---

45 Proposal for a Directive on adapting non contractual civil liability rules to artificial intelligence, COM(2022) 496 final, https://ec.europa.eu/info/sites/default/files/1_1_197605_prop_dir_ai_en.pdf.

46 Proposal for a Directive of the European Parliament and of the Council on liability for defective products COM(2022), 495 final, https://single-market-economy.ec.europa.eu/document/download/3193da9a-cecb-44ad-9a9c-7b6b23220bcd_en?filename=COM_2022_495_1_EN_ACT_part1_v6.pdf.

47 See Art. 9 of the Product Liability Directive and Art. 11 of the Belgian law of 25 February regarding liability for defective products.

48 Art. 5.34 Belgian Civil Code; Cass. 31 October 1966, *Arr.Cass.* 1967, 301; Cass. 3 March 1967, *Arr.Cass.* 1967, 829; Cass. 27 October 1995, *Arr.Cass.* 1995, 920; Cass. 24 September 2007, *TBBR* 2009, 216, annotation D. Philippe; Cass. 28 November 2013, *Arr.Cass.* 2013, 2572; Luik 4 November 1997, *TBBR* 1998, 374; Rb. Hasselt 2 April 2001, *RW* 2004-05, afl. 19, 751; Rb. Leuven 2 November 2016, *TBO* 2017, 89; J.H. Herbots, D. Clarysse and J. Werckx, 'Overzicht van rechtspraak: Bijzondere overeenkomsten (1977-1982) Deel 1' (1985) TPR 790; A. De Boeck, *Informatierechten en -plichten bij de totstandkoming en uitvoering van overeenkomsten* (Intersentia 2002) 225, no. 520; A. De Boeck, 'De wilsgebreken dwaling en bedrog vandaag Responsabilisering en ankerplaats voor de precontractuele informatieverplichting' in R. Van Ransbeeck (ed), *Wilsgebreken* (die Keure/la Charte 2007) 42; B. Demarsin, *Handel in kunstvoorwerpen* (die Keure/la Charte 2009) 191; J. del Corral, *Dwaling* (Larcier 2011) 48; A. Maes, 'De dwaling in rechte: een nieuw paardenmiddel?' (2014) TBBR 176, 177; S. Stijns, *Verbintenissenrecht: Boek 1* (die Keure/la Charte 2022) no. 105.

49 Art. 5.34 Belgian Civil Code; Cass. 27 October 1995, *RW* 1996-97, 298; Cass. 24 September 2007, *TBBR* 2009, 216, annotation D. Philippe, *RW* 2009-10, 1735; Antwerp 7 Mai 2012, *TBBR* 2016, afl. 4, 232; Bergen 3 juni 2014, *JLMB* 2017, 14; Luik 19 maart 2019, *JLMB* 2019, afl. 17, 791; A. De Boeck, *Informatierechten en -plichten bij de totstandkoming en uitvoering van overeenkomsten* (Intersentia 2002) 230-231; B. Demarsin,

A first obstacle in this regard is that the buyer often does not directly buy the target company but rather the shares in a corporation – raising the question of whether a mistake regarding some aspect of the company itself might be considered a mistake regarding an aspect of the shares.[50]

This should be nuanced, however. The so-called 'corporate veil' should not be applied too strictly because the sale concerns shares rather than the corporation's assets. This applies, for example, when it is clear to the seller that the buyer acquires the shares specifically to obtain the company's assets.[51]

A second obstacle is that it is often said that a mistake about the value of a good is, by definition, a mistake that may not lead to annulment (Art. 5.34 fourth para Belgian CC).[52] This is particularly challenging, as mistakes in an M&A context often concern or at least impact the target company's value. The buyer may, for example, be mistaken about the performance of the target company or its size or client portfolio.

This, too, should be nuanced. Only mistakes regarding the *subjective valuation* of the goods sold are excluded. Mistakes concerning an element that *does* impact the price may thus lead to an application of the mistake regime (Art. 5.34 fourth para Belgian CC). The *ratio legis* of the exclusion of mistakes regarding the value of an object – i.e., to dismiss the general possibility of annulment on the basis of an imbalance in the contract (Art. 5.38 Belgian CC)[53] – does not apply in such instances. A mistake regarding a crucial element of the good sold may thus lead to the application of the mistake regime, even though it also impacts the value of the good. Furthermore, we are convinced that the exclusion of Article 5.34, fourth para Belgian CC, should not be applied to mistakes

Handel in kunstvoorwerpen (die Keure/la Charte 2009) 204; J. del Corral, *Dwaling* (Larcier 2011) 48; S. Stijns, *Verbintenissenrecht: Boek 1* (die Keure/la Charte 2022) no. 105.

50 Luik 24 April 2004, *TBBR* 2004, 253, annotation A. De Boeck; K. Reniers, *Gemeenrechtelijke beschermingsmechanismen bij de koop-verkoop van aandelen* (Intersentia 2017) 185.

51 Also see F. Hellemans and B. Heynickx, 'Wilsgebreken in het vennootschapsrecht' in R. Van Ransbeeck (ed), *Wilsgebreken* (die Keure/la Charte 2007) 223-224; K. Reniers, *Gemeenrechtelijke beschermingsmechanismen bij de koop-verkoop van aandelen* (Intersentia 2017) 188 ff.

52 Brussels 11 January 2011, *TBBR* 2013, 98, annotation J. Callebaut; S. Stijns, D. Van Gerven and P. Wéry, 'Chronique de jurisprudence. Les obligations: les sources (1985-1995)' (1996) JT 689, 709; C. Goux, 'L'erreur, le dol et la lésion qualifiée: analyse et comparaisons' (2000) TBBR 14; B. Demarsin, *Handel in kunstvoorwerpen* (die Keure/la Charte 2009) 222 ff.; E. Swaenepoel, *Toetsing van het contractuele evenwicht* (Intersentia 2011) 106; K. Swerts and others, 'Toestemming' in J. Roodhooft (ed), *Bestendig Handboek Verbintenissenrecht* (Wolters Kluwer 2021) II.4 – 60. See specifically regarding the sale of shares: K. Reniers, *Gemeenrechtelijke beschermingsmechanismen bij de koop-verkoop van aandelen* (Intersentia 2017) 191-192.

53 C. Parmentier, 'La volonté des parties', *Les obligations contractuelles* (Jeune barreau 1984) 61-62; A. De Boeck and J. Waelkens, 'Dwaling' in E. Dirix, B. Tilleman and M. Dambre (eds), *Bijzondere overeenkomsten Artikelsgewijze commentaar met overzicht van rechtspraak en rechtsleer* (Wolters Kluwer 2017) 10.

regarding the price amount rather than the value of the good, as the discussed *ratio legis* does not credibly apply in such instances.[54]

Furthermore, the excusability requirement is particularly interesting. A mistake is deemed excusable if a reasonable contracting party would also commit it.[55] This raises the question of whether a reasonable contracting party would also deploy an AI system. Interestingly, this notion of excusability largely – though not fully[56] – corresponds to the notion of diligence in Belgian law.[57] The relevant question is thus whether the use of the AI system is diligent.

Although this question may be tackled in different ways,[58] it generally concerns a balancing exercise between two conflicting perspectives. On the one hand, the use of an AI system is, in fact, very diligent, as it helps cut costs and provide cheaper, faster and better services. As a result, someone deploying an AI system in due diligence will help cut transaction costs and will thus help make the resulting transaction cheaper,

54 Also see M. Herbosch, 'De dwaling van het consensualisme' (2022) TPR 797, 835.

55 Cass. 6 January 1944, *Arr.Cass.* 1944, 66; Cass. 10 April 1975, *Arr.Cass.* 1975, 871; Cass. 28 November 2013, *Arr.Cass.* 2013, 2572; Arbh. Luik 27 April 2001, *RRD* 2001, (193) 199; Antwerp 12 June 2006, *RW* 2008-09, afl. 7, 279, annotation B. van den Bergh; Gent 25 February 2009, *RW* 2010-2011, 746, annotation F. Haentjens; Brussels 7 September 2009, *T.Not.* 2010, afl. 4, 198; Antwerp 5 December 2011, *RW* 2013-2014, 866 (implicit); Gent 9 January 2012, *TBBR* 2014, afl. 4, 174, annotation A. MAES; Luik 19 December 2013, *TBBR* 2018, 432, annotation N. Tissot and J. Buyle; Rb. Dendermonde 18 september 1970, *RW* 1971-1972, afl. 13, 630, annotation R. Kruithof; Rb. Namen 24 November 2006, *Rev.not.b.* 2007, afl. 5, 260; Rb. Brussels 2 March 2012, *Res Jur.Imm.* 2013, 144; Orb. Brussels 5 April 2018, *TBBR* 2019, 139; C. Goux, 'L'erreur, le dol et la lésion qualifiée: analyse et comparaisons' (2000) TBBR 18; S. De Jonghe, 'Dwaling omtrent de zelfstandigheid van de zaak' (2004) RABG 409; J. del Corral, *Dwaling* (Larcier 2011) 63; A. De Boeck and J. Waelkens, 'Dwaling' in E. Dirix, B. Tilleman and M. Dambre (eds), *Bijzondere overeenkomsten Artikelsgewijze commentaar met overzicht van rechtspraak en rechtsleer* (Wolters Kluwer 2017) 29; F. Peeraer, *Nietigheid en aanverwante rechtsfiguren in het vermogensrecht* (Intersentia 2019) 150; K. Swerts and others, 'Toestemming' in J. Roodhooft (ed), *Bestendig Handboek Verbintenissenrecht* (Wolters Kluwer 2021) II.4 – 62, no. 1475; P. Wéry, *Droit des obligations. 1: Théorie générale du contrat* (Larcier 2021) 242, nr. 234; S. Stijns, *Verbintenissenrecht: Boek 1* (die Keure/la Charte 2022) no. 107.

56 See Cass. 28 June 1996, *Arr.Cass.* 1996, 664.

57 The excusability is closely related to the requirement of 'good faith' as to its knowledge component (not knowing and not being supposed to know), see more extensively M. Herbosch, *Intelligent contracteren* (Kluwer 2023) no. 349. This closely relates to the requirement of 'acting in good faith' (see A. Van Oevelen, 'De zogenaamde "subjectieve" goede trouw in het Belgische materiële privaatrecht (in het bijzonder in de materies die het notariaat aanbelangen)' (1990) TPR 1097-1099; A. De Boeck, *Informatierechten en -plichten bij de totstandkoming en uitvoering van overeenkomsten* (Intersentia 2002) 236, which is a requirement that is very similar to the Belgian duty of diligence.

58 See, e.g., extensively on an approach based on an analogy between the use of an AI system and the engagement of a risk: M. Herbosch, 'The Diligent Use of AI Systems: A Risk Worth Taking?' (2022) EuCML 14, 14 ff.

benefitting both contracting parties. Similarly, a Canadian judge ruled that a Canadian lawyer should have used an AI system to help a client.[59]

On the other hand, one might argue that the fact that AI systems occasionally and inevitably result in undesirable and incorrect output means that the use of such a system is generally not all that diligent. Someone who decides to use an AI system would thus be faced with the benefits of using an AI system, but also with the consequences, along the lines of the adage *eius damnum, cuius commodum.*[60]

Consequently, a contracting party that wants to use an AI system and act diligently may thus be required to implement safeguards to ensure that system errors do not cause too much damage. This would also help show the system user's diligence if damage arises. An important example of such a safeguard is human supervision. Depending on the performance of the AI system, the diligent deployment of that system might even require that the user does not unquestioningly trust the system results, but it takes some time to verify them.[61]

An essential challenge to applying the mistake regime in an M&A context is that the preliminary contracts usually stipulate that it is up to the buyer to verify all the relevant information. As a result, it is more difficult for the buyer to show that they have acted diligently.

In this regard, it is helpful to stress that such clauses have certain limitations. First, such clauses cannot fully exclude the whole regime of mistake.[62] The mistake regime is a protective, mandatory legal regime.[63] It may only be renounced after the mistaken

59 It should be noted, however, that this case was also determined by a Canadian requirement for lawyers to use the technological tools where available; see Superior Court of Justice Ontario 22 November 2018 (*Cass v. 1410088 Ontario Inc.*, 2018 ONSC 6959), http://canlii.ca/t/hw728.

60 See, e.g., R. Janal, 'Extra-Contractual Liability for Wrongs Committed by Autonomous Systems' in M. Ebers and S. Navas (eds), *Algorithms and Law* (Cambridge University Press 2020) 194.

61 See similarly in Art. 14 of the AI act, the requirement of human oversight for high-risk systems.

62 B. Demarsin, 'Clausules in verband met dwaling' in G.-L. Ballon and others (eds), *Gemeenrechtelijke clausules, vol I en II* (Intersentia 2013) 454-455; T. Vansweevelt and B. Weyts, 'Geldigheidsvereisten van de overeenkomst' in B. Weyts and T. Vansweevelt (eds), *Handboek Verbintenissenrecht* (Intersentia 2019) 193. While some authors appear to claim that the mistake regime *can* be excluded (see e.g., A. De Boeck, 'De wilsgebreken dwaling en bedrog vandaag Responsabilisering en ankerplaats voor de precontractuele informatieverplichting' in R. Van Ransbeeck (ed), *Wilsgebreken* (die Keure/la Charte 2007) 67 ff; K. Reniers, *Gemeenrechtelijke beschermingsmechanismen bij de koop-verkoop van aandelen* (Intersentia 2017) 209; P. Wéry, *Droit des obligations. 1: Théorie générale du contrat* (Larcier 2021) 245-246, they seem to base this on the fact that the mistake conditions can be modulated (*infra*). As a result, their view may be quite similar although slightly less nuanced.

63 In this sense, see S. Stijns, 'De sanctionering van de wilsgebreken' in R. Van Ransbeeck (ed), *Wilsgebreken* (die Keure/la Charte 2007) 137.

party has learnt the truth (Art. 5.61 Belgian CC).[64] It is, however, possible for parties to contractually modulate the varying conditions that must be met for the application of this regime.[65] This is often done in varying sectors. For example, in the art sector, a seller of a piece of art will often explicitly state that they do not guarantee the authenticity of that piece of art.[66] In this way, parties may describe the object of the sale. As a result, the buyer may not hold the seller contractually liable if the piece of art does not turn out to be what the buyer had hoped for. This also impacts the mistake regime. If the contract explicitly states that the work of art is not sold as a work by a specific artist, the buyer will have a hard time showing that the conditions of the mistake regime are met.

While we thus do not dogmatically adhere to the idea that *l'aléa chasse la nullité pour erreur*,[67] such contractual clauses may have a crucial impact on the mistake regime's requirements. They may, for example, render the burden of proof substantially more

---

64 See, more generally: S. Stijns, 'De sanctionering van de wilsgebreken' in R. Van Ransbeeck (ed), *Wilsgebreken* (die Keure/la Charte 2007) 137; A. De Boeck and J. Waelkens, 'Dwaling' in E. Dirix, B. Tilleman and M. Dambre (eds), *Bijzondere overeenkomsten Artikelsgewijze commentaar met overzicht van rechtspraak en rechtsleer* (Wolters Kluwer 2017) 50; F. Peeraer, *Nietigheid en aanverwante rechtsfiguren in het vermogensrecht* (Intersentia 2019) 360-361; T. Vansweevelt and B. Weyts, 'Geldigheidsvereisten van de overeenkomst' in B. Weyts and T. Vansweevelt (eds), *Handboek Verbintenissenrecht* (Intersentia 2019) 181; I. Claeys and T. Tanghe, *Algemeen contractenrecht* (Intersentia 2022) 535-537.

65 Cass. 24 April 2003, *Arr.Cass.* 2003, 1038; Luik 30 November 2009, *JLMB* 2011, 457; Rb. Brussels 6 April 2007, *TMR* 2008, 342 (implicit); H. De Page, *Traité élémentaire de droit civil belge, Tome I: Introduction. Théorie générale des droits et des lois. Les personnes – la famille* (Bruylant 1962) 63; R. Kruithof, 'Verbintenissen Overzicht van rechtspraak (1974-1980)' (1983) TPR 555; A. De Boeck, *Informatierechten en -plichten bij de totstandkoming en uitvoering van overeenkomsten* (Intersentia 2002) 248; B. Tilleman, 'Dwaling bij de aan- en verkoop van kunst en antiek' in E. Dirix and others (eds), *Liber Amicorum Jacques Herbots* (Kluwer 2002) 455-456; R. Dekkers and others, *Handboek Burgerlijk Recht – deel III* (Intersentia 2007) 29; R. Timmermans, 'Dwaling en bedrog bij koop en verkoop van onroerend goed' in R. Derine and others (eds), *Het onroerend goed in de praktijk* (Wolters Kluwer 2007) XV.F.42; D. Philippe, 'A propos de la substance de l'erreur' (2009) TBBR 218, 219; J. del Corral, *Dwaling* (Larcier 2011) 76; P. Wéry, *Droit des obligations. 1: Théorie générale du contrat* (Larcier 2011) 238; B. Demarsin, 'Clausules in verband met dwaling' in G.-L. Ballon and others (eds), *Gemeenrechtelijke clausules*, vol I en II (Intersentia 2013) 457; P. Van Ommeslaghe, *Traité de droit civil – Tome II: Les obligations* (Bruylant 2013) 262; A. De Boeck and J. Waelkens, 'Dwaling' in E. Dirix, B. Tilleman and M. Dambre (eds), *Bijzondere overeenkomsten Artikelsgewijze commentaar met overzicht van rechtspraak en rechtsleer* (Wolters Kluwer 2017) 43 ff; T. Vansweevelt and B. Weyts, 'Geldigheidsvereisten van de overeenkomst' in B. Weyts and T. Vansweevelt (eds), *Handboek Verbintenissenrecht* (Intersentia 2019) 192; P. Wéry, *Droit des obligations. 1: Théorie générale du contrat* (Larcier 2021) 245-246.

66 See for some concrete illustrations E. Dirix, 'Dwaling en bedrog bij koop van kunst en antiek' in K. Rimanque (ed), *Kunst en recht* (Kluwer 1985) 103-104; B. Demarsin, *Handel in kunstvoorwerpen* (die Keure/la Charte 2009) 169 ff.

67 See on this adage: M. von Kuegelgen, 'Réflexions sur le régime des nullités et des inopposabilités' in P.-A. Foriers (ed), *Les obligations contractuelles* (Jeane Barreau 2000) 327. See similarly in France (J. Ghestin and Y.-M. Serinet, 'Erreur', *Répertoire de droit civil* (Dalloz 2018) nos. 58 ff.) and the Netherlands (H. Drion, 'Algemene problemen', *De dwaling in het privaatrecht* (Algemene Vergadering van de Broederschap der Candidaat-Notarissen 1972) 6). A. De Boeck, *Informatierechten en -plichten bij de totstandkoming en uitvoering van overeenkomsten* (Intersentia 2002) 248-249; S. Bar, 'Quand le compteur kilométrique trompe l'acheteur d'un véhicule d'occasion' (2004) TBBR 46, 48; A. De Boeck and J. Waelkens, 'Dwaling'

complicated because the author of the work is crucial to the buyer. After all, if the buyer cared so much about the element concerned, would they not have examined it more closely to resultingly find that it did not match his or her expectations? Similarly, and closely related to this, such clauses increase the threshold of excusability. In the application of 'forewarned is forearmed' a diligent buyer would analyse an element more thoroughly after being warned about its potential problematic status. It thus becomes substantially more difficult to fulfil the burden of proof regarding the varying mistake requirements.

To the same effect, a contractual clause that states that the buyer has received access to all the relevant information and that it is up to him or her to verify this information is thus likely to increase the standard required for the buyer to be mistaken in an excusable way.[68] While this cannot be entirely excluded, it can be made very difficult.

More generally, the excusability of using an AI system as a source of information closely relates to using external advisors. Even when someone hires an external expert for advice, the relevant question remains whether or not the mistaken party should have reasonably noticed the mistake.[69] Hence, when a part of the due diligence is left up to an AI system, this does not lead to a more flexible application of the mistake regime. Nevertheless, the fact that a person deploys modern tools may help demonstrate the diligence of the mistaken party, much like it may be diligent and prudent to seek the help of an external expert.[70]

However, using an AI system may impact the excusability requirement negatively if the AI system is selected negligently or when it is deployed negligently. The latter may be the case if the system is used in violation of the user manual. More generally, users of AI systems may take several steps to ensure the diligence of their system use.[71] Such elements may subsequently help highlight the excusability of AI system users.

---

in E. Dirix, B. Tilleman and M. Dambre (eds), *Bijzondere overeenkomsten Artikelsgewijze commentaar met overzicht van rechtspraak en rechtsleer* (Wolters Kluwer 2017) 45.

68 The contract can, for example, stipulate what types of investigative measures a contracting party should take, before contracting. See, for example, Rb. Nijvel 9 September 2011, *Rev.not.b.* 2013, 265.

69 L. Herve, 'Du caractère inexcusable de l'erreur commise par l'acheteur d'un terrain à bâtir' (1991) ActDr 216, 230; A. De Boeck, *Informatierechten en -plichten bij de totstandkoming en uitvoering van overeenkomsten* (Intersentia 2002) 244-245; A. De Boeck and J. Waelkens, 'Dwaling' in E. Dirix, B. Tilleman and M. Dambre (eds), *Bijzondere overeenkomsten Artikelsgewijze commentaar met overzicht van rechtspraak en rechtsleer* (Wolters Kluwer 2017) 38; I. Samoy and others, 'Legal Ignorance in Belgian Private Law' (2021) European Review of Private Law 161, 172.

70 See, at least implicitly in this sense, J. Stevens, 'Hoe gemeen is het gemene recht?' (1979-1980) RW 1602, 1617; A.-S. Baudry and C. De Koker, *Valkuilen bij aankoop van een onroerend goed: Wilsgebreken, verborgen gebreken en verborgen non-conformiteit* (Larcier 2016) 37.

71 M. Herbosch, 'The Diligent Use of AI Systems: A Risk Worth Taking?' (2022) EuCML 14, 14 ff.

The fact that there is *some* chance that the AI system may have resulted in incorrect output and that the contracting party may be mistaken should not all too easily be generalised to deduce that this party's mistake was not excusable. Even in a non-AI context, there is always *some* – usually minimal – probability that things are not as the party contracting had imagined them.[72] Both in a non-AI and in an AI context, this uncertainty only becomes relevant when the degree of the uncertainty increases, and the behaviour of the contracting party thus becomes reckless, failing to meet the standard of reasonableness.[73]

Regardless of whether the buyer uses an AI system, the relevant question remains whether or not a 'reasonable buyer' would also have been mistaken. Even if a preliminary contract dictates increased care, this may still be the case, for example, if the provided documents contain incorrect information that was impossible for the buyer to verify. Nevertheless, such preliminary contracts often significantly curtail the possibility of the buyer to annul the contract in the case of a mistake. As a result, from a mistake perspective, it is usually of limited importance that the buyer uses an AI system.

4.3 *Contractual Liability*

Suppose the buyer purchases the shares of a company due to incorrect advice by an AI system. In that case, he may also be able to hold the provider or user of the system contractually liable. He might hold the provider liable, for example, if the buyer himself used an AI system. If his (legal) counsel used the system, he might want to hold the latter liable for the resulting damage.

Even though our previous discussion clarified that the buyer who, either directly or via an advisor, used an AI system will usually be barred from annulling the sale altogether, given the prevalence of preliminary agreements that render this more complicated, the buyer may thus attempt to seek compensation from the person who provided them with the system.[74]

72 Some uncertainty cannot be excluded; see J. Ghestin and Y.-M. Serinet, 'Erreur', in *Répertoire de droit civil* (Dalloz 2018) nos. 68 ff. See in a similar sense: K. de la Durantaye, *Erklärung und Wille* (Mohr Siebeck 2020) 17-19.

73 In a liability context, the resulting risk that was taken is then said to become 'abnormal'; see more extensively M. Herbosch, 'The Diligent Use of AI Systems: A Risk Worth Taking?' (2022) EuCML 14, 19 ff.

74 In a traditional context, where someone hires an external expert (and not an AI system), it is sometimes even argued that this should be the *only* redress for the mistaken party, i.e. with exclusion of the mistake regime; see M. Dambre, 'Informatieplicht en actiemogelijkheden van partijen bij de aankoop van kunstvoorwerpen' (1990) TBBR 38, 44-45.

For the potential contractual liability of the system provider in relation to the system user, it is crucial to assess whether or not the contract meets the contractually agreed upon standards. If this is the case, for example, because the contract only stipulates that the system should achieve an average performance of a certain level, e.g., by performing with a certain recall[75] or precision[76] when qualifying contract clauses, then the mere fact that the system user did not achieve a desirable result in an individual instance does not qualify as a contractual breach. As we have discussed earlier, it is, in fact, inherent to AI systems that they may occasionally result in undesirable output. The relevant question is thus whether the AI system's performance exceeds the boundaries to the extent that this should be deemed permissible.

When the contract does not explicitly stipulate the standards the system should meet, Belgian law entails that the system provider should ensure that the system presents a reasonable degree of accuracy.[77] The system provider, hence, has a duty of best efforts – i.e., a duty of diligence – to optimise the system performance to a reasonable extent. Such a duty of diligence does not require the system provider to make unreasonable efforts.[78] After some system training, further optimisation of the system would require increasingly more time, effort and investment for an increasingly slight improvement of the system. At some point, these investments are no longer reasonable in light of the marginally improved performance of the system.

Until now, we have discussed whether the system provider might be held contractually liable for potential harm that a system user suffers due to the inadequate performance of the system. In addition, assessing whether a counterparty of the system user might hold that system user contractually liable for harm caused by erroneous AI system output may be relevant. This may, for example, be relevant when a client is dissatisfied with their counsel's use of an AI system. In that regard, we might think of a lawyer who uses an AI system to perform a due diligence analysis for their client. In such relations, the client may seek liability of the lawyer-system user when they suffer damage due to an incorrect analysis.

---

75 The recall of a classification system is a measure for the amount of correct predictions, compared to the total amount of elements that should have been predicted to belong to a certain category.

76 The precision of a classification system is a measure for the amount of correct predictions, compared to the total amount of predictions made for a certain category.

77 See for a similar case in the Netherlands, concerning a traditional IT-system (and not an AI system): Rb. Amsterdam 18 December 2019, ECLI:NL:RBAMS:2019:9635, *Computerrecht* 2020, no. 85, annotation by W.F.R Rinzema.

78 See in the same vein G. Jocqué, 'Bewustzijn en subjectieve verwijtbaarheid', *Aansprakelijkheid, aansprakelijkheidsverzekering en andere schadevergoedingssystemen* (Kluwer 2007) 37-38.

Concerning their client, such service providers are responsible for the people they employ and the tools they use.[79] To hold a service provider contractually liable, the client needs to show that there was a contractual breach, i.e., that the lawyer-system user did not meet the required standards of care in his or her analysis,[80] e.g. by recklessly deploying an unfit AI system. This question is closely related to the diligence of the use of AI systems (. However, the burden of proof, in this case, resides with a party who does not readily have access to information about the system's performance.

To meet the required standard of proof, the client might attempt to invoke the new Belgian Article 5.230 Civil Code, which states that a service provider is liable if the service fails to fulfil his or her obligations due to the use of a defective tool. This requires, however, that the client is able to show the defectiveness of the tool used – i.e., the AI system. This is, again, somewhat problematic as the client does not readily possess information related to the system performance as discussed earlier.

Based on the previous discussion, it is clear that many hurdles hinder someone seeking compensation for damage resulting from an incorrect AI system due diligence analysis. Furthermore, parties will often incorporate clauses limiting or excluding contractual liability[81] in addition to clauses that detail the parties' contractual obligations. Without discussing these clauses in depth,[82] it should be clear that they may constitute an additional obstacle for a party seeking compensation in case of erroneous AI system output. This applies to the system user, who may have a hard time invoking the mistake regime, and to their ability to hold the system provider contractually liable.

5 Conclusion

In this chapter, we have examined the use of AI systems in M&A due diligence from a legal perspective. We started with the unique properties of AI systems that make them intriguing, although challenging, tools to use for M&A transactions. Considering these properties, we could examine their legal implications in an M&A context. To that end, we discussed the legal regime that applies when AI systems are used to form contracts while contemplating what this means for M&A transactions.

79 See for the general principle: S. Stijns, *Verbintenissenrecht: Boek 1* (die Keure/la Charte 2022) nos. 200 ff.

80 To this end, we are implicitly qualifying the duty of a lawyer to perform a qualitative due diligence analysis as a duty of best efforts in the sense of Art. 5.72 first para. of the Belgian Civil Code.

81 See Art. 5.89 Belgian Civil Code.

82 See in more detail: H. Claes and M. Herbosch, 'Artificial Intelligence and Contractual Liability Limitations: A Natural Combination?' (2023) 31 European Review of Private Law 469 ff.

This helped clarify that AI-supported due diligence analysis is inherently imperfect, much like a more traditional human analysis. It is impossible to guarantee that an AI system will achieve the desired result in all situations. As a result, situations where AI systems lead to mistakes will arise when these systems are used sufficiently often in M&A due diligence. The question then arises as to whether the party using the system can invoke the protection of the legal regime of mistake.

This largely depends on the challenging condition of excusability. An analysis of the diligence of the use of the system in the given circumstances determines this condition. Furthermore, it is also influenced by potential preliminary contracts between the parties, allocating due diligence risks to the buyer. It may be very tough to show that this requirement is met, although contracting parties cannot entirely exclude this possibility.

In addition to the legal regime of mistake, undesirable system output might also give rise to questions of liability. This applies both to the system provider, in his or her relationship with the party using the system, and to service providers that use an AI system in the context of their services, such as a lawyer using an AI system to perform due diligence, in their relations with their clients. In both instances, a particularly challenging property of the contractual liability regime is that the burden of proof resides with the party who suffered the damage, even though they cannot readily access information about the system's performance.

The new Belgian provision stating that service providers are liable for contractual breaches caused by defective tools they employ does not fully mitigate this challenge. The latter requires, inter alia, that the client can show that the system used was defective. In this situation, the client faces the same hurdle: they do not readily have access to information about the system's performance.

Contractual clauses may further limit the liability of the system user or provider. While a detailed analysis of such clauses exceeds the scope of the present contribution, it should be clear that they may make it virtually impossible for the client or lawyer-system user to obtain damages from the lawyer-system user or the system provider, respectively.

Part II
Art Authentication

The Use of Artificial Intelligence to Secure Art Transactions – Some Thoughts of an Art Lawyer

*Bert Demarsin**

1 'What We Are All Striving for Is Authenticity!'

Do you like *real* butter? Do you have a taste for *real* champagne? You probably prefer to give and receive *real* flowers, or perhaps you have a weakness for *real* Italian fashion. Do you write with an *authentic* Mont-Blanc? Are you tempted by German cars for their *authentic* driving pleasure, and do you avoid the beaten track during holidays in order to experience that piece of *authentic* Southern atmosphere? "What we are all striving for is authenticity!"[1] Oprah Winfrey proclaimed some time ago, when talking about the important things in life.

While it is generally not recommended to take this lady's quotes for granted without any critical thinking, I have to admit that her statement on authenticity does seem to hold true. After all, in our consumer society, a significant part of the economy seems to be aimed at *ersatz* and reproduction. As far back as the 1930s, the philosopher Walter Benjamin proclaimed, "Was Menschen gemacht hatten, das konnte immer von Menschen nachgemacht werden".[2] Since then our reproductive skills have obviously not declined, considering the further development of science and technology. They have even reached a symbolic end point, as in contemporary society, technically, a living creature, such as a sheep or even a human being, can be duplicated.[3]

In tandem with the technical possibilities of reproduction, the question of authenticity has become an important one in our society. The 'authenticity' or 'genuineness' of an object or experience has become an economic factor of importance in a society that has come to understand that often things are not what they seem. In today's economy, the

* Prof. dr. Bert Demarsin – KU Leuven, Faculty of law (Belgium).

1 O. WINFREY, *The Oprah Magazine*, March 2002.

2 W. BENJAMIN, *Das Kunstwerk im Zeitalter seiner technischen Reproduzierbarkeit*, Frankfurt, Suhrkamp, 2007, 10.

3 S. LEQUETTE-DE KERVENOAËL, *L'authenticité des œuvres d'art*, Paris, L.G.D.J., 2006, 1.

original product somehow ironically became the exception, as imitations on the market are infinitely more common than 'the real thing'.

For a considerable period of time, that sensitivity to the authentic existed mainly in the art trade. From the beginning of the nineteenth century onwards, the issue of authenticity took the lead, at a time when in other economic fields or sections of society the concern about authenticity was simply non-existent. Case law can testify to this since for the past two centuries purchasers of works of art have considered lack of authenticity to be important enough to take the matter to court.[4]

The art trade may not only have been the first industry to fully recognise the importance of 'genuineness' or 'authenticity'; it is also the field in which these qualities seem to have the biggest impact. Just think about some notorious works of art that at first seem to be just some children's drawing, some trivial painting or some perfectly common urinal. Without any physical change happening, these objects turn into invaluable works of art because of the simple fact that they prove to descend from a great artist. And so it occurs that the seventeenth-century painting a buyer was able to purchase at a public auction for $288,000 was suddenly valued at $18,000,000 the moment it turned out to be the work of the famous baroque artist Nicolas Poussin (1594-1665). The painting remained unaltered, but its value increased times 60. Similarly, an unsightly sculpture was found to be a piece of bravura from the renaissance sculptor Zoppo. As a result, the price increased from FF. 4,500 to some FF. 3,200,000. Out of the blue, the same sculpture turned out to be seven hundred times more expensive![5] Yet it is not all roses, as the exact opposite can happen as well. The news that the portrait of the young man that figured in a Sotheby's auction catalogue was not made by Rembrandt caused the estimated value to tumble from 70 to 4 million.[6]

Due to its far-reaching impact in the art trade, the average citizen almost spontaneously relates the idea of authenticity with the trade in works of art. Somehow, the subject seems to appeal to the public's imagination, as authenticity issues are discussed at length in the press. That happens not only in specialised magazines, such as *Artnews*, *The Burlington Magazine*, *The Art Newspaper*, *L'estampille - L'objet d'art* or *Connaissance des arts* but also in mainstream newspapers.

---

4 *Jendwine v. Slade* (1797) 170 *Eng. Rep.* 459; *Lowther v. Lord Lowther* (1806) 33 *Eng. Rep.* 230; *Lomi v. Tucker* (1829) 172 *Eng. Rep.* 586; *Hill v. Grey* (1816) 171 *Eng. Rep.* 521; *Pennell v. Woodburn* (1835) 173 *Eng. Rep.* 52; *De Sewhanberg v. Buchanan* (1832) 172 *Eng. Rep.* 1004; CA Paris, 17 June 1813, *S.* 1814, II, 85; Trib. civ. Seine, 14 March 1840, *Le Droit* 15 March 1840.

5 CA Paris, 1e ch., sect. B, 15 November 1990, *Juris-Data* nr. 1990-025479.

6 S. LEQUETTE-DE KERVENOAËL, *L'authenticité des œuvres d'art*, Paris, L.G.D.J., 2006, 1.

Although the question of whether the authenticity of a work of art affects the way in which it is aesthetically experienced is an interesting one, we will not discuss it the course of this article. We retain from the foregoing that authenticity has an unmistakable financial impact. In the commercialisation process of a work of art, authenticity indeed plays first fiddle. It is precisely the hand of the master that determines the art-historical and financial value. The fact that Picasso allegedly gave the following answer when he was asked to interpret one of his own cubist canvases may be evidence of this: "Ce que cela représente, Madame? … Et ben …, cela représente un million".

Furthermore, it seems that the financial importance of authenticity in the art trade is only increasing, since all sorts of studies show that prices have undergone exponential growth over the last 40 years.[7] For example, a couple of months prior to the outbreak of the financial crisis, which also severely affected the art market, the 2007 Artprice market report showed another year of substantial growth, with its peak moment appearing in November 2007. At that time, the art market was surely flourishing, given its seventh year of continuous price increases. The average annual growth amounted to no less than 18%. Let us consider a few examples: a portrait of Liz Taylor by Andy Warhol was sold at \$21 million, while the seller obtained it for 'only' \$3.25 million six years earlier. Monet's *Waterloo Bridge* was sold in London in 2007 at £16 million, whereas in 1990 the same work changed owners for a tenth of that price. Besides, such price increases are not reserved for the 'extremely rich'. On the market for works priced below €20,000, which still makes up 90% of the total number of transactions on the art market, the same upward trend can be seen.[8] The sale at Christie's – Paris of an ink drawing by Odilon Redon, *Jeune fille avec chat et fleurs*, yielded €3,200, while three months later the gavel at Sotheby's – London closed the deal at €9,500. In 2006, €4,500 was paid for the pastel *Relief sur l'idée du Requiem* by Jean Tinguely. At the end of December 2007 the same pastel was traded at the Parisian auction house Piasa for €10,100. Even without instances of contested authenticity there are enormous price fluctuations due to speculative growth of the market. It goes without saying that authenticity issues make prices soar or drop even further.

It is clear that in the art trade authenticity issues have an enormous financial impact. Nor are they a rare phenomenon at all. They were not rare in the past and will not be rare in the future. After all, a great deal of expertise is required to authenticate works

7 We mention a few: valuable are the Art Market Trends, an extensive report that Artprice publishes every year (www.artprice.com) and the analysis of *Kusin & Company*, an international economic research institute for the trade in works of art (http://www.kusin.com). Also of interest are the research reports of *The European Fine Art Foundation* (www.tefaf.com). See Y. GAILLARD, *Le marché de l'art français aux enchères*, Paris, Economica, 2000, 249 p.

8 http://web.artprice.com/AMI/AMI.aspx (accessed 15 August 2023).

of art, and mistakes are easily made. Here new technologies come in, such as the use of artificial intelligence, which is the central topic of this contribution. However, in order to fully grasp how AI may or may not change the art industry and the legal position of collectors, dealers and experts, it is probably wise to briefly analyse the notion of authenticity, as it is the key concept that all cases flow from.

2 THE CONCEPT OF AUTHENTICITY?

What does it actually mean when a work of art is said to be authentic? Have you ever thought about that? Despite the ubiquity of the term, defining the true meaning of the notion of authenticity turns out to be rather difficult. Most people tend to focus on the object to determine what requirements it must meet to be authentic. The key, however, lies in understanding that no work of art is authentic by itself, as 'authenticity' is not an intrinsic or objective quality of an art object. An art object is authentic only in relation to a certain attribution, which is added (usually by the seller) to the art object.[9] In previous research, I therefore called authenticity to be a 'relational' or 'functional' concept:[10] The authenticity of a work of art should always be assessed in relation to the attribution that goes with it for commercial purposes. Indeed, the notion 'authentic' acquires its full meaning only from the attribution, to which, strangely enough, it is completely redundant. An authentic painting by Rubens is no different from a painting by Rubens. The authentic Mona Lisa is just ... the Mona Lisa, whereas an inauthentic Picasso is actually not a Picasso at all.[11] As such, authenticity is not a quality of the paintings by Rubens but what sets them apart from a much larger group of paintings that were not made by Rubens. Since these works could not be termed paintings by Rubens in the first place, the adjective 'authentic', strictly speaking, does not add anything to the category of paintings by Rubens.[12]

We just pointed out that when it comes to authenticity, everything depends on the attribution linked to the object or the collectible. Accordingly, 'authenticity' can be

9 J.L. AUSTIN, *Sense and Sensibilia*, London, Oxford University Press, 1964, 69; D. DUTTON, 'Authenticity in Art', in J. LEVINSON (ed.), *The Oxford Handbook of Aesthetics*, Oxford, Oxford University Press, 2003 (258), 258; L. STEPHAN, 'Le vrai, l'authentique et le faux', *Cahiers du musée national d'art moderne* 1991, afl. 36 (7), 7; N. HEINICH, 'Art contemporain et la fabrication de l'inauthentique', *Terrain* 1999, afl. 33 (5), 5; F. BALLON, 'L'authenticité d'une œuvre d'art. Expertise: modalités et techniques', *Petites Affiches* 2005, afl. 149 (4), 5-6.

10 In 2008, the author of this article obtained a PhD in law from KU Leuven with a comparative law dissertation devoted to the issue of authenticity in the art trade. See B. DEMARSIN, *Authenticiteit en contracteren omtrent kunst: een rechtsvergelijkende analyse*, Bruges, die Keure, 2008, 801 p.

11 N. GOODMAN, 'Authenticity', in *Grove Art Online*, Oxford, Oxford University Press, https://www.oxfordartonline.com/groveart (accessed 15 August 2023).

12 J.L. AUSTIN, *Sense and Sensibilia*, London, Oxford University Press, 1964, 70-71.

defined as "the quality of an (art) object to actually be what it purports to be".[13] Affirming a work's authenticity therefore comes down to substantiating the relationship between what the attribution to a work states and what the work actually is.[14] Accordingly, inauthenticity occurs when there are discrepancies between what the artwork claims to be and reality or – to put it succinctly – discrepancies between the putative and the effective.[15]

Due to its functional or relational nature, the notion of authenticity can be attuned to the endless diversity in artworks and collectibles. Hence, the notion need not be limited to the identity of the artist (*e.g.* a panel by Rembrandt or a canvas by Vermeer), a placement in time and space (*e.g.* an Egyptian figurine of the XIIIth dynasty or Meissen porcelain of the early 18th century) a ritual context of use (*e.g.* a Dogon mask), the material used (*e.g.* silver, ivory or platinum) or the technique employed (*e.g.* a drawing, an engraving or a lithograph). 'Authenticity' can actually concern any possible feature of the object. "Puisqu'un objet présente toujours une infinité de caractéristiques, il est toujours pourvu d'une infinité d'identités spécifiques distinctes.... Un objet, par ailleurs, peut être authentique ou non de plus d'un point de vue".[16] In other words, since an attribution can concern just about any conceivable quality of an art object, the same applies to the concept of authenticity. According to this pragmatic interpretation, authenticity becomes but the expression of the hypersingular, depending entirely on what you as an *attributor* (or the art expert you consult) choose to mention. Hence, it becomes clear that authenticity does not concern the quality of the art object but rather pertains to the quality of the attribution activity. Accordingly, our attention shifts from the art object to the doings of the authenticating subject.[17] So let us focus on the role of these *authenticators* and *attributors*: who are these art experts and how do they go about?

---

13 E. SOURIAU and A. SOURIAU, *Vocabulaire d'esthétique*, Paris, PUF, 1990, 200-201; S.M. LEVY, 'Authentication and Appraisal of Artwork', in R.S. KAUFMAN (ed.), *Art Law Handbook*, Gaithersburg, Aspen Law and Business, 2000 (829), 833; F. DURET-ROBERT, 'L'authenticité des œuvres d'art dans la pratique du marché de l'art', in M.-A. RENOLD, P. GABUS and J. DE WERRA (eds.), *L'expertise et l'authentification des œuvres d'art*, Geneva, Schulthess, 2007 (29), 29. See also S. LEQUETTE-DE KERVENOAËL, *L'authenticité des œuvres d'art*, Paris, L.G.D.J. 2006, 160; E.J.H. SCHRAGE, *De Regelen der Kunst III*, Amsterdam, Russell Advocaten, 2007, 78-79.

14 F. BALLON, 'L'authenticité d'une œuvre d'art. Expertise: modalités et techniques', *Petites Affiches* 2005, afl. 149 (4), 4; N. HEINICH, 'Art contemporain et la fabrication de l'inauthentique', *Terrain* 1999, afl. 33 (5), 5; O. DE BAECQUE, 'L'authenticité d'une œuvre d'art. Rapport de synthèse', *Petites Affiches* 2005, afl. 149 (36), 36.

15 B. DEMARSIN, *Authenticiteit en contracteren omtrent kunst: een rechtsvergelijkende analyse*, Bruges, die Keure 2008, 41-42.

16 L. PRIETO, 'Le mythe de l'original', in G. GENETTE (ed.), *Esthétique et poétique*, Paris, Editeur du Seuil, 1992 (131), 133-134.

17 B. DEMARSIN, *Authenticiteit en contracteren omtrent kunst: een rechtsvergelijkende analyse*, Bruges, die Keure, 2008, 100.

3 Meet the Art Expert

If you want to trade an art object, you have to make known to the world what you have on sale. In other words, the art object needs an attribution, a suitable description put together to indicate the quality or main features of the product. If the seller is a professional art dealer, he will probably formulate that attribution himself. Of course, that will happen when the seller considers himself sufficiently competent to make that judgment call. It may, however, occur that the complexity of the assessment forces the seller to engage an art expert to perform this difficult job for him.[18] But who are these art experts' owners and dealers call upon to assist them in case of need?

First, there are the academic art scholars: (art) historians/archaeologists/ anthropologists, whose expertise is the result of training and research at a university or specialised research institution. As scholars, they focus their entire work on the oeuvre of a particular artist, a time period, a school or even a culture. They act on their own initiative and carry out independent research without being driven by questions that potential stakeholders, such as owners or dealers, may address to them.[19]

Unlike academic art scholars, commercial art experts do not examine art objects on their own initiative but provide their services at the behest of a client. Usually, their intervention must facilitate or secure a pending sale, by formulating an attribution at the request of one or even both parties.[20] Few commercial art experts devote themselves exclusively to authentication and appraisal services; most of them combine this with other commercial activities, such as running a gallery or antiques shop.[21] They mostly acquired their authentication skills through some sort of academic or professional

18 P.H. KARLEN, 'Fakes, Forgeries and Expert Opinions', in P. LALIVE (ed.), *International Sales of Works of Art - La vente internationale d'oeuvres d'art*, I, Geneva, Institute of International Business Law and Practise, 1988 (219), 221.

19 F. CHATELAIN, C. PATTYN and J. CHATELAIN, *Œuvres d'art et objets de collection en droit français*, Paris, Berger-Levrault, 1997, 134; M. CORNU and N. MALLET-POUJOL, *Droit, œuvres d'art et musées: protection et valorisation des collections*, Paris, C.N.R.S. Editions, 2004, 45-48; P.H. KARLEN, 'Fakes, Forgeries and Expert Opinions', in P. LALIVE (ed.), *International Sales of Works of Art - La vente internationale d'oeuvres d'art*, I, Geneva, Institute of International Business Law and Practise, 1988 (219), 221; H. VEROUGSTRAETE-MARCQ, 'L'expertise scientifique des peintures: les faux et les nouveaux faux', *Annales de droit de Louvain* 1988 (415), 415.

20 M. ROETHLISBERGER, 'Le statut de l'expert dans la pratique', in Q. BYRNE-SUTTON (ed.), *L'expertise dans la vente d'objets d'art - Aspects juridiques et pratiques*, Zürich, Schulthess, 1992 (111), 112.

21 F. CHATELAIN, C. PATTYN and J. CHATELAIN, *Œuvres d'art et objets de collection en droit français*, Paris, Berger-Levrault, 1997, 172-173; S. LEMOINE, 'Le rôle de l'expert dans la pratique', in Q. BYRNE-SUTTON (ed.), *L'expertise dans la vente d'objets d'art - Aspects juridiques et pratiques*, Zürich, Schulthess, 1992 (67), 68.

training.[22] The lion's share, however, have been formed empirically, through their presence in the field as gallery owners or antique dealers. Years of experience as a dealer have turned them into knowledgeable art attributors.[23]

Finally, there are the so-called *connaisseurs* or *art connoisseurs*, a term commonly used to refer to the very diverse group of people that frequent art exhibitions, art museums, art galleries, art fairs. Their keen interest in art is the only thing they actually have in common. Unlike the art scholars and commercial art experts, they are not professionally engaged in the art industry. In fact, anyone call can themselves an art connoisseur. No education or specific training as an art historian, restorer or archaeologist is required, nor is there any need to know all the tricks of the business. As self-educated experts, they gained a certain 'familiarity with the art object'. Of course, *art connoisseurs* are not bound by any professional code, since – strictly speaking – they are no formal part of the official art industry. And yet in certain cases (be it for free or otherwise) these *art connoisseurs* make public statements on the authenticity, the provenance and the value of art objects. The faith put in these 'expert opinions' may vary widely. In most other sectors, statements of such non-professional 'connoisseurs' would lack any gravitas or meaning, and therefore the group of self-proclaimed *connaisseurs* would not deserve to be mentioned. However, this analysis does not hold true for the art trade. In fact, some *connoisseurs* possess extraordinary expertise.[24] Just think of the partner or closest friend of a deceased artist, his next of kin or the bearers of his moral rights. Some *connoisseurs* clearly demonstrate that outstanding ability which they have acquired as 'initiates' or 'insiders' of the world of art.[25] Through their immediate experience, these people may have acquired exceptional familiarity with the oeuvre of a particular artist. Out of emotional involvement, they may pronounce on authenticity matters, even though they did not receive any formal education to do so. And yet the market often considers these judgments to be very authoritative.[26]

Within each of the three aforementioned categories some experts claim to be generalists, whereas others present themselves as specialists.[27] A generalist covers a large field

---

22 S. LEMOINE, 'Le rôle de l'expert dans la pratique', in Q. BYRNE-SUTTON (ed.), *L'expertise dans la vente d'objets d'art – Aspects juridiques et pratiques*, Zürich, Schulthess, 1992 (67), 67.

23 H. BOUNAMEAUX, 'Expertise des œuvres d'art', in F. DEREME (ed.), *La fiscalité des œuvres d'art et antiquités*, Brussels, Larcier, 2004 (315), 326; H. VEROUGSTRAETE-MARCQ, 'L'expertise scientifique des peintures: les faux et les nouveaux faux', *Annales de droit de Louvain* 1988 (415), 415.

24 F. CHATELAIN, C. PATTYN and J. CHATELAIN, *Œuvres d'art et objets de collection en droit français*, Paris, Berger-Levrault, 1997, 134.

25 M. CORNU and N. MALLET-POUJOL, *Droit, œuvres d'art et musées: protection et valorisation des collections*, Paris, C.N.R.S. Editions, 2004, 50-52.

26 F. DURET-ROBERT, *Ventes d'œuvres d'art*, Paris, Dalloz, 2001, 125-126.

27 M. ROETHLISBERGER, 'Le statut de l'expert dans la pratique', in Q. BYRNE-SUTTON (ed.), *L'expertise dans la vente d'objets d'art – Aspects juridiques et pratiques*, Zürich, Schulthess, 1992 (111), 112.

of the arts (*e.g.* modern painting, furniture, ceramics and porcelain, manuscripts...) and has considerable knowledge of these fields. The public will usually turn to one of these generalists for expertise and assessment. Besides acquiring general knowledge, some experts (generalists) have concentrated on the work of one artist or, at most, a couple of artists and have grown into specialists in that particular field. Within the triad mentioned above, specialists are usually found among university professors and museum curators or among research teams. Niche traders and people belonging to the artist's inner circle are usually seen as specialists as well. It goes without saying that the specialist's opinion carries more weight in a debate on authenticity than the view of a generalist.[28]

Since the authenticity of an art object depends entirely on the quality of the expert's work, it would not be strange to expect him to give proof of his skills prior to authenticating pieces or providing attribution services to the market. Yet the above overview shows that anyone who wishes to do so can claim to be an art expert.[29] Accordingly, our expectations are not met. It is indeed remarkable that in Belgium the legal position of the '*expert in works of art*' has not been regulated, as opposed to the status of other experts who do enjoy a protected professional title, such as accountants, doctors, lawyers or architects.[30] In fact, this appears to be a worldwide phenomenon: even in major art trade countries such as the United States,[31] the United Kingdom,[32] France[33]

28 F. DURET-ROBERT, *Ventes d'œuvres d'art*, Paris, Dalloz, 2001, 103-124 (in particular 115); H. BOUNAMEAUX, 'Expertise des œuvres d'art', in F. DEREME (ed.), *La fiscalité des œuvres d'art et antiquités*, Brussels, Larcier, 2004 (315), 326-327; F. DURET-ROBERT, 'L'authenticité des œuvres d'art dans la pratique du marché de l'art', in M.-A. RENOLD, P. GABUS and J. DE WERRA (eds.), *L'expertise et l'authentification des œuvres d'art*, Geneva, Schulthess, 2007 (29), 32-33.

29 B. KNAPP, 'La réglementation de la profession d'expert en objets d'art – Aspects juridiques et pratiques', in Q. BYRNE-SUTTON and M.-A. RENOLD (eds.), *L'expertise dans la vente d'objets d'art – Aspects juridiques et pratiques*, Geneva, Schulthess, 1992 (93), 93 and 98; O. SANDROCK, 'General Report: Appraisal', in M. BRIAT (ed.), *International Sales of Works of Art - La vente internationale d'œuvres d'art*, II, Deventer, Kluwer, 1990 (611), 622.

30 H. BOUNAMEAUX, 'Expertise des œuvres d'art', in F. DEREME (ed.), *La fiscalité des œuvres d'art et antiquités*, Brussels, Larcier, 2004 (315), 325; F. DE GERADON, 'Naar een bescherming van de beroepen verbonden aan kunstvoorwerpen en het cultureel patrimonium', *T. Desk.* 2002 (16), 17.

31 D.B. HOMER, 'Fine Art Appraisers: The Art, the Craft and the Legal Design – Proposed Model Fine Art Appraiser Act', *Columbia-VLA Journal of Law & the Arts* 1983-1984 (457), 462; O. SANDROCK, 'General Report: Appraisal', in M. Briat (ed.), *International Sales of Works of Art - La vente internationale d'œuvres d'art*, II, Deventer, Kluwer, 1990 (611), 622; R. LERNER and J. BRESLER, *Art Law: The Guide for Collectors, Artists, Investors, Dealers and Artists*, I, New York, Practising Law Institute, 2005, 553.

32 Hailsham of St. Marylebone, *Halsbury's Laws of England*, IL, London, Butterworths, 1984, v° *valuers and appraisers*, 2; O. SANDROCK, 'General Report: Appraisal', in M. BRIAT (ed.), *International Sales of Works of Art - La vente internationale d'œuvres d'art*, II, Deventer, Kluwer, 1990 (611), 622.

33 J. GHESTIN, 'Le droit interne français de la vente d'objets d'art et de collection', in P. LALIVE (red.), *International Sales of Works of Art - La vente internationale d'œuvres d'art. Volume I*, Genève, Institute of International Business Law and Practise, 1988 (131), 151; J.-L. DELVOLVE, 'Aspects juridiques du

and Germany,[34] the title of art expert can be used freely, without being subject to any quality control or regulation. In France and Germany, however, there are experts who enjoy state recognition. Yet even there the profession is not really regulated, as state recognition as *expert agréé* or *Öffentlich Bestellter Sachverständiger* is by no means necessary for professional practice.[35] The title only refers to these experts' ability to play a role in official court proceedings.[36] We would therefore have to conclude not only that access to the profession is open to anyone but also that people who call themselves art experts are not subject to any *strict* professional or deontological code at all.[37]

Yet we believe that the absence of any title protection for art experts (or even any specific legal framework) does not need to be an insurmountable problem, provided that civil liability can play its full part.[38] In our opinion, this mechanism proves perfectly fit to hold art experts liable whenever they fail to meet the standards of proper service.[39] It is immediately clear why the rest of this contribution deals precisely with the civil liability of experts. However, before commencing our legal analysis, it seems wise to devote some attention to the art expert's methodology, or should we say methodologies. Here the use of artificial intelligence comes into the story.

---

commerce internationale de l'art: quelques positions du droit français', in M. BRIAT (red.), *International Sales of Works of Art – La vente internationale d'œuvres d'art.* Volume II, Deventer, Kluwer 1990 (725), 725.

34 T. GERLACH, *Die Haftung für fehlerhafte Kunstexpertisen*, Munich, Institut für Urheber- und Medienrecht, 1998, 32-33; H. SCHACK, *Kunst und recht*, Cologne, Carl Heymanns Verlag, 2004, 62; G. PICKER, *Kunstgegenstände & Antiquitäten*, Munich, Stiebner, 2000, 301; T.K. DREIER, 'The Legal Status of the Art Expert in Germany', in Q. BYRNE-SUTTON (ed.), *Etudes en droit de l'art*, Geneva, Schulthess, 1992 (99), 99.

35 For more on this state recognition of experts in France and Germany, see S. LEQUETTE-DE KERVENOAËL, *L'authenticité des œuvres d'art*, Paris, L.G.D.J., 2006, 176-179; F. DURET-ROBERT, *Droit du marché de l'art*, Paris, Dalloz, 2004, 176-178; T. GERLACH, *Die Haftung für fehlerhafte Kunstexpertisen*, Munich, Institut für Urheber- und Medienrecht, 1998, 32-33; H. SCHACK, *Kunst und recht*, Cologne, Carl Heymanns Verlag, 2004, 62; G. PICKER, *Kunstgegenstände & Antiquitäten*, Munich, Stiebner, 2000, 301; T.K. DREIER, 'The Legal Status of the Art Expert in Germany', in Q. BYRNE-SUTTON (ed.), *Etudes en droit de l'art*, Geneva, Schulthess, 1992 (99), 99.

36 See on that topic: B. DEMARSIN, *Expertise, veiling en certificaten in de kunsthandel – Authenticiteit en aansprakelijkheid rechtsvergelijkend onderzocht*, Bruges, die Keure 2008, 564 p.

37 S. LEQUETTE-DE KERVENOAËL, *L'authenticité des œuvres d'art*, Paris, L.G.D.J., 2006, 174-175; O. SANDROCK, 'General Report: Appraisal', in M. BRIAT (ed.), *International Sales of Works of Art – La vente internationale d'œuvres d'art*, II, Deventer, Kluwer, 1990 (611), 622.

38 S. LEQUETTE-DE KERVENOAËL, *L'authenticité des œuvres d'art*, Paris, L.G.D.J., 2006, 175.

39 B. DEMARSIN, *Authenticiteit en contracteren omtrent kunst: een rechtsvergelijkende analyse*, Bruges, die Keure 2008, 113.

4 The Methodologies of Art Experts

Art experts may revert to a range of methodologies to authenticate a work of art or formulate a suitable attribution. Depending on the case, each of these methods may do the job, yet often their outcomes will be combined to minimise the risk of misattribution. Until recently, there were said to be four types of expertise.[40] They all consider the art object from a specific perspective.[41] With the use of AI, a fifth method is currently being established. In what follows, we will critically assess its true meaning. Since the activity of attributing and authenticating artworks is rarely an exact science, it is often recommended to combine various forms of expertise to obtain a higher degree of certainty.[42] Even though they are not the main focus of this contribution, it seemed wise to provide a brief overview of the technical analysis, the style analysis, the historical analysis and the forensic analysis before we go on to focus on the use of artificial intelligence as a fifth, emerging type of expertise.

4.1 Technical Analysis

In order to authenticate a work of art, experts may perform a visual analysis of the object from a technical point of view. This means the expert will concentrate on the object in its material existence.[43] The expert will examine the materials that have been used and the way they have been assembled, the support (wood, canvas, paper,...);[44] the frame;[45] the presence of hallmarks, stamps, inscriptions or signatures;[46] the state of conservation

---

40 See B. DEMARSIN, *Authenticiteit en contracteren omtrent kunst: een rechtsvergelijkende analyse*, Bruges, die Keure 2008, 113-120.

41 S. LEMOINE, 'Le rôle de l'expert dans la pratique', in Q. BYRNE-SUTTON (ed.), *L'expertise dans la vente d'objets d'art - Aspects juridiques et pratiques*, Zürich, Schulthess, 1992 (67), 70.

42 F. CHATELAIN, C. PATTYN and J. CHATELAIN, *Œuvres d'art et objets de collection en droit français*, Paris, Berger-Levrault, 1997, 139.

43 S. LEMOINE, 'Le rôle de l'expert dans la pratique', in Q. BYRNE-SUTTON (ed.), *L'expertise dans la vente d'objets d'art - Aspects juridiques et pratiques*, Zürich, Schulthess, 1992 (67), 70; R.S. LEVINSON, 'Examining the Techniques and Materials of Paintings', in R.D. SPENCER (ed.) *The Expert versus the Object - Judging Fakes and False Attributions in the Visual Arts*, Oxford, Oxford University Press, 2004 (111), 112-117.

44 For more, see: R.H. MARIJNISSEN, *Schilderijen: Echt-fraude-vals - Moderne onderzoeksmethoden van de schilderijenexpertise*, Elsevier, Brussels, 1985, 61-79; R.S. LEVINSON, 'Examining the Techniques and Materials of Paintings', in R.D. SPENCER (ed.), *The Expert versus the Object - Judging Fakes and False Attributions in the Visual Arts*, Oxford, Oxford University Press, 2004 (111), 112-114.

45 For more, see R.H. MARIJNISSEN, *Schilderijen: Echt-fraude-vals - Moderne onderzoeksmethoden van de schilderijenexpertise*, Elsevier, Brussels, 1985, 91-92.

46 For more, see: P. SIEGEL, 'Signature Identification: From Pen Stroke to Brush Stroke', in R.D. SPENCER (ed.), *The Expert versus the Object - Judging Fakes and False Attributions in the Visual Arts*, Oxford, Oxford University Press, 2004 (89), 89-93; R.H. MARIJNISSEN, *Schilderijen: Echt-fraude-vals - Moderne onderzoeksmethoden van de schilderijenexpertise*, Elsevier, Brussels, 1985, 66-70; S. LEQUETTE-DE

(*e.g.* craquelure, varnish, discoloration of pigments, patina, presence of mould, insect damage and retouches or restorations),[47] taking into consideration the object's function and the wear and tear that normal usage would have brought to the object over the years.[48]

4.2 Style Analysis

In performing a style analysis, the expert will establish how the work was created and how the artist developed the theme. The expert will attempt to identify the work stylistically within the oeuvre of a certain artist, style period, community of origin or region by comparing it with works that are authentic beyond discussion.[49] Among the four traditional types of expertise, this was always the most controversial, and the most likely to provoke sceptical reactions from observers with a less trained eye.[50] Actually, they are not entirely wrong, as a style analysis is largely a subjective matter, entirely based upon the expert's conviction. What is more, style analysis seems to depart from the assumption that the artist always created works of comparable quality, even though it is rather unlikely that even Picasso or Rembrandt never experimented or experienced a lesser day....[51] Nevertheless style analysis is generally considered to be a very useful technique,[52] if only for the fact that it allows experts to formulate an initial attribution, which may later be confirmed or falsified through additional examinations.[53]

KERVENOAËL, *L'authenticité des œuvres d'art*, Paris, L.G.D.J., 2006, 186-192; F. DAULTE, 'Les éléments de l'expertise', in M. Briat (ed.), *International Sales of Works of Art - La vente internationale d'œuvres d'art*, II, Deventer, Kluwer, 1990 (719), 721.

47 For more on this topic, see: R.H. MARIJNISSEN, *Schilderijen: Echt-fraude-vals - Moderne onderzoeksmethoden van de schilderijenexpertise*, Elsevier, Brussels, 1985, 111-125; O. KURZ, *Fakes: A Handbook for Collectors and Students*, London, Faber and Faber, 1948, 28-30.

48 R.H. MARIJNISSEN, *Schilderijen: Echt-fraude-vals - Moderne onderzoeksmethoden van de schilderijenexpertise*, Elsevier, Brussels, 1985, 54-55 and 125.

49 F. CHATELAIN, C. PATTYN and J. CHATELAIN, *Œuvres d'art et objets de collection en droit français*, Paris, Berger-Levrault, 1997, 139; S. LEQUETTE-DE KERVENOAËL, *L'authenticité des œuvres d'art*, Paris, L.G.D.J., 2006, 196-197; S. LEMOINE, 'Le rôle de l'expert dans la pratique', in Q. BYRNE-SUTTON (ed.), *L'expertise dans la vente d'objets d'art - Aspects juridiques et pratiques*, Zürich, Schulthess, 1992 (67), 70.

50 R.H. MARIJNISSEN, *Schilderijen: Echt-fraude-vals - Moderne onderzoeksmethoden van de schilderijenexpertise*, Elsevier, Brussels, 1985, 137-138; F. CHATELAIN, C. PATTYN and J. CHATELAIN, *Œuvres d'art et objets de collection en droit français*, Paris, Berger-Levrault, 1997, 139; P. ROSENBERG, 'Expertise : l'avis d'un conservateur de musée', in M. BRIAT (ed.), *International Sales of Works of Art - La vente internationale d'œuvres d'art*, II, Deventer, Kluwer, 1990 (715), 716.

51 S. LEQUETTE-DE KERVENOAËL, *L'authenticité des œuvres d'art*, Paris, L.G.D.J., 2006, 200-201.

52 F. DAULTE, 'Les éléments de l'expertise', in M. BRIAT (ed.), *International Sales of Works of Art - La vente internationale d'œuvres d'art*, II, Deventer, Kluwer, 1990 (719), 722; F. DURET-ROBERT, *Marchands d'art et faiseurs d'or*, Paris, Belfond, 1998, 155; A.K.J. BOLZ, *A Regulatory Framework for the Art Market ? - Authenticity, Forgery and the Role of Art Experts*, Maastricht, Maastricht University, 2019, 178-179.

53 S. LEQUETTE-DE KERVENOAËL, *L'authenticité des œuvres d'art*, Paris, L.G.D.J., 2006, 200; F. CHATELAIN, C. PATTYN and J. CHATELAIN, *Œuvres d'art et objets de collection en droit français*,

4.3 Historical Analysis

The historical analysis attempts to get to the bottom of an art object's history based on historical sources.[54] Here, experts try to establish the artwork's pedigree (*i.e.* the chain of successive owners) through historical research. If they manage to do so, without any gap, from the creation of the work until the present, the work's authenticity is said to be 'proven'.[55] To do so, the expert will try to trace the work's presence in private or public collections, in public sales and in exhibitions.[56] Unfortunately, this is often impossible. Because of wars, revolutions or changing fashions experts may lose track of the work.[57] Some works have an incredible history; others travel around the world as a result of events that are difficult to trace, such as private sales, or even thefts.[58] It is also far from evident to establish an unquestionable pedigree, due to the large numbers of copies that circulate on the market.[59] Historical research, however, does not focus exclusively on the pedigree or, more generally, the *provenance*[60] or origin of the art object. The expert also looks for elements in the composition that might give clues as to its age. To test an artwork's authenticity, the expert will try to discover anachronisms in the object that render the attribution impossible. These anachronisms can pertain to various elements. They may be found, for instance, in inscriptions, because language, characters and fonts are products of their time.[61] The same can be said of heraldry,[62] clothing,[63] iconology

Paris, Berger-Levrault, 1997, 139; T. GERLACH, *Die Haftung für fehlerhafte Kunstexpertisen*, Munich, Institut für Urheber- und Medienrecht, 1998, 35-38.

54 See *Hahn v. Duveen*, 234 N.Y.S. 185 (N.Y. Sup. Ct., 1929).

55 S. LEMOINE, 'Le rôle de l'expert dans la pratique', in Q. BYRNE-SUTTON (ed.), *L'expertise dans la vente d'objets d'art - Aspects juridiques et pratiques*, Zürich, Schulthess, 1992 (67), 71; S. LEQUETTE-DE KERVENOAËL, *L'authenticité des œuvres d'art*, Paris, L.G.D.J., 2006, 229; F. CHATELAIN, C. PATTYN and J. CHATELAIN, *Œuvres d'art et objets de collection en droit français*, Paris, Berger-Levrault, 1997, 138; R.H. MARIJNISSEN, *Schilderijen: Echt-fraude-vals - Moderne onderzoeksmethoden van de schilderijenexpertise*, Elsevier, Brussels, 1985, 147-152.

56 S. LEQUETTE-DE KERVENOAËL, *L'authenticité des œuvres d'art*, Paris, L.G.D.J., 2006, 229.

57 F. CHATELAIN, C. PATTYN and J. CHATELAIN, *Œuvres d'art et objets de collection en droit français*, Paris, Berger-Levrault, 1997, 138.

58 M. RHEIMS, *Les collectionneurs de la curiosité, de la beauté, du goût, de la mode, et de la spéculation*, Paris, Ramsay, 1981, 132.

59 S. LEQUETTE-DE KERVENOAËL, *L'authenticité des œuvres d'art*, Paris, L.G.D.J., 2006, 230.

60 See F. DAULTE, 'Les éléments de l'expertise', in M. BRIAT (ed.), *International Sales of Works of Art - La vente internationale d'œuvres d'art*, II, Deventer, Kluwer, 1990 (719), 719-720.

61 R.H. MARIJNISSEN, *Schilderijen: Echt-fraude-vals - Moderne onderzoeksmethoden van de schilderijenexpertise*, Elsevier, Brussels, 1985, 140.

62 Ibid., 1985, 141.

63 Ibid., 142-144.

and iconography.[64] Certain important indications may also be hidden in bibliographical references.[65]

4.4 *Forensic Analysis*

Experts also have a wide range of forensic research techniques at their disposal that make up the fourth type of expertise. In practice, a diverse set of techniques and tests are possible. Common to all of them is the fact that the expert examines in a laboratory setting the support base, the pigments or other materials, in an attempt to establish whether or not these findings can be reconciled with a particular attribution.[66]

Although greeted with a lot of scepsis in the early years, forensic analysis has by now undeniably proven its capacity to generate crucial insights. Accordingly, this fourth form of expertise is generally considered to contribute in the most valuable way to the work of authenticators and art experts. Still, it is important to understand that the results are not always as unambiguous as we would expect them to be and that these forensic techniques remain to depend (at least in part) on the interpretation by the researcher.[67] Therefore, it is generally said that forensic analysis can be successful only when combined with other types of expertise.[68] Laboratory tests may help to date an object of art as precisely as possible but will not allow experts to attribute the work to a specific artist.[69] It immediately becomes clear that the technique is of greater value for the attribution of objects to classical antiquity, rather than for the identification of the creator of a nineteenth-century painting. In addition, forensic analyses are pre-eminently useful to refute an already existing attribution, which has led some to observe that this form of expertise actually works *a contrario*.[70] The greater part of these highly advanced laboratory techniques also come at considerable prices. Hence, for the test to be cost-effective, the object should represent a considerable financial value.[71] Forensic

---

64 T. GERLACH, *Die Haftung für fehlerhafte Kunstexpertisen*, Munich, Institut für Urheber- und Medienrecht, 1998, 144.

65 R.H. MARIJNISSEN, *Schilderijen: Echt-fraude-vals - Moderne onderzoeksmethoden van de schilderijenexpertise*, Elsevier, Brussels, 1985, 152-154.

66 S. LEMOINE, 'Le rôle de l'expert dans la pratique', in Q. BYRNE-SUTTON (ed.), *L'expertise dans la vente d'objets d'art - Aspects juridiques et pratiques*, Zürich, Schulthess, 1992 (67), 71; S. LEQUETTE-DE KERVENOAËL, *L'authenticité des œuvres d'art*, Paris, L.G.D.J., 2006, 241.

67 See A.K.J. BOLZ, *A Regulatory Framework for the Art Market ? - Authenticity, Forgery and the Role of Art Experts*, Maastricht, Maastricht University, 2019, 292.

68 S. LEQUETTE-DE KERVENOAËL, *L'authenticité des œuvres d'art*, Paris, L.G.D.J., 2006, 247.

69 H. VEROUGSTRAETE-MARCQ, 'L'expertise scientifique des peintures: les faux et les nouveaux faux', *Annales de droit de Louvain* 1988 (415), 423.

70 S. LEQUETTE-DE KERVENOAËL, *L'authenticité des œuvres d'art*, Paris, L.G.D.J., 2006, 245-246.

71 L. DUBOFF and C. KING, *The Deskbook of Art Law*, Dobbs Ferry, Oceana Publications, K-16.

analysis automatically implies the involvement of a specialised research facility, with costly equipment at its disposal. It therefore falls outside of the reach of the average art expert.[72] It should also be understood that some tests require a sample to be taken from the artwork and are thus somewhat harmful. Therefore, professional experts, applying utmost care, are certainly required.[73]

4.5 AI Analysis

Recently, the use of AI has also increasingly been mentioned as a fifth and new technique to authenticate art, especially paintings.[74] It is fair to say that, at this point, the technology is still in its infancy and definitely far from universally applicable. It is important to note that any AI analysis requires large scale data sets and reliable algorithms, which are not available or developed (yet) for the vast majority of artists. Consequently, it is too early to make any meaningful statements as to whether AI will (over time) become a truly convenient, (cost-)effective and accurate means of assessing an artwork's authenticity. Of course, from a mere theoretical perspective, the technique has potential, as over the past years AI models have proven their value in a wide range of industries. Why would the art business be an exception?

An AI analysis of paintings basically works as follows: first, an algorithm is developed and trained by feeding the computer as many images as possible from a certain artist. Based on that data (and, of course, the more the better), the algorithm extracts and saves all elements, features, techniques, brushstrokes, etc. that are typical for the artist at hand. Once developed and trained on the basis of a reliable data set, images of potential works are submitted to the system. The computer will then do the comparison and will indicate whether or not the new image matches the artist algorithm.[75]

Whether the use of AI for the analysis of art and cultural goods will really grow into a powerful fifth form of expertise is in my opinion yet to be seen. There certainly is

---

72 F. CHATELAIN, C. PATTYN and J. CHATELAIN, *Œuvres d'art et objets de collection en droit français*, Paris, Berger-Levrault, 1997, 136; S. Lequette-de Kervenoaël, *L'authenticité des œuvres d'art*, Paris, L.G.D.J., 2006, 243-244.

73 F. CHATELAIN, C. PATTYN and J. CHATELAIN, *Œuvres d'art et objets de collection en droit français*, Paris, Berger-Levrault, 1997, 136-137; S. LEQUETTE-DE KERVENOAËL, *L'authenticité des œuvres d'art*, Paris, L.G.D.J., 2006, 244-245.

74 See F. LU, 'Introducing the Latest Tool in Art Authentication: AI', available on https://jingdailyculture.com/art-recognition-ai-art-authentication (last consulted on 10 March 2024); C. BENGHOZI, 'Authentification des œuvres d'art. Les experts face à l'Intelligence artificielle', available on https://www.meer.com/fr/72853-authentification-des-oeuvres-dart (last consulted on 10 March 2024).

75 For more reading on the technical aspects, please consult the contribution by Prof. Postma in this book "Artificial Intelligence Is a Powerful Tool for Art Attribution".

potential, yet I cannot but see significant obstacles. As I feel it, it may be easier to have AI recognise images of, say, houses and cats with great accuracy than to authenticate paintings by artists such as Van Gogh,[76] Da Vinci,[77] or Raphaël.[78] Bearing in mind how AI analytics basically work, it is fair to say that an algorithm only becomes reliable on the basis of *big* data. Given the fact that there are millions of pictures of houses and millions of pictures of cats, an AI system based on a massive amount of data can actually be developed. Yet there are only a few dozen paintings by Vermeer, and the same goes for Da Vinci. Are such numbers really enough material for a performant algorithm? In addition, to be reliable, the algorithm has to be developed on the basis of input that is undoubtedly correct. While it is easy to submit a long and unquestionable series of images depicting a house or a cat, the same is not possible for master paintings. It is therefore to be feared that the algorithm will inevitably get contaminated with wrong inputs, which, in turn, will lead to wrong output. Only if the model is 100% accurate will the responses it generates be equally reliable.[79]

As with forensics, it is immediately clear that any AI analysis far exceeds the capabilities of the average art expert. In addition, most forensic and AI analyses are highly technical and specialised, often going beyond what the majority of the art world tends to grasp. Sadly enough, results are not always univocal, and hence the need to interpret them in relation to broader historical, stylistic and technical evidence.[80] That is true for forensic analyses and no different for AI-based art research. What is more, given the few players that are currently pioneering this novel technique and the very limited number of 'artist-algorithms' developed, the actual use of AI for authentication services is currently far below 1%. Unlike forensics, AI analysis is by no means part of the toolbox of today's art expert. But what is not can still be….

---

76 See https://art-recognition.com/case-studies/vincent-van-gogh-self-portrait (last consulted on 10 March 2024).

77 See A. SCHRADER, 'Two A.I. Models Set Out to Authenticate a Raphael Painting and Got Different Results, Casting Doubt on the Technology's Future', available on https://news.artnet.com/art-world/ai-art-authentication-will-not-replace-humans-2340290 (last consulted on 10 March 2024).

78 See S. HECKER; 'Authenticity in Art: What if Artificial Intelligence is Not Objective? A Reflection After Raphael', available on https://www.artlawyersassociation.com/post/authenticity-in-art-what-if-artificial-intelligence-is-not-objective-a-reflection-after-raphael (last consulted on 10 March 2024).

79 For more critical reservations about how AI can be used for art expertise purposes, see the contribution by Prof. Van der Stighelen and Prof. Büttner in this book "'Painted by Rubens? No, Says AI' On Connoisseurship and Algorithmic Verification of Paintings". See also A. SCHRADER, 'Two A.I. Models Set Out to Authenticate a Raphael Painting and Got Different Results, Casting Doubt on the Technology's Future', available on https://news.artnet.com/art-world/ai-art-authentication-will-not-replace-humans-2340290 (last consulted on 10 March 2024); S. HECKER, 'Authenticity in Art: What if Artificial Intelligence Is Not Objective? A Reflection after Raphael', available on https://www.artlawyersassociation.com/post/authenticity-in-art-what-if-artificial-intelligence-is-not-objective-a-reflection-after-raphael (last consulted on 10 March 2024).

80 A.K.J. BOLZ, *A Regulatory Framework for the Art Market? – Authenticity, Forgery and the Role of Art Experts*, Maastricht, Maastricht University, 2019, 292.

5 First Scenario: Inauthenticity and the Loss of the Contractual Balance between Buyer and Seller

Since authenticity disputes are essentially attribution problems, they arise pre-eminently in the art trade. Indeed, attributions are only really relevant for marketing purposes. Usually, cultural objects are attributed in the very context of the art trade. Undoubtedly, sellers make up the prime attributors, as they want to advertise their merchandise. As a result, these sellers tend to be the first to be legally challenged in case of misattributions. This makes sense, because inauthenticity upsets the contractual balance between the buyer and the seller. After all, contracts are typically designed to benefit both parties, as they will obtain something more dear or useful to them than the performance they provide in return. When later, one of those performances turns out to fall short, the goal of and logic behind the contract are fundamentally compromised. Fortunately, the victim (usually the aggrieved buyer) should not have to endure this without redress. As in virtually all other jurisdictions, also under Belgian law purchasers of non-authentic artworks will find (all kinds of) remedies to undo the damage by having the contract annulled or terminated or by pursuing financial compensation. In Belgium, there is a lot of published case law to illustrate this.[81]

In addition, numerous authors have analysed the parties' legal remedies under sales law or under general contract law.[82] In Belgian legal practice, the doctrine of error is probably the most important basis for obtaining legal redress in case of authenticity issues. In addition, aggrieved buyers also successfully invoke the seller's duty to deliver conforming goods.[83]

---

81 For a chronological overview, up to 1 January 2008 of all published case law on authenticity disputes litigated before the Belgian courts, see B. DEMARSIN, *Authenticiteit en contracteren omtrent kunst: een rechtsvergelijkende analyse*, Bruges, die Keure 2008, 755-760. Here we add more recent cases: Court of Appeal Brussels 15 November 2011, ECLI:BE:CABRL:2011:ARR.20111115.1; Court of Appeal Brussels 12 November 2008, *TWVR* 2009, vol. 4, 242, note F.M.; Court of Appeal Brussels 25 October 2006, ECLI:BE:CABRL:2006:ARR.20061025.1; Trib. Brussels 2 January 2012, *DAOR* 2012, 195.

82 See M. DAMBRE, 'Informatieplicht en actiemogelijkheden van partijen bij de aankoop van kunstvoorwerpen', *TBBR* 1990, 33-45; B. TILLEMAN, 'Dwaling bij de aan- en verkoop van kunst en antiek', in E. DIRIX (ed.), *Liber amicorum Jacques Herbots*, Antwerpen, Kluwer, 2002, 443-459; E. DIRIX, 'Dwaling en bedrog bij koop van kunst en antiek', in K. RIMANQUE (ed.), *Kunst en Recht*, Antwerpen, Kluwer, 1985, 95-116; M. FONTAINE, 'Les aspects juridiques de la commercialisation des oeuvres d'art', *Annales de droit de Louvain*, 1988, 383-413; J. SACE, 'Quelques réflexions sur l'erreur dans les ventes d'objets d'art', in K. BERNAUW (ed.), *Liber amicorum Yvette Merchiers*, Brugge, die Keure, 2001, 239-252; C. OLSBURGH, *Authenticity in the Art Market*, Leicester, Institute of Art and Law, 2005, 100 p.; S. LEQUETTE-DE KERVENOAËL, *L'authenticité des œuvres d'art*, Paris, L.G.D.J., 2006, 265-416.

83 M. DAMBRE, 'Informatieplicht en actiemogelijkheden van partijen bij de aankoop van kunstvoorwerpen', *TBBR* 1990 (33), 41 and 43-44; A. MEINERTZHAGEN-LIMPENS, *Traité élémentaire de droit civil belge. Tome I*, Brussel, Bruylant, 1997, 210; B. DEMARSIN, *Authenticiteit en contracteren omtrent kunst: een rechtsvergelijkende analyse*, Bruges, die Keure, 2008, 382-390; B. TILLEMAN, 'Dwaling bij de aan- en verkoop van kunst en antiek', in E. DIRIX (ed.), *Liber amicorum Jacques Herbots*, Antwerpen, Kluwer 2002

6 Second Scenario: Inauthenticity and the Liability for Professional Malpractice of a Service Provider

Not only do authenticity issues have consequences in the direct relationship between the seller and the buyer of an inauthentic art object; often professional intermediaries and service providers are involved as well. Their role is to facilitate or optimise the sales process at the request of one of the parties or even both of them. Usually, the service provided by such a professional is essentially aimed at providing information by making statements on the authenticity of the artworks, attributing them or assessing their value. Sometimes, the expert's intervention is even entirely aimed at this, for instance when he is being asked to issue a certificate of authenticity. Much more often, however, such expert statements are part of a more comprehensive service package. Think of auction catalogues, which are dressed up as an important sub-aspect of the organisation of a public sale.

The reason why parties engage an expert is to ensure a flawless transaction. If things still go wrong, despite the involvement of a service provider, they will obviously try to hold the latter liable. That is perfectly understandable, as, with his poor judgment, the expert is at the root of the authenticity problem. Hence, professional liability for damage caused by wrongful expert advice should be an essential part of any legal analysis of authenticity disputes in the art trade. It complements the earlier analysis on inauthenticity and its effect in the direct relationship between the buyer and the seller.[84]

---

(443), 449; E. DIRIX, 'Dwaling en bedrog bij koop van kunst en antiek', in K. RIMANQUE (ed.), *Kunst en Recht*, Antwerpen, Kluwer 1985 (95), 112-113.

84 Very detailed on this second scenario, see: B. DEMARSIN, *Expertise, veiling en certificaten in de kunsthandel - Authenticiteit en aansprakelijkheid rechtsvergelijkend onderzocht*, Bruges, die Keure 2008, 3 *et seq.*; T. GERLACH, *Die Haftung für fehlerhafte Kunstexpertisen*, Munich, Institut für Urheber- und Medienrecht, 1998, 134 p.; A.K.J. BOLZ, *A Regulatory Framework for the Art Market ? - Authenticity, Forgery and the Role of Art Experts*, Maastricht, Maastricht University, 2019, 199 *et seq.*; S.M. LEVY, 'Liability of Art Experts for Professional Malpractice', *Wisconsin Law Review*, 1991, 595-652; M. VON KUEGELGEN, 'La responsabilité des professionnels de la vente d'oeuvres d'art', *Rev. not. b.*, 1994, 302-341; S. LEQUETTE-DE KERVENOAËL, *L'authenticité des œuvres d'art*, Paris, L.G.D.J., 2006, 417-564; K.B. SINGER, 'Sotheby's Sold Me a Fake!' - Holding Auction Houses Accountable for Authenticating and Attributing Works of Fine Art', *Columbia-VLA Journal of Law & the Arts*, 1999-2000, 439-455; R.D. SPENCER, 'The Risk of Legal Liability for Attributions of Visual Art', in R.D. SPENCER (ed.), *The Expert versus the Object - Judging Fakes and False Attributions in the Visual Arts*, Oxford, Oxford University Press, 2004, 143-187; N. PALMER, 'The Civil Liability of the Professional Appraiser or Attributer of Works of Art under English Domestic Law', in Q. BYRNE-SUTTON (ed.), *L'expertise dans la vente d'objets d'art - Aspects juridiques et pratiques*, Zürich, Schulthess, 1992, 19-36.

7 Third Scenario: Inauthenticity and the Actions to Silence All Critics

Both in the direct relationship between the buyer and the seller and in the ancillary relationship linking the aggrieved party to a professional service provider, authenticity disputes essentially amount to the aggrieved party's attempt to find redress against the person who formulated the attribution that caused the former to buy or sell a certain piece.[85]

Yet there is even a third scenario that gives rise to authenticity disputes and case law. Instead of claiming legal redress from the seller and/or the expert who lured the purchaser into the deal, the latter sometimes tries to uphold the authenticity of his purchase by initiating legal proceedings to silence the third party who compromised the artwork's reputation with unfavourable (and unsolicited) statements. This third scenario has been extensively described in the literature[86] as well, and even case law can be found.[87]

8 Resolving Authenticity Issues in Court: The Significance of AI for Art Authentications

In all three scenarios just described, the plaintiff will have to prove in a first step that the art object at hand was actually misattributed. If he fails to do so, no action will lie, as in the court's opinion there is just no clearly established problem. Indeed, before the court has to consider at all whether a purchase transaction should be annulled or rescinded or whether experts should be held liable for their misjudgement, it is first up to the plaintiff

85 B. DEMARSIN, *Expertise, veiling en certificaten in de kunsthandel – Authenticiteit en aansprakelijkheid rechtsvergelijkend onderzocht*, Bruges, die Keure 2008, 3.

86 See B. DEMARSIN, *Authenticiteit en contracteren omtrent kunst: een rechtsvergelijkende analyse*, Bruges, die Keure, 2008, 128-153; P. KRAUS, 'The Role of the Catalogue Raisonné in the Art Market', in R.D. SPENCER (ed.), *The Expert versus the Object – Judging Fakes and False Attributions in the Visual Arts*, Oxford, Oxford University Press, 2004, 63-71; A.K.J. BOLZ, *A Regulatory Framework for the Art Market ? – Authenticity, Forgery and the Role of Art Experts*, Maastricht, Maastricht University, 2019, 239 *et seq.*; F. DURET-ROBERT, *Droit du marché de l'art*, Paris, Dalloz, 2004, 199 *et seq.*; R.D. SPENCER, 'The Risk of Legal Liability for Attributions of Visual Art', in R.D. SPENCER (ed.) *The Expert versus the Object – Judging Fakes and False Attributions in the Visual Arts*, Oxford, Oxford University Press, 2004, 143-187; T.E. Jr. STEBBINS, 'Possible Tort Liability for Opinions Given by Art Experts', in F. FELDMAN, S.E. WEIL and S.D. BIEDERMAN (eds.), *Art Law – Rights and Liabilities of Creators and Collectors*, II, Boston, Little, Brown and Co., 1986, 517-533; L. DUBOFF and C. KING, *The Deskbook of Art Law*, Dobbs Ferry, Oceana Publications, K-57; R. LERNER and J. BRESLER, *Art Law: The Guide for Collectors, Investors, Dealers and Artists*, II, New York, Practising Law Institute, 2005, 579 et seq.

87 For a comprehensive overview of these types of cases, we refer to B. DEMARSIN, *Authenticiteit en contracteren omtrent kunst: een rechtsvergelijkende analyse*, Bruges, die Keure, 2008, 138-153.

to establish that the art object around which the dispute revolves is not authentic, or, in other words, has been wrongly attributed. The emergence (or even complete breakthrough) of AI-based art expertise does not change any of this fundamentally. The only thing that really matters is whether the court considers the inauthenticity proven, regardless of whether the plaintiff called in AI-based or any other form of art expertise. Yet that does not mean that there are no interesting reflections to be made.

From a comparative perspective, there are generally two different ways to establish in court that an authenticity issue actually exists.[88] In common law jurisdictions, juries and judges will decide this factual issue based on the statements of a (sometimes very long) list of expert witnesses each party calls upon to testify in court. In the common law world, the parties do the hard work of gathering all relevant expertise and presenting this to the court. The parties are in command, by examining and cross-examining the expert witnesses called upon during a trial. It is important to understand that in the common law world, the parties basically choose whom they wish to call as a witness. As a result, they control what evidence is brought before the court and what underlying types of analysis – technical, stylistic historical, forensic or even AI – the court can take into account. Accordingly, in common law proceedings, AI-based authenticity arguments can be presented to court, just as much as arguments stemming from other types of expertise. The downside of this approach is that highly complex factual matters, such as authenticity disputes, tend to result in what is often called a battle of experts fought before a court that has to decide what even eminent art experts cannot agree on. As a result, both sides come trotting in with the longest possible list of witnesses who support their position. And as a judge, what do you do when 67 experts claim to be in favour of authenticity, while 43 are against? In the process of weighing the evidence, numbers undoubtedly matter, but can one testimony of a world renowned expert outweigh the views of 25 others? These examples immediately highlight the difficulties inherent in the common law approach based on expert witnesses called upon by the parties. Thus, as far as the UK and US courts are concerned, it is clear that AI analyses of artworks can already effectively come into play. As soon as one of the parties' expert witnesses calls in arguments based on an AI analysis, these courts will have to weigh the evidence that flows from it in their overall assessment of the matter. To date, however, we do not have any indication that this already happens a lot, let alone that in their assessment of authenticity issues, courts give more weight to AI-based expertise over other expert testimonies. But again, what is not may someday be....

---

88 For more on that topic, see: R.D. SPENCER, 'Authentication in Court – Factors Considered and Standards Proposed', in R.D. SPENCER (ed.), *The Expert versus the Object – Judging Fakes and False Attributions in the Visual Arts*, New York, Oxford University Press, 2004, 189-215.

On the European continent (*e.g.* Belgium, France, Netherlands, Germany,...) judges tend to appoint a single expert to advise the court and act as master on the issue of authenticity. Hence, courts keep lists of designated, judicial experts in all sorts of areas, including artworks and collectibles. Unlike the approach used in Britain and America, the continental European approach avoids having judges clear factual issues that even eminent specialists on the matter cannot resolve in unison. That seems like a big step forward. However, the continental European way to tackle the issue also has huge drawbacks, as everything depends on the quality of the experts that figure on the list. What happens if the court-appointed expert sees things wrong, is not scrupulous or simply less specialised than the expert the plaintiff consulted? What if the appointed expert does not know about the new insights in the field or is unfamiliar with or just not open to new techniques, such as certain forensic tests or AI analyses? In practice, the list approach will almost inevitably result in court authentications of works that the world's true specialists reject and vice versa. In addition, listing systems tend to offer little by way of innovation: they usually include almost exclusively established experts, who ground their judgments on traditional, uncontroversial methods. Therefore, given that this form of expertise is still entirely in its infancy, we believe it will require years, if not decades, before the art experts on the list generally revert to AI analyses. Today, the few pioneers of AI authenticity analysis are simply not included on the lists of experts that continental European courts may appoint. But again, what is not may someday be....

9 Resolving Authenticity Issues in Court: The Significance of AI for Cases of Expert Liability

To be successful, any claim for liability brought against an art expert, either in contract or in tort, basically requires the plaintiff to provide proof of the former's failure to comply with his duty of care. Accordingly, the aggrieved party has to convince the court that a normally diligent service provider under the contract would not have made the same erroneous attribution. In case of a tort claim, the situation is not fundamentally different, as the plaintiff will have to prove that the art expert's behaviour fell short. Again, the emergence (or even complete breakthrough) of AI-based art expertise does not fundamentally change any of this. After all, all forms of expertise, including AI analyses, could be used to prove that the appropriate standard of care was not met. Again, in common law jurisdictions, juries and judges will decide this issue themselves, based on the statements of expert witnesses, while in civil law jurisdictions courts will tend to call in the help of some court-appointed expert to assist in making this assessment. Since AI analysis of artworks is currently still in its infancy, it is certainly not the widespread, ubiquitous and standard technology on which there is consensus. Hence, there is currently not a single court decision known to me that holds an art expert liable for failure to employ AI analyses as an authentication technique or method of art research. But what is not may someday be…: once more the proverb says it all.

10 Conclusion

Over the past few years, artificial intelligence certainly seems to be on the rise as a new methodology for art research, resulting in some first interesting findings. Given the incredible power of AI, it would be stupid to remain blind to these new developments by bluntly rejecting the technology as inadequate per se. Sure, certain aspects require fine-tuning, and obvious methodological questions and criticisms require clearance. There is clearly a long way to go for AI to become an established form of expertise to authenticate artworks and secure art transactions. True art lawyers, however, cannot afford to ignore the phenomenon, given the shift that AI may potentially bring to this field as well. Instead, they should keep track of further evolutions in this very interesting field. Therefore, as a form of general take-away, the maxim bears repeating: what is not may someday be.

Artificial Intelligence Is a Powerful Tool for Art Attribution

*Eric Postma**

1 Introduction

For the last 25 years, together with various collaborators, I have been developing and studying artificial intelligence (AI) algorithms for art attribution.[1] Perhaps surprisingly, the research was motivated not by my interest in art but by a deep curiosity about human perception and how it can be modelled computationally. Since then, quite a few people tried to seduce me into commercialising the art-attribution algorithms we[2] have developed because of their conviction that such an endeavour would have potential economic value. I always declined, however, not just because I knew that I did not possess the required entrepreneurial skills but also because my chief interest is in the scientific merit of the algorithms and what they reveal about human vision. A couple of years ago, the Swiss-based company Art Recognition invited me to become one of their scientific advisers. We collaborate on developing algorithms for art attribution and authentication in joint research projects, but even in that collaborative effort, I am never involved in specific assessments of authorship. Debates about authenticity get heated and I leave it up to experts in the domain to determine the usefulness of information that experts on the science of visual perception and its computational modelling can provide.

* Prof. dr. Eric Postma. Cognitive Science & AI, Tilburg University, the Netherlands, Jheronimus Academy of Data Science (JADS), Eindhoven University of Technology/Tilburg University.
I am grateful for the constructive comments of anonymous reviewers that helped improve an earlier version of this text.

1 I.J. Berezhnoy, E.O. Postma and H.J. van den Herik (2007). Computer Analysis of Van Gogh's Complementary Colours. *Pattern Recognition Letters*, 28, 703-709; I.J. Berezhnoy, E.O. Postma and H.J. van den Herik (2009). Automatic extraction of brushstroke orientation from paintings. *Machine Vision and Applications Journal*, 20, 1-9; L.J.P. van der Maaten and E.O. Postma (2010). Texton-Based Analysis of Paintings. In A. Tescher (Ed.), *Proceedings of the SPIE Optical Engineering and Applications*, 7798, 7789OH, San Diego: The International Society for Optical Engineering; N. van Noord, E. Hendriks and E. Postma (2015). Toward Discovery of the Artist's Style: Learning to Recognize Artists by Their Artworks. *IEEE Signal Processing Magazine*, 32(4), 46-54; N. van Noord and E. Postma (2017). Learning Scale-Variant and Scale-Invariant Features for Deep Image Classification. *Pattern Recognition*, 61, 583-592; L. Schaerf, C. Popovici and E.O. Postma (2023). Art Authentication with Vision Transformers. *Neural Computing and Applications*. https://doi.org/10.1007/s00521-023-08864-8; J. Ostmeyer, L. Schaerf, P. Buividovich, T. Charles, E.O. Postma and C. Popovici (2024). Synthetic Images Aid the Recognition of Human-Made Art Forgeries. *PLoS ONE*, 19(2), e0295967. https://doi.org/10.1371/journal.pone.0295967.

2 In this article, 'we' refers to the team of researchers with whom I collaborated in the cited articles.

I am fascinated by the skills of experts (e.g., *connoisseurs*) who can recognise the style of a painter by simply viewing a picture of an artwork. These experts have gained an extraordinary ability to pick up the visual cues that reveal the identity of a painter. Such specialised pattern-recognition abilities are intriguing to AI researchers like me, whether connoisseurs, medical experts or astronomers display them. Following Feynman's famous quote "What I cannot create, I do not understand", together with my team I attempt to create models that could mimic the art-attribution skill of connoisseurs. We obtain quite promising results when using the so-called deep-learning algorithms, which exhibit an impressive pattern-recognition ability.[3] Deep-learning algorithms are at the heart of the 'AI revolution' of the last ten years. Unfortunately, their depiction in the media is misguided, which leads to many misconceptions about the virtues and vices of AI. This chapter intends to provide a nuanced view of the use of AI in art attribution. The research question addressed reads: To what extent do AI algorithms contribute to art attribution? Although the emphasis is on art attribution, many of the described considerations apply to other AI application domains as well.

2 Artificial Intelligence for Visual Recognition

During the last decade, powerful 'deep-learning' algorithms emerged that seem to match and even outperform humans in visual pattern recognition.[4] One of the most notable examples is the AI system AlphaGo, which learned to play the Chinese board game Go. AlphaGo played against the best human Go player and won.[5] It was an enormous breakthrough because the game of Go is one of the most complex board games. Another more recent example is the AI system AlphaFold, which predicts how proteins fold from a chain of amino acids,[6] a task that is notoriously difficult for humans. AlphaFold is revolutionising structural biology and will have a major impact on medicine. A specific class of AI algorithms made great strides in the automatic classification of images. These algorithms are now being deployed worldwide to support medical experts.[7]

---

3 See, e.g., Schaerf et al., 2023.

4 Cf. Y. LeCun, Y. Bengio and G. Hinton (2015). Deep Learning. *Nature*, 521, 436-444.

5 See, e.g., D. Silver, et al. (2017). Mastering the Game of Go Without Human Knowledge. *Nature*, 550, 354-359.

6 J. Jumper, et al. (2021). Highly Accurate Protein Structure Prediction with AlphaFold. *Nature*, 596, 583-589.

7 See, e.g., N. Hendrix, E. Scholten, B. Vernhout, S. Bruijnen, B. Maresch, M. de Jong, S. Diepstraten, S. Bollen, S. Schalekamp, M. de Rooij, A. Scholtens, W. Hendrix, T. Samson, S. Ong, E. Postma, B. van Ginneken and M. Rutten (2021). Development and Validation of a Convolutional Neural Network for Automated Detection of Scaphoid Fractures on Conventional Radiographs. *Radiology: Artificial Intelligence*, 3(4), e200260. https://doi.org/10.1148/ryai.2021200260.

To appreciate the strengths and limitations of AI algorithms, we consider the following example that compares the description of images by machines and humans.[8] AI algorithms can assign adequate descriptions to everyday images.[9] It requires training an algorithm on millions of image-description pairs. During training, the algorithm learns to translate the visual characteristics of an image into an appropriate textual description. After being confronted with a sufficiently large number of image-description pairs, the algorithm can generalise the translation to novel images. For instance, when presenting the trained AI system with the previously unseen image shown in Figure 1, it generates the description 'A small boy throwing a frisbee in a park'. The ability of the trained AI algorithm to generate an adequate description suggests that it understands the image. After all, humans would be likely to give the same or a similar description.

Figure 1 Whereas a properly trained AI system may generate an adequate description of the image (i.e. 'boy throwing a frisbee in a park'), it does not perceive the image in the same way as humans do.

However, the similarity of descriptions given by humans and machines does not imply that their perceptual abilities are similar. Whereas AI systems solely translate the visual characteristics of the image into a description, human perception gives rise to a very rich experience that goes far beyond such a translation. The perceiver of Figure 1 may have experienced what it is like to throw or catch a frisbee, has likely been in parks similar to the one depicted, may have recollections of the smells and sounds in parks, and understands that playing with a frisbee may be an individual or a joint activity. These are only a few of the many thoughts associated with the picture. Stating that an

8 R. Brooks (2017). The Seven Deadly Sins of AI Predictions. *MIT Technology Review*, 6 October 2017. https://www.technologyreview.com/2017/10/06/241837/the-seven-deadly-sins-of-ai-predictions/.

9 Cf. LeCun et al., 2015.

AI algorithm 'recognises' or 'understands' an image is misleading because it suggests that it is a synthetic analogue of human perception. AI algorithms rely on only those visual features that contribute to the description and have no sense of the meaning of the picture. Statements that AI systems recognise or understand images are partly responsible for the widespread belief that AI algorithms perform visual tasks on a par with humans. In reality, AI algorithms excel only on visual tasks that are extremely narrow in scope when compared to the breadth of everyday human visual tasks. Therefore, the abilities of AI algorithms are not comparable to the broad visual abilities of humans.

Paradoxically, the narrow nature of their pattern-recognition abilities can give AI algorithms an edge over humans. In case the visual context can obscure or mislead human perception, AI algorithms may benefit from their ignorance of the 'wider picture' and succeed in recognising where humans fail. AI algorithms do not suffer (or benefit) from 'contextual biases' that may hamper human visual perception. A good example of such a contextual bias is the famous 'Invisible Gorilla' experiment. In this experiment, researchers instructed human participants to watch a video of a group of students handing over a ball and to count how often the ball is changing hands. At the end of the video, most participants may have correctly counted the number of ball handovers but completely missed the man in a gorilla suit that crossed the scene halfway through the video.[10] The contextual bias arises from the task instruction leading to selective attention to the ball, effectively suppressing visual input that is irrelevant to the task. Lacking contextual bias, an AI algorithm would detect the gorilla and any other visual shapes independent of their relevance.

3 Artificial Intelligence for Art Attribution

Human experts (or connoisseurs) engaged in art attribution and authentication benefit from their rich cultural, domain-specific, and artist-specific expertise. Well-trained experts can integrate the vast body of knowledge about an artwork to arrive at an assessment of its authenticity. Besides the visual appearance of the artwork, experts rely on knowledge about its provenance, 3D structures of the applied brushstrokes, chemical composition of pigments, various imaging methods (x-ray, multispectral), dendrochronological analysis of its wooden frame, historical context, ageing effects, provenance, and many more. Current AI algorithms for art attribution consider the visual

10 D.J. Simons and C.F. Chabris (1999). Gorillas in Our Midst: Sustained Inattentional Blindness for Dynamic Events. *Perception*, 28(9), 1059-1074.

appearance of an artwork only. This limits AI-based assessments to two-dimensional projections of paintings.

3.1 Why AI Is Promising for Art Attribution

The main strength of AI algorithms is in the 'single-minded' translation of (digital) images into predefined classes. Automatic art attribution classifies digital reproductions of artworks by, say, Van Gogh, Gauguin and Monet, into one of three classes, each representing an attribution to one of the three painters. Automatic art attribution requires a training set of undisputed artworks for each artist. During training, the deep-learning algorithm adapts its internal mapping to ensure that visual features that are associated with Van Gogh's, Gaugain's, or Monet's artworks translate into the proper attribution. The training results in a hierarchical sequence of 'pattern detectors', each of which detects detailed visual characteristics in the image of relevance to the attribution task. The pattern detectors in the initial stages of the deep-learning hierarchy detect simple visual structures, such as the contours of a brushstroke. In subsequent stages of the hierarchy, the pattern detectors detect increasingly complex visual structures, ranging from detecting combinations of brushstrokes to partial or complete objects.

After having trained the deep-learning algorithm on the training set, we assess the attribution performance on a test set that contains (digital reproductions of) artworks by the three artists, previously unseen by the algorithm. The performance on the test set provides an estimate of how well the trained algorithm can correctly attribute artworks. Typically, deep-learning algorithms perform well on art-attribution tasks (in most cases involving over three artists) with accuracies ranging from about 85% to 95% correct attributions on previously unseen paintings.[11] Interestingly, over the past years, we have observed a steady increase in performance because of improvements in the pattern-recognition abilities of deep-learning algorithms.[12]

3.2 Why AI May Fail in Art Attribution

Despite the potential of AI algorithms to support art attribution, there are four main pitfalls relating to their use. In what follows, we briefly review these pitfalls regarding (i) the validity of the attribution, (ii) the veridicality of reproduction, (iii) scarcity of training examples and (iv) scale variance and invariance.

11 See, e.g., Schaerf et al., 2023.
12 van Noord et al., 2015; van Noord and Postma, 2017; Schaerf et al., 2023.

(i) The validity of attribution.

The 'single-minded' approach of an AI algorithm is also its weakness. Suppose that, in our art-attribution task, all artworks by Van Gogh contain specific reproduction artefacts. For instance, there may be a very subtle spherical distortion in the image arising from the type of lens used by the photographer that created the photograph. Although such distortions may be very subtle and undetectable by humans, a deep-learning algorithm can use it as a cue to determine its authorship. In that case, the deep-learning algorithm develops one or more detectors that recognise the characteristics of the photo camera, rather than the characteristics of the artist! The spherical distortion is only one of the many ways that artefacts may provide hidden cues to the deep-learning algorithm.

(ii) The veridicality of reproduction.

It is virtually impossible to get a veridical digital reproduction of an artwork. Every reproduction method may leave a mark on the resulting reproduction, whether it is an RGB image, multispectral image, X-ray image or any other type of image. Our early work on quantifying the complementary colours of Van Gogh offers a good illustration.[13] We aimed to measure the use of complementary colours in Van Gogh's artworks throughout his oeuvre. To do so, we got Ektachromes of his artworks with colour reference cards attached to the frames. The colour reference cards offer a ground truth for the reproduced colour. Using a digital scanner, we created reproductions of the Ektachromes and measured the digital values of the colours on the reference cards. Even though the colours on the different cards were identical, their digital values showed considerable variation. Distortions introduced by photographing the artwork and by creating the Ektachrome caused the variation. When relying on reproductions, variations in colour and other image characteristics are unavoidable. The digitisation process that transforms the physical artwork into a digital image may introduce pitfalls for art attribution because the AI algorithms use anything in the digital data to optimise their performance.

(iii) Scarcity of training examples.

Deep-learning algorithms require several thousand examples per class. The reason for this 'data-hungriness' of deep-learning algorithms is their abundance of visual detectors, which all have to be trained by the learning algorithm. We need several thousands of artworks per artist to train a deep-learning algorithm from scratch on an art-attribution task. Most artists did not create that many artworks, which makes it impossible to satisfy the data-hungriness of deep-learning algorithms.

---

13 Berezhnoy et al., 2007.

(iv) Scale variance and invariance.

The fourth pitfall that may hamper AI-based art-attribution concerns the resolution of digital reproductions. When viewing a painting in the museum, you may examine it from different distances. Stepping backward provides you with a full view of the entire depicted scene. Stepping forward may allow you to recognise the individual brushstrokes. When visiting a museum website, you may do the same, provided the image resolutions of the artworks depicted on the site are sufficiently large. In principle, AI systems may strive to use high-resolution images for art attribution. However, there is a problem. Artworks vary in size. Some paintings are tiny, e.g. the size of a half A4 page, whereas others are huge, e.g. covering an entire wall. Depending on the artist and artwork, accurate art attribution may rely on large-scale features, e.g. the depicted scene, or on details, e.g. the depiction of an eye or the detailed application of a brushstroke. In our early art-attribution studies, we relied on 'scale-normalised' reproductions. In these reproductions, a single pixel represents a fixed surface area of the artwork. The AI algorithm always 'sees' paintings to be likened to a human observer that examines paintings at a fixed distance. Scale normalisation is appropriate if the visual cues revealing the artist are at the level of brushstrokes. However, if the painted eye provides a cue to the artist, then the size of the painted eye may depend on the size of the painting, and scale normalisation may negatively affect the attribution performance.

It may be clear that AI algorithms are not infallible. The four pitfalls show that, for a variety of reasons, extraneous factors that have nothing to do with the artwork or its artist may affect outcomes.

3.3 How AI May Succeed in Art Attribution

The four main pitfalls of art-attribution algorithms do not invalidate their usefulness. In what follows, we discuss how to overcome the four pitfalls to improve AI-based attributions.

(i) The validity of attribution.

The validity of AI-based attributions depends on how the algorithm arrives at its decision. Although often argued to be black boxes, it would be more appropriate to refer to AI systems as 'grey boxes'. In particular, for visual applications, the inner operation of trained AI systems can be examined in two main ways. The first way is through an exploration of the visual detectors that make up the trained deep-learning algorithm. Because of the hierarchical nature of deep-learning algorithms, the visual detectors associated with different levels of the hierarchy reveal the elementary and more complex visual characteristics that support the final decision. Art scholars can interactively explore the nature of these detectors and assess their effects on the final attribution. With the proper software, they can perform a kind of reverse engineering on the trained deep-learning algorithm to discover previously unknown visual characteristics associated with a specific painter or to detect characteristics that have nothing to do with authorship signalling a reproduction artefact. The second way in which scholars can examine the trained AI algorithm is by highlighting the regions of the painting that contribute to the attribution. Several algorithms are available to highlight the image regions that contribute positively or negatively to the attribution outcome. In our previous work with a trained art-attribution algorithm, we applied such highlighting to show the estimated contributions of Jan Luyken and Caspar Luyken (father and son), who collaborated on the artwork depicted in Figure 2.[14]

Figure 2 Visualisation of how characteristic each image region is for the artists Jan Luyken (yellow) and Caspar Luyken (blue). (N. van Noord, E. Hendriks and E. Postma (2015). Toward Discovery of the Artist's Style: Learning to Recognize Artists by Their Artworks. IEEE Signal Processing Magazine, 32(4), 46-54).

14 van Noord et al., 2015.

(ii) The veridicality of reproduction.

As stated previously, unavoidable variations in appearance hamper the veridicality of reproduction. The best manner to deal with this limitation is to use a range of reproductions, each of which represents a variation in one of the appearance characteristics. In deep-learning, data augmentation is a method that uses many variants of the same image (typically used to expand the size of the training set). Typically, researchers realise data augmentation by digitally generating variants of the original image that are zoomed out or in, subtly skewed in terms of perspective, slightly rotated, and so forth. For art attribution, it would be preferable to perform 'physical' data augmentation by collecting many reproductions (with different illumination, various cameras, multiple viewpoints, and so forth). In preliminary experiments, we found that such data augmentation is an effective means of avoiding reproduction-specific distortions from affecting the attribution.

(iii) Scarcity of training examples.

To address data-hungriness of deep-learning algorithms, 'transfer learning' can reduce the number of required examples per class considerably. Applied to art attribution, transfer learning implies pre-training the AI algorithm on a related task (e.g. the task of recognising the style of artworks) for which more data is available. The transfer-learning method even works for a less related task, for instance, pre-training on an object-recognition task and subsequently fine-tuning the AI algorithm on the art-attribution task. Pre-training on the object-recognition task ensures that the deep-learning algorithm develops visual detectors suitable for the processing of natural images. Subsequent fine-tuning on the art-attribution task adapts the visual detectors to deal with painted images. Our preliminary investigations of both forms of transfer learning (i.e., pre-training on paintings versus pre-training on natural images) did not result in significant differences in attribution performance.

(iv) Scale variance and invariance.

There are several ways to deal with the pitfall of scale variance and invariance. The most straightforward way is to ignore the scale variations altogether while training the AI algorithm. The result will be that some of the visual detectors developed by the algorithm will become 'scale invariant', so their responses are (largely) independent of the size (scale) of the visual pattern they detect. Human perception exhibits scale invariance because the recognition of persons, objects and scenes is (largely) independent of the distance to the observer in a range from, say, 0.5 to 5 metres. We explored scale-invariant art attribution using a dedicated deep-learning algorithm that also preserved scale variations and found it to perform successfully.[15] There are many alternative routes to dealing with the different scales of artwork that are currently being explored in our group. For instance, we explore the use of deep-learning algorithms with in-built scale invariance (so-called 'equivariant networks', see, e.g., Sosnovik, Szmaja, & Smeulders, 2020)[16] for automatic art attribution. The selection of the proper route should be informed by domain knowledge about the painter, the painting style and the sizes of the artworks involved.

4 AI Algorithms Are Fallible; Humans Are Too

The broad intelligence of human art experts is an advantage for making sense of artworks but also introduces a liability. The ambition to discover an artwork can lead experts astray. Probably the most dramatic example is the Van Meegeren case.[17] In 1937, the renowned Dutch art historian and Vermeer expert Abraham Bredius encountered a new painting titled *Christ and the Disciples at Emmaus* shown in Figure 3. The ambition of Bredius to discover a new Vermeer led him to attribute the painting to Johannes Vermeer. He published his discovery in the *Burlington Magazine for Connoisseurs*:

> It is a wonderful moment in the life of a lover of art when he finds himself suddenly confronted with a hitherto unknown painting by a great master, untouched, on the original canvas, and without any restoration, just as it left the painter's studio. And what a picture! Neither the beautiful signature ... nor the pointillés on the bread which Christ is blessing, are necessary to convince us that we have here – I am inclined to say – the masterpiece of Johannes Vermeer of Delft ... quite different from all his other paintings and yet every inch a Vermeer. In no other picture by the great master of Delft do we find such sentiment, such a profound understanding of the Bible story – a sentiment so nobly human expressed through the medium of highest art.[18]

15 van Noord and Postma, 2017.

16 See, e.g., I. Sosnovik, M. Szmaja and A. Smeulders, (2020). Scale-Equivariant Steerable Networks. *International Conference on Learning Representations (ICLR).* https://openreview.net/forum?id=HJgpugrKPS.

17 Described in F.H. Kreuger (2007). *A New Vermeer, Life and Work of Han van Meegeren.* The Netherlands: Quantes, Rijswijk.

18 A. Bredius (1937). A New Vermeer. *Burlington Magazine for Connoisseurs*, 71(416), 210-211, 210; reproduced from http://www.essentialvermeer.com/misc/van_meegeren.html.

Figure 3 "Christ and the Disciples at Emmaus" Han van Meegeren (1936–1937) Old canvas, relined, 115 x 127 cm. Museum Boijmans Van Beuningen, Rotterdam. The renowned art expert Abraham Bredius attributed the painting to Johannes Vermeer. An AI algorithm would have detected this image as being different in style from authentic Vermeers. (Image copied from http://www.essentialvermeer.com/misc/van_meegeren.html)

Later, it turned out that the artwork was a forgery created by the master forger Han van Meegeren. In hindsight, the style of *Christ and the Disciples at Emmaus* differed from other works by Vermeer. Present-day AI algorithms would detect the anomalous style of the forgery, in the same way that we and our colleagues were able to detect the famous Wacker forgery (F419) that was introduced on the market as a painting by Van Gogh by Otto Wacker.[19]

Considering the weaknesses and strengths of human and AI-based art attribution, AI algorithms are not infallible but do provide a potentially powerful tool to support the examination of painting styles, support art attribution and authentication. Their strengths and limitations complement those of humans. The research question stated in the introduction read: to what extent do AI algorithms contribute to art attribution?

19 C.R. Johnson, E. Hendriks, I.J. Berezhnoy, E. Brevdo, S.M. Huges, I. Daubechies, J. Li, E.O. Postma and J. Wang (2008). Image Processing for Artist Identification. *IEEE Signal Processing Magazine*, 25(4), 27-48.

From our analysis of the potential failures and successes of artificial and human intelligence, our answer to the question is: to the extent that AI algorithms complement the strengths and weaknesses of human intelligence.

5 The Future of AI in Art Attribution

Soon, AI algorithms will be commonplace in museums and art institutes to assist art experts and connoisseurs in their assessments of artworks. After the debacle of Bredius, the attribution of artworks became a more rigorous scientific endeavour. Nowadays, imaging, pigment analysis and many other tools are standard tools to support the attributions of art scholars. Each of these tools provides a unique and limited view of the artwork. There are two reasons it will take some time before AI algorithms for art attribution become mainstream tools in the art domain. First, the algorithms are still in development. Future algorithms will not only be more powerful but also allow for interactive exploration and correction by the user. Second, art scholars must be trained in the virtues and vices of AI algorithms and learn how to integrate the narrow pattern-recognition skills of deep learning with their broad expertise. Ultimately, AI algorithms will be another powerful tool in the extensive toolbox of art scholars to enhance the validity of art attributions.

‘Painted by Rubens? No, Says AI’ On Connoisseurship and Algorithmic Verification of Paintings

*Katlijne Van der Stighelen and Nils Büttner**

1 Introduction

On 26 September 2021, *The Guardian* reopened the public discussion surrounding Peter Paul Rubens’ painting *Samson and Delilah*:

> Was famed Samson and Delilah really painted by Rubens? No, says AI … Long-held doubts about the authenticity of the National Gallery’s masterpiece, bought for £ 2.5m in 1980, are backed by pioneering technology.[1]

What does this statement suggest? It presumes that the advantages of an artificial intelligence (AI) system for art authentication are clear. A new era has begun. An ‘unbiased, objective and independent algorithm’ is available that can be used for *legal adjudication* regarding the attribution of paintings. This newspaper article announces that an objective authority such as ‘artificial intelligence’ is capable of making a definitive judgment on the authenticity of a painting. The assumption seems to be that the problem of authenticity has been solved once and for all. At last, scientific criteria are available to substantiate attribution to a specific artist. Such a method would be particularly welcome to art historians, art dealers and auction houses and could also be used in legal disputes regarding the authenticity of a work of art – in this case, a painting. This chapter asks whether an AI system for the authentication, in its current state of development, provides an objective algorithm for the unquestionable attribution of paintings. The test case in applying this research is *Samson and Delilah*, until now assumed to have been painted around 1610 by Peter Paul Rubens for Antwerp burgomaster Nicolaas Rockox (Figure 1 + details Figure 1.1; 1.2; 1.3). That this particular painting was chosen

* Prof. dr. Katlijne Van der Stighelen is professor at the KU Leuven Department of Art History. Prof. dr. Büttner is a professor at the Staatliche Akademie der bildenden Künste Stuttgart.

1 Dalya Alberge, ‘Was Famed Samson and Delilah Really Painted by Rubens? No, Says AI’, *The Guardian*, 26 September 2021; URL: https://www.theguardian.com/artanddesign/2021/sep/26/was-famed-samson-and-delilah-really-painted-by-rubens-no-says-ai (accessed 4 February 2022).

is hardly a coincidence. It is believed to have been made by one of the most famous artists in Western art history and is currently held in one of Europe's most important museums, the National Gallery in London. It was precisely the painting's prominent location and the high price it commanded that sparked controversy long before the digital age, as is discussed below.

Figure 1 Peter Paul Rubens, *Samson and Delilah*, panel, 185 × 205 cm, London, The National Gallery, c. 1609-1610.

Figure 1.1-1.3 Peter Paul Rubens, *Samson and Delilah*, panel, 185 × 205 cm, London, The National Gallery, c. 1609-1610 [3 details of Fig. 1].

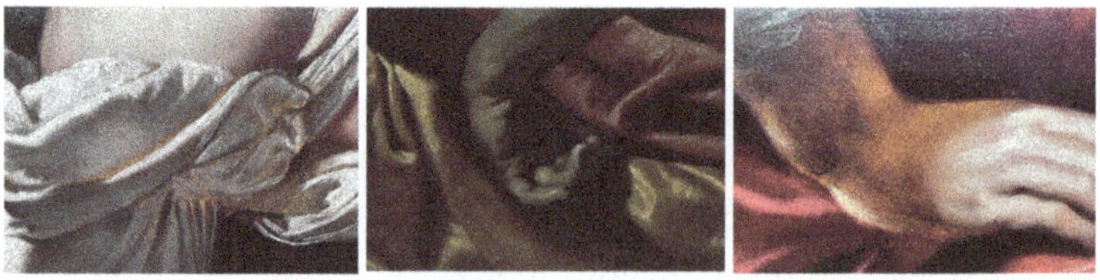

Rubens experts, art historians and conservators have never doubted the painting's authenticity. Indeed, in all the monographs and articles on the artist in which it is discussed, it is touted as one of the most representative expressions of his early stylistic period when he returned to Antwerp in 1608 after a roughly eight-year stay in Italy.[2]

2 Rubens, *Samson and Delilah*, c. 1609-10, panel, 185 × 205 cm, London, The National Gallery, inv. no. 6461. See Roger-Adolf d'Hulst and Marc Vandenven, *The Old Testament* (Corpus Rubenianum Ludwig

Curiously, non-specialists occasionally raised their voices, claiming that the painting was not by Rubens himself, as referred to in the journal article quoted previously: there have been "[l]ong-held doubts about the authenticity of the National Gallery's masterpiece".[3] The tension between the unanimity of the specialists, on the one hand, and the criticism of the outsiders, on the other, made *Samson and Delilah* an excellent test case for AI to uncover the 'truth' about the painting. Thus, the 'connoisseurship' of specialists would be put to a trial by fire and judged on its merits.

2 The Term Connoisseurship

The consensus among specialised art historians regarding the attribution of the panel to Rubens is based on 'connoisseurship'. To understand the uniqueness of this phenomenon, it is important to examine its historiography. In this way, one can determine the principle from which it derives its authority and demonstrate that it is still an extremely valid approach, even in the current context. This article first briefly reviews how people thought about connoisseurship and attribution in the past and, second, critically examines the application of AI.

The word 'connoisseur' first appears in the early eighteenth century. It circulated in England as a term derived from the French *conoisseor*, 'an expert, a judge, one well-versed', from *conoistre* and the Latin *cognoscere*, 'to get to know or to recognise'.[4] Art criticism initially emerged in France, where the Salons of the Académie des Beaux-Arts stimulated discussion of aesthetics between 1725 and 1890. The 'application of connoisseurship' was a prerogative of the 'gentleman'. In this context, it is interesting to note that the question raised was whether the ability to make aesthetic judgments was determined by rank and education or depended on a kind of "'aesthetic feeling' that would be stronger in one [man] than in another".[5]

Burchard, III), London and New York, 1989, pp. 107-113, cat. no. 31; David Jaffé, 'Rubens Back and Front. The Case of the National Gallery "Samson and Delilah"', *Apollo*, CLII, 2000, pp. 21-25. In *Rubens. A Master in the Making*, exh. cat. National Gallery of Art London, London, 2005, pp. 159-168, nos. 72-77, *Samson and Delilah* is considered by David Jaffé one of the important touchstones of the artist's production shortly after his return from Italy. See also, Marcello Francone (ed.), *Samson and Delilah: A Rubens Painting Returns*, exh. cat. Rockoxhuis, Antwerp; Liechtenstein Museum, Vienna, Milan, 2007; Aneta Georgievska-Shine, 'Rubens and the Tropes of Deceit in Samson and Delilah', *Word & Image, A Journal of Verbal/Visual Enquiry*, XXIII, 4, 2007, pp. 460-470; Hans Jakob Meier, 'Peter Paul Rubens and His Brother Philip's Poems on Samson and Judith', *Journal of the Warburg and Courtauld Institutes*, LXXVII, 2014, pp. 241-245.

3 See notes 1 and 2.

4 Arturo Tosi, *Language and the Grand Tour: Linguistic Experiences of Travelling in Early Modern Europe*, Cambridge, 2020, p. 231.

5 Francesco Ventrella, 'Art and Aesthetics', in Richard Whatmore and Brian Young (eds.), *A Companion to Intellectual History*, London, 2016, pp. 358-376, esp. p. 369.

Strictly speaking, connoisseurship did not exist in England until the early eighteenth century. The first recorded use of the word 'connoisseur' in English is by the Dutch immigrant physician and satirical author Bernard de Mandeville (1670-1733), who refers to 'connoisseurs' as 'judges of painting' in the first edition of his *Fable of the Bees* (1714).[6] De Mandeville used the word just once but added some very pertinent comments. According to him, attribution, which he calls judgment, hardly plays a role when it comes to works by unknown painters; however, when paintings by grand masters are judged, then connoisseurs show another side and different opinions immediately arise:

> how strangely have they differed as to the works of eminent masters! There are parties among ***connoisseurs*** [emphasised by the authors]; and few of them agree in their esteem as to ages and countries.

It is obvious that copies are worth less than originals: 'a noted original will be ever worth more than any copy that can be made of it by an unknown hand.' Furthermore, he notes that when connoisseurs determine the value of a painting, they are guided not only by the fame of the artist but also by 'the scarcity of his works' and the distinction of the collection from which the painting comes. In short, according to De Mandeville, 'connoisseurs' often disagree and are particularly interested in works by 'eminent masters'.[7]

The British portraitist and art critic Jonathan Richardson (1667-1745) can be credited with formulating a theoretical understanding of the concept, describing connoisseurship as a "science of judgment regarding the value, both monetary and cultural, of paintings".[8]

6 Brian Cowen, 'An Open Elite: The Peculiarities of Connoisseurship in Early Modern England', *Modern Intellectual History*, 1, 2, 2004, pp. 151-183, esp. pp. 151-152.

7 Bernard de Mandeville, *The Fable of the Bees: or, Private Vices, Publick Benefits*, London, 1714, pp. 206-207: 'Judges of painting will never disagree in opinion, when a fine picture is compared to the daubing of a novice; but how strangely have they differed as to the works of eminent masters! There are parties among connoisseurs; and few of them agree in their esteem as to ages and countries; and the best pictures bear not always the best prices: a noted original will be ever worth more than any copy that can be made of it by an unknown hand, though it should be better. The value that is set on paintings depends not only on the name of the master, and the time of his age he drew them in, but likewise in a great measure on the scarcity of his works; but, what is still more unreasonable, the quality of the persons in whose possession they are, as well as the length of time they have been in great families; and if the Cartons, now at Hampton-Court, were done by a less famous hand than that of Raphael, and had a private person for their owner, who would be forced to sell them, they would never yield the tenth part of the money which, with all their gross faults, they are now esteemed to be worth'. URL: https://www.gutenberg.org/files/57260/57260-h/57260-h.htm (edition London, 1806) (accessed 14 December 2022).

8 Carol Gibson-Wood, 'Richardson, Jonathan, the Elder (1667-1745)', in *Oxford Dictionary of National Biography*, Oxford, 2004; online edition, January 2008; See also Carol Gibson-Wood, 'Jonathan Richardson and the Rationalization of Connoisseurship', *Art History*, 7, 1, 1984, pp. 38-56; Carol Gibson-Wood, *Studies*

By 1715, he had already published *An Essay on the Theory of Painting*, considered to be the first art-theoretical treatise in English, and four years later (1719) his *Two Discourses*, part I: *The Connoisseur. An Essay on the Whole Art of Criticism, as it Relates to Painting*, and part II: *An Argument in Behalf of the Science of a Connoisseur; Wherein is Shewn the Dignity, Certainty, Pleasure, and Advantage of it* (Figure 2).[9] The treatises sparked discussions on the nature and finality of connoisseurship. According to Richardson, 'connoisseurship' focuses on the attribution of works and verification of originality (read authenticity) and secondarily on aesthetic pleasure.[10] He regards this ambiguity as strictly elitist. Based on his knowledge, the connoisseur can see 'les beautés invisibles aux yeux ordinaires' (the beauties invisible to ordinary eyes) and can derive from it a pleasure inaccessible to 'non-connoisseurs'.[11]

Figure 2 Jonathan Richardson, *Two Discourses*, I: *The Connoisseur. An Essay on the Whole Art of Criticism, as it Relates to Painting*, and II: *An Argument in Behalf of the Science of a Connoisseur; Wherein is Shewn the Dignity, Certainty, Pleasure, and Advantage of it'*, London, 1719.

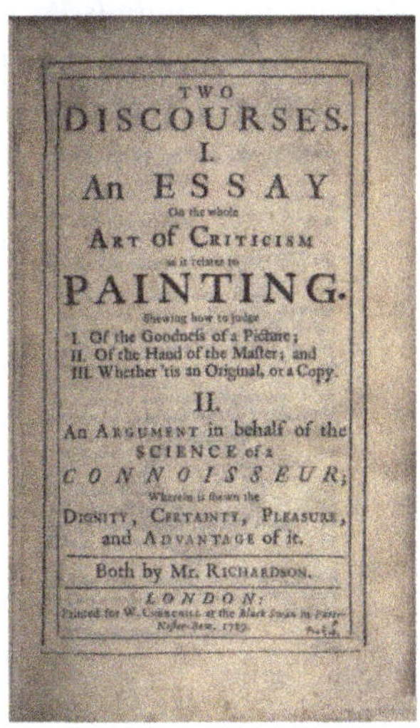

TWO
DISCOURSES.
I.
An ESSAY
On the whole
ART of CRITICISM
as it relates to
PAINTING.
Shewing how to judge
I. Of the Goodness of a Picture;
II. Of the Hand of the Master; and
III. Whether 'tis an Original, or a Copy.
II.
An ARGUMENT in behalf of the
SCIENCE of a
CONNOISSEUR;
Wherein is shewn the
DIGNITY, CERTAINTY, PLEASURE,
and ADVANTAGE of it.

Both by Mr. RICHARDSON.

LONDON:

in the Theory of Connoisseurship from Vasari to Morelli*, New York, 1988, esp. chap. 7; Carol Gibson-Wood, *Jonathan Richardson: Art Theorist of the English Enlightenment*, New Haven, 2000.

9 Full title of part I: 'Shewing how to judge I. Of the Goodness of a Picture; II. Of the Hand of the Master; and III. Whether 'tis an Original, or a Copy'.

10 See Carol Gibson-Wood (note 8).

11 Frédéric Elsig et al, 'Le *connoisseurship* et ses révisions méthodologiques.' Connoisseurship and Its Methodological Revisions', *Perspective Actualité en histoire de l'art*, 3, 2009, pp. 344-356, esp. p. 345; URL: https://journals.openedition.org/perspective/1303 (accessed 4 February 2023).

From then on, the term 'connoisseur' was used appropriately and inappropriately, its original meaning becoming blurred and applied more as a derogatory term than a category of knowledge.[12] This changing tide in the British context and the criticism of anyone who pretended to be a 'connoisseur' is clearly illustrated in a print Hogarth designed for the catalogue of the Society of Artists exhibition in 1761 entitled *The Tailpiece*. In it, the connoisseurs are personified by an elegantly dressed monkey. He waters the dead trees that represent the 'old' master paintings (inscribed with 1502, 1600 and 1606), indicating that a 'real connoisseur' prefers traditional art to that of the modern painters.[13] The monkey was later replaced by a group of boisterous onlookers who pay no heed to the painting being shown to them upside down. This satire of those posturing as 'connoisseurs' was far sharper.

3 Traditional Methods of Attribution

The nineteenth century saw a turning point, with connoisseurship manifesting itself as a new epistemological model. This meant that connoisseurship was no longer seen as an amateur activity but aimed to reach the level of an 'objectifying science'. The way in which connoisseurship fitted in with the new approach to science was demonstrated by Italian historian Carlo Ginzburg (*1939). Ginzburg is considered the inventor of 'microhistory', a historical method that focuses on small units of research, such as an event or an individual, rather than the larger picture.[14] In 1976 he published *Il formaggio e I vermi*, translated as *The Cheese and the Worms*, a monograph on the cosmogony of the Italian miller Menocchio (1532-1599) from Montereale. The life of this one heretic opens up the broader sixteenth-century life and the mediaeval religious beliefs of his contemporaries.[15] In his article *Clues: Roots of an Evidential Paradigm* (published in English in 1989), Ginzburg noted the strong relationship between his micro-historical approach and the practice of nineteenth-century connoisseurship. To understand 'the versatility and multi-applicability of connoisseurship' he revisited the history of previous interpretations of the phenomenon and focussed on the nineteenth-century

12 Harry Mount, 'The Monkey with the Magnifying Glass: Constructions of the Connoisseur in Eighteenth-Century Britain', *Oxford Art Journal*, 29, 2, 2006, pp. 167-184, esp. p. 171.

13 See URL: https://www.metmuseum.org/art/collection/search/392616; https://www.royalacademy.org.uk/art-artists/work-of-art/tailpiece-to-the-catalogue-of-pictures-exhibited-in-spring-gardens (accessed 4 February 2023).

14 On the concept and history of 'microhistory', see Carlo Ginzburg, *Threads and Traces: True, False, Fictive*, Berkeley, 2012, pp. 193-214. – See also: David Freedberg, 'Why Connoisseurship Matters', in Katlijne Van der Stighelen (ed.), *Contributions on Rubens and His Colleagues in Honour of Hans Vlieghe*, Pictura Nova X, 1, Turnhout, 2006, pp. 29-43.

15 Paola Zambelli, 'From Menocchio to Piero Della Francesca: The Work of Carlo Ginzburg', *The Historical Journal*, 28, 4, 1985, pp. 983-999. See also Carlo Ginzburg, 'Microhistory: Two or Three Things That I Know about It', *Critical Inquiry*, 20, 1, 1993, pp. 10-35.

art historian Giovanni Morelli (1816-1891). The latter also wrote under the pseudonyms Ivan Lermolieff (an anagram of his own name) and Johannes Schwartze, and his method of attribution marks the invention of modern *connoisseurship.*[16] A painting can be attributed to a specific master thanks to 'a careful study of particular and (...) highly distinctive characteristics'. It is not the conscious characteristics of a picture that must be analysed but 'the most trivial details', 'the unconscious and unwitting ones'. These are 'the clues' by means of which the identity of the artist can be established. At its core, the Morellian method is based on the belief that painters reveal their *true* identity in the parts of the painting about which they care least. In his *Rudiments of Connoisseurship*, written in the 1890s but published in 1902, as well as his *Three Essays on Method* of 1927, Bernard Berenson (1865-1959), a specialist in Italian Renaissance art, improved and refined Morelli's method.[17] As an American, he was more familiar with the English connoisseurial tradition than with its French origins.

The new 'Morellian technique' of scholarship makes it possible to identify the characteristic 'hands' of painters through the sharp observation of minor details.[18] However great, all painters tend to fall back on a formula for rendering details such as an ear or a fingernail. Hence, such minor details are the most characteristic parts of a picture and the surest or only guide to a reliable attribution. Morelli explored this method in his *Italian Painters: Critical Studies of Their Work* (1890; Eng. trans., 1892) (Figure 3) and rectified hundreds of false attributions. It is crucial to realise that Morelli was not educated as an art historian but studied medicine (though he never practised it).

16 Carlo Ginzburg, '*Clues: Roots of an Evidential Paradigm*', in Carlo *Ginzburg (ed.), Clues, Myths, and The Historical Method,* Baltimore, 1992, pp. 96-126, esp. pp. 96-97.

17 See Ernest Samuels, *Bernard Berenson: The Making of a Legend*, Cambridge, 1987; Hayden B.J. Maginnis, 'The Role of Perceptual Learning in Connoisseurship: Morelli, Berenson, and Beyond', *Art History*, 13, 1, 1990, pp. 104-117.

18 On the development and criticism of the Morellian method, see Anna Tummers, *The Eye of the Connoisseur: Authenticating Paintings by Rembrandt and His Contemporaries: Amsterdam Studies in the Dutch Golden Age*, Amsterdam, 2011, pp. 30-39.

Figure 3 ***Giovanni Morelli, Italian Painters. Critical Studies of Their Works. Italian Painters: The Borghese and Doria-Pamfili galleries in Rome*, London, 1892: Diagram of ears of a selection of artists, London, 1892, p. 78.**

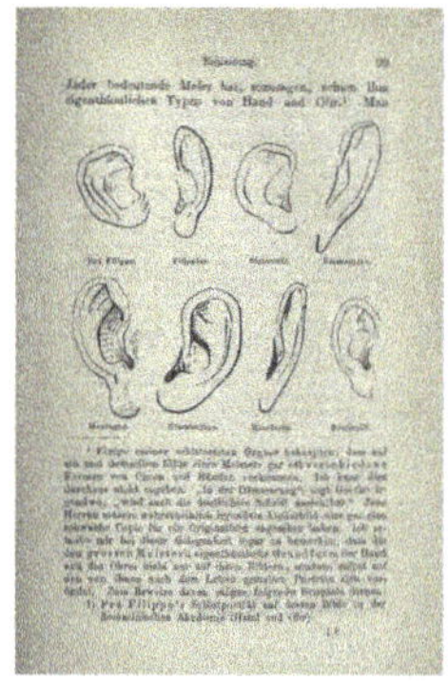

Fascinated by the history of epistemology, Ginzburg managed to connect the procedures Morelli applied to attribute paintings to those used by the author Sir Arthur Conan Doyle (1859-1930), the alter ego of Sherlock Holmes, to unmask criminals, and by Sigmund Freud (1856-1939) to interpret the body language and dreams of his patients. All three of them were educated as physicians. Painters, patients or criminals do not show themselves openly but only reveal their true identity through virtually unnoticed details. As Ginzburg stated: "In each case, infinitesimal traces permit the comprehension of a deeper, otherwise unattainable reality".[19] Where Morelli succeeded in establishing the identity of the artist by observing the way in which he painted ears, in *The Adventure of the Cardboard Box*, Sherlock Holmes unmasked the murderer by comparing the ears of the receiver of the packet, Miss Susan Cushing, with those of her sister Mary, the victim of this crime of passion (Figure 4). Freud, in turn, analysed the eyes, ears, lips and fingertips of his patient Dora as secrets of the body. In his opinion, we tend to ignore body narratives although they must be read as secrets to be 'revealed': "betrayal oozes out of him at every pore".[20] For this reason, fruitful Morellian connoisseurship must be understood as a nineteenth-century model of

19 Carlo Ginzburg (note 16), p. 101. See also Carlo Ginzburg, 'On Small Differences: Ekphrasis and Connoisseurship', *Visual History*, 2, 2016, pp. 11-29.

20 Rosemary Balsam, 'Eyes, Ears, Lips, Fingertips, Secrets: Dora, Psychoanalysis, and the Body', *Psychoanalytic Review (New York)*, 102, 1, 2015, pp. 33-58, esp. p. 33, as Freud wrote in his 'Three Essays on the Theory of Sexuality': 'He that has eyes to see and ears to hear may convince himself that no mortal can keep a secret. If his lips are silent, he chatters with his fingertips; betrayal oozes out of him at every pore.' In 1914 Freud wrote in 'The Moses of Michelangelo': 'It seems to me that his [Morelli's] method of inquiry is closely related to the technique of psycho-analysis. It, too, is accustomed to divine, secret and concealed things from unconsidered or unnoticed details, from the rubbish heap, as it were, of our observations'. See Carlo Ginzburg (note 16), p. 99.

inductive reasoning, 'a method of drawing conclusions by going from the specific to the general, also described as bottom-up reasoning'. Even now, when art historians utilise connoisseurship while looking at paintings in the flesh to assess the attribution, they apply the Morellian method. Although this method has been viewed with scepticism, in his article entitled *The Thinking Eye, the Mind That Sees*, Hal Opperman approaches the basis of connoisseurship as a "fundamental sensory faculty – that of discrimination, that is, the ability to distinguish among physical properties of nature (e.g., colours of the prismatic spectrum, notes of the scale)", an understanding that comes close to Morelli's interpretation.[21]

Figure 4 Arthur Conan Doyle, *The Adventure of the Cardboard Box, The Strand Magazine*, January, 1893, p. 204: *"He [Sherlock Holmes] examined them [the ears] minutely"*. Illustration by Sidney Paget.

4 THE NEW METHOD OF COMPARING IMAGES

Scholars of digital humanities and computational scientists are looking for instruments to rationalise and objectify the process of attributing works of art.[22] From this point of view, it is hardly surprising that exactly during the last years new interest in Morelli's strategies has emerged among scholars of digital humanities and computational scientists. Image

21 Hal Opperman, 'The Thinking Eye, the Mind That Sees. The Art Historian as Connoisseur', *Artibus et Historiae*, 1990, 11, 21, 1990, pp. 9-13, esp. p. 9.

22 A separate yet equally important debate plays on the border of connoisseurship and chemical analysis. See Anna Tummers and Robert G. Erdmann, 'The Eye Versus Chemistry? From Twentieth to Twenty-First Century Connoisseurship', in Maria Perla Colombini, Ilaria Degano and Austin Nevin (eds.), *Analytical Chemistry for the Study of Paintings and the Detection of Forgeries. Cultural Heritage Science*, Springer, 2022, pp. 3-45. URL: https://doi.org/10.1007/978-3-030-86865-9_1 (accessed 4 February 2022).

recognition is considered one of the most challenging problems in imaging science, and Deep Learning has dramatically improved the accuracy of image recognition.[23]

To give just one example, Christopher Nygren published an article titled 'On Giovanni Morelli, or How to See A Renaissance Painting Computationally'.[24] In it he remarks: 'Giovanni Morelli is probably familiar to most art historians, though that's not necessarily the case for computer scientists interested in computer-aided visual perception'. However, Nygren himself became curious about the connection between Morelli's approach and actual Computational Visual Aesthetics. He compared the Morellian method to

> something like algorithmic computation. It is an iterative procedure that draws attention to the minutia[e] of a painting (…) in the hope of saying something of consequence about the whole. Like in DNA sequencing or computing programming, it is seeking to identify minimal degrees of variance that have maximal consequence.[25]

In 2021 Nygren was one of four authors of a more extended collaborative research project focusing, among others, on the *Salvator Mundi* by Leonardo da Vinci, which was auctioned in London at Christie's on 15 November 2017. It fetched $450.3 million dollars, making it the 'most expensive painting in the world' although – and this makes the case so exceptional – expert opinion regarding its attribution was divided (Figure 5).[26]

23 Already in 2004 experiments were launched to develop computer programs with the intention of facilitating the attribution process by a team from Dartmouth College in Hanover, New Hampshire. They analysed pen lines and brushstrokes based on a technique that had been developed to recognise the digital manipulation of photographs. See Siwei Lyu, Daniel Rockmore and Hany Farid, 'A Digital Technique for Art Authentication', Proceedings of the National Academy of Sciences, 101, 49, pp. 17006-17010. Already on 13 May 2005, Daniel Rockmore was invited to KU Leuven on the retirement of Hans Vlieghe: 'To be or not to be a connoisseur? A Symposium in Honour of Hans Vlieghe'. Rockmore presented a lecture entitled 'Digital Art Authentication'.

24 Christopher J. Nygren, 'On Giovanni Morelli, or How to See a Renaissance Painting Computationally' (2015/2016). URL: https://sites.haa.pitt.edu/cva/on-giovanni-morelli-or-how-to-see-a-renaissance-painting-computationally/ (accessed 4 February 2023).

25 Ibid.

26 Alison Langmead et al, 'Leonardo, Morelli, and the Computational Mirror', *Digital Humanities Quarterly*, 15, 1, 2021. URL: http://www.digitalhumanities.org/dhq/vol/15/1/000540/000540.html (accessed 4 February 2023).

Figure 5 Leonardo da Vinci (Attributed to), *Salvator Mundi*, panel, oil on panel 65.7 x 45.7 cm, Location unknown, c. 1500.

The article examines how the process of connoisseurship may be modellable within the field of digital computation. The results, though, were somewhat disappointing:

> When we began this project, we took a leap of faith that we would uncover interesting areas of art-historical inquiry by computationally mechanising Giovanni Morelli's method of art attribution. While it was to be expected that our system could match Morelli's own at the level of the workflow - extract a set of details and compare them - we did not anticipate how our work would show us the complexity of Morelli's historical process at a more fundamental level.

The question is, to what extent is it possible to register artistic traces - such as pigments, composition, thickness of the paint, brushstrokes, form, the nature of the canvas or panel, patina and craquelures - 'at the level of pixels'? Their conclusions are extremely meaningful and significant for the dispute at hand. They argue that pixel-level information as such would never be sufficient to produce a credible attribution. As one of the outcomes of their research, the authors created a new concept in the discussion, namely that the process of attribution must be regarded as 'a social practice'. While the importance of physical traces cannot be underestimated, it is the expert's judgment that remains most important.

5 A Combination of Methods

An exemplary overview of the historical and actual application of connoisseurship in the field of seventeenth-century Dutch painting by Anna Tummers came out in 2011.[27] Comprehensive analyses of connoisseurship and its practical application are found in John H. Brown's 'Epistemology of Connoisseurship', from 2008,[28] and Joris Corin Heyder's recent and most inspiring essay on 'Doing Connoisseurship'.[29] Nils Büttner formulated an equally practice-based description of 'connoisseurship' in relation to (the workshop of) Rubens, which is of particular relevance in the context of this discussion. He concludes:

> in all fairness it must be admitted, however, that connoisseurship is less a method than a consciously-driven application of a whole set of methods. Of these the most important are undoubtedly the comparisons of material, painterly techniques and the visible traces of the production process in the paintings. This can happen within one painting, but ideally it refers to a whole body of material which is both diverse and clearly defined.[30]

His definition goes beyond that of Morelli, in that it also includes material-technical research of material and painting techniques. Researching the physical history of the work obliges art historians to work in an interdisciplinary fashion. While material-technical analyses will never answer all the questions, they might objectivise first opinions and provide additional arguments.

To illustrate the additional value of high-end technological analysis as part of the authentication process, another painting related to Rubens can be introduced.[31] A number of technological methods, such as X-radiography, X-ray computer tomography, mammographic tomosynthesis and macroscopic X-ray fluorescence, have been

27 Anna Tummers (note 18).

28 John H. Brown, 'Connoisseurship: Conceptual and Epistemological Fundamentals', in Jason Kuo (ed.), *Perspectives on Connoisseurship of Chinese Painting*, Washington, DC, 2008, pp. 137-176. URL: https://faculty.philosophy.umd.edu/jhbrown/connoisseur/index.html (accessed 4 February 2022).

29 Joris Corin Heyder, 'Doing Connoisseurship. Yesterday, Today, Tomorrow. Introductory Remarks', *Journal of Art Historiography*, 24, 2021, pp. 1-9. URL: https://doi.org/10.48352/uobxjah.00003417 (accessed 4 February 2022).

30 Nils Büttner, 'The Hands of Rubens: On copies and their Reception', in Toshiharu Nakamura (ed.), *Appreciating the Traces of an Artist's Hand, Kyoto Studies in Art History*, 2, 2017, pp. 41-53, esp. p. 43. See also, Neil de Marchi and Hans van Miegroet, 'Pricing Invention: "Originals," "Copies" and their Relative Value in Seventeenth-century Netherlandish Art Markets', in Victor A. Ginzburg and Pierre-Michel Menger (eds.), *Economics of the Arts. Selected Essays*, Amsterdam, 1996, pp. 27-70.

31 Hans Vlieghe, *Rubens Portraits of Identified Sitters Painted in Antwerp* (Corpus Rubenianum Ludwig Burchard XIX.2), London and New York, 1987, pp. 77-78, cat. no. 89.

employed to analyse the *Portrait of Young Anthony van Dyck* in the Rubenshuis in Antwerp alternatively attributed to Peter Paul Rubens and his pupil Anthony van Dyck. The results of this non-destructive analysis and characterisation of pigment are impressive and led to the conclusion that the painter's hand was rather immature, making Rubens' authorship unlikely. Moreover, it corroborates the attribution to Anthony van Dyck, which led to the conclusion that it must be an early self-portrait. Thanks to the collaboration with the University of Antwerp (Axes) and the Rubenshuis, sufficient resources were made available.[32] The results of several experiments on this portrait illustrate the range of possibilities afforded by high-technological research (Figure 6).[33]

Figure 6 Anthony van Dyck, *Self-Portrait*, panel, 36.5 × 25.8 cm, Antwerp, Rubenshuis, c. 1616/17. Top left: optical photograph; top right: copper distribution; below left: mercury distribution; below right: lead distribution.

32 Katlijne Van der Stighelen et. al, 'Young Anthony van Dyck Revisited: A Multidisciplinary Approach to a Portrait Once attributed to Peter Paul Rubens', *ArtMatters. International Journal for Technical Art History*, 6, 2014, pp. 21-35.

33 Compare to Figure 12. Anthony van Dyck, *Self-Portrait*, Antwerp, Rubenshuis: (a) black and white photograph of 'Young Anthony'; and corresponding distributions of (b) calcium (inverted), (c) iron and (d) lead obtained by MA-XRF of Figure 13. Anthony van Dyck, *Self-Portrait*, Antwerp, Rubenshuis: (a) colour photograph of 'Young Anthony' and corresponding distributions of (b) mercury, (c) copper and (d) lead obtained by MA-XRF.

Radiological examinations were carried out as well on *Samson and Delilah* in London as early as 1983.[34] X-ray diffraction powder analysis was used to determine the different lead white pigments, as well as to detect lead tin yellow, a pigment that fell into disuse after the end of the seventeenth century.[35] In addition, examination with infrared reflectography revealed that the complex composition had not been prepared with a detailed preparatory drawing in charcoal, thus typical of Rubens and proof of the maker's virtuosity.[36] The careful preparation of the composition in the drawing made it possible to apply the composition directly to the striped *imprimatura* with brown oil paint. The fact that this streaky *imprimitura* also served in many places to model the shadows by letting the panel shine through the thin layer of paint or by not covering it with paint until the end is a technique only Rubens practised in such a masterful fashion. However, as noted by the authors of the article on Leonardo and Morelli mentioned previously, the analysis and interpretation of these 'physical traces' are very important, but, in the end, it is the 'superior eye' of the connoisseur that has the last word.[37] Let it be clear that this conclusion restores to connoisseurship 'some of the disciplinary esteem it deserves', as David Freedberg put it. At first sight, one would expect that technical and digital evidence might conflict with the ability of the connoisseur "to understand something instinctively, without the need for conscious reasoning".[38] In fact, quite the opposite is true. Apparently, the combination of hard-core technological research and the intuitive application of the accumulated experience of the connoisseur guarantees the best verification of the authentication. Unfortunately, not many paintings have been subjected to thorough technological research, making the eye of the connoisseur all the more important.

Let us return to Rubens' *Samson and Delilah* in the National Gallery in London. Not a single serious Rubens scholar has ever doubted the authenticity of this painting on stylistic grounds. From a restorer's perspective, there is no doubt either. Joyce Plesters's research from 1983 can be compared to a steadily growing number of art-technological studies demonstrating the strong correspondence with other paintings by Rubens.[39] In 1997 the National Gallery issued a press release announcing that dendrochronological

---

34 For the interpretation of the X-ray, see Joyce Plesters and David Bomford, 'Samson and Delilah: Rubens and the Art and Craft of Painting on Panel', *National Gallery Technical Bulletin*, 7, 1983, pp. 30-49, esp. pp. 41-42.

35 Ibid., pp. 38-39.

36 Ibid., p. 37.

37 See Freedberg (note 14), p. 32.

38 Ibid.: 'We are all familiar with the experience of recognizing in a flash who a picture is by; and of recognizing a work as a copy, or a fake (...) even though we may be unable to set out exactly what lies at the basis of our decisions', – In the same article Freedberg points out the need to place the category of 'intuition' in its neuroscientific context too.

39 See note 60.

investigation of Rubens' *Samson and Delilah* conducted by Peter Klein proved that one of the boards used for the panel has the same felling date, 1600, as a board in Rubens' *Raising of the Cross* in Antwerp Cathedral.[40] This Baltic oak tree was probably felled in 1600, which dovetailed perfectly with the assumed date of origin and the context of its genesis. In the same statement, reference was made to no fewer than thirteen scholars who "have devoted their careers to the study of Rubens [and] unanimously agreed that the painting was one of the artist's masterpieces".[41] The National Gallery wanted to make clear that every Rubens scholar of standing, without exception, endorsed the attribution to Rubens. Moreover, by referring to all these Rubens experts, a range of international and very prestigious universities and museums became embroiled in the discussion. The same statement noted that 'none of the individuals who have doubted the painting's attribution to Rubens has published any scholarly work on the artist'. Surprisingly, this did not help. Rubens' *Samson and Delilah* has remained a subject of discussion like no other painting before. It had made the front page of a slew of newspapers published between 1992 and the Autumn of 2021 because there were 'doubts about its authenticity'.[42]

Paging through a sales catalogue of one of the major auction houses today makes it immediately clear just how much attention is paid to the provenance of a work of art. Not only does the stylistic analysis lead to the attribution but an 'external aspect' such as the provenance can also be a crucial argument. When we know who acquired a painting shortly after it was made and the family with which it stayed for centuries before surfacing on the art market, there will be little doubt that the object is not what everyone assumes it to be. Regarding Rubens' *Samson and Delilah,* there is visual and

40 See scientific report by Peter Klein, Universität Hamburg, Ordinariat für Holzbiologie (2 October 1996): "Regarding the sapwood statistic of Eastern Europe an earliest felling date can be derived for the year 1597, more plausible is a felling date between 1601 ... 1603.... 1607 + x. With a minimum of 2 years for seasoning an earliest creation of the painting is possible from 1599 upwards. Under the assumption of a median of 15 sapwood rings and a minimum of 2 years for seasoning a creation is plausible from 1605 upwards." – For the press release, URL: https://static1.squarespace.com/static/6151be4525884f7a310cc887/t/6161e47ac36999692e310376/1633805434872/The+National+Gallery+Press+Release+on+the+Samson+and+Delilah%2C+Oct+1997.pdf (accessed 23 December 2023).

41 The scholars mentioned are as follows: Professor Egbert Haverkamp-Begemann (Institute of Fine Arts, New York University); Dr. Walter Liedtke (Metropolitan Museum of Art, New York); Dr. Frans Baudouin, Professor Carl van de Velde, Dr. Hans Vlieghe and Dr. Arnout Balis (Rubenianum, Antwerp); Dr. Paul Huvenne (Rubenshuis, Antwerp); Professor Dr. Justus Müller-Hofstede and Professor Hans-Joachim Raupp (University of Bonn); Dr. Konrad Renger (Alte Pinakothek, Munich); Professor Michael Jaffé (former Director, Fitzwilliam Museum, Cambridge); Dr. Elizabeth McGrath (Warburg Institute, University of London); Professor Christopher White (Director, Ashmolean Museum, Oxford). For an overview of the arguments, see David Jaffé, 'Rubens Back and Front: The Case of the National Gallery "Samson and Delilah"', *Apollo,* 152, 2000, pp. 21-25.

42 For a full overview of sources related to the de-attribution of Rubens' painting of Samson and Delilah in the National Gallery, see URL: https://www.inrubensname.org/resources (accessed 4 February 2022).

archival evidence that it was commissioned by Burgomaster Rockox; the question, however, is whether the painting now in the National Gallery is identical to Rockox's original.

6 The Provenance of 'Samson and Delilah'

What is known about the provenance of Rubens' *Samson and Delilah*? It was commissioned by the Antwerp burgomaster Nicolaas Rockox around 1609-1610 to decorate the 'salette' (or salon) of his house in Keizerstraat in Antwerp. The house still exists and can be visited as a museum ('Snijders en Rockoxhuis').[43] Rubens had just returned to Antwerp from Italy after eight years. He introduced a new flamboyant style inspired by sixteenth-century Venetian painters, in general, and Caravaggio, in particular. Rubens' painting occupied the place above the mantelpiece. How do we know this? Because Rockox, one of the most important collectors of his time, also ordered a painting depicting his cabinet filled with pictures. The scene from the Bible is easily recognisable in the cabinet by Frans Francken II (Figure 7).[44]

Figure 7 Frans Francken II, *The 'Salette'* [Cabinet] *of Nicolaas Rockox, burgomaster of Antwerp*, panel, 62.3 x 96.5 cm, Munich, Alte Pinakothek, c. 1630-1635.

43 See URL: https://www.snijdersrockoxhuis.be/en/ (accessed 4 February 2022).

44 Frans Francke II, *Banquet in the House of Nicolaas Rockox*, c. 1630-1635, panel, 62.3 × 96.7 cm, Munich, Bayerische Staatsgemäldesammlungen, Alte Pinakothek, inv. no. 858. See Ursula Härting, *Studien zur Kabinettbildmalerei des Frans II Francken (1581-1642). Ein repräsentativer Werkkatalog* (*Studien zur Kunstgeschichte*, 21), Hildesheim, Zürich and New York, 1983, pp. 90-91, 374, no. 462; Konard Renger, with Claudia Denk, *Flämische Malerei des Barock in der Alten Pinakothek*, Munich and Cologne, 2002, pp. 202-205.

When Rockox died in 1640 an inventory of all his possessions was drawn up. His 'groote Saleth' was decorated with "*Eene schilderye oliverwe op panneel in zyne lyste beteekenende Sampsom ende Dalida van d'maecxsel van den* heere *Rubbens*".[45] The painting disappeared somehow after 1641, although a 'Samson and Delilah' was discussed in a letter the art dealer Marcus Forchondt wrote to his brother Willem.[46] In the first instance, Marcus had his doubts about the attribution and opined that it might instead be a copy after Rubens: '*soo comt het my als een coppy voor*', but he was pleased to have been informed that the connoisseurs considered it to be an original: "*geern gesien dat de liefhebbers het stuck Samson voor orrigenael houden*". In 1700, Prince Johann Adam Andreas I of Liechtenstein purchased a panel called 'Samson and Delilah' as being by Rubens from the Forchondt brothers.[47] The painting must have left the Liechtenstein collection at some point because it was sold in Paris in 1881 and bought by a German collector. The 'non-believers' have often used the argument that it is incomprehensible that the consecutive curators of one of the pre-eminent collections of seventeenth-century Flemish art would not have realised that Rubens' painting of 'Samson and Delilah' was an important work. This is a fundamental point of criticism, leading them to believe that the biblical scene could not be by Rubens. And yet the same fate befell another monumental painting by Rubens also painted shortly after 1610, the famous *Massacre of the Innocents,* now in Toronto (Figure 8). Alongside Rubens' earlier masterpiece, *Samson and Delilah,* the Forchondt brothers sold it to Hans-Adam, the Prince of Liechtenstein, around 1700. Although all Rubens scholars concur that there is conclusive evidence and are convinced that the incomplete provenance in no way undermines the attribution to Rubens, this factor of uncertainty has been played out by the 'non-believers'.

45 Erik Duverger, *Antwerpse kunstinventarissen uit de zeventiende eeuw* (*Fontes Historiae Artis Neerlandicae. Bronnen voor de kunstgeschiedenis van de Nederlanden,* I), vol. IV, Brussels, 1989, p. 383.

46 Rockox and his wife left all their movable assets, including 'conste van schilderyen', to the almoners of the city of Antwerp, who sold them on the Friday market in Antwerp in June 1641 to benefit their charitable work. See Carolien De Staelen, 'Rubens's "Samson and Delilah" in the National Gallery: New Facts Relating to Its Provenance', *The Burlington Magazine,* 146, 2004, pp. 467-469, esp. p. 467.

47 The Antwerp art dealer Marcus Forchondt expressed doubt in a letter of 17 June 1699 to his brother Willem, writing '(...) vant stuck Samson van Rubbens dat heb wel ontfangen maer nu ickt naer by besien soo comt het my als een coppy voor (...)'. In the same letter he stated: '(...) geern gesien dat de liefhebbers het stuck Samson voor orrigenael houden (...)'. For an overview of additional archival evidence related to the possible yet unlikely provenance of *Samson and Delilah* as part of the possessions of Maria de Sweerdt, widow of Jan II Moretus, and Johanna Catharina Hugens, see De Staelen (note 46), p. 468.

Figure 8 Peter Paul Rubens, *Massacre of the Innocents*, panel, 142 x 183 cm, Toronto, The Thomson Collection at the Art Gallery of Ontario, c. 1610.

While the authentication of paintings has traditionally relied on connoisseurship, additional evidence may be offered by scientific analysis and provenance research, investigation of related works, whether it be paintings, sketches, drawings or engravings. In the case of *Samson and Delilah*, there are three visual sources that reproduce the painting under discussion. First, Rubens' painting can be seen above the mantelpiece in a contemporary painting representing Rockox's 'salette'. Second, Jacob Matham made an engraving after the painting (Figure 9).[48] And, third, there is a preliminary drawing generally accepted as being by Rubens himself (Figure 10).[49] Believe it or not, the toes of Samson's right foot are what the fuss is all about. In the painting in the National Gallery, they are cropped at the edge of the picture plane. However, this is not the case either in the contemporary engraving by Jacob Matham or in the picture over the mantelpiece in the painting by Frans Francken, in which Samson's entire right foot is visible. However, undue importance should not be attached to these secondary pictorial

48 Jacob Matham after Rubens, *Samson and Delilah*, c. 1611/12, engraving, 376 × 441 mm. See d'Hulst and Vandenven (note 2), p. 111; Léna Widerkehr and Huigen Leeflang (eds.), *Jacob Matham* (Part I), Amsterdam, 2007, pp. LVI-LVII, p. 23, no. 10; Hans Jakob Meier, *Die Kunst der Interpretation: Rubens und die Druckgraphik*, Berlin, 2020, pp. 127-130, no. 5. A copy of this print preserved in the British Museum (inv. no. 1857,0613.528) is inscribed in pen and brown ink lower right: 1611.

49 Rubens, *Samson and Delilah*, c. 1609, pen and brown ink and brown wash, 164 × 162 mm, Private Collection. See d'Hulst and Vandenven (note 2), pp. 113-114, no. 31a; Anne-Marie Logan and Kristin Belkin, *The Drawings of Peter Paul Rubens. A Critical Catalogue, II (1609-1620)*, Turnhout, 2023, pp. 202-204, no. 248.

sources. The foot is not shown in its entirety in the drawing either, or in the oil sketch in Cincinnati, which later served as a model for Matham's engraving.[50]

Figure 9 Jacob Matham after Peter Paul Rubens, *Samson and Delilah*, engraving, 376 × 441 mm, London, British Museum (inv. no. 1857,0613.528). This copy of the engraving is inscribed in pen and brown ink lower right '1611'.

Figure 10 Peter Paul Rubens, *Samson and Delilah*, pen and brown ink and brown wash, 164 × 162 mm, Private Collection, c. 1609.

50 Rubens, *Samson and Delilah*, c. 1609, panel, 51.8 × 50.6 cm, Cincinnati, Ohio, Cincinnati Art Museum, inv. no. 1972-459. See d'Hulst and Vandenven (note 2), pp. 114-115, no. 31b.

Figures whose feet are not completely depicted or are cropped by the edge of the picture also occur in other paintings by Rubens, as evidenced by the sketch of *The Annunciation of the Death of the Virgin* (Figure 11).[51] Should one wish to use this phenomenon as an argument, it is sooner confirmation of a common practice in his workshop. For example, the toes of the child kneeling prominently on the steps in the foreground of *The Miracles of St Ignatius* are missing.[52] Rubens does not seem to have been bothered by such details. This is also substantiated by *The Drunken Hercules*, in which several figures and their limbs are cut by the right edge of the picture and the foreground on the right is not executed completely.[53]

Figure 11 Peter Paul Rubens, *Annunciation of the Death of the Virgin*, panel, 92 × 74.3 cm, London, Courtauld Institute of Art, Princes Gate Collection, c. 1611.

51 Rubens, *Annunciation of the Death of the Virgin*, c. 1611, panel, 92 × 74.3 cm, London, Courtauld Institute of Art, Princes Gate Collection, inv. no. 300.The cropped foot was taken over by the painter Frans Luyckx, who copied the picture and whose copy was reproduced in an engraving by Frans van der Steen.

52 Rubens, *The Miracles of St Ignatius*, c. 1618, canvas, 535 × 395 cm, Vienna, Kunsthistorisches Museum, inv. no. 313. See Hans Vlieghe, *Saints* (*Corpus Rubenianum Ludwig Burchard*, VIII), II, Brussels, London and New York, 1973, pp. 73-74, no. 115.

53 Rubens, *The Drunken Hercules*, c. 1613-1615, panel; 220 × 200 cm, Dresden, Staatliche Kunstsammlungen, Gemäldegalerie Alte Meister, inv. no. 987. Nils Büttner, *Allegories and Subjects from Literature* (*Corpus Rubenianum Ludwig Burchard*, XII), I-II, London and Turnhout, 2018, pp. 138-145, no. 11.

7 AI ANALYSIS OF 'SAMSON AND DELILAH'

This article is not the place to focus on the arguments forwarded by the sceptics, as the issue under discussion is to the extent to which AI can deliver new 'proof'. An initial attempt to examine the controversial painting with the tools of AI was made by Erica Gasparini at Tilburg University in 2010.[54] Although the study yielded no clear results, further research was nevertheless conducted.[55] However, in 2021 *Artnet news* could print a headline reading, 'The National Gallery's Prized Peter Paul Rubens Painting Is Actually a Fake'.[56] This article by Sarah Cascone was based on *The Guardian's* initial report, which quoted the statements of representatives of a Zurich-based start-up. The sceptics, who had shown little interest in serious arguments by art historians or conservators, were thrilled and spread the news across all social networks. Specialised in the authentication of artworks using AI, the young company achieved a veritable media coup with the help of *The Guardian* article. Within a few days it was quoted worldwide and was exploited and reprinted by journalists from all countries. Yet none of them posed the question of how this AI actually works and which images were used for comparison.

As the company's homepage and all published articles claim, the Art Recognition algorithm was trained with the help of 'images of verified authentic works of art'.[57] This information is important because the authentication is not carried out with original works of art but is based exclusively on digital images. Such a digital image reduces the relief of the three-dimensional surface of the oil painting to a plane that can then be analysed pixel by pixel. So it is not an 'original' that is analysed but rather a digital reproduction.

8 COMPARING WHAT SHOULD NOT BE COMPARED

This raises the problem of standardising the digital images used for this comparison. Anyone searching Google for digital images of famous paintings can easily see how much the colour values of digital images differ, and often so much that the colouristic quality of the original painting cannot be determined in a digital picture. These colour

---

54 Erica Gasparini, *The Attribution of Samson and Delilah: Digital Analysis of a Masterpiece*, HAIT Master Thesis series no. 10-004, Tilburg, 2010; Thesis committee: E.O. (Eric) Postma, P.H.M. (Pieter) Spronck, M.M. (Menna) van Zaanen.

55 Ibid., p. 38: 'Unfortunately, the results achieved applying the four digital analysis methods mentioned above do not allow us to determine the attribution of the target painting'.

56 Sarah Cascone, 'The National Gallery's Prized Peter Paul Rubens Painting Is Actually a Fake, New Artificial Intelligence Testing Has Found', *Artnet News*, 27 September 2021, URL: https://news.artnet.com/art-world/ai-national-gallery-rubens-not-authentic-2013830 (accessed 4 February 2023).

57 URL: https://art-recognition.com/our-technology/ (accessed 5 February 2023).

differences become a potential source of error for the algorithm. To solve this problem, colour and brightness variants of all available images are produced. But what does the colour scale of the pixels generated in this way have to do with the original work of art? Moreover, the images used "might have deformations and loss of information because of factors such as image resolution, lighting conditions, camera type, and post-processing compression rate".[58] The next problem is the resolution of the images and the relation of the pixels of the digital image to the real painting. The company uses 'high quality images' according to its own advertising statements. What is meant by this is unknown because the stock of images is a company secret. However, in addition to the expert opinion, private clients also receive a list of the images used for comparison, and this proves to be an interesting read. A large part of the material used stemmed from a photo agency, which provides all its data on its homepage. All the images offered have an average resolution of 300 dpi. The indication of 'dots per inch' refers to the digital image and not to the painting itself. The agency offers its customers the painting *Samson and Delilah* in a standard size, whereby the digital image is 4961 × 4551 pixels in size, i.e. 42 × 38.5 cm. Those wishing a larger file can also purchase a 44 × 40.4 cm image, which is also 300 dpi. The original painting is almost five times as large. Anyone who buys an image of the oil sketch in Cincinnati there can purchase a special size image that measures 60.9 × 54.9 cm at 300 dpi, which is thus larger than the original! If one acquires a digital image of the central panel of the altarpiece with the *Deposition from the Cross*, in reality 420 cm x 320 cm, the photo again measures only 43.4 cm × 57.6 cm. Very few of the photos supplied by the agency include a colour reference card that would allow the colour values to be adjusted. A standardisation of the colour values is therefore impossible. It is not documented whether the AI relates the digital images in such a way that it is always based on an equal number of pixels per square centimetre in the original. If this were done, it would mean a significant loss of quality in many images because the digital originals are rarely as large as the originals. However, if one takes the digital images as they are delivered, an oil sketch image with more than 300 pixels per square centimetre can be compared with the London painting, the best available image of which has only 118 pixels per square centimetre of the original. If one then adds the *Deposition from the Cross* for comparison, one is likening a painting with not even 50 pixels per square centimetre in the best available image. This deficit can only be compensated for at the price of working with digital images, which are anything but 'high quality images'. Alternatively, one can ignore this problem and compare what should not be compared. Either choice ends in a catch-22 situation and yields an unreliable result. The fact that the company seems unconcerned about the problem of the quality of the images used for

58 Ludovica Schaerf, Eric Postma and Carina Popovici, 'Art Authentication with Vision Transformers', *Neural Computing and Applications*, August 2023, URL: https://doi.org/10.1007/s00521-023-08864-8 (accessed 23 December 2023).

comparison is quite clear from the recommendation made to the customers regarding the image quality required for the analysis under the FAQs: 'I have taken a photo of my artwork with my iPhone. Is the quality sufficient for the analysis?' Answer: 'Absolutely. Please make sure that the photo is upfront [*sic*] and with no shadows coming from lamps or other objects'.

9 QUALITY AND QUANTITY OF WORKS USED FOR COMPARISON

Apart from the poor quality of the digital images, another obvious problem with the result of the AI analysis is the quantity of works used for comparison. The company endeavours to make use of all available comparisons, but 'normally a dataset of around 200 images is enough to produce accurate results'. However, the often quoted AI analysis fell far short of their standards in the study of Rubens' *Samson and Delilah*. "We gathered a total of 148 original paintings by Peter Paul Rubens to train, optimize and validate our model, results," says the report. Separate from the fact that they did not analyse '148 original paintings' but 148 unrelated digital images of dubious quality, the number of reference images was very small. There are 1800 painted compositions by Rubens (not counting oil sketches). The reference quantity was thus less than 10% of his oeuvre. However, it would be wrong to try to answer the question of comparative material quantitatively. What is necessary is a qualitative comparison that takes into account the historical and material aspects of the pictures. As already indicated, Rubens' paintings vary greatly in size, ranging from works measuring a mere 20 × 40 cm to ones that are almost 10 metres high. How was the selection made, which images were entered? Did the selection of comparisons take into account the varying technique according to the support or the stylistic developments in the painter's oeuvre, whose works were often largely executed by the studio? More important still, with the procedure used for the AI analysis, it is impossible to check who held the brush when the picture was painted. The AI compares patterns and can only determine whether the general characteristics of a digitally reproduced composition, the distribution of colour and brightness values match the patterns of the technical reference images. The technique cannot compare brushstrokes because it lacks knowledge of the plasticity of the paint applied. What is certain is that the people behind the AI were not aware of the fact that the structure of the paint layers and the painterly technique of Rubens in works executed on panel differ greatly from those executed on canvas. Instead of a streaky *imprimitura*, canvas paintings have an opaque grey underpainting that appears completely different not only in reality but also in the digital image. To compare the reproductions of such works with the digital reproduction of a painting executed on a wooden panel only compounds the problems mentioned previously. It is not known whether the 148 digital reference images also included photographs of paintings on canvas. This essential distinction did not play a role in a report we have on another painting. Against this background, what is the validity of the statement that "the result was always the same: Every patch, every single square, came out as fake, with more than 90% probability".[59] This statement is unobjective because the term 'fake' calls the painting into question in a way that is utterly unjustified, because the result generated by the computer is based 'solely on optical information'.[60] The mere comparison of visual patterns that AI performs cannot overrule the results of research obtained through the inclusion of contextual information, which includes provenance research and related knowledge, the results of art-technological investigation and much more. The statement is therefore as promotional as it is ahistorical.[61]

In addition, the results of the optical comparison carried out by the computer cannot be compared with the results of the Rubens research as long as it is not clear which pictures were used for comparison: the data and the results it generated are utterly unreliable. This is also, and above all, proven by the 'heat map', which is meant to provide visual evidence on the algorithm's evaluation. While these hotspot areas do not directly indicate a passage as being 'fake' or 'original', they 'have the highest importance for the final decision'. A closer look at one of these passages in the London painting, for example Delilah's breast and shoulder (Figure 12), reveals that it is, in fact, a particularly masterful demonstration of Rubens' painterly technique. This visible trace of *imprimitura*, which is also regularly encountered in oil sketches, is entirely characteristic of Rubens' original painting technique and has often been described as such.[62] At this point, one detail may suffice as a comparison (Figure 13).[63]

59 *The Guardian* (note 1).

60 This limitation of AI technology is also identified by Schaerf, Postma, and Popovici (note 58).

61 On the early modern concept of the original, see Nils Büttner, 'Echtheitsfragen. Kunsthistorische Überlegungen zum Begriff des Originals in der Malerei der frühen Neuzeit', in von Reinmar Emans and Martin Geck (eds.), *Echtheitskritik bei Bach. Bericht über das 5. Dortmunder Bach-Symposion 2004*, Dortmund, 2008, pp. 9-23.

62 See Nico Van Hout and Arnout Balis, *Rubens Unveiled. Notes on the Master's Painting Technique*, Antwerp, 2012, esp. pp. 45, 58–59.

63 Rubens, *Venus Frigida*, 1614, panel, 143 × 184 cm, Antwerp, Koninklijk Museum voor Schone Kunsten, inv. no. 709. See Büttner, *Allegories* (note 53), pp. 414-420, no. 54. See also, Rubens, *The Holy Family with St Anne, St John and a Dove*, 1609, panel, 66 × 51 cm, Private Collection; Rubens, *The Coronation of a Hero*, c. 1613-1615, panel, 221.5 × 200.5 cm, Munich, Bayerische Staatsgemäldesammlungen, Alte Pinakothek, inv. no. 997. See Büttner, *Allegories* (note 53), pp. 145-152, no. 12; Rubens, *Venus in Front of a Mirror*, 1613-1615, panel, 123 × 98 cm; Vaduz-Vienna, Liechtenstein, The Princely Collections, inv. no. GE120. See Nadja Lowitzsch, in Johann Kräftner et al. (eds.), *Vorbild Rubens*, exh. cat. Kunsthistororisches Mueum Wien, Vienna; Gemäldegalerie Akademie der Bildenden Künste, Vienna, 2004, pp. 95-98, no. 20.

Figure 12 Peter Paul Rubens, *Samson and Delilah*, panel, 185 × 205 cm, London, The National Gallery, c.1609-1610, detail.

Figure 13 Peter Paul Rubens, *Venus Frigida*, panel, 143 × 184 cm, Antwerp, Koninklijk Museum voor Schone Kunsten, 1614, detail.

10 Conclusion

Considering the results of art-technological research, this comparison of individual parts of a painting, which Morelli had already recommended, is key to understanding Rubens' painting technique and proof that the central connoisseurship method of carefully chosen comparison is suitable for achieving valid results. Nygren tried to connect Morelli's strategies with actual Computational Visual Aesthetics. In 'Reflections on connoisseurship and computer vision' published in 2021, Peter Bell and Fabian Offert state: "Here [using AI] connoisseurship is not reinvented but modelled in a way that seems to stay close to the human connoisseur: as learning from examples".[64] Their statements endorse and respect the principles of traditional attribution skills and reflect their awareness of the fact that the way in which AI has been applied so far is

64 Peter Bell and Fabian Offert, 'Reflections on Connoisseurship and Computer Vision', *Journal of Art Historiography*, 24 June 2021, p. 1.

but the beginning of a process that might take years before adequate procedures are developed which are smart and refined enough to apply data sets such that it can enrich traditional connoisseurship. It is to be hoped that further technological development and an incipient dialogue between art historians and AI experts will be able to combine the potential of different technical, technological and traditional methods of connoisseurship.[65]

65 The competition of new and old methods proclaimed by the press should become a fruitful collaboration, as emphasised in 2023 by Wolfgang Reuter, 'Original oder Schüler? Einsatzmöglichkeiten Künstlicher Intelligenz bei Zuschreibungsfragen am Beispiel des Rembrandt Research Projects', *Kunstgeschichte Open Peer Reviewed Journal*, 21 February 2023, cf. URL: https://www.kunstgeschichte-ejournal.net/600/1/Reuter%20-%20Rembrandt_DE_15.02.2023.pdf (accessed 23 December 2023).

Part III
Human Resources

AI and HR Policy: The Role of AI in the Formation of Employment Contracts

*Satya Staes Polet and Laura Llangozi**

Artificial intelligence[1] (AI) sits at the heart of the global trend towards digitalisation, and its various applications have a huge potential to improve the ways in which businesses run and in which we, as consumers, interact with them and with one other. AI can also play a crucial role at many stages of employment relationships, including recruitment, work allocation and employee monitoring.

This article focuses on the role of AI in different stages of employment contract formation. It aims to provide its readers with an overview of the relevant examples and the main legal points of attention when it comes to using AI in (work-related) contract formation, in light of market practice and an analysis of current and future legislation. However, the purpose of this article is not to perform an in-depth analysis of each of these examples and points of attention. We have chosen this structure, which consists of a mosaic of key aspects of the use of AI in employment contract formation in order to demonstrate how AI has naturally penetrated into the workplace, how it can impact employment contract formation, how the existing legislation is and can be used to regulate the use of AI in this case, and, finally, how the expected legislation will interfere with the current landscape.

---

* Lawyers at Freshfields Bruckhaus Deringer, Brussels.

1 According to recital 71 of the AI Act, artificial intelligence is a rapidly developing family of technologies that requires regulatory oversight and a safe and controlled space for experimentation, while ensuring responsible innovation and integration of appropriate safeguards and risk mitigation measures. According to academia, however, AI is a generic term that refers to any machine or algorithm that is capable of observing its environment, learning, analysing and reasoning, and based on the knowledge and experience gained, taking intelligent action or proposing decisions, to solve a problem at hand, comparable to human intelligence. See 'A brief introduction to AI systems and their use in legal tech', Georges Gielen, p. 3, basing this definition on Rémy Bonnafé, 'New Technologies and the Law: The Impact of Artificial Intelligence on the Practice of Law', https://medium.com/@remybonnaffe/new-technologies-and-the-law-the-impact-of-artificial-intelligence-on-the-practice-of-law-c456904688d1 and Annoni Alessandro, Benczur Peter, Bertoldi Paolo, Delipetrev Blagoj, De Prato Giuditta, Feijoo Claudio, Fernandez Macias Enrique, Gomez Gutierrez Emilia, Iglesias Portela Maria, Junklewitz Henrik, Lopez Cobo Montserrat, Martens Bertin, Figueiredo Do Nascimento Susana, Nativi Stefano, Polvora Alexandre, Sanchez Martin Jose Ignacio, Tolan Songul, Tuomi Ilkka and Vesnic Alujevic Lucia, 'Artificial Intelligence: A European Perspective', Publications Office of the European Union, Luxemburg, 2018.

Towards this end, we provide concrete examples of uses of AI in the employment relationship, before parties enter into such a relationship, both during the initial contract formation (AI in recruitment and drafting automated contracts, including in an environment like the metaverse), under Section 1, and during the employment relationship (AI in the employment relationship and termination of employment relationship), under Section 2. Second, we set out an overview of the key current legal provisions and the challenges that they pose in relation to the use of AI in the workplace (protection of personal data, the role of workers' representatives, neutrality), under Section 3. Furthermore, we examine the impact of the expected legislation (EU AI Act, EU Liability Directive, CoE's CAI proposal), the challenges that may be associated with them, and how employers can prepare to comply with them, under Section 4.

While this chapter refers to the formation of employment contracts, a number of topics that it covers are also relevant for other types of working relationships (e.g. self-employed relationships).

The article takes into account the developments in its subject matter up to 5 March 2024.

1 AI in Initial Contract Formation

This section looks at the phase that preceded the effective formation of the employment contract. Hence, it explores the role that AI can play from the first contact between the potential employer and the candidate (read more under point 1. AI in recruitment) to the way AI can contribute to drafting contracts (read more under point 2. Automated contracts). This section, just like Section 2, also explores some of the key aspects of the metaverse, respectively, in the initial contract formation, under this Section 1, and in the ongoing contract formation, under Section 2. We also tackle a few related challenges in the process of and while concluding employment contracts in a virtual reality, like the metaverse.

1.1 AI in Recruitment

AI is not only a means for drafting or signing an employment contract (as will be elaborated on under 'Automated contracts'), but it also facilitates the contract formation by helping Human Resources (HR) departments during the recruitment phase. Forbes has identified AI in recruitment to be one of the top hiring trends for many years and expects that the use of AI tools in recruitment will continue in 2024.[2]

In recent years, an increased use of AI systems[3] across different recruitment processes has been noted, from CV and voice analytics to chatbots and self-assessment tools. One of the most common uses is that of AI systems that scan job applicants' CVs in the recruitment phase. Although it is widely used to filter the applicants for many recruiters, both in-house or external recruiting companies, this comes with a number of challenges. The main one is likely the risk of discrimination if the AI system has not been fed with a sufficiently representative set of data or if it comes across practical examples that had not existed before and hence was not taught to recognise them. This risk, of course, goes beyond the recruitment phase and can be present in other stages of employment relationship (see under 'Neutrality').

Other AI systems used during the recruitment phase are those that analyse candidates' speech and facial expressions (and even gesticulations). Such systems are used during video interviews in order to generate and compare reports of their emotional intelligence or credibility. While this is another innovative aspect of AI in the workplace, it seems that, to the extent they are used to infer emotions, such systems could become prohibited in the EU, as soon as the proposed Regulation laying down harmonised rules on AI (the AI Act) enters into force (see Section 4 for more details).

Chatbots are another trend noted among employers who have embraced the use of AI in recruitment. Chatbots can help employers with everything from recruiting passive job candidates to pre-screening applicants over written applications and video interviews. They can interpret, score and compare human responses in order to come up with a comparison or a ranking between the candidates.[4]

---

2 Isaiah Hankel, 'Don't Let Chatbots Throw Off Your Job Search Game', Forbes, 28 March 2022. Serenity Gibbons, 'How AI Might Impact the Job Market in 2024', Forbes, 7 December 2023.

3 AI Act defines an AI system as a machine-based system designed to operate with varying levels of autonomy and that may exhibit adaptiveness after deployment and that, for explicit or implicit objectives, infers, from the input it receives, how to generate outputs such as predictions, content, recommendations or decisions that can influence physical or virtual environments. During the trilogue negotiations on the AI Act, EU policymakers agreed to wait for the OECD to review its definition on AI systems, which was eventually fully incorporated into the political agreement reached in December 2023, even though minor tweaks were made in relation to the order. The OECD definition itself was considered broad by many stakeholders who were waiting for the publication of its explanatory memorandum, which only became public on 5 March 2024, and it contains information to help to interpret the definition by adding more background on how AI systems are built and operate, as well as focusing on key words from the definition such as 'autonomy' and 'adaptiveness'. Details are available in the 'Explanatory memorandum on the updated OECD definition of an AI system', OECD Artificial Intelligence Papers, March 2024, No.8.

4 See note 2 above.

Although not directly linked with AI, it is worth mentioning that one of the most fashionable yet innovative topics of discussion among tech enthusiasts in employment has been the metaverse.[5] Some of the biggest tech names have been noticed hosting recruitment fairs and meetings in the metaverse.[6] On the one hand, events of these kinds hosted in a virtual reality can be associated with the benefit of having the risk of discrimination based on protected characteristics[7] mitigated. On the other hand, virtual reality might lead to further biases. In the metaverse everyone can choose their own avatar. Hence, gender, race and other elements that may lead to discrimination during the recruitment process are not necessarily visible or do not necessarily reflect the reality, depending on the choice of the avatar (see 'Contracting in the metaverse' for more details). When this is the case, the question being debated is whether an invisible characteristic will be considered as a cause for discrimination. For instance, if the avatar has a characteristic that the real person does not have and they are discriminated against for this characteristic presented in virtual reality, will the discrimination apply to the avatar or to the real person? According to certain legal scholars,[8] it cannot be excluded that discrimination can apply to both, as they argue that discrimination can be established based on a perception created in the metaverse. As Rácz-Antal explains, numerous pieces of national legislation specify that discrimination is unlawful even if based on perceptive characteristics, meaning that an individual is treated unfairly because it is believed that he or she possesses a protected characteristic.

Other software are designed to avoid biases in recruitment, by scanning the job posts when they are drafted in order to identify discriminatory words.[9]

Next to the various uses of AI systems listed previously, the predictive analytics is another aspect of how AI systems contribute to recruitment.[10] As opposed to the systems explained previously, the predictive analytics do not analyse the profile of the

5 Metaverse is an immersive and constant virtual 3D world where people interact by means of an avatar to carry out a wide range of activities. Tambiama Madiega, Polona Car and Maria Niestadt with Louise Van de Pol, 'Metaverse Opportunities, Risks and Policy Implications', European Parliamentary Research Service, June 2022.

6 See the LinkedIn example: Rime El Haddi, 'The Metaverse: A Glimpse into the Future of Technical Recruitment', 6 May 2022.

7 In this article we refer to protected characteristics as defined by the ILO Convention No. 111, Discrimination (Employment and Occupation) Convention, 1958, which lists as protected characteristics race, colour, sex, religion, political opinion, national extraction or social origin.

8 Ildikó Rácz-Antal, 'Labour Law and Metaverse –Can They Fit Together?', p. 36, Italian Labour Law e-Journal Issue 1, Vol. 16(2023) ISSN 1561-8048.

9 Carmen Nobel, 'Simple Ways to Take Gender Bias Out of Your Jobs', Harvard Business Review, 5 January 2017.

10 Chiradeep BasuMallick, '3 Ways Predictive Analytics Is Changing Recruitment Practices', Spiceworks, 16 December 2021.

candidate but rather the data gathered from current employees, such as their personal details, education, family details, performance and behaviour. Based on such data, the AI systems then generate the preferred new hire profile(s) for the organisation that is recruiting. However, organisations must be careful about the extent to which they use predictive analytics and the type of information that they want to collect. While organisations are continuously looking to diversify their teams, collecting and processing personal data in order to identify candidates that meet companies' diversity goals can raise concerns from a data protection perspective. For instance, asking questions about gender, ethnicity, sexual orientation or disability may not be allowed or, at least, may be sensitive in some jurisdictions.[11]

1.2 Automated Contracts

Other important aspects of employment in which AI can contribute include drafting, negotiating and signing employment contracts. Any of these can take place not only in the real world, in a meeting room or in a physical (home) office but also in a virtual reality, such as the metaverse. This is why this section analyses the automated drafting of contracts, but at the same time also what contracting in the metaverse can mean.

1.2.1 Automated Drafting

Automated contract drafting already exists, with products that offer the user the comfort of drafting a contract within a short period. These programs are usually designed as templates, allowing the user to change specific data, such as details of the parties, remuneration, start date and some other components of the contract. Such programs contribute to the efficiency of the organisation that is hiring by saving time and building consistency in all contracts of the same kind or category.

However, automated contracts are not produced entirely by the program. Even if the developments of generative AI have the potential to reduce them further, they require human attention and intervention, at least to insert the personal details of the parties, prompt the AI system to produce the right template and provide other details. Hence, it is important to emphasise that, in this context, the AI system does not impact the worker directly, because the product of such a system is reviewed by a human. The individual is impacted by the commercial agreement that is reached between the parties

11 Notably under Art. 9 of the GDPR '1. Processing of personal data revealing racial or ethnic origin, political opinions, religious or philosophical beliefs, or trade union membership, and the processing of genetic data, biometric data for the purpose of uniquely identifying a natural person, data concerning health or data concerning a natural person's sex life or sexual orientation shall be prohibited'.

but not by the AI system itself that is used to produce the contract. The latter does not (help to) take any decision; it only helps to draft the contract.

Finally, although we are not aware that this is being done in practice, AI could, in our view, be used not only in the negotiation or formation of individual contracts but also in the negotiation of collective bargaining agreements (CBAs), to support collective negotiations of social partners. For instance, an AI system could be used to scan existing CBAs with the same subject matter and, on this basis, propose an initial draft which the social partners would further discuss and negotiate. Also in this case, the result of the AI system would not be final, as the draft would be reviewed and further negotiated by the social partners. Therefore, the employees will only be affected indirectly, and human intervention of social partners will mitigate the related risks of a contract drafted by an AI tool.

1.2.2 Contracting in the Metaverse

Metaverse was briefly touched on under Section 1.2.1, but how about concluding an employment contract in the metaverse? This is another example of how AI could facilitate contract formation. In the metaverse, whether in the case of individual or collective negotiation, a contract could be negotiated entirely in a virtual environment, which has its core functions based on AI systems.

Multiple scenarios are possible, including when contract automation systems (as described previously) are used in the metaverse. The drafting of the contract could be supported by one automated drafting system based on AI (and that can also be used outside the metaverse), whereas the virtual space where the parties meet to negotiate and conclude the agreement is created by another AI system. The latter is designed to be similar to the real workplace in the sense that participants meet in meeting rooms, can share documents on screen or make presentations, very much like in a physical meeting room, where all the five senses are activated, rather than a simpler virtual meeting.[12] Hence, the parties can draft, negotiate, review and sign a contract in the metaverse. It is also possible for parties to generate the contract in the metaverse and then review and sign it in the real world (e.g. because the law applicable to the contract requires wet-ink signatures).

There are different approaches towards how the metaverse will impact the existing legal landscape. Certain legal scholars[13] argue that it is just a new environment in which

---

12 Marco Biasi, 'Guest Editorial. The Labour Side of the Metaverse', p. 2, Italian Labour Law e-Journal Issue 1, Vol. 16 (2023) ISSN 1561-8048.

13 Valerio De Stefano, Antonio Aloisi and Nicola Contouris, 'Metaverse Is a Labour Issue', Social Europe, 1 February 2022.

existing rules will apply to traditional contractual relationships, as the metaverse does not change these relationships. However, their view is also that the metaverse will come with new challenges and that the existing legislation might have to be adjusted in order to address them. As the metaverse is still in its early days, it remains to be seen whether and how it will impact the current regulations. What seems certain, however, is that it will definitely be another environment in which parties will potentially find themselves negotiating and concluding employment contracts and which will, in essence, be based on AI.

2 AI in Ongoing Contract Formation

Employment relationships are, in essence, contractual relationships that constantly evolve in time. Indeed, in the course of an employment relationship, the role, the compensation, the work location, etc. can be modified at regular intervals.

Every time a term of the employment relationship is changed, a new contract is formed between the parties, regardless of whether the modification is reflected in a written contract (e.g. the verbal amendment of a clause does not necessarily require that the written contract be amended). Consequently, contracts can be formed at multiple points in time during an employment relationship. This view is also shared by certain trade unions, such as the Italian CGIL and the French Force Ouvrière,[14] who have expressed the concern that the use of AI systems may lead to contractual changes and significantly alter the relationship between workers and employers.

2.1 AI during the Employment Relationship

AI systems that trace productivity, guide the discipline of employers or monitor employee emails can play a role in ongoing contract formation. As any other AI systems, those listed in the preceding paragraphs are associated with a number of benefits, but also pitfalls. One of the concerns about these types of AI systems is that they can put employees in a position where they feel that they are being monitored by robots and, consequently, that they are also treated as such.[15] This is because the AI systems usually do not consider the personal aspects that might influence the performance of an employee, for example, a system that counts the number of working hours or the movements of the keyboard/

14 Valerio De Stefano and Simon Taes, 'Algorithmic Management and Collective Bargaining', Foresight Brief, European Trade Union Institute, 10 May 2022.

15 Colin Lecher, 'How Amazon Automatically Tracks and Fires Warehouse Workers for "Productivity"', The Verge, 25 April 2019.

mouse and calculates productivity based solely on objective criteria. It does not, however, calculate the time spent in office meetings, for business development and other activities that do not take place in front of the screen. Neither does it consider the time when the employee (or worker) was absent from work for justified reasons (e.g. due to sickness or parental leave) and hence clocked lower working hours than another colleague for objective and legitimate reasons.[16]

AI systems are also coded by humans, and in order to make them work properly, a large data set is often required. Still, even in the best case, AI systems might make mistakes. According to Gizmodo, in 2017, drivers of Amazon Flex (Amazon's 'last-mile' delivery that operates the delivery from a local facility to the customer) mentioned that the delivery time automatically calculated by the AI system was sometimes longer but more often too short to effectively complete the delivery and that the two did not compensate.[17]

Nevertheless, despite the critics and challenges, monitoring AI systems keep being developed. According to ComputerWorld in 2021, AI systems that detect concentration levels by tracking facial expression and muscle movement are a real thing and one of the companies that has already created it expects it to be applicable to online classes, meetings and sales activities as hybrid work continues.[18] The innovation goes even further, with an AI-supported sales performance management solution provider that wants organisations to rethink the way sales compensation is managed and optimised, according to Venture Beat.[19]

2.2 *AI in the Termination of an Employment Relationship*

AI can also be used for the termination of the employment relationship in various ways. The first one is to draft and sign a termination letter or contract. This can be an AI system that generates a template and/or through which the contract or the letter of termination is signed.

16 This has also been confirmed by a ruling of November 2023 of the Tribunal of Palermo, Italy. See Section 3.3, under 'Neutrality'. Even though the case was related to platform workers, the reasoning was the same as that in the foregoing.

17 Bryan Menegus, 'Amazon's Last Mile', Gizmodo, 16 November 2017.

18 Matthew Finnegan, 'Rise in Employee Monitoring Prompts Calls for New Rules to Protect Workers', Computer World, 30 November 2021.

19 Chris Preimesberger, 'Forma AI Poised to Grow AI-supported Sales Compensation Management Platform', Venture Beat, 17 May 2022.

The second form of using AI systems in the process of termination is related to the employee monitoring that was discussed previously. The reports generated after monitoring employees' performance through an AI system, regardless of it being email monitoring, mouse movements or any other, can lead employers not only to reward good performance but also to make decisions related to termination of a working relationship. It seems that these kinds of AI systems are also used by certain employers to decide, during a redundancy process, where they have to select those employees that have to be redundant. According to Game World Observer, a game company decided to lay off 150 employees, after using big data and AI analysis, which indicated to the employer who the 'unproductive' employees were, based on their activities in email, documents, dashboards and so on.[20]

3 Challenges under Existing Legal Frameworks

The use of AI systems in the employment context, and particularly in the employment contract formation, is associated with a number of legal challenges, which we summarise on a high level in this chapter, such as the protection of personal data, the potential involvement of employee representatives and the neutrality of the used systems.

3.1 Protection of Personal Data[21]

A first challenge arises from the rules concerning the protection of personal data.[22]

First, AI systems very often involve the use of (large) data sets which may include personal data. Data sets are used to develop or 'train' the AI or are input in the AI to produce the results that the user expects. For instance, employers can store and analyse candidates' data collected during the recruitment phase as well as analyse the personal data of employees in order to build the profile of a potential 'ideal candidate' or assess their performance.

20 Evgeny Obedkov, 'Xsolla Fires 150 Employees Using Big Data and AI Analysis, CEO's Letter Causes Controversy', Game World Observer, 4 August 2021.

21 For the purpose of this article, we focus only on the rules concerning the protection of personal data, as they will be the most relevant in the context of the formation of a working relationship. For challenges related to the use of non-personal data, please refer to Data Act and the interplay with existing regulations, Freshfields Bruckhaus Deringer, 30 September 2022.

22 Under Art. 4(1) of the GDPR, personal data means 'any information relating to an identified or identifiable natural person ("data subject")'.

As with any processing of personal data, the above is subject to the provisions of the General Data Protection Regulation (GDPR).[23] In particular, the personal data used by or for AI systems must be processed lawfully, fairly and transparently in relation to the data subject. In addition, personal data should be collected for specified, explicit and legitimate purposes and not further processed in a manner that is incompatible with those purposes.[24]

The data controller[25] is responsible for, and must be able to demonstrate, compliance with, the aforementioned requirements.[26] This is known as the concept of accountability, which is central to the GDPR.

Furthermore, the processing of personal data must be based on one of the legal grounds listed in the GDPR.[27] Among such legal grounds are the following:

- the consent of the data subject;
- that the processing is necessary for the performance of a contract to which the data subject is party or in order to take steps at the request of the data subject prior to entering into a contract; or
- that the processing is necessary for the purposes of the legitimate interests pursued by the controller or by a third party, except where such interests are overridden by the interests or fundamental rights and freedoms of the data subject.

Also, data subjects are entitled to receive information about the processing of their personal data.[28]

Second, and more specifically related to the subject of this article, when AI systems are used to make decisions either about recruiting a candidate by analysing their CVs, their facial expressions or voices during an audiovisual interview or about the performance

23 In this article, we focus only on the rules concerning the protection of personal data that derive from the Regulation (EU) 2016/679 of the European Parliament and of the Council of 27 April 2016 on the protection of natural persons with regard to the processing of personal data and on the free movement of such data, and repealing Directive 95/46/EC (General Data Protection Regulation or GDPR).

24 Art. 5.1 of the GDPR.

25 'Controller' means the natural or legal person, public authority, agency or other body which, alone or jointly with others, determines the purposes and means of the processing of personal data; where the purposes and means of such processing are determined by Union or member state law, the controller or the specific criteria for its nomination may be provided for by Union or member state law. Art. 4 (7) of the GDPR.

26 Art. 5.2 of the GDPR.

27 Art. 6.1 of the GDPR.

28 Arts. 13 and 14 of the GDPR.

of an employee or worker by analysing their behaviour, the GDPR provides for strict restrictions.

The candidate or the employee will have the right not to be subject to a decision based solely on automated processing, including profiling, which produces legal effects concerning him or her or similarly significantly affects him or her.[29] There is space for exceptions when automated decision-making is necessary for entering into, or performing, a contract between the data subject and a data controller, when national law allows, or when the data subject has given his or her consent on this.[30]

In practice, this means that (outside the scope of the exceptions) employers using AI systems to help decision-making processes should provide for (the possibility of) a meaningful human intervention in such a process.[31]

This requirement of the GDPR is also reflected to a certain extent in the latest legislative proposals that concern AI (see Section 4.1.2),[32] but also in the positions of trade unions which require human control of algorithms. In addition, the EU Commission's proposal for a Directive on platform workers calls for more transparency in the use of such AI systems and for a 'human in command' approach.[33]

Finally, looking beyond the EU, the UK Information Commissioner's Office (ICO) has issued guidance on the need for human oversight and auditing of AI systems when they are used to make important decisions. According to the ICO, most of the automated decisions actually involve human intervention, but what should be required is an active human intervention where a human reviews the decisions before they are applied and has the discretion to alter it.[34]

---

29 Art. 22.1 of the GDPR.

30 Arts. 22.2 and 22.3 of the GDPR.

31 Guidelines WP 251 of the Art. 29 Data Protection Working Party on Automated individual decision-making and Profiling for the purposes of Regulation 2016/679, as last revised and adopted on 6 February 2018 and endorsed by the European Data Protection Board, p. 20 et seq.

32 Art. 14 of the proposed AI Act.

33 Proposal for a directive of the European Parliament and of the Council on improving working conditions in platform work, 9 December 2021, COM (2021) 762 final, 2021/0414 (COD).

34 Website of the UK Information Commissioner's Office, What does the UK GDPR say about automated decision-making and profiling?

3.2 *The Role of Employee Representatives*

The Directive establishing a general framework for informing and consulting employees in the European Community[35] (Directive) requires employers to engage in social dialogue where decisions likely to lead to substantial changes in work organisation or in contractual relations are concerned.[36] It mandates both *ad hoc* and regular information and consultation duties on the part of the employer.

Even though the Directive does not refer directly to information and consultation requirements due to the use of technology and, in particular, of AI, if the use of such systems leads to substantial changes in work organisation or contractual relations, then the Directive's information and consultation requirements could be triggered, obviously depending on local applicable laws and concrete circumstances. The AI Act, the impact of which is further explored in Section 4, also refers to the Directive and to the potential need for information and consultation of workers' representatives.[37]

In light of the foregoing, it should be noted that in some member states, the introduction of automated machinery or the use of AI technology may already require consultation with, or the consent of, the employee representative bodies. For instance, the German Works Constitution Act[38] grants works councils a co-determination right with respect to the introduction of new technologies that can monitor or assess employees. As for the case in Spain, the Rider Law[39] introduced *inter alia* an amendment to the section of the Workers Statute in order to give works councils the right to be informed by the company of the parameters, rules and instructions that algorithms or AI systems are based on, provided that they affect decision-making, working conditions, access to employment and its maintenance, including profiling.[40]

In Italy, since 2017, a national collective agreement for the manufacturing sector[41] provides for a specific individual right for employees to receive training to cope with changes related to the transformation of work brought by technological innovations.

---

35 Directive 2002/14/EC of the European Parliament and of the Council of 11 March 2002 establishing a general framework for informing and consulting employees in the European Community – Joint declaration of the European Parliament, the Council and the Commission on employee representation, Official Journal of European Union L80/29, 23 March 2002.

36 Art. 4.2 (c) of the Directive.

37 Recital 58b of the AI Act text agreed in December 2024, interinstitutional file 2021/0106(COD), of 26 January, p. 56, see here.

38 German Works Constitution Act (Betriebsverfassungsgesetz), section 87, para. 1, no. 7.

39 Spanish Royal Decree 9/2021 of 11 May, BOE no. 113 of 11 May, pp. 56733-56738.

40 Raquel Flórez and Juan Pastor, 'WorkLife 2.0: A New "Rider Law" in Spain that Will Affect a Part of the Gig Economy', Freshfields Bruckhaus Deringer, 17 May 2021.

41 CCNL impiego privato – 05/02/2021, n.9000963.

In parallel, trade unions are actively looking into the use of AI systems in the workplace. In particular, they are trying to promote ethical standards that employers should comply with when using AI systems.

Moreover, global trade unions themselves are being more and more vocal about issues concerning 'algorithmic management'. UNI Global Union (UNI), a global union federation with affiliates in 150 countries, suggests[42] that algorithmic management should be a topic of collective bargaining at all levels, with the social partners playing a role in the implementation and governance of the tools that serve such a purpose. According to UNI, there are not yet many collective agreements that focus directly on algorithmic management, but some of them include language regarding issues related to algorithmic management.

Next to voicing concerns and encouraging ethical use of AI, employees and workers' organisations and trade unions are also using it to their benefit.[43] Some of them have developed chatbots to exchange with workers. For example, WorkIt[44] is an app that enables workers to ask questions about workplace policies. It was designed by United for Respect, a US-based non-profit organisation acting for the workers in the retail industry.[45] Another example is UNIONSMART,[46] an app which intends to give personalised advice to members of United Workers Union, the Australian trade union that developed it.

3.3 *Neutrality*

One of the most prominent challenges associated with the use of AI in the employment relationship is the risk of unequal treatment and discrimination.

While the use of AI is often considered as a positive asset, precisely as it removes potentially biased human judgment from work-related decisions, it has appeared in a number of instances that AI was not always as neutral as it seemed.

42 Uni Global Union, Professional & Managers, 'Algorithmic Management – A Trade Union Guide', 1 September 2020.
43 Frances Flanagan and Michael Walker, 'How Can Trade Unions Use Artificial Intelligence to Build Power?', November 2021, published by IndustriALL, here.
44 See WorkIt app, here.
45 Privacy statement of United for Respect's WorkIt app, see here.
46 See UNIONSMART app, see here.

This is illustrated by the comment made by the labour tribunal of Brussels in the context of a case brought to it by the public prosecutor and supported by social security office and platform workers as intervening parties:

> It cannot … be denied that, behind the creation of an algorithm, there is always a human intervention for the design of this one, this algorithm being created to "fill" human needs.[47]

Even though this case was not directly related to the issue of employee discrimination by AI systems, the tribunal's reference to the human intervention points out that AI systems, because they are (initially) created by humans, are not necessarily totally immune to (unconscious) biases.[48]

We have seen and continue to see a number of examples of biases in AI systems. For instance, in the mid-2010s, Amazon used an AI-based recruitment tool to rate applicants. According to Reuters,[49] by 2015 the tech giant realised that its system was not rating candidates for software developer jobs and other technical posts in a gender-neutral way. The AI systems had been fed with the resumes of programmers hired in the preceding ten years, and they realised that these resumes were essentially coming from men, given that the tech industry was dominated by male employees at that time. The result was that the AI system was inadvertently biased to favour male candidates, against its initial goal.

Potential neutrality issues are further illustrated in a case brought to the tribunal of Bologna by a local trade union.[50] In this case, the platform used an AI system that, according to the tribunal, determined the reliability of riders based on their behaviour and would then allocate more rides to those riders with a higher reliability index. For instance, if a rider did not cancel a pre-booked shift 24 hours in advance, his or her reliability would be automatically impacted negatively. The tribunal found that this treatment did not take into account the reasons why the shift was cancelled, which could sometimes be due to illness, serious emergency or the will to exercise a legitimate right to collective action. Consequently, the tribunal concluded that the lack of ability to take such reasons into account unjustly penalised riders having legitimate reasons for not working and, hence, resulted in an indirect discrimination.

---

47 Trib. Trav. Bruxelles (Fr.) (25e ch.), 8 December 2021, J.L.M.B. 2022, liv. 9, p. 390.

48 Satya Staes Polet and Brunhilde Van Den Haute, 'L'intelligence artificielle dans la relation de travail: état des lieux', Orientations – Wolters Kluwer, 2023/4, p. 37.

49 Jeffrey Dastin, 'Amazon Scraps Secret AI Recruiting Tool that Showed Bias against Women', Reuters, 11 October 2018.

50 Tribunal of Bologna, case no. 2949/2019, see here.

Another case of indirect discrimination caused by the use of algorithms by a platform was found because of a claim brought to the tribunal of Palermo.[51] The algorithm used by the platform advantaged workers carrying out their shifts in the high demand hours of the day/week and penalised workers for not showing up for the shifts that they had booked. Based on a similar reasoning as the tribunal of Bologna in the aforementioned case, the tribunal of Palermo ruled that the system created indirect discrimination by treating every worker identically without considering individual circumstances, particularly their family situations, age, disability, etc. It might also cause indirect discrimination based on religion as it disadvantages those workers who, because of their religion, cannot work on some of the high demand hours (e.g. Jewish workers on Saturdays) or based on their trade union activities, as the system does not consider that the reason why some of the workers do not show up for a pre-booked shift might be linked to the exercise of their right to strike (as was also taken into account by the tribunal of Bologna).

4 What Is Next?

According to statistics of the Council of Europe (CoE), the number of AI-related initiatives in Europe has been continuously increasing over the past few years.[52] In the recent years before this article was published, however, it has been noticed that initiatives were coming increasingly from the EU institutions. This also reflects the central role that the EU has taken in this regard, especially with its latest proposals which include the AI Act and a proposal for an AI Liability Directive (AI Liability Directive).[53] These, however, are not the only legal frameworks put forward in Europe. The CoE has come up with a proposal for a legal framework that regulates AI. All these three proposals and their main aspects are the subject of this chapter.

Before looking at these proposed legislative frameworks, it is important to emphasise that the practitioners, academics or simple users of AI should not be content only with the introduction of legislative initiatives that regulate the digital sphere. But it is essential to expect that such initiatives are robust, evidence-based, and capable of

51 Employment Tribunal of Palermo, case no. 9590/2023 R.G.L.

52 Website of the Council of Europe, see here.

53 Proposal for a directive of the European Parliament and of the Council on adapting non-contractual civil liability rules to artificial intelligence (AI Liability Directive), 28 September 2022, COM (2022) 496 final, 2022/0303 (COD).

steering digital technology in the direction that guarantees their compatibility with human rights, democracy and the rule of law.[54]

4.1 The AI Act

On 21 April 2021, the EU Commission published a proposal for an AI Act, and, after lengthy amendments and negotiations, the EU institutions agreed on a final text in December 2023. The AI Act attempts to strike a balance between addressing perceived risks linked to the use of AI, on the one hand, and not unduly constraining or hindering technological development or otherwise increasing the cost of placing AI solutions on the market, on the other.

4.1.1 Employment-related Considerations

The AI Act, once it is adopted,[55] will be the only binding instrument at the EU level that covers AI in a transversal way and covers many of its aspects. It also impacts the use of AI systems in the workplace and includes employment-related considerations.

For instance, Recital 36 of the AI Act acknowledges the risk of the use of AI systems in the recruitment process or for the purpose of monitoring the performance or the behaviour of employees. AI systems used in employment relationships are considered as high-risk in the AI Act, given that they have an impact in the career prospects and in the livelihoods of the population. This approach is also consistent with the EU Commission's digital strategy that aims to promote a technology that works for people, which is one of the three main pillars of the EU Commission's policy 'Shaping Europe's digital future'.[56] The rules that would apply to AI systems under the AI Act depend on their risk classification.

In the context of the formation of employment contracts, it should first be noted that the AI Act prohibits placing on the market, putting into service for this specific purpose, or using AI systems to infer emotions of individuals in the areas of, *inter alia*, workplace (with certain exceptions).[57]

---

54 Nathalie Smuha, 'Digital Sovereignty in the European Union: Five Challenges from a Normative Perspective', SSRN, 19 July 2023, p. 18.

55 The final text of the AI Act was agreed in December 2023. However, until this article was finalised (February 2024), the European Parliament and the European Council were refining the details, before the act is finally adopted. See Section 4.1.4 for more details.

56 Communication from the Commission, Shaping Europe's Digital Future, COM/2020/67 final.

57 Art. 5.1.(dc) of the AI Act.

Further, Article 6.2 and Annex III of the proposed AI Act refers to a list of high-risk AI systems, which includes, among others, AI systems used in employment, workers management and access to self-employment:

- AI systems intended to be used for recruitment or selection of natural persons, notably to place targeted job advertisements, to analyse and filter job applications and to evaluate candidates;
- AI intended to be used to make decisions affecting terms of the work-related relationships, promotion and termination of work-related contractual relationships, to allocate tasks based on individual behaviour or personal traits or characteristics and to monitor and evaluate performance and behaviour of persons in such relationships.

The foregoing list is not exhaustive. According to the AI Act, this is only a limited number of AI systems whose risks have already materialised or are likely to materialise in the near future. The EU Commission has reserved the right to expand this list by applying a set of criteria and risk assessment methodology.[58]

The AI Act also foresees the involvement of workers' representatives prior to putting into service or using high-risk AI systems. According to the AI Act, this information shall be provided, where applicable, in accordance with the rules and procedures laid down in EU and member states' law and practice on information of workers and their representatives. On a literal reading of the provision, it is not entirely clear whether the AI Act creates a stand-alone information obligation or whether it merely intends to confirm that existing rules on information of employees and their representatives should also be followed, where applicable laws so require.

4.1.2 Link with the Charter of Fundamental Rights of the EU[59] ('Charter') and Ex ante Testing

The proposed AI Act intends to identify different sources of risk that derive from the use of AI systems and to ensure the protection of fundamental rights. In the explanatory memorandum[60] of the proposed AI Act, it is acknowledged that the use of AI with its specific characteristics (such as opacity, complexity, dependency on data and autonomous behaviour) can adversely affect a number of fundamental rights enshrined

58 Art. 7 of the AI Act.

59 Charter of Fundamental Rights of the European Union, 2012/c 326/02, Official Journal of European Union C 326/391, 26 October 2012.

60 Explanatory memorandum of the Proposal for a regulation of the European Parliament and of the Council laying down harmonised rules on artificial intelligence (Artificial Intelligence Act) and amending certain union legislative acts, p. 14.

in the Charter. Also, the final text of the AI Act makes reference to and requires the respect of the Charter.[61]

For the purpose of this article, it is worth mentioning the following rights provided by the Charter: right to human dignity (Art. 1), right to respect for private life and protection of personal data (Arts. 7 and 8), right to non-discrimination (Art. 21), right to equality between women and men (Art. 23) and workers' rights to fair and just working conditions (Art. 31).

In order to ensure that fundamental rights are safeguarded, the proposed AI Act requires an ex ante testing of the AI systems in order to ensure that they work consistently with their intended purpose.[62] It stipulates that such testing can be done at any phase of the development process before the AI system is used and that testing should be done based on what is necessary to achieve this purpose and not go beyond it. This testing requirement will be one of the crucial obligations that the providers of high-risk AI systems will have to comply with (and deployers of these AI systems have to make sure it is fulfilled) in order to minimise the risk of biased AI systems that might then have an impact in several areas, including HR processes, at any stage of the contract formation.

4.1.3 Relevant Obligations for High-Risk AI Systems

The proposed AI Act sets out a number of obligations concerning the high-risk AI systems, which companies that develop or use such technology in their contract formation or other employee-related processes should consider.

While it is not the subject matter of the present contribution to analyse these obligations in detail, we would like to briefly set out what we believe are the most relevant ones in this context.

The AI Act requires the establishment, implementation, documentation and maintenance of a risk management system in relation to the high-risk AI systems. It also requires a regular, systemic update of such risk management system, which comprises:[63]

- identification and analysis of the known and foreseeable risks associated with each high-risk AI system;

61 See recitals and Art. 1 of the AI Act.

62 See, in particular, Section 3.5 of the explanatory memorandum of the AI Act.

63 Art. 9 of the AI Act.

- estimation and evaluation of the risks that may emerge when the high-risk AI system is used in accordance with its intended purpose and under conditions of reasonably foreseeable misuse;
- evaluation of other possibly arising risks based on the analysis of data gathered from the post-market monitoring system referred to in the AI Act; and
- adoption of appropriate and targeted risk management measures (further specified in the AI Act).

Other noteworthy obligations include:
- data and data governance:[64] data sets used to train, validate and test AI models must meet quality criteria defined in the AI Act;
- technical documentation:[65] technical documentation should be drawn up before the system is put on the market or used and should be updated;
- record-keeping:[66] high-risk AI systems will be designed and developed with capabilities allowing the automatic recording of events ('logs') over the duration of the lifetime of the system;
- transparency and provision of information to users:[67] the AI systems should be sufficiently transparent to enable users to interpret their output and use them appropriately;
- human oversight:[68] AI systems should be effectively overseen by natural persons during the period in which they are in use (see our foregoing comments pertaining to human oversight); and
- accuracy, robustness and cybersecurity:[69] the AI Act requires an appropriate level of accuracy, robustness and cybersecurity and to perform consistently in these respects throughout the system's life cycle.

The personal scope of the obligations provided in the proposed AI Act is rather broad.[70] It is no surprise that most (if not all) of the obligations lie on the shoulders of the providers of the high-risk AI systems.

Therefore, the relevance of the AI Act in the employment contract formation may be more indirect than direct,[71] noting that employers that use high-risk AI systems (i.e. as

64 Art. 10 of the AI Act.
65 Art. 11 of the AI Act.
66 Art. 12 of the AI Act.
67 Art. 13 of the AI Act.
68 Art. 14 of the AI Act.
69 Art. 15 of the AI Act.
70 Title III, Chapter 3 of the AI Act.
71 Simon Taes, 'Robotisering en artificiële intelligentie op de werkvloer. Het recht op privacy van werknemers in het licht van de mensgerichte agenda', R.D.S. 2022, liv. 1, p. 15.

deployers) will have to be careful that their contractual relationships with providers[72] take into account the requirements that are associated with the use of high-risk AI systems.

In addition, we believe that the AI Act can be directly relevant for employers that use high-risk AI systems, on the following grounds.

First, deployers also have specific obligations under the proposed AI Act. In particular, they will:

- monitor the operation of the high-risk AI system on the basis of the instructions of use, inform the provider (or distributor) when they have reasons to consider that the use in accordance with the instructions of use may result in the AI system presenting a risk and suspend the use of the system;
- to the extent deployers exercise control over the high-risk AI system, ensure that the natural persons assigned to ensure human oversight of the high-risk AI systems have the necessary competence, training and authority as well as the necessary support;
- keep the logs automatically generated by that high-risk AI system, to the extent that such logs are under their control for an appropriate period of at least 6 months; and
- where applicable,[73] carry out a data protection impact assessment.[74]

Second, the proposed AI Act also provides that deployers could acquire the capacity of providers in the following circumstances:

- they put their name or trademark on a high-risk AI system already placed on the market or put into service, without prejudice to contractual arrangements stipulating that the obligations are allocated otherwise;
- they make a substantial modification to a high-risk AI system that has already been placed on the market or that has already been put into service and in a way that it remains a high-risk AI system; or
- they modify the intended purpose of an AI system, including a general-purpose AI system, which has not been classified as high-risk and which has already been placed on the market or put into service in such a manner that the AI system becomes a high-risk AI system.[75]

Third, the combination of the AI Act with the AI Liability Directive may potentially place an additional burden on the deployers that are faced with damage claims, for which they should be prepared (see under 'Proposal for an AI Liability Directive').

72 Or potentially with importers or distributors.
73 See Art. 35 of the GDPR.
74 Art. 29 of the AI Act.
75 Art. 28 of the AI Act.

Fourth, as we have seen throughout the foregoing examples, it is not unusual for companies to themselves develop the AI systems that they use in the context of the employment relationship. In these circumstances, it cannot be excluded that they could be considered as providers in the meaning of the proposed AI Act.

4.1.4 Entry into Force

The proposed AI Act is still making its way in the EU legislative process, and it seems to be in its final steps before adoption. On 2 February 2024, the European Council ('Council') endorsed the interinstitutional agreement reached on 9 December 2023, which finalised the main provisions of the AI Act. Each of the two institutions, the Council and the European Parliament (EP) will have to formally adopt the AI Act, before it is published in the EU official journal.

The Council's vote of 2 February paves the way for the formal voting of the AI Act by the EP in the plenary expected to take place in March 2024, once it is first adopted in the parliamentary committees. Should the EP vote in favour, a formal vote would take place in the Council in late March or April 2024. Only when this and the official translation works have been achieved will the AI Act be published in the EU official journal.

The legal instrument that the EU has chosen for the AI Act is a regulation, which will have horizontal direct effect across all member states, since the day when it will enter into force. Therefore, organisations that develop or use AI systems should familiarise themselves with the requirements of the final version of the AI Act in order to identify the areas in which they can start preparing.

4.2 Proposal for an AI Liability Directive

In September 2022, the EU Commission proposed the AI Liability Directive, which introduces rules governing damages caused by AI systems. This proposal is of particular interest because of two key provisions:

- access to evidence: the AI Liability Directive intends to empower the courts across member states to order providers or users of a high-risk AI system to (under certain conditions) disclose relevant evidence about such system that is suspected of having caused damage. In the context of a claim for damages, the court will only order the disclosure of the evidence by the provider or the user if the claimant has undertaken all proportionate attempts at gathering the relevant evidence from the defendant (including where the latter is the provider or the user); and
- rebuttable presumption of causality: the AI Liability Directive provides that, under certain conditions, national courts will presume, for the purposes of applying liability

rules to a claim for damages, the causal link between the fault of the defendant and the output produced by the AI system (or the failure of the AI system to produce an output). It will be for the national courts to decide whether such presumption can be rebutted or not and, consequently, whether the defendant is liable.

The proposed rules aim at ensuring that victims of harm caused by AI systems can access reparation, in the same manner as if they were harmed under any other circumstances. By accessing evidence as set out previously, they will be able to identify the person that could be held liable and to find out what went wrong. The disclosure will, however, be subject to appropriate safeguards to protect sensitive information, such as trade secrets.[76]

This proposed directive is also making its way through the legislative process of the EU, albeit at a slower pace than the AI Act. At the time of finalising this article, the negotiations on the AI Liability Directive have been suspended and are expected to resume only after the EU elections, in the second half of 2024. It will take a long time for this legislation to produce effects on employers that fall in its ambit, given that, unlike the AI Act, the AI Liability Directive will have to be implemented by the member states within two years after it has been adopted at the EU level. Only when it is transposed to their respective local legislation of the individual member states will it be able to bring effects for employers and more broadly for those that fall within its scope.

4.3 Proposal of the CoE for a Legal Framework[77]

The CoE has set up an *ad hoc* committee on AI (CAHAI).[78] The CAHAI's mission was, among others, to contribute to AI standards, coordinate work and establish an international negotiations process in the AI space. In December 2021, the CAHAI put forward a proposal for a legal framework on AI based on the CoE's standards on human rights, democracy and the rule of law.[79] The proposed legal framework would consist of a combination of legal instruments aimed at mitigating the risks deriving from the use of AI, particularly those that interfere with human rights, rule of law and the functioning of democracy. This proposal attempts to maintain a balance between, on the one hand, the

76 Recital no. 20 to the AI Liability Directive.

77 For a more detailed description of this proposed framework, see P. Valcke and M. Sas, 'Intelligence Artificielle (I.A.): tour d'horizon d'un cadre juridique émergeant', R.D.T.I. 2021, liv. 84/2021, p. 59 et seq.

78 Now succeeded by the Committee on Artificial Intelligence (CAI).

79 Possible elements of a legal framework on artificial intelligence, based on the Council of Europe's standards on human rights, democracy and the rule of law, CAHAI (2021)09rev, 3 December 2021.

benefits of AI systems and the progress of innovation and, on the other hand, the risks associated with the use of AI systems.

According to this proposal, potential elements of a legal framework for the development, design and application of AI could include impact or risk assessment, risk ranking and principles applicable to the development of AI systems.

Although the components of this proposal appear to be relatively similar to those of the AI Act, some consider that it would complement the AI Act in that it would tend to protect not individuals (as the AI Act does) but the interests of society as a whole.[80]

5 Conclusions

Employment relationships constitute one of the areas that cannot remain unaffected by the development of technology and of AI, more specifically. The large number of examples of the use of AI systems in work-related contexts, from recruitment to performance management to termination, are a proof not only of its impact on working relationships but also of the contribution of AI in the social development.

However, the use of AI is accompanied by challenges that are considered to impact not only the tasks, but also the career prospects, the mental health and the livelihoods of workers. Therefore, different actors: legislators, regulators, courts, trade unions and employers themselves have started to be vocal, first, in raising awareness about such risks and, second, and most importantly, in taking steps to regulate the use of AI systems in a work-related context.

The challenges for organisations developing or using AI in the context of the employment relationships seem to be numerous, arising from data protection rules to potential involvement of employee representatives, compliance of AI systems with all legal requirements, and avoiding the risk of discriminating employees.

The legal frameworks proposed by the EU and the CoE should put some restrictions on the use of AI systems, in order to protect fundamental rights and to avoid abuse. It remains to be seen how these restrictions will be addressed in practice, without stifling the trust and the potential for innovation that are necessary to allow AI to deploy its potential to help all actors in the employment relationship.

80 Valcke and Sas, 'Intelligence Artificielle (I.A.)', p. 65.

Discrimination in AI Human Resources: An Overview of the EU Legal Framework

*Ana Maria Corrêa**

1 Introduction

For the past five years, European Union (EU) policymakers have worked relentlessly to create a regulatory framework for artificial intelligence (AI) systems. This framework has high ambitions regarding the ethical and legal principles AI developers must comply with. In this regard, the European Commission proposed AI Act aims to ensure that AI systems used in the EU are safe, transparent, traceable and non-discriminatory.[1] The proposed act sets out rules based on different risk levels associated with AI. In addition, fairness and non-discrimination have been mobilised as key values in the Ethics Guidelines for Trustworthy AI[2] prepared by the High-Level Expert Group on AI. Efforts were mustered to create a horizontal regulatory framework applicable to multiple sectors with a common aim: enabling the emergence of human-centric and trustworthy AI.

The concerns to create human-centric and trustworthy AI are not unmotivated. Human Resources (HR) departments have increasingly implemented AI to support or fully take decisions in work-related environments, including in recruitment, staff performance appraisals and dismissal.[3] Job applicants have seen their CVs assessed

---

* Dr. Ana Maria Corrêa is a postdoctoral researcher at CiTiP KU Leuven.

1 Proposal for a Regulation of the European Parliament and of the Council laying down harmonised rules on artificial intelligence (Artificial Intelligence Act) and amending certain union legislative acts. COM/2021/206 final.

2 High-level expert group on artificial intelligence (HLEG AI). *Ethics Guidelines for Trustworthy AI* (2019). In other policy documents, fairness and non-discrimination have been directly or indirectly addressed. *See* COM (2020) 65 final. 'White Paper on Artificial Intelligence: A European Approach to Excellence and Trust'. European Commission, Brussels (2020); High-level expert group on artificial intelligence (HLEG AI). *Assessment list for Trustworthy Artificial Intelligence (altai) for Self-Assessment* (2020).

3 Tambe, Prasanna, Peter Cappelli and Valery Yakubovich. 'Artificial Intelligence in Human Resources Management: Challenges and a Path Forward'. *California Management Review* 61.4 (2019): 15-42; Van Esch, Patrick, J. Stewart Black and Joseph Ferolie. 'Marketing AI Recruitment: The Next Phase in Job Application and Selection'. *Computers in Human Behavior* 90 (2019): 215-222; Baiocco, Sara, et al. *The Algorithmic Management of Work and Its Implications in Different Contexts*. No. 2022/02. JRC Working

by AI screening tools and their facial expressions analysed in video interviews by AI technologies before being able to have real contact with HR professionals or hiring managers.[4]

So far, litigation and research have documented biased data sets used to train machine learning systems and discrimination against protected groups in algorithmic supportive decision-making technologies.[5] Individuals have experienced worse treatment based on their irrelevant demographic aspects, such as their gender, ethnic origin and age.[6] This reality raises several ethical and legal questions. From the ethical point of view, Frank Pasquale argues that AI should not entirely replace human reasoning in areas involving the fate of human lives: such as deciding who gets shot or who gets fired.[7] The main reason for this argument is that automated decision-making is based on efficiency and often dissociated from human empathetic reflection. Besides this ethical dimension, legal questions regarding AI decision-making are equally pressing. For instance, is data related to employees' gender taken into account in automated CV's screening? Should this serve as sufficient basis for *prima facie* direct or indirect discrimination claims based on sex?

The proposed EU AI Act contains instruments to potentially address discrimination against protected classes in AI systems in the employment field. First, it classifies AI technologies that fully make or assist work-related decisions as high-risk category AI.[8] These decisions include recruitment, allocation of personalised tasks and termination of employment contracts. Second, the proposal sets down extra safeguard obligations

Papers Series on Labour, Education and Technology, 2022; De Stefano, Valerio. '"Negotiating the Algorithm": Automation, Artificial Intelligence and Labour Protection'. Artificial Intelligence and Labour Protection (May 16, 2018). *Comparative Labor Law & Policy Journal* 41.1 (2019):15-46; Adams-Prassl, Jeremias. 'What If Your Boss Was an Algorithm? Economic Incentives, Legal Challenges, and the Rise of Artificial Intelligence at Work'. *Comparative Labor Law & Policy Journal* 41 (2019): 123.

4 'The Impact of Artificial Intelligence on the Future of Workforce in the European Union and the United States of America'. Available at: https://www.whitehouse.gov/wp-content/uploads/2022/12/TTC-EC-CEA-AI-Report-12052022-1.pdf, p. 26.

5 *See NJCM et al. v. the Netherlands* – District Court of the Hague,5/02/2020, ECLI:NL:RBDHA:2020:1878: This case concerned the digital welfare fraud detection system (SyRI) used in the Netherlands. A court, in the Hague, ruled that SyRI posed risks of discrimination and bias by linking data related to socio-economic status and national origin with the likelihood of committing fraud to the Dutch social system. Concerning the legal literature, see: Barocas, Solon and Andrew D. Selbst. 'Big Data's Disparate Impact'. *California Law Review* 104 (2016): 671-732.

6 Köchling, Alina and Marius Claus Wehner. 'Discriminated by an Algorithm: A Systematic Review of Discrimination and Fairness by Algorithmic Decision-Making in the Context of HR Recruitment and HR Development'. *Business Research* 13.3 (2020): 795-848.

7 Pasquale, Frank. *New Laws of Robotics*. Harvard University Press, 2020.

8 Annex III, 4 on the Proposal for a Regulation of the European Parliament and of the Council laying down harmonised rules on artificial intelligence (Artificial Intelligence Act) and amending certain union legislative acts. COM/2021/206 final.

for high-risk AI. In cases in which AI may pose a threat to the fundamental rights of individuals, the proposal requires from AI developers and deployers the implementation of risk management systems that might be able to estimate and identify the threats related to their technologies, including the discriminatory one. The proposal invites AI developers to mitigate these threats with specific practical measures, such as explanation methods apt to make AI decision-making more transparent. Other safeguards involving data governance, accuracy and robustness are also relevant to the extent to which high-quality data and proper data training may mitigate the risk of discrimination against individuals with protected grounds. Finally, the proposal's call for more diversity of AI development teams may serve as extra support in the fight against discrimination. Evidence has shown that the "more-gender equal tech teams are, on the whole, the better positioned to create more gender-equal technology".[9] The legal scholarship has devoted enormous efforts to analyse, assess and contribute to the debate on the EU proposal for AI Act.[10]

Even though this EU emerging regulatory framework has focused on fundamental rights and AI ethics, one should bear in mind that the EU non-discrimination law has developed solid concepts to address bias, prejudice and worse treatment to individuals because of demographic aspects such as their gender, ethnic origin, age, religion, disability or sexual orientation. Concepts such as those of positive action, direct and indirect discrimination have been developed and construed by the Court of Justice of the European Union (CJEU) and member states' courts since the creation of the European Economic Community. Concerning more particularly the employment field, EU non-discrimination law provides the most robust rules through numerous directives.[11]

Similarly to the approach of personal data protection and the General Data Protection Regulation (GDPR), the European Union has opted to regulate AI through a horizontal legal framework applicable to technologies in multiple sectors of the market.[12]

9 West, Mark, Rebecca Kraut and Han Ei Chew. *I'd Blush if I Could: Closing Gender Divides in Digital Skills through Education.* UNESCO, 2019.

10 De Stefano, Valerio and Mathias Wouters. 'AI and Digital Tools in Workplace Management and Evaluation: An Assessment of the EU's Legal Framework' (March 1, 2022). Available at: https://www.europarl.europa.eu/stoa/en/document/EPRS_STU(2022)729516; Cefaliello, Aude and Miriam Kullmann. 'Offering False Security: How the Draft Artificial Intelligence Act Undermines Fundamental Workers' Rights'. *European Labour Law Journal* 13.4 (2022): 542-562; Veale, Michael and Frederik Zuiderveen Borgesius. 'Demystifying the Draft EU Artificial Intelligence Act—Analysing the Good, the Bad, and the Unclear Elements of the Proposed Approach'. *Computer Law Review International* 22.4 (2021): 97-112.

11 *See* Barnard, Catherine. *EU Employment Law*, 4th ed., Oxford, 2012.

12 Veale, Michael and Frederik Zuiderveen Borgesius. 'Demystifying the Draft EU Artificial Intelligence Act—Analysing the Good, the Bad, and the Unclear Elements of the Proposed Approach'. *Computer Law Review International* 22.4 (2021): 97-112.

Concerning AI, this option has advantages and challenges. The main challenge is the proposed Act's broad scope and approach to the discrimination concept.

With those challenges in mind, the purpose of this contribution is to provide an overview of the EU non-discrimination legal framework, aimed at addressing discrimination perpetrated by AI systems. This chapter is organised as follows. In Section 2, the chapter addresses uses of AI by HR departments, including recruitment, appraisal and dismissal. Section 3 showcases instances of litigation regarding discrimination against protected classes in appraisal, dismissal and recruitment processes. Sections 4, 5 and 6 provide an overview of the main instruments put in place by EU non-discrimination laws to address discrimination by AI systems in the employment sector. In this regard, Section 4 maps the EU non-discrimination law framework that is relevant for this chapter. Section 5 focuses on direct and indirect discrimination. Section 6 explores the intersection of AI technical measures with positive action.

2 Uses of AI for HR Purposes

HR departments have implemented AI in multiple workforce-related activities, including recruitment of new employees and management and dismissal of the existing workers.[13] Recruitment, management and dismissal of workers are complex processes and may involve several stages. The use of AI is documented in different stages of each of these processes.

In recruitment, for instance, AI is used in sourcing candidates online. Notably, some practices involve targeting job offers to individuals based on specific demographic traits, including their gender, ethnic origin, age and sexual orientation.[14] Google, Microsoft, LinkedIn and Facebook provide advertisers with tools and filters to target with specific metrics the audience that they want to reach. This practice was the focus of several class actions in which potential employment candidates alleged they were discriminated against when excluded from receiving the targeted advertisements based on criteria related to their sex, ethnic origin and age.[15] In addition, AI is employed for screening CVs. Applicant tracking systems are able to scan text documents for selecting

13 Chevalier, Françoise and Cécile Dejoux. 'Intelligence artificielle et management des ressources humaines: pratiques d'entreprises'. *Enjeux Numériques* 15 (2021): 94-105.

14 Corrêa Harcus, Ana Maria and Isabelle Rorive. 'Digital Profiling: Challenges for Equal Opportunities in Online Targeted Employment Advertising'. *European Journal of Human Rights* 3 (2022): 221-241.

15 *Onuoha v. Facebook, Inc*, No. 5:16-cv-06440-EJD (United States District Court. Northern District of California San Jose Division, 7 April 2017); *Bradley v. T-Mobile US, Inc*, No. 17-cv-07232-BLF (United States District Court. Northern District of California San Jose Division, 4 June 2019); *National Fair Housing Alliance v. Facebook, Inc*, No. 1:18-cv-02689-JGK (United States District Court. Southern District

CVs with employers' preselected keywords and phrases.[16] An AI tool developed by Amazon was in the media spotlight for being trained with biased data. The tool selected CVs predominantly from male candidates.[17] Moreover, AI is applied in employment interviews to assess candidates' facial expressions and voice intonation.[18] HireVue, a business developer of AI used in employment interviews and for screening CVs, has performed more than seventy million interviews.[19] The potential discriminatory effects of such application of AI have been raised to public authorities.[20]

In management processes, AI is implemented to reduce repetitive tasks traditionally assigned to HR.[21] In this context, administrative and legal support are provided by AI virtual assistants to respond to inquiries frequently presented by employees, such as the number of days off they are entitled to or clarifications regarding remuneration. Moreover, HR departments have increasingly applied AI systems in performance assessment.[22] Assessing employees' performance is fundamental for companies to decide talent retention, develop skills and promote employees in structured careers. The use of AI in performance reviews is praised for its potential neutrality and avoidance of similarity bias. The sector recognises that

> when managers have to do all this for a large number of employees, it can be taxing and can result in human errors like personal biases, conclusions based on incomplete data, and favoritism.[23]

Performance reviews conducted by AI-powered technologies are heavily data-driven and based on the collection of data from multiple sources. These sources may include written communication among employees, their calendars, their time connected to

---

of New York, 8 August 2018); *Riddick v. Facebook, Inc*, No. 3:18-cv-04429 (United States District Court. Northern District of California San Jose Division, 19 March 2019).

16 Laumer, Sven, Christian Maier and Andreas Eckhardt. 'The Impact of Business Process Management and Applicant Tracking Systems on Recruiting Process Performance: An Empirical Study'. *Journal of Business Economics* 85 (2015): 421-453.

17 Goodman, Rachel. 'Why Amazon's Automated Hiring Tools Discriminated Against Women', *American Civil Liberties Union* (12 October 2018). Available at: https://www.aclu.org/blog/womens-rights/womens-rights-workplace/why-amazons-automated-hiring-tool-discriminated-against.

18 Suen, Hung-Yue, Kuo-En Hung and Chien-Liang Lin. 'Intelligent Video Interview Agent Used to Predict Communication Skill and Perceived Personality Traits'. *Human-centric Computing and Information Sciences* 10 (2020): 1-12.

19 Information available on their website, available at: https://www.hirevue.com.

20 *EPIC v. HireVue*. Federal Trade Commission (6 November 2019). Available at: https://epic.org/wp-content/uploads/privacy/ftc/hirevue/EPIC_FTC_HireVue_Complaint.pdf.

21 https://www.hec.edu/en/knowledge/articles/ai-hr-how-it-really-used-and-what-are-risks.

22 Köchling and Wehner, 'Discriminated by an Algorithm'.

23 *See* the HR support business website. Profit.co, available at: https://www.profit.co/blog/performance-management/use-of-artificial-intelligence-in-performance-reviews/.

their desktop device, and data from past performance review.[24] Despite the promise that AI may solve human bias in worker performance appraisals, the specialised literature has pointed out that AI may, in some cases, deepen stereotyping and discrimination against protected classes.[25]

Finally, the use of AI is also documented in redundancy and dismissal of workers. The press reported that workers have been dismissed based on either combined AI human or sole AI decision-making from companies such as the multinational make-up business Estée Lauder,[26] software company Xsolla[27] and Amazon.[28]

In the next section, I delve into litigations and controversies surrounding discrimination against protected classes in dismissal, appraisal and recruitment of workers. These instances of litigation challenge the idea that technology is neutral. Given that technology, such as AI, may be embedded with political and moral values, a regulatory framework should attempt to frame AI in ways that align with societal goals, values and principles. The complex interplay between technology, moral and political meanings must be taken into account when establishing a legal framework for AI.

3 AI and Ontology of Discrimination: A Sample of Disputable Cases

Do technical tools have political qualities? This question was addressed in a seminal article written by Langdon Winner in 1980.[29] This text was written much before AI had become a buzzword and is often introduced in discussions involving the meaning of technology. Langdon argues that technical tools, machines and infrastructure "embody specific forms of power and authority".[30] In this sense, objects and technologies have

24 *Ibid.*

25 De Stefano, Valerio and Mathias Wouters. 'AI and Digital Tools in Workplace Management and Evaluation: An Assessment of the EU's Legal Framework' (March 1, 2022). Available at: https://www.europarl.europa.eu/stoa/en/document/EPRS_STU(2022)729516.

26 Thompson, Susan and Andrew Lloyd. 'Sacked by an Algorithm: Can Employment Law Keep Up with Advances in Technology?', *Relocate Magazine* (17 May 2022). Available at: https://www.relocatemagazine.com/sacked-by-an-algorithm-can-employment-law-keep-up-with-advances-in-technology-0522-talent-management.

27 Miquel Echarri. 'One Second, 150 Dismissals: Inside the Algorithms that Decide Who Should Lose their Job', *El País* (14 October 2021). Available at: https://english.elpais.com/usa/2021-10-14/one-second-150-dismissals-inside-the-algorithms-that-decide-who-should-lose-their-job.html.

28 Soper, Spencer. 'Fired by Bot: Amazon Turns to Machine Managers and Workers Are Losing Out', *Bloomberg* (28 June 2021). Available at: https://www.bloomberg.com/news/features/2021-06-28/fired-by-bot-amazon-turns-to-machine-managers-and-workers-are-losing-out.

29 Winner, Langdon. 'Do Artifacts Have Politics?' *Daedalus* 109.1 (1980): 121-136.

30 *Ibid.*, p. 123.

embedded values of their designers. And more. Objects and technologies are ontologically normative and shape which groups of individuals can make the best use of them. The embodiment of these values in objects and technologies may or may not be intentional. This idea is quite provocative and challenges the common knowledge that: (1) objects/ technologies are neutral, (2) what makes them good or bad is the use given to them.

Winner illustrates his reasoning that objects have political qualities with multiple real examples, including the extraordinarily low bridges in Long Island, New York, that were built to prevent the presence of buses in the region. The bridges were intentionally designed to achieve a particular social effect: the eviction of social groups that used buses as a mean of transportation. In this case, African-Americans and low-income groups were over-represented among the ones who did not have access to Long Island. In Europe, other examples include the broad straight streets designed by Haussmann in Paris to prevent the building of barricades.

These ideas can be illuminating to the way we perceive AI as the outcome of human engineering. Can the design of AI tools implemented by HR departments have adverse consequences on individuals with certain demographic traits? The following examples respond affirmatively to this question. The meaning of the AI design deserves further investigation. This adverse impact can be intentional or unintentional.

The multinational cosmetics company Estée Lauder got on the spotlight of labour lawyers for using AI technology in a dismissal process.[31] The company's HR team allegedly used AI to support its decision-making to reduce its team of make-up artists. The technology had been originally designed for employment interviews and counted with more than fifteen thousand data points. Voice intonation, inflections and emotions were among the data assessed by the AI technology. Some concerned employees brought the claim to a court in the UK. The company opted to settle the case aside. This example showcases the complexity of using AI in dismissal processes for two reasons: first, when fifteen thousand data points are processed, it remains unclear what the exact reasons for dismissing the employee are. Among the reasons, some could be related to measurable skills and others to factors that may not be considered, such as the voice intonation. Voice intonation differs according to a person's gender, cultural background and age. Voice intonation may not be considered in an employment dismissal decision because it may lead to discrimination against protected classes, such as gender, ethnic origin or even age. This would be a case when the AI technology relates worse performance

31 Mitchell, Irwin. 'Computer Says No: Unpicking the Employment Risks of AI' (20 November 2022). Available at: https://www.lexology.com/library/detail.aspx?g=0639439a-42a5-48ac-b7fd-5f56908bb4b8.

with a certain voice intonation that is more representative among certain groups, for instance.

Potential discrimination against workers has been reported in appraisal processes as well. The Italian labour union CGIL filed a case regarding the algorithmic evaluation of Deliveroo's riders.[32] Riders were evaluated based on the aspects of reliability and participation on the platform. These two metrics combined determined the raking of riders on the platform. The riders' position in the raking determined which riders would take more convenient work shifts and the most inconvenient ones. The main issue was that these metrics did not consider the reasons for the absence of drivers to determine their reliability and participation. Riders were automatically downgraded even if they were absent for legitimate reasons such as health issues and family commitments. The Italian court ruled that the algorithm could give rise to indirect discrimination.[33]

A case of potential algorithmic discrimination in the recruitment sector also concerned Amazon Mechanical Turk (AMT), a subsidiary of the popular company Amazon. AMT operates a crowdsourcing platform that brings together business and independent workers. These workers are selected after they create an account and provide information via a form available on AMT website. Once, trying to provide work through the platform, a female worker located in Germany received an email from the company indicating that AMT decided that she would not be allowed to provide her services through the platform. The email mentioned that "our account review criteria are proprietary and we cannot disclose the reason why an invitation to complete registration has been denied".[34] After several unsuccessful attempts to obtain information on how her personal data had been processed to generate the refusal to provide work through the platform, the worker filed a complaint with the Luxembourg data protection authority. The complainant wondered: "Did they [AMT] reject me because of my location, level of education, gender?"[35]

Another case in recruitment involved an AI hiring tool in development by Amazon that was fed and trained with data about successful engineers who were predominantly men.[36] When the tool was implemented, women were vastly under-represented in the

32 Court of Bologna (1st Instance, Labour Section), Filcams CGIL Bologna & al. c. Deliveroo Italia SRL, 12 December 2020, n. 2949/2019.

33 Gramano, Elena and Miriam Kullmann. 'Algorithmic Discrimination, the Role of GPS, and the Limited Scope of EU non-Discrimination Law', in De Stefano, V., Durri, I (eds), *A Research Agenda for the Gig Economy and Society*. Edward Elgar Publishing, 2022, pp. 53-72.

34 Noyb, 'Complaint Commission Nationale Pour la Protection des Données' (December 2021). Available at: https://noyb.eu/sites/default/files/2021-12/AMT%20Complaint%20-%20FR%20redacted.pdf.

35 *Ibid.*

36 Goodman, 'Why Amazon's Automated Hiring Tools Discriminated Against Women'.

selection of candidates. This happened because the system did not consider female candidates who had degrees from colleges that were not attended by many existing Amazon male engineers. In addition, the system gave priority to resumes with verbs that men had statistically used more often, such as 'executed' and 'captured'.

Finally, a trade union in Denmark reported having found an automated hiring system being trained with data correlating Asian women with cleaning work. The outcome was priority to work allocation for this group on cleaning chores and the exclusion of other groups from the same kind of work.[37]

These sorts of unequal treatment based on demographic traits are addressed by the EU non-discrimination legal framework.[38] The idea behind this chapter is to present the current legal framework that can serve as a support to address discrimination perpetrated by AI systems. The limits of this legal apparatus will not be addressed for two reasons: first, the author considers that the current legal framework already provides answers to several cases involving discrimination by AI. Second, various scholars have already explored certain limits of existing equality laws in addressing cases of discrimination by AI systems.[39]

4 EU Non-discrimination Legal Framework

The designation non-discrimination laws refers to a multi-layered framework of legal rules composed of the European Union, international and member states sources.[40]

Initially, the European Economic Community focused on gender discrimination in the employment field for reasons that were economic.[41] In the context of intensive

---

37 Soper, Spencer. 'Fired by Bot at Amazon: It's You against the Machine' (28 June 2021). Available at: https://www.bloomberg.com/news/features/2021-06-28/fired-by-bot-amazon-turns-to-machine-managers-and-workers-are-losing-out.

38 For an overview of the EU non-discrimination framework on the labour, advertising and housing sectors online, *see* Ana Maria Corrêa. *Discrimination in Online Platforms.* Intersentia, 2022.

39 To cite a few: Wachter, Sandra. 'The Theory of Artificial Immutability: Protecting Algorithmic Groups Under Anti-Discrimination Law'. *Tulane Law Review* 97:2 (2022): 149:199. Gerards, Janneke and Federik Borgesius Zuiderveen. 'Protected Grounds and the System of Non-Discrimination Law in the Context of Algorithmic Decision-Making and Artificial Intelligence'. *Colorado Technology Law Journal* 20 (2021): 1-28. Xenidis, Raphaële and Linda Senden. 'EU Non-Discrimination Law in the Era of Artificial Intelligence: Mapping the Challenges of Algorithmic Discrimination', in Ulf Bernitiz et al. (eds), *General Principles of EU Law in the EU Digital Order.* Kluwer Law International, 2020, pp. 151-182.

40 Bribosia, Emmanuelle and Isabelle Rorive. 'Anti-discrimination Law in the Global Age'. *Journal Européen des droits de l'homme* 1 (2015): 3-10.

41 Ellis, Evelyn and Philippa Watson. *EU Anti-Discrimination Law.* OUP Oxford, 2012.

economic integration, member states that fostered gender equality by promoting equal payment would be at a competitive disadvantage with respect to member states that did not provide for the same equal employment conditions.

In the EU, early documents such as the Treaty of Rome, 1957, placed gender equality as the foundation of equality law. The Treaty established the right to equal pay between men and women.[42] It also conferred the European Economic Community with the competence to legislate on matters of equal treatment. This legal framework led to the development of two relevant directives focused on gender equality: the equal pay directive of 1975[43] and the Equal Treatment Directive of 1976,[44] which prohibited discrimination based on gender in access to employment, vocational training and promotion and working conditions.

In 1997, the Treaty of Amsterdam remarkably expanded the scope of protection beyond workplace discrimination and the grounds deserving protection from EU law. The Treaty introduced specific competence to address discrimination based on sex, racial or ethnic origin, religion or belief, disability, age or sexual orientation.[45] This development significantly impacted the enactment of the Equality Directives in the early 2000s.

At the dawn of the twentieth-first century, following the Amsterdam Treaty, European secondary law provided member states with a legal framework to address inequality beyond gender discrimination and the employment field. On the one hand, the Directive 2000/43 implementing the principle of equal treatment between persons irrespective of racial or ethnic origin (hereinafter Race Equality Directive) laid down a framework for combating discrimination on the grounds of racial or ethnic origin in the context of employment but also social protection, health care, education and access to and supply of goods and services.[46] On the other, the Directive 2000/78 established a framework for equal treatment in employment and occupation (hereinafter Employment Equality Directive) on the grounds of religion or belief, disability, age, and sexual orientation. In

42 Art. 119, Treaty establishing the European Economic Community (Treaty of Rome), 25 March 1957.

43 Council Directive 75/117/EEC of 10 February 1975 on the approximation of the laws of the member states relating to the application of the principle of equal pay for men and women, OJ L 45, 19.2.1975, pp. 19-20. (No longer in force. Replaced with Directive 2006/54/EC of the European Parliament and of the Council of 5 July 2006 on the implementation of the principle of equal opportunities and equal treatment of men and women in matters of employment and occupation (recast)).

44 Council Directive 76/207/EEC of 9 February 1976 on the implementation of the principle of equal treatment for men and women as regards access to employment, vocational training and promotion, and working conditions, OJ L 39, 14.2.1976, pp. 40-42. (No longer in force. Replaced with Directive 2006/54/EC (recast).

45 Art. 6a, Treaty of Amsterdam amending the Treaty on European Union, the Treaties establishing the European Communities and certain related acts OJ C 340, 10.11.1997, pp. 1-144.

46 Art. 3, Race Equality Directive.

2006, the Directive 2006/54 (hereinafter Gender Equality Directive) on equal treatment of men and women in matters of employment has put together some earlier directives concerning gender discrimination.

In 2009, the Treaty of Lisbon substantially strengthened the equality principle in the core of the Union, by conferring the EU Charter of Fundamental Rights with the same status as the Treaty of the European Union and the Treaty of the Functioning of the European Union. This development was relevant because beyond member states' bodies, all EU institutions, including the European Parliament and the European Commission, shall comply with the Charter of Fundamental Rights in developing and implementing EU law. The EU Charter on Fundamental Rights has more grounds of protection than the Equality Directives. It forbids discrimination on the grounds of sex, race, colour, ethnic or social origin, genetic features, language, religion or other belief, political opinion, membership of a national minority, property, birth, disability, age or sexual orientation.[47]

This extensive non-discrimination law framework has been developed and implemented by the CJEU to address direct and indirect discrimination in different economic sectors. The articulation of direct and indirect discrimination that may be perpetrated by AI systems are refined in the following section.

5 DIRECT OR INDIRECT DISCRIMINATION AGAINST INDIVIDUALS WITH PROTECTED GROUNDS

Concerning work-related environments, the purpose of the Equality Directives is to prohibit direct and indirect discrimination on the grounds of gender, race or ethnic origin, religion or belief, disability, age and sexual orientation in access to employment and conditions of work. The Gender Equality Directive also aims at promoting gender equality.

Direct discrimination takes place when one person is treated less favourably than another is, has been or would be treated in a comparable situation on the grounds of their sex, race, religion or belief, disability, age and sexual orientation.[48] The concept of direct discrimination relies on the principle "likes should be treated alike".[49] Therefore, the determination of less favourable treatment requires a comparator.

47 Art. 21, Charter of Fundamental Rights of the European Union OJ C 326, 26.10.2012, pp. 391-407.

48 Art. 2 (a), Race Equality Directive. Art. 2 (a), Employment Equality Directive. Art. 2 (a), Gender Equality Directive.

49 Fredman, Sandra. *Discrimination Law.* Oxford University Press, 2011, p. 166.

In practice, the victim of direct discrimination must point to the treatment another person without the protected ground has received, receives or would receive in a similar situation. The wording 'is, has been or would be treated' makes it clear that the victim of discrimination may find support in similar situations in the present, past or even hypothetical situations. Direct discrimination is often assessed through the 'but-for' test, in which the complainant may ask "but for the existence of x, would y have occurred?"[50] In the case concerning AMT, the female complainant should question "but for the existence of my gender, would I have been hired"? or "if not my gender, would I have been hired"? Employers are able to justify direct discrimination based on sex only if there is either genuine occupational requirement[51] or the situation falls within the circumstances where positive action is allowed.[52]

Genuine occupational requirement shall be case-based, exceptional and proportionate in cases of direct discrimination. There must be a link between the employer's preference to a protected ground, such as the gender of an employment candidate, for instance, and the qualifications required for a particular type of work. The threshold for justifying direct discrimination is higher than that in the indirect one. A test of proportionality might assess whether the occupational requirement is genuine and legitimate. Moreover, the concept of genuine occupational requirement evolves in time. The CJEU decided in early cases, e.g., that sex should be a legitimate genuine occupational requirement in the case of restricting the role of midwives to women, considering the sensitivity of the activity with regard to women giving birth.[53] Sex was also considered a genuine occupational requirement defence in the *Sirdar v Army Board* case in which positions were restricted to men.[54] Sirdar was a female chef and complained that she was banned from taking a position in a unit of the British Army. The unit in question was intended to be the first line of attack. The court considered the limitation based on sex proportional, given the unit was small and its members should be able to act as fighting members. Both understandings evolved in time and were fully criticised as stereotyping the role of women.[55] However, there are more recent examples of how sex can be considered a genuine occupational requirement in situations regarding access to work, including the performance of artistic work.[56]

50 Bell, Mark. 'Direct Discrimination', in D. Schiek, L. Waddington and M. Bell (eds), *Non-Discrimination Law*. Hart Publishing, 2007, chapter 2.

51 Art. 14.2, Gender Equality Directive.

52 Art. 3, Gender Equality Directive.

53 *Commission v. United Kingdom* ECLI:EU:1983:311.

54 *Sirdar v. Army Board* ECLI:EU:C:1999:246.

55 Holzleithner, Elisabeth. 'Gender Equality and Physical Requirements in Employment'. *European Equality Law Review 2017*.1 (2017): 13-21.

56 European Union Agency for Fundamental Rights and Council of Europe, *Handbook on European Non-Discrimination Law*, 2018, p. 98.

Direct discrimination is conditioned neither to intentional nor to overt practices. Direct discrimination occurs when someone is treated less favourably than another or has been or would be in a comparable situation. Therefore, no proof of intentional or overt discrimination is required. Direct discrimination can be demonstrated through the 'but-for' test.[57] Moreover, the identification of the victim is not necessary to demonstrate direct discrimination.[58] Conceiving discriminatory practices perpetrated by AI systems in employment-related decisions has one important benefit. In the EU, defences or justifications for direct discrimination are much more limited than those accepted in circumstances of indirect discrimination. In the aforementioned case regarding AMT, the female candidate should reference a comparator of the other sex to make a case of direct discrimination. The burden of proof in this case is shifted.[59] AMT would have to demonstrate that the candidate was not excluded from the selection because of her gender.

Indirect discrimination occurs where an apparently neutral provision, criterion or practice would put persons of one sex at a particular disadvantage compared with other persons without the protected grounds.[60] The discriminatory outcome of a certain neutral general provision, criterion or practice is fundamental to the determination of indirect discrimination. The disadvantage must be related to a specific ground, such as, for instance, one of sex or ethnic origin. In the European Union, typical examples include the general neutrality policy certain employers adopt that forbids employees from wearing any religious symbols in the workplace.[61] The policy applies to all employees, despite their gender and religious affiliations. However, in Western Europe, such a 'neutral' policy affects in higher numbers Muslim women who wear headscarves. Such a neutral policy has an adverse impact on this group of people, considering that statistically, Muslim men, catholic and Jewish women do not wear visible religious symbols. In companies with such a neutrality policy, Muslim women may be incentivised to resign or not apply for an employment position. Moreover, the CJEU has consolidated precedents of indirect discrimination concerning general policies for part-time employment schemes, given their adverse effect on a far greater number of women than men.[62] The use of statistics is not mandatory to prove indirect

57 Bell, 'Direct Discrimination'; N. Bamforth, M. Malik and C. O'Cineide. *Discrimination Law: Theory and Context*. Sweet & Maxwell, 2008, p. 237.

58 *Feryn NV* ECLI:EU:C:2008:397.

59 Art. 19, Gender Equality Directive.

60 Art. 2.1.(b) Gender Equality Directive.

61 See cases *Achbita v. G4 solutions* NV ECLI:EU:C:2017:203; *Asma Bougnaoui and Association de défense des droits de l'homme (ADDH) v. Micropole* SA ECLI:EU:C:2017:204; and *IX v. WABE eV and MH Müller Handels GmbH v. MJ*, ECLI:EU:C:2021:594.

62 *Bilka – Kaufhaus GmbH v. Karin Weber von Hartz* ECLI:EU:C:1986:204.

discrimination, even though it can significantly contribute to making a case for indirect discrimination.[63]

Indirect discrimination has three main elements: (i) there must be equal treatment; (ii) despite being equal, the treatment has an adverse impact on persons with the protected grounds; (iii) the adverse impact may be justifiable by good reasons, such as business necessity.[64]

The CJEU has had a conservative approach to the defence of indirect discrimination.[65] Justification of indirect discrimination has been accepted in controversial instances. In a case related to a neutrality policy, in which the company did not accept the use of religious symbols by their employees, the CJEU understood that although such a policy was disadvantageous to Muslim women, it was justifiable, given employers have the right to project an image of neutrality protected by their freedom to conduct business.[66] Moreover, the CJEU concluded that the general policy was a necessary and proportionate means to project the company's image of neutrality.

Transposing the elements of indirect discrimination to a concrete case involving AI may be enlightening. Estée Lauder allegedly used AI technology in a dismissal process. The technology in question was designed to take voice intonation, inflections and facial expressions reflecting emotions into account. The case was set aside. However, complainants could make a case for indirect discrimination, considering that the company used an apparent neutral practice - the AI technology - to assess all their employees. The element of equal treatment seemed present in the case. Despite being equal, the use of AI could have an adverse impact on persons with protected grounds, considering it used data related to voice intonation, inflections and facial expressions to support a dismissal decision.[67] Voice intonation, inflections and facial expressions vary according to gender, cultural background and age and may serve as a proxy for these protected grounds. If the AI technology relates a certain voice intonation to bad performance, for instance, and this voice intonation is proportionately more present

63 Seymour-Smith, Nicole and Laura Perez. ECLI:EU:C:1999:60. & *Instituto Nacional de la Seguridad Social v. BT*, ECLI:EU:C:2021:55.

64 Fredman, *Discrimination Law*, p. 178.

65 Bribosia, Emmanuelle, Robin Medard Inghilterra and Isabelle Rorive. 'Femmes Voilées au Travail Face aux Errements du Droit de la Non-Discrimination : Observations Relatives à l'Arrêt du 12 Octobre 2020 de la Cour du Travail de Gand (Achbita c. G4S Secure Solutions)'. *Journal des Tribunaux du Travail* 1393 (2021): 145-154.

66 Which is protected by Art. 16 of the Charter of Fundamental Rights of the European Union; *Achbita v. G4 solutions* NV ECLI:EU:C:2017:203, para. 38.

67 *EPIC v. HireVue*. Federal Trade Commission (2019, November 6). Available at: https://epic.org/wp-content/uploads/privacy/ftc/hirevue/EPIC_FTC_HireVue_Complaint.pdf.

within the male population, men would be negatively impacted in this dismissal decision. Estée Lauder could allege that it had a legitimate reason for using AI, including the large number of employees to be assessed. Moreover, the company would have to demonstrate that using AI in this situation was proportionate and that it could not have achieved the same result in a less discriminatory way. Proving this would be certainly more challenging.

6 FAIRNESS METRICS AND POSITIVE ACTION

Another non-discrimination law concept that has been mobilised in the context of HR uses of AI in the selection of employees is that of positive action.[68] In the past decade, data science research has focused on technical methods to counter discrimination in algorithmic systems.[69] This literature aims to address problems such as the one raised by the tool in development by Amazon to select employees. The Amazon AI system greatly under-represented women when selecting the most suitable CVs among a pool of CVs.

In order to address this sort of bias, specialised data research has developed measures that include statistical parity, casual modelling and counterfactual fairness.[70] In statistical parity, for instance, the fairness of the mathematical model is conditioned to demographic parity. In this case, the model must predict a certain result for individuals belonging to different demographic groups with equal probability. In simpler words, the statistical parity approach equalises outcomes across protected and non-protected groups. In the case of Amazon, for instance, women should have the same rate of success as their male counterparts. Measures to address the sort of bias faced by Amazon often include what the specialised literature names as “Fairness through awareness”.[71] These measures have in common the fact that they take into account a protected aspect, such as sex, in order to make a prediction or decision.

68 More on the topic, see Corrêa, Ana Maria and L. Naudts. ‘When Fairness Through Awareness Is Legal Positive Action’ 2023 (forthcoming).

69 Dwork, Cynthia, et al. ‘Fairness through Awareness’. *Proceedings of the 3rd Innovations in Theoretical Computer Science Conference*. 2012; Hardt, Moritz, Eric Price and Nati Srebro. ‘Equality of Opportunity in Supervised Learning’. *Advances in Neural Information Processing Systems* 29 (2016): 1-22; Mehrabi, Ninareh, et al. ‘A Survey on Bias and Fairness in Machine Learning’. *ACM Computing Surveys (CSUR)* 54.6 (2021): 1-35.

70 Dwork, et al. ‘Fairness through Awareness’.

71 *Ibid.*

In the past years, legal scholars and data scientists have framed the technical concept of fairness through awareness as positive action.[72] Researchers have affirmed that this sort of fairness metrics requires algorithms to take protected characteristics into account and use them to counteract other unidentified sources of bias.[73] In the European Union, the understanding that fairness through awareness metrics translate into the legal concept of positive action should be taken with caution, given the high threshold positive action must adhere to in order to be legal.

The term positive action generally involves a series of measures to achieve substantive equality for groups of individuals that have historically faced discrimination in sectors such as employment one.[74] They may reach individuals with disabilities, minorities and under-represented individuals of a certain age group or gender. Positive action measures comprise inclusive policies, funding targeting special groups and preferential treatment (also known as quotas).[75]

EU law does not prevent member states from adopting measures to achieve substantive equality. In this light, the principle of equal treatment should not restrain any member states

> from maintaining or adopting measures providing for specific advantages in order to make it easier for the under-represented sex to pursue a vocational activity or to prevent or compensate for disadvantages in professional careers.[76]

EU secondary law also contemplates the possibility of positive measures in the employment sector regarding the compensation of disadvantages related to several grounds, including sex, ethnic origin, age and disability.[77]

---

72 Gajane, Pratik and Mykola Pechenizkiy. 'On Formalizing Fairness in Prediction with Machine Learning'. *arXiv preprint arXiv:1710.03184* (2017), p. 3; Bent, Jason R. 'Is Algorithmic Affirmative Action Legal'. *Georgetown Law Journal* 108 (2019): 803, 808; Chander, Anupam. 'The Racist Algorithm'. *Michigan Law Review* 115 (2016): 1025.

73 Chander, Anupam. 'The Racist Algorithm'. *Michigan Law Review* 115 (2016): 1023. For further implications on personal data protection, see Art. 22, GDPR.

74 Van Caeneghem, Jozefien. *Legal Aspects of Ethnic Data Collection and Positive Action*. Springer, 2019.

75 Oppenheimer, David B. 'The Ubiquity of Positive Measures for Addressing Systemic Discrimination and Inequality: Comparative Global Perspective'. *Brill Research Perspectives in Comparative Discrimination Law* 3(3-4) (2019): 1-114, p. 3.

76 Art. 157(4) TFEU. Art. 23 of the EU Charter of Fundamental Rights is one the same direction.

77 Art. 3, Directive 2004/113/EC; Art. 3, Directive 2006/54/EC; Art. 5, Directive 2000/43/EC; Art. 7 (Directive 2000/78/EC).

What the CJEU case law entirely rejects is the possibility of establishing strict quotas for access to employment based solely on a demographic trait, such as one of ethnic origin and gender.[78] In this regard, the Court has deemed aligned to the principle of non-discrimination the promotion of equality of opportunities instead of equality of results. In the past, the CJEU has considered quotas for training positions and interview as legal positive action related to the concept of equality of opportunity.[79] Also, quotas for women for promotion in a public career were accepted as legitimate if men had their merits assessed as well.[80]

In sum, in the EU, legal positive action should not be confused with any pure form of preferential treatment based exclusively on protected grounds, such as gender and ethnic origin. If any quotas are established in the context of equality of opportunities, including interviews for employment, selection of CVs or training programs, all candidates should also be assessed on their individual merits. According to this understanding, technical fairness measures for AI systems, designed to take demographic traits, such as gender, into account should also consider all other data related to the merits of the candidates.

7 Conclusion

HR departments have increasingly implemented AI in employment decision-making processes, including recruitment, management and dismissal of workers. In these processes, litigation and research have documented discrimination against individuals based on irrelevant demographic aspects, such as their gender and ethnic origin. In light of these pressing issues, this chapter aimed to provide an overview of the main non-discrimination law concepts that can be mobilised in cases of discrimination against protected classes perpetrated by AI systems. This chapter highlights that the notions of direct, indirect discrimination and positive action have been intensively construed and developed in the EU for more than sixty years. Even though the AI Act proposal presents relevant contribution to advance the fight against discrimination in AI systems used by HR, such as including AI employment decision-making tools in high-risk category, it should be complemented with the EU non-discrimination law framework in order to provide meaningful tools to address bias and worse treatment against workers and employment candidates.

---

78 *Eckhard Kalanke v. Freie Hansestadt Bremen* ECLI:EU:C:1995:322.

79 *Georg Badeck and Others, interveners: Hessische Ministerpräsident and Landesanwalt beim Staatsgerichtshof des Landes Hessen* ECLI:EU:C:2000:163.

80 *Hellmut Marschall v. Land Nordrhein-Westfalen* ECLI:EU:C:1997:533.

Part IV
Dispute Resolution and Settlements

The (Un)Limited Use of AI Segmentation in the Insurance Sector

*Julie Goetghebuer**

1 Introduction

It is imperative for insurers to identify the type of risks they are underwriting. This identification involves an estimation of the 'claims probability' (i.e. the risk of claims occurring and their magnitude) of each prospective policyholder, which results in the establishment of a risk profile. This so-called segmentation technique enables insurers to determine whether to underwrite a risk and, if so, on what terms (i.e. the premium and conditions of an insurance contract).

Wielding the segmentation technique not only necessitates the amassment of certain information regarding prospective policyholders and the insured risk but also processing the harvest. In this respect, statistics are essential in the insurance industry. After all, without the analysis of historical data, it is impossible to predict the risk of existing or prospective policyholders. Of late, a new wind is blowing in the insurance industry. The availability and variety of innovative technologies, which support the provision of financial services, have increased considerably. Insurtech, the convergence of insurance and technology, is being significantly transformed by artificial intelligence (AI), as AI could lead to replacing human experts. Whereas in the past risk data was static and incomplete, the insurance industry can now rely on AI and big data.[1] The latter supplements the standard data with new and non-traditional information, and the former opens avenues for the accurate prediction of individual risks of policyholders

* PhD-student at Ghent University and Financial Law Institute.

1 In the context of this chapter, the term 'AI' predominantly denotes a technological framework characterised by inherent self-learning capabilities, placing significant emphasis on the deployment of 'machine learning'. In essence, it pertains to systems that progressively enhance their proficiency in executing specific tasks through the accumulation of experience and data. Such emphasis on machine learning aligns with the prevailing trend in contemporary AI discourse. This implies that within the context of this chapter, the term 'AI' does not encompass less advanced AI algorithms, commonly known as 'symbolic AI'. As a result, this chapter does not delve into the domain of 'expert systems', in which human experts formulate exact rules, encapsulated as 'if-then-else' instructions, for a computer to meticulously adhere to when making decisions within specific scenarios.

and, consequently, more tailored premiums and policy conditions.[2] AI data analytics play a pivotal role in analysing vast data sets to identify patterns and could ultimately lead to more efficient and data-driven decision-making processes within the insurance industry.[3]

This chapter addresses the following profound question: can (Belgian) insurance companies use AI to determine a policyholder's claim probability? Answering these questions requires, first of all, some contextual guidance, which is provided by clarifying the segmentation technique and the concepts of AI and big data (A.).[4] Second, this chapter discusses both the potential benefits and the pitfalls of AI segmentation for both insurers and policyholders (B.). Focusing on the Belgian Insurance Act,[5] the final part of this contribution sketches the insurer's freedom to use AI as well as the relevant legal (in)direct limitations. In addition, that section also examines whether the aforementioned restrictions protect the policyholder from erroneous decisions made by an AI system (C.).[6]

2 AI and Insurance Segmentation

2.1 Data Collection and Analysis for the Purpose of Segmentation

The assessment of the risk potential policyholders represent is crucial for insurers. After all, it is in the insurer's interest to underwrite risks that are not too big. Likewise, the

2 DELOITTE, *From Mystery to Mastery: Unlocking the Business Value of Artificial Intelligence in the Insurance Industry*, 2017, www2.deloitte.com/, 99; SCOR, *The Impact of Artificial Intelligence on the (Re)Insurance Sector*, March 2018, www.scor.com, 8; BEUC, *The Use of Big Data And Artificial Intelligence in Insurance*, May 2020, www.beuc.eu, 6; M. Eling, D. Nuessle and J. Staubli, "The Impact of Artificial Intelligence Along the Insurance Value Chain and on the Insurability of Risks", *The Geneva Papers on Risk and Insurance – Issues and Practice* 2021, 7; BaFin, *Big Data Meets Artificial Intelligence: Challenges And Implications for the Supervision and Regulation of Financial Services*, July 2018, www.bafin.de, 96 and 107; AFM, *The Personalisation of Prices and Conditions in the Insurance Sector: An Exploratory Study*, June 2021, www.afm.nl, 12-13.

3 Regarding the more technical aspects of AI and profiling, *see* the Chapter of Prof. Gielen "A Brief Introduction to AI and Its Use in the Legal Practice".

4 This chapter focuses on the use of AI for the analysis of big data. To facilitate reading, we have opted to use only the term 'AI', instead of 'AI and big data'.

5 Wet van 4 April 2014 betreffende de verzekeringen, *BS* 30 April 2014.

6 This chapter focuses exclusively on the interaction between the insurer and its policyholder. Public-law sanctions, that could be imposed by the Financial Services and Markets Authority in Belgium (FSMA) and the impact of AI segmentation on the prudential supervisory framework are not within this contribution's ambit. Additionally, it is important to note that while privacy aspects are prevalent in this context, this chapter does not provide a comprehensive exploration of the data protection regulation and its relation to AI segmentation. Discussing this matter in detail would require a substantial expansion beyond the chapter's scope. Consequently, certain privacy-related issues are only briefly alluded to, primarily in footnotes.

insurer must be able to neutralise larger risks with smaller ones.[7] This implies that the insurer must estimate the claims probability of each prospective policyholder. By means of such estimations, the insurer can establish risk profiles and divide policyholders into risk groups with the same (or similar[8]) profile.[9]

This division of policyholders into homogeneous groups with the same risk profile based on statistics and prediction models is called 'segmentation'.[10] Segmentation is beneficial for both the insurer and the (potential) policyholder. On the one hand, segmentation enables the insurer to differentiate the terms of an insurance contract according to some specific characteristics of the risk ('segmentation criteria').[11] On the other hand, this delineation confers advantages on the policyholder as well, as it ensures the insurance agreement is customised to their specific circumstances, potentially resulting in a more accurate premium and terms.

Segmentation criteria are used to calculate both the probability of a claim occurring and the size of the claim if it actually occurs.[12] Each policyholder in the same risk group will be designated an equal probability and size of the claim warranting an equal treatment, for instance, with respect to insurance terms. As such, segmentation determines underwriting, pricing, terms and/or scope of coverage of an insurance contract.[13] The insurer will charge high-risk policyholders a higher premium and stricter conditions or can decide not to grant them any coverage. Lower risk policyholders will obtain lower risk premiums and/or better conditions and are less likely to be excluded from coverage.[14]

---

7 E. Goessens, *Private verzekering en solidariteit*, Mortsel, Intersentia, 2018, 21.

8 A complete equivalence of claim probability and size of the claim within each group is almost impossible as the insurer cannot always consider all types of factors to calculate the risks.

9 T. Vansweevelt and B. Weyts, *Handboek Verzekeringsrecht*, Antwerpen, Intersentia, 2016, 42; Goessens, *Private verzekering en solidariteit*, 16; Ph. Colle, *Algemene beginselen van het Belgische verzekeringsrecht (zevende editie)*, Mortsel, Intersentia, 2019, 3.

10 M. Fontaine, *Verzekeringsrecht*, Brussel, Intersentia, 2017, 15; Y. Thiery, *Discriminatie en verzekering*, Antwerpen, Intersentia, 2011, 188.

11 T. Vansweevelt and B. Weyts, "Deel I. Het belang, de kenmerken en situering van het verzekeringsrecht", in T. Vansweevelt and B. Weyts (eds.), *Handboek Verbintenissenrecht*, Antwerpen, Intersentia, 2016, 42; D.E. Palmer, "Insurance, Risk Assessment and Fairness: An Ethical Analysis", in P. Flanagan, P. Primaux and W. Ferguson (eds.), *Insurance Ethics for a More Ethical World, Research in Ethical Issues in Organizations*, Vol. 7, Oxford, Elsevier, 2007, 114.

12 K. S. Abraham, "Efficiency and Fairness in Insurance Risk Classification", *Virginia Law Review* 1985, Vol. 71, Issue 3, 408; Fontaine, *Verzekeringsrecht*, 15.

13 Abraham, "Efficiency and Fairness in Insurance Risk Classification", 408; Fontaine, *Verzekeringsrecht*, 15.

14 J. Amankwah, "Chapter 15. Insurance Underwriting on the Basis of Telematics: Segmentation and Profiling", in J. De Bruyne and C. Vanleenhove (eds.), *Artificial Intelligence and the Law*, Mortsel, Intersentia, 2021, 407.

To apply the segmentation technique, the insurer needs to obtain data regarding the prospective policyholder and the insured risk.[15] Traditionally, the insurer collects information by presenting the policyholder with an insurance proposal. The policyholder must complete this form to inform the insurer of the transaction's nature and of the facts, as well as the circumstances that enable the insurer to assess the risks.[16] Belgian insurance law obligates the policyholder to spontaneously and accurately communicate all known information that may influence the insurer's risk assessment. This obligation is restricted to data the policyholder deems relevant. He need not communicate circumstances that the insurer already knew or should reasonably have known.[17] The information asymmetry and, in this respect, the vulnerable position of the insurer vis-à-vis the policyholder justifies this spontaneous disclosure obligation. The former has little or no knowledge of the characteristics of the risk. This legal obligation of the policyholder allows the insurer to trust the policyholder to correctly communicate the characteristics of the risk.[18]

The traditional method set out previously is, despite the obligation of the policyholder, somewhat one-sided. Nowadays, risks represented by policyholders can be predicted by employing AI. The new era of AI gives the insurers access to (non-traditional) information that is (more) comprehensive, accessible from multiple (external) sources and available on a real-time basis.[19] This data often involves actions that occur in the online world, such as banking app transactions, e-mail traffic, videos, images, clickstream, search queries, social media interactions and so on. These sources include information about users' private lives, such as their interests and certain life events. Social data, such as likes or posts on social media, in addition to traditional data, could predict whether or not a potential policyholder exhibits a high claim probability. As a fictional example, a page on Facebook is called '*I like driving fast*', and statistical analysis of historical data shows people that like this page are more likely to crash their car. The AI algorithm could pick up on this correlation and could conclude that this risk will not be underwritten or that the premium for those policyholders will increase.[20] Needless to say, this wide array of information gives insurers increased insights regarding existing and prospective policyholders.[21]

15 BEUC, *The Use of Big Data and Artificial Intelligence in Insurance*, 3.

16 Art. 55, 6° of the Insurance Act.

17 Art. 58, the first paragraph, of the Insurance Act.

18 Colle, *Algemene beginselen van het Belgische verzekeringsrecht (zevende editie)*, 58.

19 Deloitte, *From Mystery to Mastery*, 99; SCOR, *The Impact of Artificial Intelligence on the (Re)Insurance Sector*, 8; BEUC, *The Use of Big Data and Artificial Intelligence in Insurance*, 6; Eling, et al., "The Impact of Artificial Intelligence Along the Insurance Value Chain and on the Insurability of Risks", 7.

20 BaFin, *Big Data Meets Artificial Intelligence*, 185.

21 Eling et al., "The Impact of Artificial Intelligence Along the Insurance Value Chain and on the Insurability of Risks", 7.

Access to a large(r) amount of data regarding policyholders increases the accuracy of the assessment of claim probability and surpasses the information asymmetry between the policyholder and the insurer.[22] An insurer who has vast amounts of data and advanced analytical capabilities at its disposal could even be said to tilt the informational imbalance in its favour, rendering the insurance proposal and the spontaneous disclosure requirement obsolete. After all, insurers will be better equipped to collect and process information regarding the risk of policyholders without having to ask them. This makes it a lot harder for a policyholder to commit fraud by feeding the insurer misleading information.[23]

2.2 *The Benefits and Challenges of AI Segmentation*

2.2.1 Benefits

Fully grasping the advantages of AI and big data requires us to illuminate the traditional method and its outcomes. After all, the traditional method is the benchmark. Compared to the traditional method, AI and big data allow for *(i)* a realistic risk prediction, *(ii)* hyper-individualisation, *(iii)* (theoretically) a true chance solidarity, *(iv)* an advantage in the marketplace and *(v)* a better prevention of risks from occurring and/or a better minimisation of their effects.

AI empowers insurers to fine-tune their risk assessments *(i)* by expanding their capacity to identify and analyse a broader range of segmentation criteria.[24] The combination of AI and big data uncovers correlations that (simple) statistics may not be able to find. Whereas traditionally proxies are used to estimate the risk (e.g. the driver's age), AI enables insurers to use real risk-prediction factors. For example, insurers could use criteria, such as aggressive driving style, which can be detected through telematics. In vehicle insurance, AI can be used to automatically record information about the policyholder and the vehicle (so-called 'telematics': the use of *tele*communications and infor*matics*, also called 'usage-based insurance' or 'UBI'). In this process, the insurer installs a device in the vehicle that collects the data used to estimate risk. With telematics, the risks are assessed based not only on secondary (proxy) data (such as the place of residence and age of the policyholder or data concerning the vehicle) but

22 SCOR, *The Impact of Artificial Intelligence on the (Re)insurance Sector*, 8; C.P. Holland, M. Mullins and M. Cunneen, "Creating Ethics Guidelines for Artificial Intelligence (AI) and Big Data Analytics: The Case of the European Consumer Insurance Market", *Patterns* 2021, Vol. 2, Issue 10, 2.

23 SCOR, *The Impact of Artificial Intelligence on the (Re)insurance Sector*, 8.

24 A. J. Heras, P.-Ch. Pradier and D. Teira, "What Was Fair in Actuarial Fairness?", *History of the Human Sciences* 2020, Vol. 33, Issue 2, 91; OECD, *The Impact of Big Data and Artificial Intelligence (AI) in the Insurance Sector*, 2020, www.oecd.org, 14.

also on primary data regarding the driving behaviour of the policyholder (braking behaviour, speeds used, the way of cornering, distance travelled, etc.) as well as the driving conditions (weather, surrounding traffic, time of day, the road used, etc.). The collected, dynamic data leads to a more accurate risk assessment and calculation of insurance premiums, possibly even in real time.[25]

AI could establish a hyper-individualisation of risks in the insurance sector and leads to a so-called 'customised insurance' *(ii)*.[26] The traditional statistical method enables the insurer to delineate risk groups and to identify several sub-groups.[27] The number of parameters correlates negatively with the size and heterogeneity of the risk groups.[28] Individual segments would thus technically decrease in size and increase in number.[29] AI intensifies this process. It makes it possible to thoroughly differentiate risks represented by policyholders until it shifts from macro to rather micro-segmentation, and even to the extent where risks could be identified at an individual level.[30] Due to this customisation, insurers can more accurately match their prices and terms to the risk represented by each policyholder.[31]

In some cases, AI could lead to achieving a true chance solidarity *(iii)*. The idea of solidarity is one of the roots of insurance. All policyholders commit to paying the costs of future damage, and they do so without knowing who will suffer the consequences in case the underwritten risk occurs. Solidarity, in this respect, entails a transfer of wealth. After all, when the underwritten risk materialises, members of the risk group who did not suffer damages collectively carry the burden with those who did. The token

---

25 NAIC and CIPR, *Usage-Based Insurance and Vehicle Telematics: Insurance Market and Regulatory Implications*, March 2015, www.naic.org, 2; R. Verbelen, K. Antonio and G. Claeskens, "Unraveling the Predictive Power of Telematics Data in Car Insurance Pricing", *Journal of the Royal Statistical Society*, 2018, Vol. 67, Issue. 5, 1276; J. Amankwah, "Chapter 15. Insurance Underwriting on the Basis of Telematics: Segmentation and Profiling", in J. De Bruyne and C. Vanleenhove (eds.), *Artificial Intelligence and the Law*, Mortsel, Intersentia, 2021, 412-413; Rathenau Instituut (J. Timmer, I. Elias, L. Kool and R. van Est), *Berekende risico's. Verzekeren in de datagedreven samenleving*, 2015, www.rathenau.nl, 29 and 48.

26 SCOR, *The Impact of Artificial Intelligence on the (Re)insurance Sector*, 8 and 26; BaFin, *Big Data Meets Artificial Intelligence*, 122; The Geneva Association, *Insurance in the Digital Age A View on Key Implications for the Economy and Society*, September 2018, www.genevaassociation.org, 7; EIOPA, *Big Data Analytics in Motor and Health Insurance: A Thematic Review*, 2019, https://register.eiopa.europa.eu/, 29; Eling et al., "The Impact of Artificial Intelligence Along the Insurance Value Chain and on the Insurability of Risks", 19.

27 BaFin, *Big Data Meets Artificial Intelligence*, 102.

28 SCOR, *The Impact of Artificial Intelligence on the (Re)insurance Sector*, 8; BaFin, *Big Data Meets Artificial Intelligence*, 107, 122.

29 BaFin, *Big Data Meets Artificial Intelligence*, 102; EIOPA, *Big Data Analytics in Motor and Health Insurance*, 32; AFM, *The Personalisation of Prices and Conditions in the Insurance Sector*, 21.

30 BaFin, *Big Data Meets Artificial Intelligence*, 102-103.

31 Ibid., 122; The Geneva Association, *Insurance in the Digital Age A View on Key Implications for the Economy and Society*, 7.

of this wealth transferring solidarity is the payment of the premium by every member of the risk group while only those who suffer a loss receive compensation.[32]

At least two kinds of solidarity can be distinguished when considering the homogeneity of risk groups: 'chance solidarity' and 'subsidising solidarity'.[33] Chance solidarity involves a wealth transfer by chance, since the risk groups of policyholders are completely homogeneous. Every member of the group has an equal chance of the risk occurring, and the lucky ones thus pay for the unlucky ones.[34] Heterogeneous risk groups give rise to subsidising solidarity. Heterogeneous groups do not consist of members with a comparable risk profile. In this situation, some members will be insured with disproportionate conditions compared to the actual risk they represent. These low-risk members are forced to subsidise the high-risk members.[35] A vehicle liability insurance that requires every policyholder to pay the same premium exemplifies subsidising liability. After all, cautious drivers will inevitably pay a share of the claims cost caused by high-risk drivers.[36]

Sidestepping or minimising subsidising solidarity is closely connected to segmentation. The more refined the segmentation, the less subsidising solidarity occurs.[37] Segmentation, thus, benefits insurers. The pursuit of establishing chance solidarity and the need to make risk groups as homogeneous as possible are driven by the insurer's desire to counteract policyholder's subsidy aversion[38] and to combat particular

32 Thiery, *Discriminatie en verzekering*, 191; B. Weyts, "Het segmentatiebeleid van de verzekeraars: krachtlijnen en wijzigingen ten gevolge van de Verzekeringswet van 4 april 2014", in T. Vansweevelt en B. Weyts, *De Verzekeringswet 2014*, Mortsel, Intersentia, 2015, 31; Goessens, *Private verzekering en solidariteit*, 22-23; J. Amankwah, "Chapter 15. Insurance Underwriting on the Basis of Telematics: Segmentation and Profiling", in J. De Bruyne and C. Vanleenhove (eds.), *Artificial Intelligence and the Law*, Mortsel, Intersentia, 2021, 417.

33 Thiery, *Discriminatie en verzekering*, 192; Goessens, *Private verzekering en solidariteit*, 22-23.

34 N. De Pril and J. Dhaene, *Rapport van de werkgroep Segmentering*, September 1995, https://feb.kuleuven.be, 12; Thiery, *Discriminatie en verzekering*, 192.

35 De Pril and Dhaene, *Rapport van de werkgroep Segmentering*, 12; Thiery, *Discriminatie en verzekering*, 192; Goessens, *Private verzekering en solidariteit*, 23; J. Amankwah, "Chapter 15. Insurance Underwriting on the Basis of Telematics: Segmentation and Profiling", in J. De Bruyne and C. Vanleenhove (eds.), *Artificial Intelligence and the Law*, Mortsel, Intersentia, 2021, 418.

36 AFM, *The Personalisation of Prices and Conditions in the Insurance Sector*, 20.

37 L. Schuermans and C. Van Schoubroeck, *Grondslagen van het Belgische verzekeringsrecht, 3de editie*, Mortsel, Intersentia, 2015, 32; AFM, *The Personalisation of Prices and Conditions in the Insurance Sector*, 20.

38 A policyholder who believes that he has a contract that is not aligned with his risk might opt to seek another insurer that offers him better, more appropriate, conditions.

economic insurance perils, such as adverse selection[39] and moral hazard.[40,41] Thorough segmentation allows insurers to charge premiums and offer conditions that are as close as possible to the actual risk.[42] AI has the potential to limit subsidising solidarity and could help to obtain true chance solidarity in some cases. These prospects sharply contrast with traditional insurance methods, which can only occasion subsidising solidarity. After all, the traditional method's narrow scope is unable to identify all risk factors.[43] Through AI, subsidising solidarity could be limited, and it could theoretically become possible to achieve true chance solidarity in some cases.[44]

Harnessing AI allows insurers to differentiate themselves from their competitors *(iv)*. The (informational) advantage enables the development of more sophisticated risk models. Building on these models, insurers may offer more competitive rates, allowing them to attract smaller risks as these risks may be covered by an insurance contract at a lower premium.[45] Risk model sophistication allows insurers to focus predominantly on positive risks and, consequently, to reduce claim payouts, but also to charge higher premiums to those policyholders who show a higher risk. In addition, insurers using AI applications could lower their operational and administrative costs by realising efficiency gains (e.g. by eliminating the need for analysing the information provided by the policyholder, i.e. the spontaneous information disclosure).[46]

---

39 The higher a policyholder thinks his risk is, the more important he will consider underwriting his risk. When insurance contracts are virtually the same for all policyholders (both those who represent a high risk and those who represent a low risk), policyholders who represent a low risk will cancel the insurance over time, given that their premium is not balanced and they are informed that they have little or no need for the insurance. When the low risks drop out, the premium will increase for those left behind.

40 Moral hazard refers to the potential negative effect insurance has on loss prevention. Without insurance, the prospect of accidents and damages provides an incentive to avoid losses by taking precautions. When a person chooses to underwrite his risk, this incentive disappears, and he will behave less carefully as he knows that the occurrence of his claim is covered and that he will not have to take responsibility for the adverse financial consequences.

41 W.P.J. Wils, "Insurance Risk Classifications in the EC: Regulatory Outlook", *Oxford Journal of Legal Studies* 1994, Vol. 14, Issue 3, 452-454; D.E. Palmer, "Insurance, Risk Assessment and Fairness", 124; FTC, *Credit-Based Insurance Scores: Impacts on Consumers of Automobile Insurance: A Report to Congress*, July 2007, www.ftc.gov, 43-44; R. Swedloff, "Risk Classification's Big Data (R)evolution", *Connecticut Insurance Law Journal* 2014, Vol. 21, Issue 1, 346; R. Cooter and T. Ulen, *Law and Economics, 6th edition*, Boston, Pearson, 2016, 49; Eling, et al., "The Impact of Artificial Intelligence Along the Insurance Value Chain and on the Insurability of Risks", 14.

42 J. Amankwah, "Chapter 15. Insurance Underwriting on the Basis of Telematics: Segmentation and Profiling", in J. De Bruyne and C. Vanleenhove (eds.), *Artificial Intelligence and the Law*, Mortsel, Intersentia, 2021, 418.

43 Abraham, "Efficiency and Fairness in Insurance Risk Classification", 409; Wils, "Insurance Risk Classifications in the EC: Regulatory Outlook", 454.

44 G. W. De Wit and J. Van Eeghen, "Rate Making Society's Sense of Fairness", *Astin Bulletin* 1984, Vol. 2, 156.

45 BaFin, *Big Data Meets Artificial Intelligence*, 122.

46 Ibid., 99; The Geneva Association, *Insurance in the Digital Age A View on Key Implications for the Economy and Society*, 14.

AI also allows insurers to advise policyholders more accurately on the precautionary measures they can take to prevent risks from occurring or to minimise their effects *(v)*.[47] For example, in the context of vehicle liability insurance, AI-based telematics can motivate policyholders to modify their driving behaviour to receive premium refunds.[48] Telematics can also display important relevance in fire insurances. Smart home devices, such as Hive (a home security product) and Nest (a thermostat), could inform insurance companies. These digital controlled products, which monitor, among other things, the security and the energy consumption of the policyholder's home, could also enable insurers to intervene when risks occur. For example, by giving insurers access to these devices,[49] they can be notified in real time if a water leak occurs and even shut off the water supply if the policyholder fails to respond.[50]

2.2.2 Challenges

Although the implementation of AI and big data benefits insurers, pervasive segmentation through AI also has downsides. The benefit of detailed assessments of risks can be subverted by the *de facto* uninsurability (i.e. the financial impossibility of covering the risks) of certain policyholders. After all, excess in segmentation may create several small segmentation groups of (very) high-risk policyholders who, due to a substantial increase in the premium, are unable to pay the premium and, consequently, cannot get insurance coverage.[51] The Belgian Insurance Law, however, somewhat mitigates this downside by establishing so-called 'pricing agencies ("*Tariferingsbureaus*")' for the most important (compulsory) and most common insurances, such as vehicle liability insurance ('*Tariferingsbureau BA*'). These pricing agencies insure those who cannot

---

47 BaFin, *Big Data Meets Artificial Intelligence*, 100; The Geneva Association, *Insurance in the Digital Age A View on Key Implications for the Economy and Society*, 8; Insurance Europe, *QAs on the Use of Big Data in Insurance*, 23 January 2019, www.insuranceeurope.eu, 2; Eling et al., "The Impact of Artificial Intelligence Along the Insurance Value Chain and on the Insurability of Risks", 19 and 21.

48 J. Amankwah, "Nieuwe technologische ontwikkelingen in verzekeringen", in C. Van Schoubroeck and I. Samoy (eds.), *Themis 106 – Aansprakelijkheids-en verzekeringsrecht*, Brugge, die Keure / la Charte, 2018, 77-78 and 81-82; BaFin, *Big Data Meets Artificial Intelligence*, 118-119; Insurance Europe, *QAs on the Use of Big Data in Insurance*, 2-3; EIOPA, *Big Data Analytics in Motor and Health Insurance*, 34.

49 Within the confines of data regulation, such as the GDPR (Regulation (EU) 2016/679 of the European Parliament and of the Council of 27 April 2016 on the protection of natural persons with regard to the processing of personal data and on the free movement of such data, and repealing Directive 95/46/EC (General Data Protection Regulation), *O.J.* 4 May 2016, iss. 119, 1-88.

50 The Geneva Association, *Insurance in the Digital Age A View on Key Implications for the Economy and Society*, 8; OECD, *The Impact of Big Data and Artificial Intelligence (AI) in the Insurance Sector*, 13.

51 BaFin, *Big Data Meets Artificial Intelligence*, 126; The Geneva Association, *Insurance in the Digital Age A View on Key Implications for the Economy and Society*, 15; OECD, *The Impact of Big Data and Artificial Intelligence (AI) in the Insurance Sector*, 6-7; J. Amankwah, "Chapter 15. Insurance Underwriting on the Basis of Telematics: Segmentation and Profiling", in J. De Bruyne and C. Vanleenhove (eds.), *Artificial Intelligence and the Law*, Mortsel, Intersentia, 2021, 420; BEUC, *The Use of Big Data and Artificial Intelligence in Insurance*, 8-9; Holland et al., "Creating Ethics Guidelines for Artificial Intelligence (AI) and Big Data Analytics", 6.

obtain coverage by commercial insurance companies. In this respect, individuals who cannot afford insurance or individuals who represent a risk that commercial insurers are unwilling to underwrite are not excluded from being insured.

AI-based segmentation could also occasion (increased[52]) opacity regarding policy conditions and criteria. Thorough segmentation inevitably leads to risk differentiation and individualisation of policy conditions. This customisation of policy conditions complicates the comparison of services/coverage and corresponding prices and potentially disables the policyholders from identifying the best offer in the market. Although increasingly sophisticated comparison tools somewhat mitigate this obstruction, these will be useful only if insurers are open about the criteria they use.[53] The Belgian Insurance Law requires insurers to publish the segmentation criteria they use in terms of underwriting, pricing and/or scope of the coverage on their website, and to explain why these criteria are used.[54] However, this disclosure does not obligate insurers to explain exactly how the employed AI model works and to what extent the various criteria influence the final decision.[55]

In addition, the insurers' freedom to adjust their segmentation policy and their segmentation criteria throughout the life of the contract adds to the discussed opacity and contributes to uncertainty as well. After all, policyholders who represent a small risk will never be sure they will maintain this position long-term.[56] Transparency, therefore, is crucial.

The importance of disclosure regarding segmentation processes should, however, not be overstated. After all, transparency is a double-edged sword. Whereas openness about segmentation has the potential to reduce opacity and uncertainty, it could equally lead to data manipulation.[57] The ability to identify the deployed segmentation criteria allows policyholders not only to adjust their behaviour but also to conceal jeopardising

52 Without the use of AI, the varied prices and exclusions included in each contract make it difficult for policyholders to accurately compare insurance proposals.

53 BaFin, *Big Data Meets Artificial Intelligence*, 99.

54 Art. 45, §1 of the Insurance Act.

55 De Pril and Dhaene, *Rapport van de werkgroep Segmentering*, 19-21.

56 J. Amankwah, "Chapter 15. Insurance Underwriting on the Basis of Telematics: Segmentation and Profiling", in J. De Bruyne and C. Vanleenhove (eds.), *Artificial Intelligence and the Law*, Mortsel, Intersentia, 2021, 421.

57 Mainly social data could easily be manipulated by, for example, creating a fake Facebook or Instagram account or posting messages that are not based on reality. Such data manipulation could result in fraud committed by the policyholder, which may be more difficult to detect compared to fraud (currently) committed through insurance proposals.

conduct to obtain a more favourable risk estimation. To avoid distortion, legislators could ban malleable data from being used in segmentation policies.[58]

AI may encourage insurers to utilise criteria that do not show a direct link to the insurance risk in order to determine the premium and conditions. AI could enable price optimisation practices, such as 'behavioural pricing', i.e. determining premiums and conditions of an insurance product based on policyholders' (online) behaviour.[59,60] Based on this online behaviour, data insurers could determine which customers would be more inclined to switch after the renewal date of their policy.[61] Based on their loyalty and willingness to pay, the price for coverage is thus calculated individually. The insurer could lower its prices at renewal for the policyholders that are more price sensitive and increase its prices at renewal for policyholders who are less likely to switch. Policyholders who are less inclined to switch and who will renew their insurance products rather than look for an alternative could be subjected to a 'loyalty penalty'.[62] When using behavioural pricing, the value of (part of) the premium is completely independent of the individual insurer's risk profile and the costs associated with the insurance product. This situation involves price discrimination.

However, price discrimination could be problematic for policyholders who find themselves in a weaker position, such as policyholders with a low income or with a low level of education or elderly policyholders who lack the resources or expertise to search and switch to a cheaper provider.[63] In addition, policyholders often do not know how their information is used in calculating the premium, so they are often unaware of whether price discrimination has occurred.[64] Unfortunately, current transparency requirements are not sufficient to address this problem. The Belgian Insurance Act only requires an explanation of the segmentation criteria used by the insurer[65] but does not compel the insurer to be transparent about the criteria that are independent

58 This will, however, have some societal impact, as this is how legislators determine which behaviour the policyholder can or cannot adapt.

59 Even though technically this practice bears no relation to the segmentation technique, it is still important to address this practice, and the legislature cannot ignore this issue.

60 EIOPA, *Big Data Analytics in Motor and Health Insurance*, 39.

61 AFM, *The Personalisation of Prices and Conditions in the Insurance Sector*, www.afm.nl, 15.

62 Ibid.; EIOPA, *Big Data Analytics in Motor and Health Insurance*, 39.

63 EIOPA, *Big Data Analytics in Motor and Health Insurance*, 39 and 47.

64 Europese Commissie, *Consumer Market Study on Online Market Segmentation through Personalised Pricing/Offers in the European Union (Request for Specific Services 2016 85 02 for the Implementation of Framework Contract EAHC/2013/CP/04), Final Report*, June 2018, 118; FCA, *General Insurance Pricing Practices: Interim Report, Market Study (MS18/1.2)*, October 2019, www.fca.org.uk, 23.

65 *See* Art. 45, §1 of the Insurance Act.

of the segmentation technique.[66] The transparency requirement imposed by the Unfair Commercial Practices Directive is also inadequate, as it only requires insurers to provide information regarding the final price (the premium), without disclosing information about the (non-segmentation) criteria that led to this price.[67] In other words, it could be desirable that the legislature creates an additional transparency requirement which requires insurers to explain to policyholders how and why they use the criteria. However, there is currently no conclusive evidence which proves that information regarding behavioural pricing can change a policyholder's behaviour or will fully protect them from paying a higher price, as information disclosure has only a limited effect on a policyholders' ability to recognise and understand individual price optimisation based on online behaviour.[68,69]

66 The used criteria for price optimisation cannot be considered segmentation criteria as these criteria have nothing to do with risk represented by the policyholder and show no relation to the claim probability. However, it is also possible that a criterion could be simultaneously related to the claims probability of a policyholder as to his price sensitivity.

67 Arts. 6 and 7 of this Directive only requires the insurer to provide information regarding the price *or* the manner in which the price is calculated: "*the price **or** the manner in which the price is calculated* (Article 6, 1., (d))" and "*the price ..., **or** where the nature of the product means that the price cannot reasonably be calculated in advance, the manner in which the price is calculated* (Article 7, 4., (c)" (own emphasis)).

68 Europese Commissie, *Consumer Market Study on Online Market Segmentation through Personalised Pricing*, 104, 167-168 and 247; OECD, *The Effects of Online Disclosure about Personalised Pricing on Consumers Results from a Lab Experiment in Ireland and Chile, OECD Digital Economy Papers, nr. 303*, January 2021, www.oecd-ilibrary.org, 27-28.

69 So merely being transparent to the policyholder is not sufficient, and legislators could consider imposing an absolute ban on using unfair, non-risk-based criteria to calculate the premiums and conditions of an insurance contract (for example, in the United Kingdom and the United States: *see* FCA, *FCA Confirms Measures to Protect Customers from the Loyalty Penalty in Home and Motor Insurance Markets, Press Release*, 28 May 2021; and CFA, *Protection Against Unfair and Excessive Rates Removed by Actuarial Group Despite Unanimous Request by Regulatory Actuaries, CAS Refuses to Undo Action*, 29 March 2021, 2). The question arises as to whether the legislature is allowed to just intervene and restrict the freedom of insurers to set rates. Solvency II Directive states that member states must ensure that the insurance products offered can be marketed in their territory without any obstacles and prohibits them from requiring prior approval or systematic notification of tariffs. This means that insurers are not required to seek prior authorisation for their premiums and can bring their (new) insurance terms to the insurance market without prior supervision. However, not all provisions involving restrictions on insurance prices will be impermissible. A provision that does not result in the direct setting of premium rates by the state which allows insurers still to be free to set the amount of the basic premium will not be in breach of the freedom to set rates. That being said, such restrictions do still interfere with the freedom to provide services and the freedom of establishment and must be justified. A restriction on these may be justified where it serves overriding requirements relating to the public interest, is suitable for securing the attainment of the objective which it pursues and does not go beyond what is necessary in order to attain it (*see* CJEU 28 April 2009, C-518/06, *Commission of the European Communities v. Italian Republic*, ECLI:EU:C:2009:270, para. 72). If the legislature stipulates that the insurer may not increase its prices when policyholders are price-insensitive, the insurer still retains its freedom to determine the basic premium. However, this does constitute a restriction on the aforementioned freedoms and must thus be justified. It could be argued that such a rule serves the public interest (i.e. consumer protection and, more specifically, protecting consumers from unfair price increases) and can achieve this objective. It also seems proportionate and does not go beyond what is necessary.

AI analytics intensify concerns that insurers will identify risks that have no causal relationship whatsoever to the insured loss. AI applications can find subtle correlations previously undetected by traditional statistics, which could lead to identifying segmentation criteria that merely correlate with the risk, without any (proven) causal link.[70,71] AI could identify spurious correlations: two random variables appear causally related to one another but are not, due to either coincidence or the presence of a certain third, unseen factor).[72,73] This means it could be important for the legislature to create an obligation that requires the insurer to use only segmentation criteria that show a causal relationship (if possible[74]), or at least an increased correlative relationship with the claims probability.

2.3 Restrictions on AI Segmentation Imposed by the Belgian Insurance Act

The question arises as to whether the insurer can simply use AI to analyse big data and an infinite number of parameters in order to individualise risks. Each insurer is free to contract with anybody on the terms and the price it wants.[75] In theory, based on the freedom of contract, the insurer is thus free to pursue its own segmentation policy. This

70 Correlation refers to two variables being statistically related in some way. Correlations do not explain whether a cause-effect relationship exists between two variables and whether one variable influences change in the other variable. Variables A and B could, for example, occur simultaneously, with no clarity as to whether, and why, A causes B. For example, an AI system might identify that policyholders who buy vampire novels on Amazon, like vampire-related media on Facebook, or follow authors of vampire fiction on Twitter are more likely to behave in a riskier manner. However, it is possible that a causal link cannot be found between being a fan of vampire fiction and claims probability or that an insurer, due to the complex and opaque nature of an AI-system, cannot prove this causal link.

71 Swedloff, "Risk Classification's Big Data (R)evolution", 366-367.

72 For example, there might exist a correlation between sunburn rates and ice cream sales. However, these two variables do not impact each other but are influenced by a third variable (a 'confounding variable'), the temperature.

73 *See* www.scribbr.com/methodology/confounding-variables/ and www.tylervigen.com/spurious-correlations for some examples.

74 Issues regarding machines' lack of understanding of causal relations were raised by J. Pearl, in *The Book of Why: The New Science of Cause and Effect*. However, nowadays there has been (preliminary) research regarding 'causal AI', stating that causal AI – powerful underlying algorithms that can explain cause and effect – may offer new opportunities to test causality and to reveal the causal patterns in large data sets faster and more efficiently, along with the ability to unravel the underlying complexity. The causal AI research area is still early in its development. *See* S.K. Sgaier, V. Huang and C.h. Grace, "The Case for Causal AI", *Stanford Social Innovation Review* 2020, Vol. 18, Issue 3, 50-55; E. Kiciman, E. Dillon, D. Edge, A. Foster, A. Hilmkil, J. Jennings, C.h. Ma, R. Osazuwa Ness, N. Pawlowski, A. Sharma and Ch. Zhang, "A Causal AI Suite for Decision-Making", *NeurIPS 2022 Workshop on Causality for Real-world Impact* 2022, 1-10; B. Kommadi, *Casual AI*, https://swisscognitive.ch/2022/01/18/casual-ai/.

75 T. Vansweevelt and B. Weyts, *Handboek Verbintenissenrecht*, Mortsel, Intersentia, 2019, 129; Heras et al., "What Was Fair in Actuarial Fairness?", 91.

freedom ensures that the insurer can employ an unlimited number of parameters. The number and nature of segmentation criteria used varies considerably in the insurance market. Therefore, some insurers may include only three segmentation criteria, and others may use 300 different criteria.[76] As a consequence, the same person would have to pay a higher premium for insurer X than for insurer Y if the latter, for example, omitted a certain parameter (affecting this person) that made the policyholder appear to carry a lower risk. In addition, this freedom has led to an open and highly competitive insurance market in which insurers, in pursuit of profitability, have started to apply more sophisticated segmentation.[77] Given this freedom, in principle, the insurer cannot be held responsible for (not) having taken a certain parameter into account. That being said, some existing legal restrictions may still limit this freedom.

2.3.1 Direct Restrictions: The Prohibition of the Use of Certain Segmentation Criteria

2.3.1.1 Discrimination

In addition to the Belgian anti-discrimination laws,[78] the Insurance Act contains some anti-discrimination rules for (most[79]) insurers. Article 44 of the Insurance Act imposes that any distinction must be objectively justifiable by a legitimate purpose, which means that any differentiation requires a well-founded, fair justification.[80] The anti-discrimination laws are applicable to all industries and define a few protected criteria which have to be justified if used. However, based on the obligation in the Insurance Act insurers must be able to justify *each* segmentation criterion, not merely the protected criteria listed by the anti-discrimination laws. In short, insurers are permitted to incorporate these protected factors provided they can offer a legitimate rationale. The key consideration is the utilisation of data and criteria that are actuarially robust and statistically relevant to the precise risk being assessed.

Moreover, the insurer must publish the segmentation criteria he uses[81] for each type of insurance contract on its website and in the proposal to the policyholder and provide

76 G. Werner, C. Modlin and W. Towers, "Basic ratemaking", *Casualty Actuarial Society* 2016, 15.

77 De Pril and Dhaene, *Rapport van de werkgroep Segmentering*, 30.

78 The Antidiscrimination Act (Wet van 10 mei 2007 ter bestrijding van bepaalde vormen van discriminatie (*BS* 30 mei 2007), the Gender Act (Wet van 10 mei 2007 ter bestrijding van discriminatie tussen vrouwen en mannen (*BS* 30 mei 2007) and the Antiracisme Act (Wet 10 mei 2007 tot wijziging van de wet van 30 juli 1981 tot bestraffing van bepaalde door racisme of xenofobie ingegeven daden (*BS* 30 mei 2007).

79 *See* Art. 43, §§1-2 of the Insurance Act.

80 Y. Thiery and C. Van Schoubroeck, "Fairness and Equality in Insurance Classification", *The Geneva Papers on Risk and Insurance – Issues and Practice* 2006, Vol. 31, 19.

81 That is, the criteria he employs for the purpose of segmentation in terms of acceptance, rating, and/or the extent of coverage.

guidance on the used segmentation criteria.[82] If the insurer decides not to cover a risk, he must communicate this to the policyholder. In this written communication, the insurer has to mention the data it has processed and the segmentation criteria that have led to the decision in particular.[83] Meeting these requirements is made significantly more onerous, as the use of an AI system requires the insurer to objectively justify a greater number of criteria and explain them to the insurer. In addition, AI models may select and apply criteria on their own, without the insurer having any insight or control over it.[84]

If the insurer is guilty of using discriminating segmentation criteria, Article 22 of the Insurance Act comes into effect, which requires the criteria that lead to discrimination to be retroactively removed from the segmentation policy. This may result in an adjustment of the policyholder's insurance contract, meaning that some policyholders will have to pay a higher premium or be subject to stricter conditions (and possibly have to terminate their contract when it becomes unaffordable for them). However, this sanction can never work to the detriment of the person protected by it, as this would be contrary to the purpose of the legal provision in question. Therefore, this sanction cannot be applied.

This anti-discrimination obligation in the Insurance Act is insufficient to fully ban discriminatory decisions made by an AI system. *First*, current obligations do not guarantee an adequately clear explanation or justification of the outcomes generated by an AI application. As elaborated previously, the legislature does not oblige the insurer to indicate the extent to which the various criteria are considered and how they are used in calculating risk. The legislature also fails to specify the level of detail to which the different criteria should be defined. Consequently, insurers could choose to describe them in more general overarching terms, which can still cover several

82 Art. 45, §1 of the Insurance Act and Art. 46, §1, the first paragraph of the Insurance Act.

83 Art. 46, §4, the first and second paragraphs of the Insurance Act.

84 This could prevent insurers from using AI applications to calculate policyholders' claims probability, which could help to prevent the creation of discriminatory decisions. Nevertheless, Explainable AI ('XAI)' could lend a hand, as it makes it possible to provide an explanation on the variables being used and why they can predict the risk. For more information regarding XAI-models, *see* A. Adadi and M. Berrada, "Peeking Inside the Black-Box: A Survey on Explainable Artificial Intelligence (XAI)", *IEEE* 2018, Vol. 6, 52138-52160; R. Guidotti, A. Monreale, S. Ruggieri, F. Turini, F. Giannotti and D. Pedreschi, "A Survey of Methods for Explaining Black Box Models", *ACM Computer Surveys* 2018, Vol. 51, Issue 5, 93:1-42; M. Brkan and G. Bonnet, "Legal and Technical Feasibility of the GDPR's Quest for Explanation of Algorithmic Decisions: of Black Boxes, White Boxes and Fata Morganas", *European Journal of Risk Regulation* 2020, Vol. 11, Issue 1, 18-50; B. Mittelstadt, C. Russel and S. Wachter, "Explaining Explanations in AI", *FAT* '19: Proceedings of the Conference on Fairness, Accountability, and Transparency* 2019, 279-288; R. Matulionyte, "Reconciling Trade Secrets and AI Explainability: Face Recognition Technologies as a Case Study", *European Intellectual Property Review* 2022, Vol. 44, Issue 1, 36-42.

(possibly prohibited) criteria.[85,86] In addition, the requirement to explain why the relevant criteria are used is very vague and could be easily met by simply stating that an AI system has demonstrated certain correlations. *Second*, it is still possible that insurers can justify the criteria they employ by demonstrating their effect on the outcome but at the same time still engage in (indirect) discriminatory decision-making. For example, if the insurer can prove that a policyholder's postal code is correlated to the degree of risk of a car accident, this criterion could still lead to a discriminatory policy, as this factor could discriminate against a particular ethnicity that is over-represented in this location. *Third*, the policyholder must detect and prove that the insurer uses discriminatory segmentation criteria,[87] which is not an easy task given the use of AI.[88] The specific characteristics of AI systems, such as opacity, autonomous behaviour, adaptivity and complexity, may make it excessively difficult, if not impossible, for the policyholder to meet this burden of proof. Also, based on the current transparency requirement, the policyholder has no clear view on all the (specific) criteria used in the segmentation policy and the extent to which they play a role in determining the policy. Moreover, the insurer can easily justify the use of the criteria just by arguing that the likelihood and extent of a claim vary as these criteria change. *Fourth*, the current provisions in the Insurance Act do not resolve the issues related to the aforementioned price discrimination, because the insurer is not obligated to objectively justify other criteria which are unrelated to the segmentation but which do influence the price. *Fifth*, AI applications could lead to the identification of criteria that are purely correlated with the risk to be insured, without any causal relationship (*e.g.* spurious correlations).[89] The legislature could choose to create a requirement that the insurer may only use

85 For example, insurers could list 'financial transactions' as a segmentation criterion, without specifying exactly which transactions are involved and exactly which show a correlation with the claims probability, and why.

86 However, this problem could be partially remedied by the transparency obligation in the GDPR. Based on the GDPR, data controllers (insurers) must inform data subjects (policyholders) that their data is being processed through an AI system, as well as provide meaningful information about the logic involved, the significance and the envisaged consequences of such processing for the data subject (Art. 13, 2., f) GDPR and Art. 14, 2., g) GDPR). Based on this provision, policyholders should at least be provided with information on the fact that they will be profiled, on the preferred approach and technology, on the main (categories of) input variables, and on the reasons why the profile is relevant to the decision-making process. In addition, this provision can require insurers to outline the weighting of the used (categories of) variables. *See* EPRS, *The Impact of the General Data Protection Regulation (GDPR) on Artificial Intelligence*, June 2020, www.europarl.europa.eu, 64.

87 This is a fault-based liability rule, which requires the person to prove a negligent or intentionally damaging act or omission ('fault') by the person potentially liable for that damage, as well as a causal link between that fault and the relevant damage.

88 The legislature has omitted to institute a provision for the shift of the burden of proof, as is the case in the general anti-discrimination laws, which introduces a limited presumption of discrimination.

89 Swedloff, "Risk Classification's Big Data (R)evolution", 366-367; FSB, *Artificial Intelligence and Machine Learning in Financial Services. Market Developments and Financial Stability Implications*, 1 November 2017, www.fsb.org, 6.

segmentation criteria that show a causal relationship or at least an increased correlation with the claims probability. However, the current obligation to objectively justify all segmentation criteria does not mean the insurer needs to demonstrate a causal link. After all, if we look at the pertinence criterion, presupposed in the Belgian general anti-discrimination laws, it is merely required that the measure has an impact that aggravates the nature of the risk.[90]

2.3.1.2 Genetic Information

The Insurance Act contains an exception to the aforementioned spontaneous disclosure obligation of the policyholder: the policyholder cannot disclose genetic data to the insurer, even if it benefits him.[91] Also, under no circumstances may the insurer request and process such information.[92,93] Again, AI could play a difficult role here. Even if the policyholder does not disclose his genetic data to the insurer, AI could still take genetic data into consideration by using proxies correlating with the policyholder's genetic profile. Merely denying AI model data or characteristics that have a direct link to genetic information does not necessarily prevent AI algorithms from determining the risks based on genetic predisposition. An AI system may look for other – seemingly neutral – variables that proxy for genetic information.[94] Suppose the AI system estimates a higher risk for policyholders who are members of a Facebook group dedicated to increasing the availability of genetic testing for Parkinson's, the insurer could discriminate by proxy as members of this Facebook group could be more likely to have a form of Parkinson's in their family.[95]

The Belgian legislature has failed to define the concept of 'genetic data', leaving its precise scope uncertain, which creates ambiguity and legal uncertainty, all the more now as AI becomes more prominent. It is up to the legislature to clearly delineate these concepts, and more specifically to include the obvious proxies or substitutes for prohibited characteristics. It is advisable to provide a broad interpretation, in order to avoid erosion of the absolute prohibition on the collection and use of genetic data.[96]

---

90 Y. Thiery, *Discriminatie en verzekering: Economische efficiëntie en actuariële fairness getoetst aan het juridisch gelijkheidsbeginsel, Proefschrift KU Leuven,* 2010, 198-199.

91 Art. 58(1) and (2) of the Insurance Act.

92 Unlike the non-discrimination provision, the use of genetic factors is *absolutely* prohibited, as the insurer cannot use any genetic information even if it can objectively justify it.

93 Goessens, *Private verzekering en solidariteit*, 65.

94 A.E.R. Prince and D. Schwarcz, "Proxy Discrimination in the Age of Artificial Intelligence and Big Data", *Iowa Law Review*, 2020, Vol. 105, 1303.

95 Ibid., 1261.

96 S. Defloor, *Het gebruik van medische informatie in private verzekeringen*, Mortsel, Intersentia, 2014, 200; Goessens, *Private verzekering en solidariteit*, 129.

An adequate solution could be to define genetic information as 'data relating to genetic characteristics', a similar description to the one included in the GDPR,[97] which would also prohibit the use of proxies.

The breach of the prohibition on communicating and processing genetic information is sanctioned with relative nullity, instead of legal conversion.[98] When the premium and other policy conditions have been determined based on genetic information, they will be nullified. Although the ground for nullity only applies to part of the contract (i.e. partial nullity), the entire contract will have to be declared null and void, as these conditions are essential to its continued existence.[99] Apart from the fact that the burden of proof once again rests on the policyholder, this sanction does not protect the policyholder at all, as the nullity sanction has the effect of retroactively depriving him of coverage. Again, this sanction cannot be applied when it is to the detriment of the person protected by it.[100] In light of this, the legislature should consider adapting this sanction in order to create other consequences that are in the interest of the injured policyholder.

2.3.1.3 Information from Health Trackers

The Belgian legislature has actively intervened in the use of technology within the health insurance sector. By using certain applications and wearables, such as *Fitbit* or *Runkeeper*, health data is captured, such as the number of steps, sleep habits, average heart rate and so on. The insurer could use this data to estimate the risk of the insured event and further individualise the premium. However, according to Article 46/2 of the Insurance Act, it is prohibited to refuse individual life insurance or health insurance,[101] or to charge a higher price if the prospective policyholder refuses to purchase or use such internet-connected devices. In other words, the policyholder should not be penalised if he refuses to use a connected device.[102] In addition, it is prohibited to use this data for segmentation even

---

97 *See* Art. 4, 13 GDPR: "'genetic data' means personal data *relating* to the inherited or acquired genetic characteristics of a natural person which give unique information about the physiology or the health of that natural person and which result, in particular, from an analysis of a biological sample from the natural person in question."

98 Art. 56 of the Insurance Act.

99 F. Peeraer, "Nietigheid op maat: proportionaliteit en werkzaamheid bij partiële nietigheid, reductie en conversie", *TPR* 2016, Issue 1, 187. For a more detailed explanation, *see also* T. Tanghe, *Gedeeltelijke ontbinding en vernietiging van overeenkomsten*, Mortsel, Intersentia, 2015, 149-276.

100 In addition, relative nullity can be invoked only by the individual protected by the violated legal provision.

101 Art. 46/1 of the Insurance Act.

102 Art. 46/2 of the Insurance Act. This article is in tune with what the GDPR stipulates. This regulation states that any consent must (among other things) be 'free'. This means that the prospective policyholder should be at risk of the services he has requested not being provided if he does not give his consent for his data to be processed for reasons other than those necessary to perform the contract. In this case, the legislature

if the policyholder agrees to use an internet-connected device or shares the information collected by this device.[103] As a result, prospective policyholders with a lower health risk demonstrated by such devices cannot obtain a lower premium or better conditions, and prospective policyholders with a higher health risk cannot be charged a higher premium or be excluded from coverage.

Unlike the ban on using genetic information, proxies do seem to be allowed here, enabling insurers to look at, for example, purchasing sports equipment or healthy food, or posting a completed run (tracked by Strava) on Facebook or Instagram, to check how healthy policyholders really are.

If the insurer were still to use health data from internet-connected devices for risk assessment and premium calculation, the legal conversion would come into effect again. This is predicated on Article 44 of the Insurance Act, housing the prohibition, which is integrated within Part 3 of the Insurance Act. In cases where the insurer violates the regulations outlined in Part 3 of the Insurance Act, legal conversion is set in motion, as opposed to relative nullity. Consequently, this necessitates the retroactive removal of the policy provisions based on these criteria from the segmentation policy, potentially leading to an (unjust) adjustment in the policyholder's policy.

2.3.1.4 Gender as a Criterion

The European Court of Justice has prohibited gender as a differentiation criterion for calculating insurance premiums and benefits, even if the differences would be based on reliable actuarial statistical data and could be objectively justified.[104,105] However, it is still possible to make an *indirect* distinction based on gender if the aim of the unequal treatment is legitimate and the means of achieving that aim are appropriate and necessary (*see* the general anti-discrimination law). The application of factors correlated

itself has decided that the personal data collected by health trackers are not necessary to assess the risk and calculate the premium and conditions of the insurance policy. For more information, *see* J. Goetghebuer, "De invloed van artikel 22 AVG op het gebruik van robo-advies binnen de beleggingssector. Met de rug tegen de muur?", *RDC-TBH* 2020, Issue 2, 156.

103 Art. 46/3 of the Insurance Act.

104 CJEU 1 March 2011, C-236/09, *Association belge des Consommateurs Test-Achats ASBL, Yann van Vugt, Charles Basselier v. Conseil des ministres*, ECLI:EU:C:2011:100.

105 The use of gender as a risk-determining factor is not generally prohibited. Since the prohibition refers only to the calculation of premiums and benefits, the insurer can use gender as a factor in calculating the risk policyholders could represent and use it to determine whether or not to underwrite the risk, as the underwriting process is separate from the base price of an insurance product profile. *See* European Commission, *Guidelines on the Application of Council Directive 2004/113/EC to Insurance, in the Light of the Judgment of the Court of Justice of the European Union in Case C-236/09 (Test-Achats)*, *Pb.C.* 13 January 2012, 11, 10.

with gender thus remains possible. For example, application forms can include different questions for each gender.[106] In addition, when it comes to vehicle insurance, price differentiation based on the size of a car engine should, for instance, remain possible, even though statistically men drive cars with greater engine power.[107,108]

AI can create greater indirect discrimination based on gender through the use of proxies. Friend lists on Facebook, shopping habits on Amazon or bol.com and search history on Google could easily translate into a high probability of an individual's gender. When data on shopping habits are fed to the AI system, it can easily learn to group individuals into categories labelled A and B. These categories can fairly accurately correspond to one's gender, although the system may be programmed to disregard direct data on gender.[109] However, even keeping this prohibition in mind, it is permissible to use proxies for gender and indirectly make a distinction, although the general discrimination laws require that this distinction be justified on legitimate grounds. If this indirect discrimination is not justified, the sanctions applicable to the Belgian general anti-discrimination obligations will apply. After all, the jurisprudence of the Court of Justice was incorporated into Belgian legislation via the Gender Act of 10 May 2007. When a person considers himself a victim of discrimination and can present facts that suggest the existence of discrimination, the defendant has to prove that there has been no discrimination. The Belgian legislature divided the burden of proof between parties. However, again, it would be difficult for policyholders to discover a breach and provide the necessary facts.

2.3.2 Indirect Restrictions

2.3.2.1 The Equivalence Requirement in the Belgian Insurance Act

Article 23, §1 of the Insurance Act states that contracts may not contain any clause that infringes the equivalence between the insurer's and the policyholder's commitments. The equivalence envisaged by this provision can refer to both a balance between the

---

106 European Commission, *Guidelines on the Application of Council Directive*, 11, 4 and 10.

107 For instance, a woman whose family has a history of breast cancer will generally have to pay a higher risk premium than a woman without such a family history. However, there is no reason for a man with the same family history to pay a higher premium, since the probability that he will suffer from breast cancer is extremely low. In other words, this distinction is justified and non-discriminatory [*see* European Commission, *Guidelines on the Application of Council Directive*, 11, 10]. It is important to emphasise that this example is used purely to clarify the meaning of an indirect distinction, as in Belgium it is forbidden to request and process such genetic information, as described previously.

108 European Commission, *Guidelines on the Application of Council Directive*, 11, 4.

109 A. Tischbirek, "Artificial Intelligence and Discrimination: Discriminating Against Discriminatory Systems", in T. Wischmeyer and T. Rademacher (eds.), *Regulating Artificial Intelligence*, Cham, Springer Nature Switzerland, 2020, 107-108.

rights and obligations of the contracting parties (evaluation of the secondary obligations, i.e. a legal equivalence) and a balance between the main contractual performances (evaluation of the essential obligations, i.e. an economic equivalence). While there is still debate as to which equivalence is involved in this case (a legal or an economic one), it can be argued that this article refers to an economic equivalence when we look at the regulation regarding unfair terms used in a contract concluded with a consumer. The Directive on unfair terms states that a contractual term shall be regarded as unfair if it causes a significant imbalance in the parties' rights and obligations arising under the contract to the detriment of the consumer (i.e. a legal inequivalence). The directive stipulates further that unfair terms shall not be binding on the consumer and that the contract shall continue to bind the parties on those terms if it is capable of continuing in existence without the unfair terms.[110] Consequently, national courts can only exclude the application of an unlawful contractual term and have no authorisation to revise its content and replace them with a default legal provision.[111] In other words, in case of insurance contracts concluded with consumers, the sanction of legal conversion *cannot* be applied when a manifest imbalance has been established between the rights and obligations of the contracting parties (thus, the legal equivalence). However, this is the very sanction applicable to a violation of Article 23, §1 of the Insurance Act. This sanction cannot take effect if legal inequivalence would be established. Besides, should one decide otherwise and argue that Article 22 of the Insurance Act refers to a legal equivalence, this provision would have no added value for consumers because the same obligation is already included in the unfair terms in the Belgian '*Wetboek Economisch Recht* (WER)' and in Article 5.52 of the Civil Code.

An economic equivalence must be achieved between the insurer's services – the coverage – and the premium to be paid by the policyholder. This means there will be economic inequivalence when the premium paid by the policyholder is too high (or too low) for the coverage provided by the insurer. Segmentation will not create such inequality, as segmentation is used only to determine the risk profile of the policyholder, and this risk profile will determine both the premium and the coverage (conditions). AI in the context of this article only determines segmentation, which means it will not impact the existence of an economic inequality.

To conclude that there is inequivalence, the court would have to look at what the insurer offers. This exercise requires comparing policyholders with the same risk profile. After all, besides the coverage, the premium is also influenced by the segmentation category

110 Art. 6, 1. of the Directive on unfair terms.

111 CJEU 14 June 2012, C-618/10, *Banco Español de Crédito SA v. Joaquín Calderón Camino*, ECLI:EU:C:2012:349, para. 65-71.

of the policyholder.[112] So if it is not possible to make an abstraction of part of the premium affected by the risk represented by the policyholder and the part affected by the scope of coverage, one can conclude as to the existence of inequivalence only if one can cluster the policyholders with the same risk profiles and compare their premiums with the acquired coverage. However, due to AI, making these comparisons will no longer be a simple task, as AI systems will lead to the creation of small segmentation groups clustering a (very) limited number of policyholders with the same risk profile. This makes the determination of an inequivalence nearly impossible.

2.3.2.2 The Rules of Conduct in the Belgian Insurance Act

Under the overarching rule of conduct,[113] insurers are obliged to act loyally, reasonably and professionally in the interests of their policyholders when distributing insurance products.[114] All other specific rules of conduct should always be read in light of this rule.[115] This implies that if the insurer complies with one of the specific rules without fulfilling this general duty of care, it still violates its legal obligations.[116]

When an insurer uses an AI system to determine the premium and terms of an insurance contract, this obligation obviously still applies. The insurer must comply with this principle both when developing the AI algorithms and when deploying them. Consequently, based on this duty of care, the insurer should not use an AI system if this system would make a worse decision on average than a reasonable natural person or a less complex algorithm. If, for example, the AI system obviously miscalculates risk, resulting in either the underwriting, premium or coverage not being tailored to the real risk represented by the policyholder, the insurer has not behaved in a loyal, reasonable and professional manner. Based on this obligation, the insurer could be expected to use only the (most appropriate) segmentation factors to accurately estimate the risk (e.g. the criteria showing a causal link or at least a strong correlation with the risk).

In order to hold the insurer liable, the policyholder cannot rely on a sanction contained in the Insurance Act. Hence, in the context of extracontractual liability, recourse

112 For example, if the insurer offers an annual premium of EUR 800 per year for policyholders with the same risk profile for vehicle liability insurance with the same exclusions, deductibles and discounts, but another policyholder representing the same risk has to pay EUR 1,600 for the same coverage, the court could conclude inequivalence exists.

113 The conduct of business measures contained in MiFID II also applies to the insurance sector.

114 Art. 279, §1 of the Insurance Act.

115 Vansweevelt and Weyts, *Handboek Verzekeringsrecht*, 137.

116 FSMA, *Aanpassing van de circulaire FSMA_2014_02 d.d. 16/04/2014 met betrekking tot de wijziging van de wet van 27 maart 1995 en de uitbreiding van de MiFID-gedragsregels tot de verzekeringssector*, September 2015, www.fsma.be/, 21.

is mandated under Article 6.5 Belgian Civil Code.[117,118] Under this provision, the policyholder is obliged to substantiate that the premium or policy terms did not align with the risk they posed in a manner exceeding the bounds of reasonableness. This transgression can be challenging for policyholders to detect and, once more, may present difficulties in terms of proof, especially in the case of AI.

Prior to the conclusion of each insurance contract, the insurer needs to determine the customer's wants and needs using information provided by the policyholder and must ensure that the insurance contract meets those wants and needs.[119] This obligation can also be described as the know your customer principle within the insurance sector[120] and is a concretisation of the general duty of care discussed previously.[121] The preparatory works show that this special rule of conduct serves the following purposes: (*i*) avoiding that the policyholder is covered multiple times for the same risks (problem of multiple coverage), *(ii)* avoiding under-insurance (in other words avoiding that the subject is covered for too low a value), *(iii)* avoiding over-insurance (in other words avoiding that the subject is covered for too high a value) and (*iv*) avoiding a wrong coverage (in other words avoiding that certain risks are not covered although this is the customer's wish or, conversely, avoiding that certain risks are covered although the customer does not wish this to be the case).[122]

The purpose of this legal obligation is to ensure that the coverage requested matches the coverage obtained. However, AI segmentation will have no influence in determining multiple or wrong coverage. After all, insurers' websites usually contain general terms and conditions defining the positive coverage as well as the exclusions for all (high-risk or low-risk) policyholders. It is mainly the extent of coverage (such as limits and exemptions) that will be determined by the risk represented by the policyholder, so AI will only play a role in this case. That being said, this legal provision does not oblige the insurer to ensure that the extent of coverage is adjusted to the risk represented by the policyholders, as it merely seeks to avoid the situations of over- and under-insurance.

117 Art. 1382 of the Belgian Old Civil Code.

118 The deficiencies attributed to the insurer are located primarily within the pre-contractual phase, although it is noteworthy that the resultant damages may also become apparent during the subsequent contract execution phase. *See* A. De Boeck, "De precontractuele fase als ontmoetingsplaats voor buitencontractuele en contractuele aansprakelijkheid: de schade ten gevolge van tekortkomingen tijdens de precontractuele fase nader geanalyseerd", in S. Stijns and P. Wéry (eds.), *De raakvlakken tussen de contractuele en de buitencontractuele aansprakelijkheid/Les rapports entre les responsabilités contractuelle et extracontractuelle*, Brugge, die Keure / la Charte, 2010, 139.

119 Art. 284, §1, paras 1 and 2 of the Insurance Act.

120 Vansweevelt and Weyts, *Handboek Verzekeringsrecht*, 157.

121 B. Bruyndonckx and S. Lodewijckx, "Verzekeringsdistributie in een nieuw kleedje", *BFR*, 2018, Issue 4, 258.

122 Report to the King regarding the Royal Decree of 21 February 2014.

AI could still lead to situations of under-insurance and over-insurance, as AI could create a miscalculated insured value.[123] However, since the calculation of insured value does not rely on (AI) segmentation, this issue will not be discussed any further.

3 Conclusion

Insurance is based on the segmentation technique, making it possible for insurers to assess the risks represented by (prospective) policyholders and establishing a risk profile for each policyholder. Segmentation can be used by the insurer to differentiate the terms of an insurance contract according to some specific characteristics of the risk ('segmentation criteria'). This means segmentation plays a role only in determining whether to underwrite this insurance risk and, if so, on what terms (the coverage, scope and premium of an insurance contract).

The current Belgian Insurance Act allows insurers to use AI as a tool for the segmentation technique, as, in general, each insurer is free to pursue its own segmentation policy. Given this freedom, *in principle*, the insurer cannot be held responsible for (not) taking a certain parameter into account. That being said, some legal restrictions still exist that could limit this freedom. The question arises as to whether these restrictions can protect the policyholder from erroneous decisions made by an AI system. After all, even if the sheer amount of new data available combined with AI could lead to accurately predicting the individual risk of policyholders, we must not forget that this new reality still leads to many challenges and ramifications for policyholders if their risk is incorrectly calculated. As the segmentation technique (traditionally) relies on the spontaneous communication of information by the policyholder, the current Belgian insurance regulation is aimed mainly at protecting the insurer from obtaining

123 While the insured value is determined primarily by the policyholder, there is still some room for the insurer and AI to intervene. It is, for instance, feasible for the involved parties to allocate an appraised value to specific assets through an explicit contractual provision. Establishing the agreed value is generally a straightforward task, rendering the utilisation of AI superfluous. However, in the context of ascertaining the agreed value of artworks, AI can serve as a valuable tool. The evaluation of the insured value of an artwork represents a more intricate undertaking, often necessitating the expertise of a specialist. This specialist's role could potentially be supplanted by the implementation of AI. Through the application of image and pattern recognition, AI can effectively determine the value of an artwork with precision. Furthermore, an AI system can conduct a comprehensive analysis, encompassing both visual and quantitative elements, such as the year of creation, the artist's identity, the materials employed, the artist's techniques, resale history and other pertinent data. Through the analysis of these parameters, AI can discern patterns correlated with the valuation of an artwork. While AI can augment the accuracy of insured value determination, it remains susceptible to imperfections, much like any technological system. An incorrect estimation of an artwork's value by the AI system due to an insufficiently representative training data set could, for example, result in an inaccurate insured value and potential instances of over- or under-insurance.

inaccurate or incomplete information. Nevertheless, AI could lead to retrieving a larger amount of data regarding the policyholder and the use of infinite segmentation criteria. AI segmentation could therefore solve the problem of information asymmetry between the policyholder and the insurer. The current Belgian Insurance Act is therefore not fully adapted to this new technological reality and currently contains few to no legal provisions that could protect policyholders from misjudging their risk and incorrect premiums and conditions.

First of all, the direct restrictions which prohibit the use of certain risk segmentation factors do not fully protect policyholders against incorrect AI segmentation. Although the legislature applies concrete sanctions to these prohibitions in law, such as legal conversion and relative nullity, the burden of proof, which is usually[124] on the policyholder, prevents their actual application. Besides the fact that such misconduct is difficult for policyholders to detect, proving its existence will not be easy, given that the specific characteristics of AI systems may make it excessively difficult to meet the burden of proof. Furthermore, even if the policyholder is able to prove a breach, the applicable sanctions do not protect the policyholder. After all, the application of legal conversion can lead to the adjustment of insurance contract, which may result in certain policyholders having to pay a higher premium or being subject to stricter conditions. Also, relative nullity does not protect the policyholder, as the nullity sanction has the effect of retroactively depriving him of coverage. More so, even if these restrictions are closely adhered to by the insurer, this still does not guarantee that the risk is assessed correctly and that the premium and conditions correspond to reality.

Second, indirect restrictions do not constitute a sufficient protection mechanism either. Although the equivalence requirement, which creates a mandatory balance between coverage and premium, should provide better protection, in reality this is not the case. After all, (AI) segmentation will not create an economic inequality as it will only determine the risk profile of the policyholder, and this risk profile will affect both premium and coverage, which means these two will always be coherent. Policyholders could, however, invoke the general rule of conduct when they think the insurer has made an incorrect risk assessment. But, again, the burden of proof of a breach lies with the policyholder.

Consequently, given the insurer's great freedom to use AI in its segmentation and the risks involved in doing so, there is a pressing need for an additional regulatory framework. The legislature must introduce provisions that could ensure appropriate

124 With the exception of general anti-discrimination laws, where there is a (too) limited presumption of discrimination.

(AI) segmentation techniques, as a result of which the insurers' decisions as to whether or not to underwrite the risk, as well as the insurance contract itself, are always adapted to the real risk represented by the policyholder.[125]

125 This article did not undertake a review of the proposals for the AI Act, AI Liability Directive and Product Liability Directive. Nonetheless, it is worth noting that these policy initiatives may hold the potential to address some of the aforementioned challenges, for example by alleviating the victims' burden of proof by introducing the 'presumption of causality' (in the AI Liability Directive). That being said, it is imperative to underscore that, within the current proposal, AI segmentation is not classified as a high-risk AI system. As a result, the majority of regulations outlined in the AI Act, as well as specific provisions within the AI Liability Act, remain inapplicable.

Settlement Agreements Applied to AI and Insurance Claims: A Normative Perspective

*Daan Willems and Bernard Tilleman**

1 Introduction

How should we shape settlement agreements in the future as a specific contract under Belgian law in Book 7 of the Civil Code?[1] It concerns a private law instrument that also applies to AI and insurance claims. A reformed framework for settlement agreements will therefore spill over into AI and contract formation, which is the focus of this collective work. In this respect, the future perspective of settlement agreements is discussed by depicting (i) the legal notion,[2] (ii) the contract formation, (iii) the legal effects and termination and (iv) the application to AI and insurance claims.[3] That perspective is not merely hypothetical, since a legislative proposal on Book 7 'Specific Contracts' was recently submitted (including settlement agreements in Arts. 7.7.9-7.7.16).[4]

---

* Daan Willems is a PhD Researcher at the Institute for Contract Law KU Leuven. Prof. dr. Bernard Tilleman is a professor at the KU Leuven Faculty of Law and Criminology.

1 Book 1 'General provisions' and Book 5 'Obligations' of the Belgian Civil Code entered into force on 1 January 2023. The future Book 7 'Specific contracts' is work in progress and is inherently connected to the new law of obligations. This contribution is an elaboration of the following contribution (in Dutch): B. TILLEMAN and D. WILLEMS, 'Dading: traditie met toekomst?' in P. SCHOUKENS, B. DEMARSIN, E. DE BECKER and T. KEERSMAEKERS (eds.), *Liber Amicorum Danny Pieters: Durven out of the box denken*, Ghent, Owl Press Legal, 2022, 406-418. The elaboration mainly relates to the last part concerning the application to AI and insurance claims.

2 Including the relevant aspects regarding Book 8 'Evidence' of the Belgian Civil Code that entered into force on 1 November 2020.

3 To situate the normative perspective, this contribution compares the Belgian law aspects of a settlement agreement to Dutch law (and merely punctually, to French, German and Swiss law). That is facilitated by the functional concept of *vaststellingsovereenkomst* (defined under 'legal notion').

4 Legislative proposal dating from 16 April 2024 concerning the introduction of Book 7 'Specific Contracts' in the Belgian Civil Code. It was submitted by two members of the Belgian Chamber of Representatives (*Kamer van Volksvertegenwoordigers*), and can be consulted via the parliament's website. It is further referred to in footnote as follows: Proposal Book 7 'Specific Contracts', Parl.St. Kamer 2023-24, nr. 3973/1.

2 Legal Notion

Overview – Under Belgian law, the diffuse concept of settlement agreement relates to a diverse terminology. Depending on the nature of the contract, it will be either a general (innominate) contract or a specific (nominate) contract. Specific (nominate) contracts are subject to the application of the common law of obligations (Book 5 of the Belgian Civil Code) to the extent that specific rules do not deviate from those general principles. Those rules are currently set out in Articles 2044-2058 of the old Belgian Civil Code (future Book 7 of the Belgian Civil Code).

***Sensu Stricto*: settlement agreement as a specific contract (under Belgian law)** – According to the Belgian Civil Code, a settlement agreement (in Dutch: *dading*; in French: *transaction*) constitutes a contract by which the parties merely prevent or terminate a dispute (Art. 2044(1) old Civil Code).[5] The French and Belgian Courts of Cassation additionally require that parties make mutual concessions.[6] We find this requirement explicitly in the particularly short § 779 of the German *Bürgerliches Gesetzbuch* on the *Vergleich*. The mutual concessions requirement was recently codified in Art. 2044(1) of the French Civil Code.[7] This requirement aims to ensure the reciprocal nature of the specific settlement agreement. This, in turn, was required to allow the dissolution of the settlement agreement based on Article 5.90 Belgian Civil Code (*ex* Art. 1184 old Civil Code), in case of a serious breach of the settlement agreement by one of the parties. It was disputed whether a resolution *ex tunc* of a settlement is appropriate as a remedy in case of non-fulfilment of the obligations derived from the settlement agreement (*infra*). The performance in kind of obligations stemming from a settlement agreement should, in fact, be encouraged following the example of Article 7.905, *in fine* of the Dutch Civil Code.

***Sensu Lato*: settlement agreement as a general contract (under Belgian law) and a specific contract (under Dutch law)** – The requirement of mutual concessions does not apply under Dutch law, which uses a broader concept of settlement agreement

---

5 The etymological origin of *dading* is connected to dispute resolution. The word *dading* finds its etymological origin in the following ancient words: *dag* (in the sense of bringing a case before the court) and *ding* (referring to a lawsuit). See the following etymological dictionary: Woordenboek der Nederlandsche Taal (WNT), freely accessible via https://ivdnt.org/woordenboeken/woordenboek-der-nederlandsche-taal/.

6 See, for example, in Belgian case law: Cass. 7 May 2020, C.19.0423.N, ECLI:BE:CASS:2020:ARR.20200507.1N.7 and Cass. 10 November 2016, C.16.0142.F, ECLI:BE:CASS:2016:ARR.20161110.3; See for example in French case law: Fr. Cass. 27 November 2012, 11-17.185, ECLI:FR:CCASS:2012:CO01177, *Bulletin* 2012, IV, n° 213 and Cass. 25 October 2011, 10-23.538, *Bulletin* 2011, IV, n° 173.

7 In France, this requirement of mutual concessions (in French: *concessions réciproques*) was included in Art. 2044(1) of the French *Code civil* via *LOI n° 2016-1547 du 18 novembre 2016 de modernisation de la justice du XXIe siècle (1)*.

(*vaststellingsovereenkomst*[8]) as a specific contract in Article 7:900 of the Dutch Civil Code (contrary to its general, innominate nature under Belgian law). It concerns a threefold notion: parties agree either (i) to decide together or (ii) that one party decides or (iii) that a third independent party decides, on the concerned uncertainty or dispute.[9] It is important to stress that the scope of those agreements is not limited to the settlement of disputes. At first sight, this shows a clear divide between: (i) the settlement agreement *sensu lato* (or *vaststellingsovereenkomst*), which under Dutch law includes the binding third-party decision and party decision, and (ii) the settlement agreement *sensu stricto* (or *dading*) governed by Articles 2044-2058 of the old Civil Code.

On closer inspection, the truth is more nuanced. Since the original provision in the Civil Code of 1804, the Belgian case law has defined the settlement agreement *sensu stricto* (or *dading*) in an increasingly flexible manner: (i) a dispute merely requires conflicting claims; (ii) the mutual concessions must not be expressed in the contract, not be equivalent, and not concern the dispute at hand,[10] and (iii) following the case law of the Belgian Court of Cassation, a settlement agreement does not imply that one of the parties recognises the merits of the claims of the other party.[11]

The concept of settlement agreement *sensu lato* (or *vaststellingsovereenkomst*) was gradually introduced by Belgian legal doctrine to name settlements for which mutual concessions are lacking.[12] The term is now also appearing in Belgian case law.[13] The broad concept of settlement agreement (or *vaststellingsovereenkomst*) could become

8 Dutch legal scholars introduced the concept *vaststellingsovereenkomst*, inspired by the German concept *Feststellungsvertrag*; see G. DE GROOT, *De schuldbekentenis* (diss. Leiden), Amsterdam, Kruyt, 1918, 107, referred to by E.J. NUMANN, 'Aantasting van vaststellingsovereenkomsten wegens dwaling', in *Non sine causa. Opstellen aangeboden aan* Prof.Mr. *G.J. Scholten ter gelegenheid van zijn afscheid als hoogleraar aan de Universiteit van Amsterdam* (Scholten-bundel), Zwolle, Tjeenk Willink, 1979, 277.

9 It was codified in the Dutch Civil Code as a specific contract at the end of the twentieth century. So, in 1993, it entered into force as title 15 '*Vaststellingsovereenkomst*' of Book 7 'Specific contracts' of the Dutch Civil Code (Arts. 7:900-906, and currently Arts. 7:900-910). It replaced the narrower concept *dading* that previously served as a specific contract in Articles 1888-1901 of the old Dutch Civil Code dating from 1838.The Dutch Civil Code in 1838 was strongly inspired by the French Civil Code dating from 1804. That is also true for the settlement agreement; see C. ASSER, *Het Nederlandsch Burgerlijk Wetboek vergeleken met het Wetboek Napoleon*, 's-Gravenhage, Gebroeders Van Cleef, 1838, 586-588.

10 F. GEORGE, *La convention de transaction*, Liège, Wolters Kluwer, 2021, 19 and 24 ; A. RIGOLET, *Contrat de transaction*, Brussels, Larcier, 2021, 17 and 20.

11 Cass. 10 November 2016, C.16 .0142.F, ECLI:BE:CASS:2016:ARR.20161110.3.

12 N. PORTUGAELS, *De vaststellingsovereenkomst*, Antwerp, Intersentia, 2018, 45; B. TILLEMAN, I. CLAEYS, Ch. COUDRON and K. LOONTJENS, *Dading*, in *APR*, Antwerp, Story-Scientia, 2000, 8; E. DIRIX, 'De kwijting voor saldo van rekening', *RW* 1981-1982, 192; G. GHEYSEN, *Dading*, in *APR*, Brussels, Larcier, 1966, 29.

13 Cass. 20 December 2010, C.10.0270.N, ECLI:BE:CASS:2010:ARR.20101220.5; Rb. Tongeren (3e B k.) 22 oktober 2010, *Limb.Rechtsl.* 2011, afl. 2, 158, noot B. Van den Bergh, Rev.trim.dr.*fam.* 2012, afl. 1, 276.

a practical concept under Belgian law, as its legal status did not significantly differ from the settlement agreement *sensu stricto* (or *dading*), defined in Articles 2044-2058 of the old Civil Code. In essence, these provisions merely repeat the common law of obligations, except for the requirement of a written proof (Art. 2044(2) old Civil Code) and the exclusion of error in law (Art. 2052(2) old Civil Code). The case law of the Court of Cassation shows a third deviation concerning the unilateral termination (*infra*).

Quo vadis? – The foregoing considerations do not, for the time being, allow one to argue that Belgian law should adhere to the Dutch solution (Arts. 7.900-7:906 of the Dutch Civil Code) and so give up the concept of the Belgian settlement agreement *sensu stricto* (or *dading*). This would then completely morph into the settlement agreement *sensu lato* (or *vaststellingsovereenkomst*[14]), replacing the notion of 'dispute' with 'uncertainty or dispute' and completely abandoning the notion of mutual concessions. Indeed, the question of whether one uses a stricter or broader definition is determined by the question of the extent to which the regime of the settlement agreement under future law should deviate from the common law of obligations, as recently provided for in Book 5 of the Belgian Civil Code.

While rewriting our Belgian Civil Code we should at least not give up the dominant term (*dading*), now that it is well established in practice.[15] A change may have far-reaching consequences for the derivative legislation, so far as there is no clear transitional provision.[16] In this sense, a more precise legal definition of the current specific contract that codifies established case law seems to contribute most to legal certainty under Belgian law. In this respect, the legislative proposal on Book 7 'Specific Contracts' is adhering to the dominant term, while codifying the requirement of mutual concessions.[17]

Written proof – As mentioned previously, Articles 2044-2058 of the old Civil Code deviate from the common law of obligations in a threefold way. Under the general law of obligations, a written deed is, in principle, required for juridical acts that concern

14 Or *vaststellingscontract*, taking into account the term *contract* as a pivotal concept in Book 5 of the Belgian Civil Code; see V. SAGAERT, B. TILLEMAN and A.L. VERBEKE, *Vemogensrecht in kort bestek*, 6th edition, Antwerp, Intersentia, 2022, 519; F. JUDO and D. WILLEMS, 'Noord-Zuidverschillen in de juridische terminologie: zin en onzin', in *Terminologie in Juridische Taal (TiNT-dag 2022)*, to be published in 2023.

15 The Belgian Official Gazette shows a strong presence of the term *dading* with about 300 entries (since 1996). That differs from the term *vaststellingsovereenkomst* with about four entries (since 1996).

16 See, for example, the transitional clause that accompanied the introduction of the Belgian Code of Economic Law: *handelaar* should be understood as *onderneming* (see *artikel 254 van de wet van 15 april 2018 ter hervorming van het ondernemingsrecht, BS 27 april 2018*).

17 Art. 7.7.9 'Definition' of the Proposal Book 7 'Specific Contracts', Parl.St. Kamer 2023-24, nr. 3973/1, 173.

a sum or a value of at least 3,500 EUR (Art. 8.9 Civil Code). To conclude a settlement agreement *sensu stricto* the Belgian Civil Code requires a written proof, regardless of the amount (Art. 2044(2) old Civil Code). The rationale of this deviation is that when parties terminate a dispute, the legislature wants to avoid subsequent discussion about how the dispute was terminated. Therefore, drawing up a written proof seems obvious to a careful lawyer.

However, this requirement seems to be increasingly flexible. For example, a beginning of proof by writing is accepted (Art. 8.13 Civil Code).[18] Moreover, the written proof does not apply to undertakings, as freedom of proof prevails in that respect (Art. 8.11 Civil Code). This follows from a judgment of the Court of Cassation dating from 19 March 2012.[19] In line with the definition, this requirement also seems to lose its significance over time. This is also due to the dynamic formation of a settlement agreement, where parties sometimes make (commercial) concessions through informal negotiations.

In certain methods of extrajudicial dispute resolution, such as arbitration, mediation and collaborative negotiations, the legislature does require a signed writing in a general manner (Arts. 1713, 1731-1732, and 1746 of the Belgian Judicial Code). In this respect, however, the rationale for the written contract is partly justified by the exequatur of an arbitral award or the homologation of a mediated agreement. So it seems appropriate to put forward a clear choice: a written contract or not?

In this regard, the legislative proposal on Book 7 'Specific Contracts' does not retain the eroded requirement of a written proof, but highlights its added value as a *best practice*.[20] In essence, this raises a more fundamental question: to what extent does the legislature wish to subject settlement agreements to formal requirements, either for evidence or for validity purposes? Therefore, the validity requirements are discussed in what follows.

3 CONTRACT FORMATION

Contract nature – A settlement agreement is, in principle, a consensual contract.[21] A consensual contract is created by the mere consent of the parties without its validity being

18 F. GEORGE, *La convention de transaction*, Liège, Wolters Kluwer, 2021, 131.

19 Cass. 19 March 2012, C.10.0645.F, ECLI:BE:CASS:2012:ARR.20120319.2; F. GEORGE, *La convention de transaction*, Liège, Wolters Kluwer, 2021, 133; A. RIGOLET, *Contrat de transaction*, Brussels, Larcier, 2021, 42.

20 Proposal Book 7 'Specific Contracts', Parl.St. Kamer 2023-24, nr. 3973/1, 172.

21 A. RIGOLET, *Contrat de transaction*, Brussels, Larcier, 2021, 41.

subject to a formal requirement, whereas a formal contract does have to comply with formal requirements to be valid (Art. 5.5 of the Belgian Civil Code). The fundamental validity requirements are defined in Article 5.27 of the Civil Code (*ex* Art. 1108 old Civil Code): (i) consent of will, (ii) capacity (also expressed in Article 2045 old Civil Code), (iii) a determinable and lawful object (also expressed in Article 2046 old Civil Code) and (iv) a lawful cause. Article 5.51 of the Belgian Civil Code forbids parties to contractually violate provisions stemming from rules of mandatory law or public order (defined in Art. 1.3 of the Belgian Civil Code).

A settlement agreement is also called an auxiliary agreement because it grafts itself mostly onto an existing legal relationship. To limit evasion of the law,[22] it seems appropriate to pursue a parallelism of forms when the settlement agreement relates to a formal contract. In that case, a settlement agreement is subject to formal requirements when it involves the termination or amendment of a legal act that must be recorded by an authentic deed. For example, when contracting parties conclude a settlement agreement on a donation that has been recorded by an authentic deed, the settlement agreement could be subjected to the same formal requirements as the donation. This is already the case when it concerns legal acts that are subject to the regime of immovable property publicity to ensure the opposability of real estate transactions (Art. 3.30 of the Belgian Civil Code).[23] That is made more explicit in the legislative proposal on Book 7 'Specific Contracts' that is referring to the immovable property publicity.[24] Thus, the conclusion of a settlement agreement that modifies a purchase of a real estate (with the transfer of rights *in rem*) will have to be transcribed as an authentic deed at the registry office.

The parallelism of form also applies to the extent that proof concerning a signed writing can only be provided by another signed writing, even if the sum or value does not exceed 3,500 EUR (Art. 8.9(1) of the Belgian Civil Code). We find that parallelism of forms in a general way in different legal systems, for example in Article 22(2) of the Swiss *Code des Obligations*. Dutch law expresses a parallelism for the settlement agreement *sensu lato* (*vaststellingsovereenkomst*) in Article 7:901(1) of the Civil Code. Parties are bound by the requirements that must be met in order to create the legal situation envisaged by the settlement agreement.

So a nuance to the fundamentally consensual nature of the settlement agreement seems appropriate. When, in the interest of the parties or third parties, the law makes the

22 N. VAN DAMME, *Wetsontduiking*, Antwerp, Intersentia, 2020, 317.
23 See B. VERHEYE, *Onroerende registerpubliciteit*, Bruges, die Keure, 2021, 648 p.
24 Art. 7.7.12 'Formalities concerning opposability' of the Proposal Book 7 'Specific Contracts', Parl.St. Kamer 2023-24, nr. 3973/1, 177.

validity of a contract depend on a particular form, it also applies to the settlement that concerns a dispute arising from that formal contract.

ADR scope – Originally, the same scope of disputes was able to be arbitrated (by a third party) or settled (by the parties themselves).[25] Since 2013, the scope of arbitrable disputes was extended (Art. 1676 of the Belgian Judicial Code). A dispute may touch upon the rules of public order (e.g. in competition law) as long as the arbitral award does not conflict with it.[26] Since 2018, this broadening has also been applied to mediation and collaborative negotiations (Arts. 1724 and 1738 of the Belgian Judicial Code). Meanwhile, the scope of the settlement agreement (or *dading*) as a specific contract in the Belgian Civil Code has not been changed, nor has the settlement agreement after judicial reconciliation (Art. 731/1 of the Belgian Judicial Code). When reforming settlement agreements, it seems appropriate to bring back uniformity in the matters that can be resolved outside the courts.[27] In this respect, the legislative proposal on Book 7 'Specific Contracts' entails a uniform ADR scope, adhering to the extended scope under arbitration, mediation and collaborative negotiations.[28] One may apply the general rule of Article 5.51 Civil Code that the prestation of an agreement is unlawful if it creates or maintains a situation that is contrary to public order or to mandatory statutory provisions.

4 LEGAL EFFECTS AND TERMINATION

Limited unilateral termination for settlement of an indefinite duration – On the unilateral termination of the settlement agreement *sensu stricto* (*dading*), the Belgian Court of Cassation ruled that a general principle of law (according to which contracts of indeterminate duration may be unilaterally terminated at any time and by each of the parties) does not authorise a party to unilaterally revoke an obligation that served as a concession, even if that obligation was entered into for an indeterminate term.[29] In that case, a right of occupancy was irrevocably granted for an indeterminate term. That concession did not disregard the aforementioned general principle of law, now codified in Article 5.75 of the Belgian Civil Code. In this respect, it seems appropriate for the legislature to provide an express deviation for the settlement agreement (*dading*)

25 F. VAN DEN ABEELE and D. WILLEMS, 'Arbitrage over huurgeschillen: een analyse in het licht van de recente rechtspraak van het Grondwettelijk Hof', *TBBR* 2021, 508.
26 Ibid., 509-510; see also K. WAGNER, *Handboek Arbitrage*, Antwerpen, Intersentia, 2022, 170.
27 F. VAN DEN ABEELE and D. WILLEMS, 'Arbitrage over huurgeschillen: een analyse in het licht van de recente rechtspraak van het Grondwettelijk Hof', *TBBR* 2021, 509.
28 Art. 7.7.10 'Object' of the Proposal Book 7 'Specific Contracts', Parl.St. Kamer 2023-24, nr. 3973/1, 175.
29 Cass. 10 November 2016, C.16.0142.F, ECLI:BE:CASS:2016:ARR.20161110.3.

to exclude the unilateral termination. The legislative proposal on Book 7 'Specific Contracts' is in line with that exclusion.[30]

Extrajudicial nullity and dissolution – Book 5 'Obligations' of the Belgian Civil Code enshrines the extrajudicial nullity in Article 5.59 (unless the contract has been established by an authentic deed) and the extrajudicial dissolution in Article 5.93 (without foregoing nuance).

The possibility of dissolving a settlement agreement *sensu stricto* (*dading*) has been disputed. De Page summarises the controversy as follows:[31] (i) proponents invoke the reciprocal nature of the settlement, (ii) opponents rely on the inherently extinctive nature of the contract and (iii) the 'inbetweeners' do not consider dissolution to be possible in declarative settlements (which consider the legal relationship to have always been as settled – *ex tunc*) but rather in constitutive settlements (which create a new legal relationship – *ex nunc*). As an opponent, De Page argues that a non-executed settlement agreement only gives the right to performance in kind. Similarly, the French Court of Cassation held that the *exceptio transactionis* does not apply in the case of a non-executed settlement without it being necessary to claim its dissolution.[32] It merely hinders the revival of the underlying dispute.[33] De Page concludes that dissolution is, in principle, excluded by the settlement agreement, unless otherwise agreed in a contractual clause. This can also be justified by the delicate balance of mutual concessions that the settlement embodies as an instrument of pacification (in this sense, partial dissolution is also often undesirable).[34]

Since De Page, groundbreaking case law of the Belgian Court of Cassation has intervened. In a landmark judgment of 1977, the Court of Cassation allowed judicial dissolution of a specific settlement agreement (*dading*).[35] In 2019, the Court of Cassation similarly allowed the extrajudicial dissolution of a specific settlement agreement (*dading*).[36] Parties can always contractually modify the dissolution.[37] Rigolet mentions that a

30 Art. 7.7.16 'Extinction' of the Proposal Book 7 'Specific Contracts', Parl.St. Kamer 2023-24, nr. 3973/1, 181.

31 H. DE PAGE, *Traité élémentaire de droit civil belge*, V, Brussels, Bruylant, 517.

32 Fr. Cass. 12 July 2012, 09-11.582, *Bulletin* 2012, I, n° 173.

33 H. DE PAGE, *Traité élémentaire de droit civil belge*, V, Brussels, Bruylant, 519.

34 A. RIGOLET, *Contrat de transaction*, Brussels, Larcier, 2021, 141.

35 Cass. 6 April 1977, nr. 19310, ECLI:BE:CASS:1977:ARR.19770406.4; F. GEORGE, *La convention de transaction*, Liège, Wolters Kluwer, 2021, 161 ; A. RIGOLET, *Contrat de transaction*, Brussels, Larcier, 2021, 140.

36 Cass. 23 May 2019, C.16.0254.F, ECLI:BE:CASS:2019:ARR.20190523.14; P. WÉRY and S. STIJNS, 'La résolution par voie de notification, enfin admise par la Cour de cassation', *JT* 2020, 21-25.

37 A. RIGOLET, *Contrat de transaction*, Brussels, Larcier, 2021, 141; N. PORTUGAELS, *De vaststellingsovereenkomst*, Antwerp, Intersentia, 2018, 525.

contractual exclusion is a frequent practice.[38] However, the contractual exclusion is at least not possible in B2C contracts (Art. VI.83, 7° of the Belgian Code of Economic Law).[39]

Given the stability sought by the settlement, it seems appropriate to depart from extrajudicial remedies that revive the dispute too quickly. For example, there may be *a posteriori* a fundamental debate about the legality of the notification (which brings about the extrajudicial dissolution). In Dutch doctrine, Van Rossum also observes that Article 7:905 of the Dutch Civil Code only excludes extrajudicial dissolution in the case of a settlement agreement by decision of a party or a third party but not when the parties make the decision together.[40]

In order to avoid these ambiguities depending on the type of settlement agreement, further reflection seems appropriate, given (i) the statutory extension of the extrajudicial nullity and dissolution sanction in Book 5 'Obligations' of the Belgian Civil Code and (ii) the parties' intention (*animus transactionis*) to extinguish the dispute and not to revive it. Here, it seems appropriate to exclude extrajudicial[41] dissolution as a matter of principle (which is consistent with the current practice of contractual clauses in a settlement agreement *sensu stricto* or *dading*). Similar to the limited unilateral termination, the legislative proposal on Book 7 'Specific Contracts' excludes the aforementioned extrajudicial remedies (nullity and dissolution).[42]

5 Application to AI and Insurance Claims

Settlement agreements in the context of AI-systems and insurance contracts – Artificial intelligence (AI) also has an impact on the practice of settlement agreements in the insurance sector. AI may, for example, be used for policy underwriting (e.g. in

38 A. RIGOLET, *Contrat de transaction*, Brussels, Larcier, 2021, 141; See also Art. 5 of a general model of settlement agreement J. LAMBERS and L. VERMEIREN, 'Dading in burgerlijke en handelszaken', in X., *Bijvoorbeeld. Modellen voor het bedrijfsleven*, Antwerp, Kluwer, 2011, VI.30.-1 – VI.30.-30.

39 A. RIGOLET, *Contrat de transaction*, Brussels, Larcier, 2021, 141.

40 A.A. VAN ROSSUM, *Vaststellingsovereenkomst*, Deventer, Kluwer, 2001, 36. *Contra*: A.C. VAN SCHAICK, *Asser-serie – Bijzondere overeenkomsten*, 7-VIII, *Bewaarneming, borgtocht, vaststellingsovereenkomst, bruikleen, altijddurende rente, spel en weddenschap*, 8th edition, Deventer, Kluwer, 2018, 191-192.

41 This specifies a more general stance (exclusion of dissolution) in a previous contribution: B. TILLEMAN and D. WILLEMS, 'Dading: traditie met toekomst?' in P. SCHOUKENS, B. DEMARSIN, E. DE BECKER and T. KEERSMAEKERS (eds.), *Liber Amicorum Danny Pieters: Durven out of the box denken*, Ghent, Owl Press Legal, 2022, 406-418.

42 Art. 7.7.13 'Exclusion of error in law and extrajudicial nullity' and Art. 7.7.16 'Extinction' of the Proposal Book 7 'Specific Contracts', Parl.St. Kamer 2023-24, nr. 3973/1, 179 and 181.

vehicle insurance).[43] It enables *"measuring risk exposure and determining the premium that needs to be charged to insure that risk"*.[44] The determination of a premium may be of use in a settlement context. Another example concerns AI facilitating online dispute resolution (ODR).

AI may formulate a settlement offer that a party can send to the other concerned parties (indirect application of ODR).[45] That implies some practical issues, in particular to take into account the relevant information that is not easily 'AI-inputable' (such as the human emotions that may underpin a dispute).[46]

Moreover, AI may also independently resolve a dispute (direct application of ODR). When an AI system independently determines a dispute or an uncertainty, mandated by the parties to do so, it resembles a binding third-party decision. So when the amount of damages is determined by an AI system, the determination decision is governed by the Belgian law of obligations in Book 5 of the Civil Code (Arts. 5.49 and 5.70(2)).[47] These provisions merely lay down the principle but have not elaborated the legal regime.

Both indirect and direct applications raise fundamental legal questions, such as (i) (re) qualification of a settlement agreement, (ii) the distinction between a settlement agreement and the execution of an insurance contract and (iii) the exclusion of an error in law (Art. 2052(2) old Civil Code), as a third deviation concerning the common law of obligations.

(i) (Re)qualification of a settlement agreement – As mentioned previously, the requirements of a settlement agreement *sensu stricto* under Belgian law (*dading*) are broadly understood (see previously; e.g. a dispute merely requires conflicting claims, and mutual concessions must not be expressed in the AI-made/-inspired settlement agreement). The latter may be evaluated in respect of the initial claims of the parties,[48] for example before the AI system formulated a settlement offer.

43 J. AMANKWAH, *Artificial Intelligence and the Law*, 2nd edition, Antwerp, Intersentia, 2023, 450.
44 Ibid.
45 H. ALESSA, 'The Role of Artificial Intelligence in Online Dispute Resolution: A Brief and Critical Overview', *Information & Communications Technology Law* 2022, 320.
46 Ibid., 332.
47 That differs from the Dutch approach, using the overarching concept *vaststellingsovereenkomst*, including the direct settlement agreement (*directe vaststelling*), the binding party decision (*bindende partijbeslissing*) and binding third-party decision (*bindend advies*).
48 An alternative to the 'initial claim' benchmark is to look at the legitimate claims: B. TILLEMAN, I. CLAEYS, Ch. COUDRON and K. LOONTJENS, *Dading*, in *APR*, Antwerp, Story-Scientia, 2000,33.

Of course, a merely abstract approach to the qualification exercise is not possible, it depends on the case. Two appeal cases before the Antwerp courts offer an illustration.[49] The court made a similar assessment when an insurer settled on the damages of an accident. The court held that only one party conceded. The insured party conceded by partly waiving its claim, but there was no concession from the insurer's side.[50] In the absence of mutual concessions, the court requalified the contract from a nominate settlement agreement *sensu stricto (dading)* to a settlement agreement *sensu lato (vaststellingsovereenkomst* or *vaststellingscontract)*.

(ii) Settlement agreement vs. execution of an insurance contract – So, first, it is questioned whether the mere execution of an insurance contract can be distinguished from a settlement agreement concerning an insurance contract. This may be unclear when an insurer uses an AI system to determine whether it should pay/settle or not. This discussion relates, in particular, to the receipt for partial or final payment issued by an insurer.[51] The Belgian Court of Cassation held that a mandatory statutory provision under Belgian insurance law (providing a restrictive interpretation of the receipt) did apply regardless of the qualification as a settlement agreement.[52] According to Portugaels, that mandatory statutory provision merely repeats the principles of interpretation (Arts. 5.64-5.66 Civil Code and 2048-2049 old Civil Code).[53] From that point of view, it merely reaffirms the application of the general principles. *A fortiori*, the qualification of an agreement as a settlement agreement *sensu stricto* (*dading*) or *sensu lato (vaststellingsovereenkomst)* under Belgian law does not (and will not) have

49 Both appeals concerning a police court judgment: Antwerp Court of First Instance (*Rb. Antwerpen – afd. Antwerpen*) 23 May 2016, *VAV* 2018, 33; Antwerp Court of First Instance (*Rb. Antwerpen*) 28 October 2013, *RW* 2016-17, 234.

50 Antwerp Court of First Instance (*Rb. Antwerpen – afd. Antwerpen*) 23 May 2016, *VAV* 2018, 33.

51 P. COLLE, 'Over de dading en de vergoedingskwijting in de praktijk van de verzekeringen', *RW* 1999-2000, 969, referred to by the below Antwerp courts. It distinguishes the receipt for partial or final payment from a contract, since it merely concerns a written confirmation of a payment made by the insurer to the injured party by way of compensation.

52 Cass. 20 December 2010, C.10.0270.N, ECLI:BE:CASS:2010:CONC.20101220.5. The original paragraph in Dutch reads as follows:
'Artikel 84 van de Wet Landverzekeringsovereenkomst bepaalt in het eerste lid dat een kwitantie voor een gedeeltelijke afrekening of ter finale afrekening voor de benadeelde niet betekent dat hij van zijn rechten afziet, en in het tweede lid, dat een kwitantie ter finale afrekening de elementen van de schade moet vermelden waarop die afrekening slaat.
Uit die dwingende wetsbepalingen volgt dat een kwitantie ter finale afrekening aan de benadeelde niet het recht ontneemt om vergoeding te vorderen voor andere elementen van de schade dan die waarop de kwitantie betrekking heeft.
Dit geldt ongeacht de kwalificatie van de kwitantie ter finale afrekening als een vaststellingsovereenkomst.'

53 N. PORTUGAELS, *De vaststellingsovereenkomst*, Antwerp, Intersentia, 2018, 547. The legislative proposal on Book 7 'Specific Contracts' confirms the principle of a strict interpretation if the common intent of the parties is not clear, see Art. 7.7.14 'Interpretation' of the Proposal Book 7 'Specific Contracts', Parl.St. Kamer 2023-24, nr. 3973/1, 179-180.

legal implications in this respect (according to the normative perspective discussed previously).

(iii) Exclusion of error in law (*error iuris*) – If mutual concessions are made to prevent or terminate the dispute at hand, it constitutes a settlement agreement *sensu stricto* (*dading*). Next to the discussed deviations concerning the evidence (Art. 2044(2) old Civil Code) and the unilateral termination (stemming from the case law), it is therefore appropriate to depict the exclusion of error in law (Art. 2052(2) old Civil Code).[54] Its importance was shown in a case of the Court of Cassation, concerning a settlement with the Customs and Excise Administration (qualified as settlement agreement *sensu stricto* (*dading*)).[55] This deviation is particularly interesting when a settlement agreement *sensu stricto* relates to AI and insurance claims (e.g. when an AI system merely suggests a settlement offer, as an indirect ODR application). It may imply that a party cannot invoke the nullity of the settlement agreement if the settlement agreement (e.g. the underlying settlement offer) was based on wrong assumptions about the applicable legal provision.[56]

6 Conclusion

So how should we shape settlement agreements as a specific contract under Belgian law in the future Book 7 of the Civil Code? It is of utmost importance to strive for an *up-front* correct qualification of the settlement agreement *sensu stricto* as a specific contract under Belgian law (*dading*; Arts. 2044-2058 old Civil Code). The way we shape settlement agreements as a specific contract under Belgian law in the future Book 7 of the Civil Code and deviate from the general provisions of law of obligations of Book 5 will increase or decrease the importance of a requalification of the settlement agreement. The more the legal regime of settlement agreement deviates, the more the qualification may be essential to decide on a case. AI-systems and insurance contracts may therefore be an interesting angle, for example for the discussed exclusion of the error in law.

Currently, a settlement agreement as a specific contract under Belgian law comes down to a threefold, broadly understood requirement (Art. 2044(1) old Civil Code): (i) an

---

54 The legislative proposal on Book 7 'Specific Contracts' retains the exclusion of an error in law, see Art. 7.7.13 'Exclusion of error in law and extrajudicial nullity' of the Proposal Book 7 'Specific Contracts', Parl.St. Kamer 2023-24, nr. 3973/1, 178.

55 Cass. 22 september 2011, C.10.0506.N, ECLI:BE:CASS:2011:ARR.20110922.4.

56 That relates to the doctoral research of Herbosch. See PhD-thesis of M. HERBOSCH, *Intelligent contracteren: Het precontractueel gebruik van systemen op basis van artificiële intelligentie*, Leuven, Lirias, 2023, 623 p. (commercial edition coming soon).

animus transactionis, (ii) a dispute and (iii) mutual concessions (according to the case law). The scope of application has a threefold implication: (i) a written proof is, in principle, needed (Art. 2044(2)), (ii) the error in law is excluded (Art. 2052(2)) and (iii) the unilateral termination is limited (according to the case law).

Looking to the future, first, the legal notion of the settlement agreement as a specific contract (*dading*) can be put more precise in the future Book 7 of the Civil Code (e.g. codifying the mutual concessions requirement). There is no immediate need for a paradigm shift towards a broader notion as adhered to in the Netherlands. Further, a written proof requirement may be left since the numerous exceptions have eroded the principle. Second, concerning the contract formation, a reform may accommodate the object towards a uniform scope of application for alternative dispute resolution (e.g. arbitration, mediation and collaborative negotiations). A formal parallelism should at least be made more clear when it concerns juridical acts that are subject to the regime of immovable property publicity. Third, the unilateral termination may be limited as well as the extrajudicial nullity and dissolution to preserve the *animus transactionis* and its extinctive character. As shown above, the recent legislative proposal on Book 7 'Specific Contracts' is consistent with these insights.

Finally, the AI and insurance application puts the error in law in a broader perspective. It may strengthen the traditional argument for excluding an *error iuris*. It is considered to be contrary to the very nature of the settlement (that an error in law can lead to nullity) as parties do voluntarily depart from a strict application of the law. Similarly, by entering into a settlement agreement, the parties waive their right to let a court decide the outcome of their dispute under the applicable law.

www.ingramcontent.com/pod-product-compliance
Lightning Source LLC
Chambersburg PA
CBHW082233240926
51846CB00014B/1393
9789462368149